GERTRUDE STEIN AND THE MAKING OF JEWISH MODERNISM

UNIVERSITY PRESS OF FLORIDA

Florida A&M University, Tallahassee
Florida Atlantic University, Boca Raton
Florida Gulf Coast University, Ft. Myers
Florida International University, Miami
Florida State University, Tallahassee
New College of Florida, Sarasota
University of Central Florida, Orlando
University of Florida, Gainesville
University of North Florida, Jacksonville
University of South Florida, Tampa
University of West Florida, Pensacola

GERTRUDE STEIN
and the MAKING
of JEWISH MODERNISM

AMY FEINSTEIN

University Press of Florida
Gainesville · Tallahassee · Tampa · Boca Raton
Pensacola · Orlando · Miami · Jacksonville · Ft. Myers · Sarasota

Copyright 2020 by Amy Feinstein
All rights reserved
Published in the United States of America

First cloth printing, 2020
First paperback printing, 2022

27 26 25 24 23 22   6 5 4 3 2 1

Library of Congress Cataloging-in-Publication Data
Names: Feinstein, Amy, author.
Title: Gertrude Stein and the making of Jewish modernism / Amy Feinstein.
Description: Gainesville : University Press of Florida, 2020. | Includes
   bibliographical references and index.
Identifiers: LCCN 2019032804 (print) | LCCN 2019032805 (ebook) | ISBN
   9780813066318 (hardback) | ISBN 9780813057422 (pdf) | ISBN 9780813068756 (pbk.)
Subjects: LCSH: Stein, Gertrude, 1874–1946—Criticism and interpretation. |
   Stein, Gertrude, 1874–1946—Literary style. | Modernism (Literature) |
   Jews in literature.
Classification: LCC PS3537.T323 Z5887 2020 (print) | LCC PS3537.T323
   (ebook) | DDC 818/.5209—dc23
LC record available at https://lccn.loc.gov/2019032804
LC ebook record available at https://lccn.loc.gov/2019032805

The University Press of Florida is the scholarly publishing agency for the State University System of Florida, comprising Florida A&M University, Florida Atlantic University, Florida Gulf Coast University, Florida International University, Florida State University, New College of Florida, University of Central Florida, University of Florida, University of North Florida, University of South Florida, and University of West Florida.

University Press of Florida
2046 NE Waldo Road
Suite 2100
Gainesville, FL 32609
http://upress.ufl.edu

For my parents

CONTENTS

List of Illustrations   ix

Acknowledgments   xi

A Note on Citation   xv

Introduction: The Stein Era   1

1. An Israel of the Imagination: The Sciences of Race, Matthew Arnold, and Stein's Modern Jew   20

2. Brother Singulars: The "Hidden Tradition" of Jewish Culture in Stein's First Fictions   38

3. "So much like a yid:" An Associative Genealogy of "Jewish Types" in the Notebooks for *The Making of Americans*   62

4. Pariah Modernism: Estranging Narration in *The Making of Americans*   87

5. "Can a Jew be wild": A Radical Jewish Grammar in the Voices Poems   123

6. "Everybody can persecute anybody": What's Funny about Jewish Identity in *Wars I Have Seen*   143

Conclusion: Making Sense of a Sensationally Jewish Stein   181

Notes   197

Works Cited   249

Index   269

ILLUSTRATIONS

FIGURE 1. Untitled diagram that includes "me" (Gertrude Stein) at one end   68

FIGURE 2. The Jewish group   72

FIGURE 3. The Anglo Saxon group   73

TABLE 1. Major Correspondences in Stein's Characterology for Jewish and Anglo-Saxon Types   67

ACKNOWLEDGMENTS

I spent a lot of time in libraries and archives researching and writing this book, and I am thankful for librarians. I am grateful for the H. D. Fellowship from the Beinecke Rare Book and Manuscript Library at Yale University, and for the guidance of Patricia C. Willis and Nancy Kuhl, curators of the Yale Collection of American Literature. I am grateful for a grant from the Hadassah-Brandeis Institute for Research on Jews and Gender and two Colgate University Research Council Discretionary Grants that funded my jaunts to the Bancroft Library of Western Americana at the University of California–Berkeley, the Jewish Museum of Maryland, and the Baltimore Museum of Art. I thank the access services staffs at the Beinecke, the Harry Ransom Research Center at the University of Texas at Austin, and the Schlesinger Library at the Radcliffe Institute for Advanced Study at Harvard University. I thank Leah Adler, Head Librarian of Hebraica-Judaica at Yeshiva University, for giving me access to their collections, and appreciate the interlibrary loan efforts of Mary Ann Linahan. The lion's share of my time was spent writing at the New York Public Library, and I am thrilled to thank happily retired Research Librarian Jay Barksdale and my colleagues in the Wertheim Study and Shoichi Noma Reading Room for their quiet camaraderie over the years. More recently, the librarians of the Dorot Jewish Division have been generous with shelf space and cheer.

This book began as a chapter in another work on avant-garde writers and the Jewish question. The University of Wisconsin–Madison English Department's professors and my fellow graduate students in the late 1990s formed an inspiring and warm intellectual community and have remained a source of support over the nearly two decades since my graduation. I am especially grateful to my mentor and champion, Cyrena Pondrom, and my professors Richard Begam, Jacques Lezra, and the late French and Jewish Studies professor Elaine Marks. I am also indebted to Susan David Bernstein, who first taught me Gertrude Stein, and Craig Werner, whose *Ulysses* and Multicultural Literature class brought me to the Jewish question. I benefitted from the tenacious support of my writing group, anupama jain and Eileen O'Halloran. Other cherished Wisconsinites whose support continued as some of us moved into the diaspora are Jody Cardinal, the late Devah Pager, Susan Funkenstein, Heather Hewett, Lisa Levenstein, John McGuigan, Abe Saloma, Jon Schofer, Lisa Tetrault, Sue Uselmann, Keisha Watson, and Phyllis Holman Weisbard. Heather Dubrow and Don Rowe, now in NYC, thanks for keeping champagne at the ready.

In upstate New York, as this book began to take shape, I worked closely with colleague and dear friend Sarah Bay-Cheng. Conversations with other Colgate English Department colleagues helped get the first draft off the ground. I especially thank Constance Harsh, Margaret Maurer, Phil Richards, Emily Sun, Peter Balakian, Morgan Davies, Linck Johnson, Jennifer Brice, Sarah Wider, Lynn Staley, and, finally, Kezia Page, who I also thank for cheese and bread. My Jewish Studies colleagues were an erudite *mishpokhe:* Lesleigh Cushing, Steven Kepnes, Alice Nakhimovsky, and Ben Stahlberg, *a sheynem dank!* Visiting scholars Brian McGrath and Dan Schwartz generously read and commented on portions of the book. The gracious Susan Edmunds of Syracuse University offered suggestions that improved the volume.

Leaving academia made it challenging to continue writing this book. I thank University Press of Florida editors Amy Gorelick, Shannon McCarthy, and Linda Bathgate for their interest, patience, and prompting over the years, and Stephanye Hunter for finally wrenching the manuscript from me. Were it not for the copious and constructive comments by the press's anonymous readers, I would not have completed the project. I have also relied that much more on scholars, friends, and family in New York City and in the provinces. I thank the esteemed mavens of Jewish Modernism: Maren Linett, Lara Trubowitz, Erin Carlston, Maria Damon, and Marilyn Reizbaum. I thank Stephen Paul Miller and Daniel Morris for *Radical Poetics and Secular Jewish Culture.* I thank Barbara Will for her unflagging encouragement, her insight, and for wrestling with Faÿ. The late Ulla Dydo met with me several times over the years, and I am sad not to share this book with her. Robert O. Paxton indulged my queries on Vichy.

François Vignale let me pick his brain about *Fontaine* and the intellectual resistance. And, recently, Edward Burns fielded burning questions.

Jonathan Goldman, thank you for convivial friendship, shrewd reading of my work, and for suggesting we organize the NYC Modernism Seminar. Thanks to Ernest Ialongo and Jennifer Gilchrist for high-spiritedly sustaining it. Sarah Leonard, Daphne Uviller, and Irene Siegel kept me company as writers, scholars, and friends. Marianne Prebet provided French sources and treats. Laina Bay-Cheng reminded me that I did not need to write this book and yet gave me the tools for balancing personal and professional endeavors. Walking in Fort Tryon Park, novelist Victoria Bond pinpointed the drama that helped unstick my conclusion. Neighbors, book club, and parent friends in Washington Heights have kept me sane and intellectually stimulated. Mary Di Lucia, thanks for poetry and your zeal for Stein. *Gracias*, Eneida Jiminian, for always babysitting *con mucho amor*. Sister Singulars, Alisa Braun and Stefanie Nanes, thanks for being such good company for so many years.

My Bronx principals Franklin Sim, Carmen Bardeguez–Brown (also a poet), and Jeffrey Houston have given me a professional home in public school teaching that has anchored and energized me. I would not have succeeded, however, without my colleagues, mentors, and friends on the staffs of the High School for Violin and Dance and the School for Excellence. One-time co-teacher, now long-time friend Naomi Sharlin showed me how love, rigor, and access make for good teaching. Students Tottiana Bagner and Ariel Smith checked quotes for me one summer, and Paige Hodge reminded me how much can happen from just sitting down and writing.

I am grateful for Janine Tobeck's painstaking reading of my first draft and for her mixtapes. Ed Heinemann, you are the stranger I am writing for. Jenn Rucklip, a new friend from the old country, read the final draft with acuity and expertly guided me through one last round of revisions. Lisa Schreibersdorf, it seems you know this book better than I do from just talking on the phone. Thank you for getting me through it all—and I mean *all*.

My family has been a constant source of encouragement. Thank you to all the Feinsteins, Schwartzes, Marcks, Nadels, Edensons, Costbergs, Lessers, Castons, and more recently the Kaplans, Muranakas, Sterns, Glaziers, and Hochsteins. In particular, Raymond Fogelson fed me wisdom and William James, cousins Barbara Meyers and the writers Rose

Lichter-Marck and Debra Nussbaum Cohen have been important sounding boards, and Stanley Feinstein attended an MLA talk I gave in Los Angeles and asked a good question. Andrew Schwartz and his psychoanalysis reading group's interest has cheered me. Phil and Judy Kaplan provided a warm hearth and time to write between meals. And Sharon Hochstein's once-anonymous fandom buoyed my tenure upstate, and then, coincidentally, a decade later, I married her cousin.

Bette Feinstein, thanks for modeling how to get things done. Roger Feinstein, you were a model ponderer, writer, and reader. I miss you and wish you were here to read this. Pearl, keep working on your *dunkument*, and someday you will finish a book or something. Thanks for being such delicious company while I finished mine. Aaron Kaplan opened a tab on his browser to *The Making of Americans* and never looked back. Thanks for always making this a priority, honeymooning in Stein's south of France, and being a true and loving partner.

Note: An earlier version of chapter 5 appeared in *Radical Poetics and Secular Jewish Culture* (Eds. Stephen Paul Miller and Daniel Morris. Tuscaloosa: The University of Alabama Press, 2010, 151–169). I wish to acknowledge and thank the Stein Estate for their willingness to allow me to quote lines from Stein's unpublished work. I also want to acknowledge Alida Latham, who provided the cover image, *Portrait of Gertrude Stein* by Francisco Riba Rovira, 1946.

A NOTE ON CITATION

At the center of this volume is the study of Gertrude Stein's early draft, notes, and final version of the novel *The Making of Americans: Being a History of a Family's Progress*, published in 1925, cited in abbreviation as *MA* (in italics). Stein first composed a short, five-chapter draft of the novel in 1903, which I cite using quotation marks, "The Making of Americans: Being the History of a Family's Progress," or, in abbreviation, without italics: MA. Between 1906 and 1911, Stein made notes on dozens of notebooks and *carnets* (small pocket notebooks), which she used when she resumed composing the novel. These remain unpublished and are held at the Beinecke Rare Book and Manuscript Library at Yale University. Stein's archivists have designated these writings as "Studies" for *The Making of Americans*. I cite them by box and folder number, as listed on the Beinecke Library Finding Aid for the Gertrude Stein and Alice B. Toklas papers (MSS 76) in the Yale Collection of American Literature (YCAL). When I refer to a specific page in a notebook or *carnet*, I use a librarian's numbering in brackets. For example, I cite as 38.791.[32] Stein's reference to her "long book" on the 32nd page of the undated notebook in Box 38, Folder 791, whose inscription is: "C This book follows the red note book marked B." I cite the completed novel using italics: *The Making of Americans: Being a History of a Family's Progress*.

In addition, I abbreviate the following texts by (or pertaining to) Stein, Matthew Arnold, and William James as follows:

ABT	*The Autobiography of Alice B. Toklas*
BGS	"Bequest of Gertrude Stein, Books"
EA	*Everybody's Autobiography*

GS/CVV	*Letters of Gertrude Stein and Carl Van Vechten*
LA	*Lectures in America*
MA	"The Making of Americans: Being the History of a Family's Progress"
MA	*The Making of Americans: Being a History of a Family's Progress*
MR	*Mrs. Reynolds*
TMJ	"The Modern Jew Who Has Given Up the Faith of His Fathers Can Reasonably and Consistently Believe in Isolation"
TL	*Three Lives*
WIHS	*Wars I Have Seen*
YIF	*Yes Is For A Very Young Man*
C&A	*Culture and Anarchy*
L&D	*Literature and Dogma*
FC	"The Function of Criticism at the Present Time"
CWJ	*The Correspondence of William James*
EMS	*William James on Exceptional Mental States: The 1896 Lowell Lectures*

Introduction
The Stein Era

> They accuse me of this and that but they have never accused me of being a Jew. At least I'm not typical.
> Gertrude Stein[1]

Despite the notable if negative consideration by many of her contemporaries, Gertrude Stein is just beginning to be seen among the writers "centrally expressing 'modernism,'" though not by recent scholars of Jewish modernism (Eshel and Presner 610). Long championed as an icon of American expatriates and salonnières in Paris and touted by Hemingway for dubbing his the "lost generation," Stein's writings are studied as examples of realism, naturalism, abstraction, literary cubism, and lesbian erotica. And in light of her training in psychology, philosophy, and medicine, her radically experimental styles have brought many to consider her an early philosopher of language. Stein as a Jewish writer has been more elusive and considered "not typical," even though, as I argue in this book, Stein's Jewishness underwrites our very understanding of modernism.[2]

In recent years, a wave of critical, theoretical, and biographical study has helped push Stein's writing to the forefront of contemporary avant-garde art, music, theater, and dance, although T. S. Eliot might be gratified to hear that the New York City Opera Company's production of *The Mother of Us All* (2000) was no *Cats*.[3] Stein's work remains a tough sell for readers and audiences in the twenty-first century. Today, her work still shocks, frustrates, and puzzles even as it intrigues, inspires, and pleases, whether the comparatively conventional prose of *The Autobiography of Alice B. Toklas*, whose run-on sentences, seemingly idiosyncratic chronology, and lack of standard punctuation still beguile the uninitiated, or the lengthier repetitions that turn single sentences into entire paragraphs in her epic anti-novel *The Making of Americans: Being a History of a Family's Progress* (completed 1911, published 1925). Readers of modernist literature who shy away from Stein's writing due to its repetition and abstraction miss the very qualities that are, I argue, what Stein considered to be the Jewish characteristics of her writing.

Gertrude Stein and the Making of Jewish Modernism bridges the fields of modernist studies and Jewish studies to assert the importance of avant-garde texts in the study of Jewish literary history and the importance of Gertrude Stein's specifically Jewish approaches to experimentation for the study of Anglo-American English literary history. In this book, I present Gertrude Stein as a major American Jewish writer and a Jewish voice of the avant-garde. I aim to provoke a reconsideration of the texts and contexts for modernism and Jewish literature in a study of Stein's changing articulations of Jewish nature. In contrast to many scholars who claim that Stein's embrace of textual abstraction forms a radical break from history and tradition, I argue that Stein's understanding of Jewish nature as a conventional, historically unchanging, and ethical force acted in tension with and as a seed for her constantly shifting formal experiments.

This book resituates Stein's methods of experimentation amidst the literary, scientific, and political debates over the place of the Jew in modernity. Central to Stein's thinking about Jews was British poet and cultural theorist Matthew Arnold (1822–1888), though his significance for Stein has never before been acknowledged by critics or biographers. Arnold's famed volume *Culture and Anarchy* (1869) identified a Judaized force he called "Hebraism" as one of two poles of influence—the other being "Hellenism"—moving civilization forward.

Stein was attuned to the struggle in European culture between Jew and non-Jew as depicted in the moralistic classifications of racialist scientism—something Arnold was clearly referencing. Stein did not join Social Darwinists, such as Francis Galton, Herbert Spencer, or Cesare Lombroso, who considered Jews to be an eternally alien race that was dangerously cosmopolitan and criminally intelligent—part Shylock, part Fagin, and part Svengali. Although she considered Jews from a racial perspective, and subscribed to some racial stereotypes, she did not categorize Jewish alterity and genius as immoral.

Instead, Stein's oeuvre celebrates Jewish nature. Influenced by Arnold's Hebraism and, to a lesser extent, Felix Adler's Ethical Culture, Stein considered the Jewish race and its "high average of brain-power" to be inherently intelligent and ethical (TMJ 424). Captivated, too, by the apparent plasticity of Jewish identity as a racial and ideological category in Arnold's salutary vision of civilization, Stein seized upon these and other "scientific" ideas about Jews as the key to articulating theories of identity and aesthetics in modern writing. She redeems criticisms of Jewish nature by positing them as the means to explain the iconoclastic nature of modernist writing. Jewish nature was, in her view, an integral if unassimilable component of modern art and modern nations.

Scholars generally view Stein as a nonpracticing Jew whose writing was imperceptibly Jewish at most. Those scholars of modernism and Jewish Studies who do consider Stein to have been Jewish have little documented sense of what that meant, even if, like journalist Janet Malcolm, they may fantasize about finding "a cache of letters between Stein and a rabbi" (192). From extensive archival research in Stein's papers, however, it becomes clear that the particularities of the Jew's experience of modernity and the weight of Jewish history were of enormous significance to Stein throughout her career as a writer. We see this in her early 1903 compositions and through the writing of *The Making of Americans*, completed in 1911. It continues in her "voices" writing of the 1910s and 1920s and through her final compositions written in Vichy and then occupied France.

In this book, I break new ground by showing that Stein's conception of Jewish nature relies on the work of Matthew Arnold, a heretofore unrecognized influence that unifies Stein's scientific study of psychology and character with her aesthetic interests. Beginning with her first fictions, Stein begins to articulate the role of the Jew in modern fiction as directly shaping the aesthetic concerns of modern literature. Stein makes clear that in this pairing of Jewish identity and culture she was indebted to Matthew Arnold. Many critics have claimed that Stein's formal experimentation derives from her scientific interests and work with psychologist William James or from literary or artistic forbears or contemporaries Henry James, George Eliot, Flaubert, Cézanne, Picasso, and Matisse. Others accept Stein's own mythologizing claim that her modernism was born from a *tabula rasa* and that she had no influences.[4]

Stein was not unique among modernist writers to have been schooled on the Victorian poet and critic Matthew Arnold. Her conception of Jewish character combined fin-de-siècle scientific racialism with Arnold's more platonic idea of Hebraism. Arnold supposed that Hebraism stood for the practical materialism of bourgeois capitalism, which he worried was dampening more free-spirited and "Hellenic" advances in civilization and culture. Stein reappropriates Arnoldian ideals of culture by looking at them through a Jewish lens. In early writings and drafts of *The Making of Americans*, for example, Stein casts the debates between the parents and children of a Jewish middle-class family as the opposed forces of Arnoldian Hebraism and Hellenism. Out of this struggle, Stein conceives the "Brother Singular," a class-conscious, yet rebellious American literary voice of modernity, which becomes the crux of her later and epic revisions of *The Making of Americans*.

My study of Arnold's influence on Stein unites the research on Stein's science with analyses by critics who include the novel in studies of turn-of-the-century Jewish narratives of race, sentiment, immigration, and assimilation.[5] Several critical studies of Stein's work have helpfully established her contributions to fin-de-siècle philosophy, phenomenology, and psychology.[6] In *Irresistible Dictation: Gertrude Stein and the Correlations of Writing and Science*, Steven Meyer states that after leaving neuroscience research, Stein "reconfigured science *as* writing and performed scientific experiments *in* writing" (xxi).[7] Alongside Meyer, studies of Stein's medical school research by Jaime Hovey, on pathological notions of lesbian sexuality, and Maria Farland, on debates over sexual dimorphism, make clear the intellectual, personal, and aesthetic import of fin-de-siècle science to Stein's early writings. It is clear that neither a sapphic primitivism nor a repudiation of sexual dimorphism drives Stein's early fiction. The archival evidence of Stein's notebooks demonstrates that what is queer in *The Making of Americans* and its forebears is Stein's invention of a Jewish modernism.

There are direct critical fore-mothers who inspired this work. Maria Damon launched the study of Stein's Jewish identity, looking initially at Stein's use of a "metaphoricity of Jewishness" and, more recently, at the author's interest in race science ("Gertrude Stein's Doggerel 'Yiddish': Women, Dogs, and Jews" 234). Barbara Will's *Gertrude Stein, Modernism, and the Problem of "Genius"* discusses the Jewish presence in Stein's writing. Mary Dearborn and Priscilla Wald have analyzed Stein's work in the context of Jewish-American immigration narratives.

Likewise foundational has been the vibrant critical conversation on images of Jews in British and Irish modernist literature by Andrea Freud Loewenstein, Bryan Cheyette, and Joyce scholars Neil Davison, Ira Nadel, and Marilyn Reizbaum. Two more-recent studies, Maren Linett on "imagined Jewishness" (10) and Lara Trubowitz on the "'rhetoricized' Jew" (38), provide crucial critical frameworks for my reading of Stein. In *Modernism, Feminism, and Jewishness*, Linett reads often-contradictory and often-antisemitic images of "the Jew" in the work of Britain's female modernists to illuminate their feminism, modernism, and other political or cultural ideals. Linett argues that many British feminist writers identified with Jews as outsiders while, in the case of Djuna Barnes, "Jewishness . . . comes to represent sameness, a patriarchal oneness and sign of continuity" (175). Encompassing these divergent notions, Stein, too, imagined Jews as both rebellious "singulars" and as symbols of established tradition and conformity. But Stein imagined Jews, especially in the first half of her writing career, using a "powerful but indirect rhetoric about Jewishness," akin to what Trubowitz finds in her analysis of the era's British parliamentary rhetoric concerned with Jewish immigrants, which "ironically, often [did not] mentio[n] Jews at all" (26). In *Civil Antisemitism, Modernism, and British Culture, 1902–1939*, Trubowitz links the political and literary rhetoric about Jews to modernist writing in order to outline "the elaborate rhetorical strategies, essentially stylistic and narrative in nature" that politicians and writers used "in order simultaneously to express and conceal their antisemitism" (19). Stein's "rhetoricized Jew" was mostly *not* concealing antisemitism, given the forthright philosemitism of so many of her formulations, but her rhetorical strategies in portraying Jewish nature do reveal surprising and concatenated literary, political, and scientific engagements.

Gertrude Stein and the Making of Jewish Modernism seeks to explain how Stein's diverse stylistic and aesthetic responses to racial, economic, and cultural ideas about Jews in modernity form a Jewish grammar of modernism. The composition of *The Making of Americans*—what she called her "long book"—and the role that Jewishness played in that composition are crucial to understanding Stein's oeuvre and the origins of modernism.[8] The years spent composing *The Making of Americans* and the decade to follow were precisely the years Stein was "making" her modernism, and when modernism itself was beginning to take shape. (Hugh Kenner famously dubbed this period *The Pound Era*, and the title of this Introduction evinces my reorientation.) This book centers on a study of both *The Making of Americans* and the unpublished notebooks written alongside it. The novel has been and remains one of the least studied of Stein's major works and often is dismissed as a failure. The novel and its drafting materials are crucial to an understanding of Stein's thinking about Jews as part of a racial, cultural, behavioral, and world-historical people and character type. The Jewish type is central to Stein's narrator's scientific narratology, linking Stein's collegiate and medical school studies to her entrée into modern narrative. *Three Lives* (1909) is part of this making, as are Stein's first fictions from 1903. The repetitious style, typological concerns, and interest in Jewish nature in *The Making of Americans* remain crucial features of subsequent writings, from the concentrated word clusters of *Tender Buttons* and the ambiguous conversations of the "voices" poems to the more conventional "audience writing" of *The Autobiography of Alice B. Toklas* (1933), *Everybody's Autobiography* (1937), *Paris France* (1940), and *Wars I Have Seen* (1945).[9] Building on the association of modernism with Arnold's abstraction of Jewish nature, Stein, in her later work, associates modernist repetition and abstraction with Jewish identity in the contexts of marriage, nationality, persecution, resistance, and the establishment of singularly modern subjectivities, from anybody to everybody.

I

Modernism is considered to be an international literary movement from the first half of the twentieth century that was an imagined community of creative people who were, in Ezra Pound's words, "making it new." Formal experimentation is one of the central manifestations of modernist style, whether in the free verse of modern poetry or the stream-of-consciousness narrative of modern prose. Much of the fabric of modernist writing, however idiosyncratic, has a recognizable texture marked by strategic uses of repetition, juxtaposition, and abstraction that are often pieced together into a crazy quilt that plays with grammatical and narrative conventions concerning syntax, punctuation, chronology, character, or plot. The result is often a sense of what Bruce Robbins describes as "disorientation, defamiliarization, making strange" (qtd. in Walkowitz 15).

From the start, reading modernist literature was so disorienting that experiencing it resembled suffering from a psychological malady. Psychological literary effects were the result of writers' interests in understanding the workings of the human mind and its relationship to narrative structure. Modernist writers asked: How might a person's thoughts be conveyed in prose? How is literary composition related to thinking? And, in step with American philosopher and psychologist William James, they questioned normative notions about mental states. As James famously asked, "Who shall absolutely say that the morbid [state of mental disease] has no revelations about the meaning of life? That the healthy minded view so-called is all?" (*EMS* 165). Stein and other writers dismissed the notion that sickness and other deviations from the norm added nothing of value to modern life.

As an imagined community, the practitioners and critics of literary modernism policed their own borders both encouraging and repressing innovation. While modernism has been characterized by an attention to formal and ideological experimentation, not everyone agreed on the extent to which experimentation might challenge literary convention. In 1928, Ezra Pound criticized Stein and James Joyce for misguided language use: "Gertie and Jimmie both hunting for new langwitch, but hunting, I think, in wrong ash-pile" (*Pound/Zukofsky* 7). For Pound, "oedipus Gertie" served as a marker of the psychological stream-of-consciousness aesthetic practices he despised as irresponsibly apolitical (*Pound/Joyce* 255). He repeatedly paired Stein with Joyce as the twinned icons of this style, declaring, with excremental allusion, that "this flow of conSquishousness Girtie/Jimmee stuff has about FLOWED long enuff" (256). The self-appointed paragon of "making it new" in modern literature, Pound condemned Stein and Joyce as heretics who were making it too new. With his never-shy misogyny, Pound's "langwitch"-hunt puts the "witch"—that old wise woman—in the word "language" and reveals his sense of a powerful spiritual dispossession of language by the likes of Stein and Joyce.

By yoking Joyce to Stein, Pound was adding insult to injury: he was suggesting that, like Stein's, Joyce's writing was Jewish. What seems at first to be an even-handed dismissal of the two writers turns out to be Pound's broader characterization of a distasteful and Jewish modernist method that Stein embodied.[10] For example, when Joyce sent Pound a draft of the "Sirens" episode from *Ulysses*, Pound complained that he had gone too far, beyond even Stein's clownish prose. "[E]ven the assing girouette of a postfuturo Gertrudo Steino protetopublic dont demand a new style per chapter," he wrote (*Pound/Joyce* 157). Later, Stanislaus Joyce would likewise warn his brother that his work in progress seemed like a "pose" and complained, "It riles my blood to see you competing with Miss Stein for the position of Master Boomster" (qtd. in Joyce *Letters* Vol. 3, 216). According to literary historian Karen Leick, this depiction of Stein as a graceless parvenu with a loud, crude, and senseless prose style, was commonplace in the popular press.[11] Coming from Pound, however, a writer trying to blast his way into the future of art and literature, it exposes a revulsion to Stein's Jewish identity and what he saw as her Jewish literary practice.

Though misogynistic, it was Pound's antisemitism that led him to cast Stein's literary successes as pathological symptoms of a Jewish degeneracy. He was not alone. The publication of Stein's radical experiments in *Three Lives* (1909), *Tender Buttons* (1914), *Geography and Plays* (1922), and *The Making of Americans* (1925) provoked writers to place her in the pantheon of those making it the newest. Wyndham Lewis complained, "Miss Gertrude Stein is the best-known exponent of a literary system that consists in a sort of gargantuan mental stutter. What she is exploiting in her method is the process of the demented" (*The Art of Being Ruled* 400).[12] T. S. Eliot, too, was concerned with the healthy progress of the movement, sometimes called "futurism" after the Italian modernists. As one of his contemporaries queried, what was to be "The Future of Futurism"?[13] Eliot shared Lewis and Pound's disdain for "postfuturo Gertrudo Steino," opining in a review of Stein's work that, "If this is of the future, then the future is, as it very likely is, of the barbarians. But this is the future in which we ought not to be interested" ("Charleston, Hey! Hey!" 595). Eliot also expressed "*ominous*" resignation about Stein's "crude" method that he thought comparable to jazz as a sign of the vulgar, primitive, and regressive nature of experimental literature to come (595).[14]

Perhaps the most promising early estimation of Stein was by critic Edmund Wilson, who read Stein seriously, identified her combined interests in narrative form and human psychology, and appreciated her sense of humor.[15] In *Axel's Castle* (1931), Wilson places Stein firmly among Yeats, Valéry, Eliot, Proust, and Joyce, whom he considers the brilliant children of the French Symbolists. He praises *The Making of Americans* as "masterly" for its "strong sense" of personality theory, accurately assessing the goal and success of Stein's work therein (238, 239). His chapter on Stein nonetheless begins by dismissing her achievements, with his infamous confession about the 925 pages of *The Making of Americans*. "I have not read this book all through, and I do not know whether it is possible to do so," he wrote (239).[16] Wilson loses patience and ultimately condemns Stein as a Symbolist heretic whose literary excesses push the limits of post-Symbolism to "absurdity" (25). Like the men quoted above, Wilson has trouble giving Stein the attention he admits she deserves because of the apparent manifestation of Stein's Jewish identity in the modern forms of her writing.

Unlike those men, however, Wilson goes beyond the implicit association of degeneracy with Jewish nature to explicitly read Stein as a Jew and *The Making of Americans* as Jewish. In *Axel's Castle*, Wilson suggests the afflicted genius of Stein and her writings. He diagnoses *The Making of Americans* as an intellectually sick text marked by Stein's "ruminative self-hypnosis," a "progressive slowing-up of the mind," and "a sort of fatty degeneration of her imagination and style" (239). Even in *Three Lives,* a work that he admires, Wilson attributes Stein's success to a writing style that represents the speech of its slow-minded characters who are German Americans and African Americans. The slow-mindedness of the characters, he argues, is just as appropriate for the "patient and brooding repetitiousness of the German-Jewish Americans" he identifies in *The Making of Americans* (240). For even though, in the pages of the novel, Stein describes her subjects as "middle class" families with "foreign" grandparents (*MA* 21, 43), Wilson reads the novel's aesthetic of "repetitiousness" as a trait typical to characters he deems "German-Jewish," given Stein's background.

Wilson joined Eliot, Pound, and Joyce in regarding Stein as the representative of an "*ominous*" Jewish future. They peered at her through the antisemitic lens of aberrant racial difference. Dubbed by Wyndham Lewis the "men of 1914," these men alluded to what they deemed Stein's excessively large and graceless body as a symbol of the monstrous threat posed by her body of work (*Blasting and Bombardiering* 249).[17] They feared that the future of modernism was Jewish and that the icon of the Judaized modernism they despised was a harbinger of the racial and social vulgarities to come. In sum, these misogynistic avatars of antisemitic modernism together shaped a vision of modernism in the image of Gertrude Stein and, implicitly, defined modernism as Jewish.[18]

II

The symbolic use of Jews or Judaism as the apotheosis and antithesis of European culture was nothing new. In the nineteenth century Matthew Arnold famously demonized England's non-Jewish bourgeoisie for their "Hebraic" character. He idealized "culture"—by which he meant the realms of philosophy, criticism, and creative expression—as distinct from Jewish character and religion. Arnold claimed to derive his abstractions from the racialism of contemporary science, noting, "Science has now made visible to everybody the great and pregnant elements of difference which lie in race, and in how signal a manner they make the genius and history of an Indo-European people vary from those of a Semitic people" (*C&A* 173). The "science" Arnold had in mind was the philological history and criticism of Frenchman Ernst Renan, who made it common practice to extrapolate the qualities of the Hebrew mind through Biblical exegesis in ethnographic readings that classified both ancient and modern Jewry as degenerate. English polymath Herbert Spencer, too, argued that the primitive nature of the ancient Hebrew people was discernible from the simplicity of Biblical grammar, especially when compared to contemporary prose of the "English language" which was structurally "superior" in its heterogeneity (*First Principles* 357). And French literary historian Hippolyte Taine applied these deterministic reading methods to the modern age. He identified the "Semitic" element in English literature as instinctual, uncivilized, and excessive, contending that a "precise" literary genius was a racial trait particular to Anglo-Saxons and denied to Semites and others (368, 6).[19]

These men enlisted the supposedly objective techniques of positivism to quantify human nature with weights and measurements. Yet their attempts to establish "scientific" truths proceeded from some of the era's non-empirical assumptions about race, which combined physiology, language, culture, nation, and religion. Scientific minds like Jean-Martin Charcot, Francis Galton, Joseph Jacobs, Cesare Lombroso, Richard von Krafft-Ebing, and Otto Weininger also played important roles in popularizing unpopular understandings of Jewish nature by diagnosing what they saw as pathological in people they considered to be literally or figuratively Jewish.

As the largest non-Christian minority in Europe, Jews were one of the major European referents for race and were widely considered to have different bodies, speech patterns, and morality. Jewish racial differences were thought to transcend class and conversion. Some scientists found Jews to be a race of "brain-workers" plagued by higher than average instances of mental illness, making them the prime example of a race exhibiting the twinned symptoms of genius and degeneracy (Webb 586).[20] When discussing inherent artistic or intellectual gifts, for example, these scientists almost without exception referred to Heinrich Heine (1797–1856), classifying him as a successfully assimilated Jew whose genius was proven by his willingness to abandon his distasteful origins or as a genius who was Jewish and, thus, degenerate.[21]

Contradiction seems to be the only constant in the deployment of Jewish stereotypes in social analyses. For, coinciding with the heyday of positivistic classification of Jews was the popularization of the opposite tendency: to generalize about them or appropriate them as metaphors. As literary historian Michael Galchinsky explains:

> At various times, Jewishness was abstracted and figuratively identified with every aspect of the nation and its legal system to its outbreaks of socialism to its stock exchange to its monarchy to its journalism. . . . This move to abstraction is one of the hallmarks of nineteenth-century representations of Jews. (51)

As Galchinsky notes, this abstractionism reflected the "Jews' categorical indeterminacy—their capacity to be understood multifariously in diasporic, religious, national, racial or ethnic terms" (57). Zygmunt Bauman adds that, despite widespread efforts to classify Jews, they were not just impossible to categorize, but signified the very "impossibility of order" (148). He suggests that "what Christian discourse produced was the ambivalence of the abstract Jew, the notional Jew, the Jew as mythical genus which cast its shadow on 'empirical' Jews, but was not reducible to what the 'empirical' Jews were or did" (151).

III

Is it possible, then, to look "empirically" at Stein's Jewish nature? Considerations of Stein's Jewish identity and its relationship to her oeuvre have remained hearsay and legend. One contemporary reported a conversation in which Stein identified with traditional Judaism: "I am a Jew, orthodox background, and I never make any bones about it" (Steward 9). Another reported that Stein claimed a heretical exceptionality among the chosen people: "Yes, the Jews have produced only three originative geniuses: Christ, Spinoza and myself" (McAlmon 204). In a third account, given in the epigraph to this introduction, Stein confirms her Jewish atypicality by claiming ambiguously that she must not be typical, since no one has accused her of being a Jew. While providing a frank sense that Stein thought of herself in Jewish terms, these reports lack corroboration. All were things Stein was said to have said, and not always by admirers. In contrast to these myths, my study is grounded in Stein's texts—including the rich, deep archive that provides an intriguing parallel to her published work. Key portions of this book stem from research conducted at the Beinecke Rare Book and Manuscript Library at Yale University, the Bancroft Library of Western Americana at the University of California–Berkeley, the Jewish Museum of Maryland, the Baltimore Museum of Art, the Harry Ransom Research Center at the University of Texas at Austin, and the Schlesinger Library at the Radcliffe Institute for Advanced Study at Harvard University.

Assembled from the archives, the recorded collage of Stein's early Jewish experiences helps us to rethink modern Jewish life, moving away from dualistic and historically inaccurate notions of assimilated, gentile, American experiences versus authentic, traditional Jewish ways of living. This dichotomy prevents us from understanding Stein's early Jewish life as a distinct "multiverse" of social, economic, linguistic, cultural, religious, and educational geographies.[22] The striving of Stein's German-Jewish bourgeois family shaped her early home life. Her father Daniel Stein was a capitalist who went into the clothing business with his brother in Pittsburgh and, a decade later, Gertrude was born across the river in Allegheny, in 1874. Stein's parents were from middle-class, German-Jewish families in Baltimore. They returned to Europe for extended periods as Daniel explored avenues of economic advancement. During the first few years of Stein's life, the family was tied to more traditional Jewish communities first in Vienna (1875–1878) and then in Paris (1878–1879).[23] Afterward, Daniel settled his family of seven in Oakland, California, where, for the next decade, the Steins were enmeshed in the social and cultural heterogeneity of this American city yet in its infancy.

One finds a veritable almanac of the Oakland Jewish life of the Stein family and the religious observances that shaped Stein's childhood in diaries from the 1880s kept by Gertrude's mother, Amelia (Milly) Keyser Stein.[24] Daniel was a founding member of the reformed First Hebrew Congregation of Oakland and, according to Milly's diaries, the synagogue stood at the center of the Steins' social life. The family was friendly with Meyer Levy, the rabbi who arrived from Pasadena in 1881 to head their congregation. In February of that year, Milly "heard that Rabbi Levy was coming here to lecture at the Temple" (*Amelia Stein Diaries* 4 Feb.

1881). Levy lunched with the family that summer and by August the four younger children—Bertha, Simon, Leo, and Gertrude—began attending religious school on Saturday and Sunday and, by the next year, a Thursday "heabrew school" (10 Aug. 1882). Religious practice revolved around Sunday School, holidays, and festivals, such as "Roshaschona," "Yom Kepur," "Schvouth," and the "Purum Mask Ball," rather than weekly Sabbath services that the family attended irregularly, often spending Saturdays in San Francisco shopping or going to the theater (24 Sept., 2 Oct. 1881; 24 May, 4 Mar. 1882).[25] Stein's middle brother Simon was confirmed at the synagogue in May of 1882; two weeks later, the family hosted a party for the entire confirmation class. In 1884, by the time Gertrude was ten years old—a birthday she celebrated at home with ten of her Sunday School classmates—the eclectic Jewish life in this small western community meant celebrating Passover one day, "Dying Eggs all afternoon" for Easter the next, and going to Sunday School at the synagogue the day after (12 Apr.).

Stein's upbringing was rooted culturally and linguistically in the traditions of the German-Jewish bourgeoisie. In the 1880s, when large numbers of impoverished Jews from Eastern Europe began to immigrate to the United States, the Steins of Oakland were enjoying a time of relative prosperity common to many middle-class German Jews. German *kultur* infused the Steins' life in California. They attended operas such as *Faust* and *Lohengrin* in San Francisco.[26] And as was typical of the German Jewish bourgeoisie in Europe, they had a gentile German governess. In her diary, Stein's mother recorded the comings and goings of the "Frauline" and her Jewish charges: "Frauline took the children to the sabath school for the first time" (20 Aug. 1881) and "The children were at Sunday school Frauline went to church" (13 Aug. 1882). Later, in college, Stein fictionalized her Germanophone upbringing in a story about a family who were immigrants from "Deutchland" (revised to "Germany"), and whose matriarch is referred to as "Grossmutter" ("The Radcliffe Manuscripts" 111, 117, and 111).[27]

The German-Jewish Steins had formal and informal social contact with many other internationals settled in the Bay Area. In the house there was a steady stream of German, Irish, and Mexican domestics, governesses, and dressmakers. Stein's mother went to a Chinese doctor for treatment of her long and terminal illness. The children met an array of "nationalities" in the public schools, as Stein later recalled: "Well all this time I went to school and school in California meant knowing lots of nationalities. And if you went to school with them and knew about their hair and their ways and all you were bound later not to be surprised that Germans are as they are and French and Greeks and Chinamen and Japs" (*WIHS* 8).

Unlike their Baltimore grandparents living amidst a large and entrenched Jewish community, the Oakland Steins were geographically isolated from their social set. Straddling divergent social milieux, Stein and her siblings, like the children she later described in *The Making of Americans*, spent time with the "poorer people who lived around them" (113). Their parents, meanwhile, maintained ties with other well-to-do Jewish families scattered farther afield. Stein's brother Leo remembered being the only Jewish family in their area:

> Later came the Jew complex, what I call the pariah complex. There were almost no Jewish families in East Oakland and most of the time I was the only Jewish boy in school. I can't pretend to have been persecuted, and if it had not been for my incredibly exaggerated self-consciousness nothing much would have come of it. (*Journey Into the Self* 199)

Stein's own "Jew complex" was more ideological but not without its challenges. She reflected, for example, on being a Jew in the largely Christian world of her childhood: "After all one is brought up not a Christian but in Christian thinking" (*EA* 243). And she recalled the first time she discovered Jewish tradition as distinct from the "Christian thinking" that surrounded her: "When I was about eight I was surprised to know that in the Old Testament there was nothing about a future life or eternity. I read it to see and there was nothing there. There was a God of course and he spoke but there was nothing about eternity" (114).[28] Stein gleaned an awareness of the competing ideologies present in particular contexts: she was "not a Christian" and yet had discerned the Christian basis for an idea that she had perhaps deemed universal. Jewish identity was not just a social relation for Stein as a young person, but already it was something that extended into intellectual realms.

In the fall of 1893, Stein entered the Harvard annex, which would become Radcliffe College in 1894. By her junior year, she described Harvard as a place "where to be a Jew is the least burden on the individual of any spot on earth" (*TMJ* 424). Studying with William James, Hugo Münsterberg, George Santayana, and Josiah Royce, Stein made the solid beginnings of a promising career in science as a published undergraduate researcher in the Harvard Psychology Laboratory. James was a philosemite and Münsterberg was Jewish, so Stein may have felt welcomed as a Jewish student in their classes. Stein, who was president of the Philosopher's Club, had a broad social circle, mostly of Jews but with some very significant gentile friends.[29] And yet she felt so strongly about Jewish racial separatism that, in the spring of 1896, she wrote a polemical essay on "The Modern Jew," arguing that even nonpracticing Jews should avoid intermarriage with gentiles. Many American Jews proudly embraced racial distinction, and Stein likewise presents Jews in the essay as a racially distinct group that should actively avoid assimilation within the sphere of the family.[30] Journalist Hutchins Hapgood confirmed that Stein was someone who "feels her race intensely" and remembered her discoursing passionately on the subject of intermarriage when they met that summer in Europe (535). He recalled, "she talked to me a long time about how impossible it was for a Jewish woman to marry a Gentile" (535).[31]

Stein's collegiate reflections on the ambiguous place of "The Modern Jew" are similar to recent estimations of the modern Jewish experience as a state of inbetweenness representative of modernity and tradition. Like her near contemporaries Charles Reznikoff and Louis Zukofsky, she voices an "uncanny perception of being both at home and a stranger within Western culture," reflecting the European-Jewish experiences of separation, demarcation, and expulsion over centuries (Fredman 100). Such history was made current for Stein by the Dreyfus Affair and the massive wave of Jews emigrating from Eastern Europe and fueled her collegiate concerns about the tenuous social standing of modern Jews. She feared that even those otherwise assimilated into the non-Jewish mainstream might nonetheless be perceived as outsiders "admitted on sufferance only" (TMJ 427). Stein's contradictory claims to Jewish longevity and vulnerability are prescient. A century later, literary critics have characterized modern Jewish identity as caught "between race and culture," and modern Jewish literature as inhabiting an ideological stance "between spontaneity and reflection" (Cheyette; Eshel and Presner).

IV

This book documents Stein's life and work as they unfolded against the backdrop of Matthew Arnold and changing ideas of Jewish identity.

Chapter 1 traces Stein's writing about empirical and abstract Jewish racialism and looks at her 1896 essay on intermarriage and the preservation of modern Jewish identity. Stein wrote the work at Harvard when she was both a Jewish racialist and an undergraduate scientist. Like many of her generation, Stein took inspiration from Arnold's critical yet glorified depiction of a Jewish force shaping civilization and the psyche. As mentioned above, Arnold in part had developed his ideas from racialist thinkers who often saw intellectual and creative "excesses," such as genius or virtuosity, as signs of a Jewish mental disease. That was a position and a methodology not without its dissenters, such as William James, who taught Stein at Harvard.

Stein's participation in racialist debates over culture resulted in her ethical and aesthetic interest in the experimental practices that would come to characterize literary modernism. Chapter 2 explores Stein's use of Arnold's Hebraism in her first fictions to allusively signal the Jewish morality of her middle-class characters. In 1903, in conventional prose, Stein wrote the novella *Q.E.D.* and the brief first draft of her novel "The Making of Americans." In both works, she presents ill-fated romances between ethically Jewish and more aesthetically inclined characters. In *Q.E.D.* she allusively depicts the Jewish identity of her protagonist, Adele, who finds herself in a love affair with the aptly named Helen. Stein closes the novella with her characters in a romantic stalemate, but her romance fusing Arnoldian Hebraism and Hellenism as an ideal of Jewish culture had just begun. The affianced couple in the first draft of "The Making of Americans" espouses Stein's Arnoldian fusion. In the novel, the paterfamilial voice of Hebraism dismisses as *modern* the Hellenic inclinations toward the arts and other "literary effects" by the young heroine and her fiancé (142). In her revising of Arnold, Stein imagines the modern writer as one of a plurality of individuals whose typologically Jewish cultural ideals combine the ethical traditions of the Hebrew with the intellectually liberating creativity of the Hellene.

In contrast to the coded nomenclatures for modern Jewish identity in Stein's first fictions, there is an explicit discussion of Jewish nature in the dozens of notebooks Stein filled when she resumed writing *The Making of Americans*. Chapter 3 examines Stein's early training in philosophy, psychology, and medicine to excavate an ambiguously racial conception of Jewish nature in these unpublished notebooks. Arnold's typology remains foundational for Stein between 1906 and 1911, when she begins to codify characteristic behaviors of Jewish and Anglo-Saxon types of people. Amidst a menagerie of friends, family, artists, scientists, and literary and historical figures, Stein ranks herself as a Jewish type alongside Picasso, Cézanne, Matisse, Flaubert, Darwin, and Caliban. Rather than keeping the world at arm's length and theorizing about it, Stein considered that these Jewish types shared an engagement with experience that she thought was the key to a modern aesthetics, what she called the ability to "unconventionalize" (39.814). In this characterization, the notebooks reveal Stein's matter-of-fact association of Jewish nature with modernism.

In these early writings, Stein differentiates notes that freely mention Jews from drafts destined for publication; the latter omit explicit Jewish references entirely. In chapter 4, I consider the solely metaphorical presence of Jews in the final text of *The Making of Americans*. Paralleling Stein's notebooks, the novel's narrator largely abandons storytelling in lieu of character study. Stein replaces the Jewish and Anglo-Saxon character types from the notebooks with a purely behavioral nomenclature and, as a result, the published volume contains no explicit references to Jews. The narrator nonetheless maintains a focus on a categorically Jewish and modern type: the pariah. He introduces several pariah figures, from servant girls to avant-garde writers, who join him in a fraternity of what he calls "Brother Singulars" (21). With an eye to Hannah Arendt's notion of the modern Jewish visionary or "conscious pariah," I argue that Stein's narrator, with the characterological "plot" he is writing for himself and strangers, estranges narration by increasingly abstracting his characterology with indefinite pronouns as the novel progresses. Amidst the formal experimentation of ever-increasing repetition and abstraction, the narrator's Jewish pariahs recede into textual indistinguishability while still differentiating themselves from others. Through this association, Stein sets the agenda for ethical authorship in the modern era.

In the fourteen years between the completion and publication of *The Making of Americans*, Stein found a new voice writing poetry, portraits, and plays. Chapter 5 considers the startling proliferation of explicitly Jewish motifs in Stein's formally revolutionary compositions of the 1910s and '20s. In these seemingly ahistorical nonreferential writings, Stein's Jew remains a figure of convention and difference that demonstrates the paradoxical fixity and indeterminacy of modernist poetics. Stein's Jewish lexicon expresses bourgeois family relations, the singularity of Jewish tradition, and Jewish nationalism. Beginning in the decade preceding Eliot's *The Waste Land* and Joyce's *Ulysses* and continuing through the 1920s, Stein's references to Jews in her experimental poetry radically change the story of the Jew in modernism by uniting the historical with the quotidian, the cultural with the racial, and the personal with the political.

In chapter 6, I discuss the interpenetration of Stein's experience as a Jew in Vichy France with the non-Jewish experiences of war and persecution in Europe and beyond. In her memoir of these times, *Wars I Have Seen*, Stein writes as openly about the Jewish question in Europe as she had in her college essay a half-century earlier. In the 1930s, Stein deemed the modern era Jewish; in the 1940s memoir, she finds the current wave of antisemitism to be an unwelcome archaism of bygone eras. She specifically criticizes Vichy's head of state, Maréchal Philippe Pétain, for persecuting Jews, paints Hitler as a monster, and strives to understand the historical, political, and personal forces that brought such figures to prominence. She Judaizes the experience of occupation—a rebellious, pluralist, and humanitarian gesture—at a time when Vichy decrees were sharply demarcating Jewish and French identities. Jewish experiences from the past (such as Dreyfus's wrongful imprisonment) and the present (such as roundups and deportations of Jews and her own experience of threatened internment in a concentration camp), become touchstones for the mass imprisonments and displacements of the war. She worries over situations of persecution, imprisonment, deportation, and refugeeism as they afflict the Jews and non-Jews of her acquaintance to conclude the Jewish and modern qualities of an era when "everybody can persecute anybody" (*WIHS* 62). She reinstates the specificities of Jewish experience and history while imagining the symbolic import of such experience for gentiles. She suggests that the persecution to which Jews historically were subject now has become general, afflicting Jews and non-Jews all over France.

My conclusion, "Making Sense of a Sensationally Jewish Stein," explores the ways that Stein's identity as a Jewish and modernist writer was a potent symbol of collaboration and resistance in Vichy France and today. In particular, I address and historicize concerns over Stein's Jewish identity and alleged Nazi collaboration as raised in the popular press in 2012, when the Metropolitan Museum of Art in New York City opened the exhibition, "The Steins Collect: Matisse, Picasso, and the Parisian Avant-Garde."

Claims of Stein's Nazi collaboration were unsubstantiated, historically obtuse, and prone to reading Stein out of context. Nonetheless, in their unremitting determination to know about Stein's wartime experiences and writings, they affirmed the importance of Jewish identity and modernist style to Stein's legacy as a writer.

1

An Israel of the Imagination
The Sciences of Race, Matthew Arnold, and Stein's Modern Jew

Gertrude Stein began her undergraduate years at Radcliffe when, as she later recalled, Darwin was "near," "evolution was still exciting very exciting," and "science meant everything" (*EA* 242). As a student of William James and Hugo Münsterberg in the Harvard Psychology Laboratory, she gained a formal introduction to empiricism and became a respected, published researcher before attending medical school at Johns Hopkins University. In addition to her recollected fervor for the science of the day, the young Stein was a fiercely proud Jewish racialist who wrote "The Modern Jew Who Has Given Up the Faith of His Fathers Can Reasonably and Consistently Believe in Isolation," a polemical essay on intermarriage and the preservation of modern Jewish identity. Written in a forensics class at Radcliffe, the essay provides a vital framework for understanding how Stein's interest in science shaped her thinking about Jewish nature.[1]

This chapter outlines the Social Darwinist sciences of race as they pertain to Jews in modernity in order to shed light on the later literary marriage of Jewish nature and ideas of the modern in Stein's oeuvre. The latter portion of the chapter explores how Matthew Arnold's abstractions and the pseudo-empirical methods of race science inform Stein's collegiate essay on modern Jews and how that relates to Stein's understanding of Jews in modernity.

As large numbers of Jews emigrated from Central and Eastern Europe to Western Europe and across the Atlantic over the course of the nineteenth century, parliaments, presses, and popular writers expressed concern about the "Jewish question"—an effort to determine the place of Jews in non-Jewish society. Some considered Jews to be Jews only by language, culture, and tradition, making conversion and full assimilation into the nation-state possible. However, "scientific" theories of racial difference from the fields of history, medicine and philology buttressed the more popular conception of Jews as degenerate, unassimilable wanderers.[2]

"Degeneration" began as a scientific term signifying a hereditary mental disease, but its usage eventually encompassed broader social concerns about racial difference, immigration, crime, public health, national security, and human evolution.[3] Racialists often linked degeneracy—as a symptom of human decline—with varieties of Jewish genius. Such links were fodder for antisemites looking to vilify Jewish contributions to European culture, but they were also fruitful affirmation for Jews who touted Jewish exceptionalism as a positive racial attribute. The most famous example of the latter was British statesman and novelist Benjamin Disraeli, who proudly vaunted his Jewish heritage despite his conversion to Christianity at age thirteen. Race, he proclaimed, was the key to world history, and, in several novels, he depicted an aristocratic Jewish race as one of superior and benevolent rulers. Disraeli's tendency to draw ties between a "chosen" race of ancient Semites and the English establishment led one observer to famously describe England as the "Israel of his imagination" (Skelton 258).[4]

Although Stein was a reader of Disraeli,[5] the Israel that caught her imagination was not his, but Matthew Arnold's. The work of this prolific critic and poet would provide a canvas for her earliest aesthetic and ethnographic investigations. Like Disraeli, Arnold characterized England in metaphorically Jewish terms, calling its ascendant middle class "Hebraic" Philistines even though these British strivers were mostly evangelical Protestants.[6] Arnold's Hebraism was a foil, however, for promoting his "Hellenism," an ideal of "culture" as the pursuit of knowledge and beauty. And while his essay *Culture and Anarchy* (1868) considered Hebraism and Hellenism to be competing tendencies of civilization, the title points to his thesis that without culture society descends into anarchy. His stated targets were English gentiles who he criticized by invoking antisemitic lore about the cruel Old Testament God of law and modern associations of Jews with capitalism.[7] Arnold also referenced the longstanding iconography of semitic differentiation within English literature—what Zygmunt Bauman calls *allosemitism*—by characterizing his Hebraism with Shylock's hard-nosed insistence on the letter of the law, the pound of flesh, or with the heroism of Disraeli's Hebrews.

By tapping into the antisemitic zeitgeist of the era, Arnold's abstractions gained an immensely broad reach. He was a hotly contested figure among intellectuals in his native England and in the United States, which he toured in the early 1880s. As historical anthropologist George Stocking observes:

> Arnold's polemic on culture fitted quite well with the degenerationist argument: both assumed a distinction between civilization and culture; both called into question the assumption that progress in virtue went hand in hand with progress in technique. (87)

Raymond Williams asserts that Arnold's *Culture and Anarchy*, with its critique of the utilitarianism of industrial capitalism, was "more influential than any other single work in this tradition" (115). Stephen Prickett adds that it "is one of those rare works which has actually modified the English language. . . . 'Hebrew' and 'Hellene,' 'Barbarian' and, above all in colloquial usage, 'Philistine,' have passed into the language" (138).

Despite Arnold's "preëminence" as a literary and social critic during her lifetime, Stein's interest in Arnold has been wholly absent from the study of her early writing (Raleigh 140). Studies have, instead, traced her debts to later controversial figures such as Otto Weininger, to more immediate mentors such as William James, or to the more aesthetic inspiration of Cézanne. Arnold's germinal place in Stein's pantheon nonetheless conjoins the influence of Weininger, James, and Cézanne as participants in the broadly "scientific" understanding of the Jewish question in modernity, one in which imagination and abstraction orient empirical study of race, character, and the psyche.

In concert with Arnold and other "scientific" thinkers, Stein's earliest analysis of "the Jewish problem" grounds Jewish difference in a conflation of behaviors and physiological characteristics (TMJ 423). On one hand, Stein reaffirms the biological "family tie" or "race-feeling" of Jews by advocating endogamous marriage (426). On the other, she redefines Judaism as a "religion of endeavor" in which Jews actively commit themselves to "noble aims and great deeds" (427). The result is an ambiguous definition of Jewishness not dissimilar to the conflation of morality and race by degenerationists. Unlike them, Stein, in an Arnoldian vein, maintains Jewish difference as a *necessary* facet of an ethical—and literary—modernity.

The Abstract Jews of Race Science

Social Darwinists forged many connections between race and modern culture, effectively linking eugenics to the sphere of aesthetics. My use of the term "Social Darwinists" is meant to encompass the purportedly empirical, if methodologically flawed, outlook of many nineteenth-century thinkers working in the same vein as Herbert Spencer, coiner of the phrase "survival of the fittest," and Francis Galton, the founder of eugenics. These scientists and other scientifically oriented thinkers considered Jews racially in moralistic classifications of character. They persisted in this hypothesis, even as the evident diversity of Jewish experience began to unravel the pretense of empiricism in racial explanations of Jewish identity.

Matthew Arnold was one among several well-known European thinkers of the day who considered "The Share of the Semitic People in the History of Civilization" (Renan). From Heinrich Heine, Karl Marx, Friedrich Nietzsche, and Otto Weininger to Ernest Renan and Hippolyte Taine, these thinkers considered Jews and Jewish ideas in direct opposition to a Christian European people cast in Indo-European, Aryan, Anglo-Saxon, Greek, and Roman molds.[8] Renan imagined that these "two elements [the Indo-European and the Semitic] . . . mingled in unequal proportions, have made the woof of the web of history" (151). The interwoven strands comprising Renan's image of history did not, however, form a peaceful tapestry in the work of most Social Darwinists. Empiricists and nonempiricists alike considered Jews to be indelibly and racially different from non-Jews, a difference that extended back to Biblical times and was to blame for the social and economic upheavals of the modern era. For many of these men, the narrative of history was one in which scientific and social agendas converged around a core concept of "progress" that pit Christianity against Judaism and cast Judaism as a degenerate threat to human evolution.

Various thinkers pathologized perceived Jewish differences as racially degenerate. The notable presence of Jews in European arts and letters nonetheless led some to think that Jews represented the very idea of "culture" to which the Semitic spirit supposedly ran counter. This made it difficult to dismiss them as uncivilized outsiders or Philistines, though critics certainly persevered in this endeavor.[9] As I mentioned in the introduction, Taine, Renan, and Spencer used pseudoscientific methods of literary criticism to target the language of Jews, both biblical and modern.[10] Although xenophobic discussions of genius and degeneracy were anecdotal, biographical, and quantitatively and physiologically inconclusive, they were hugely influential.[11] Jewish physician Max Nordau was instrumental in popularizing this questionable practice in his book *Degeneration* (*Entartung* 1892–1893, in English 1895).[12]

There were, however, numerous dissenters to degenerationism. George Bernard Shaw responded to Nordau with "An Exposure of the Current Nonsense About Artists Being Degenerate," and the leading German psychologist William Hirsch asked, "How far can we, from a work of art or literature, diagnose a mental disease of its author?" (Shaw's work was later published as "The Sanity of Art" in 1895; Hirsch 218). Agreeing with Hirsch, William James railed against the authors of what he called the "genius books" for using the language of empiricism as a pretense for objectivity (*EMS* 164). In his 1896 Lowell Lectures on "Exceptional Mental States," James declared:

> The medical terms become mere appreciative clubs to knock a man down with. Call a man a cad and you have settled his social status. Call him a degenerate, and you've grouped him with the most loathsome specimens of the race, in spite of the fact that he may be one of its most precious members. (164)[13]

James's mention here of the human race's "most precious members" is likely a refutation of the claim that Jews were degenerate. Although James does not specifically name Jews in his public lectures, his letters indicate that he was a fervent philosemite who criticized antisemitism, admired Jews categorically, and, as a young man, romantically exoticized Jews he encountered.[14] James often referred to Jews with superlatives as "the ablest [nation] in the world" and, throughout the 1890s, expressed a matter-of-fact disapproval of antisemitism, whether his wife's, an innkeeper's, or that of degenerationists (*CWJ* 8: 128).[15] In his marked impatience with prejudice of all kinds,[16] James exhibited a healthy skepticism of the Social Darwinists' empirical methods; he was, however, swimming against the tide.

The most notorious example of Jewish degeneration theory was the misogynistic treatise, *Sex and Character* (*Geschlecht und Charakter* 1903, in English 1906), by Otto Weininger (1880–1904), a Viennese Jewish apostate. The book became a sensation, especially when the author committed suicide a few months after it was published, and its influence extended to modern writers such as James Joyce, Ford Maddox Ford, and Gertrude Stein.[17] Scholars have long pointed to Weininger as a major influence on Stein's ideas about Jewish identity, gender, and character.[18]

Weininger's approach to the Jewish question was psychological and anti-empirical; it exemplified the contradictions inherent in Social Darwinian usages of the term "race." Weininger admired William James, despite the latter's largely empirical methods, holding that James felt "almost instinctively that psychology cannot really rest upon sensations of the skin and muscles" (82). Although Weininger disputes racial understandings of Jewish nature and the notion that "genius is supposed to be a form of madness," his conclusions are indistinguishable from antisemitic purportedly empirical classifications of Jews as degenerate geniuses (329). For Weininger, Judaism was:

> neither a race nor a people nor a recognised creed. . . . [but] a tendency of the mind . . . a psychological constitution which is a possibility for all mankind, but which has become actual in the most conspicuous fashion only amongst the Jews. (303)

Weininger's antisemitism, inextricable from his misogyny, makes explicit the moralistic underpinning that Arnold and others only implied when adopting the intellectual patrimony of Heine's dualistic notions of Jew and non-Jew. Frustrated by his sense of the broad social malady looming, since "Judaism is the spirit of modern life," Weininger, in *Sex and Character*, desires to cure Judaic ill-health by eradicating what he considers to be female and Jewish imperfections in society (329). For Weininger, male nature was inherently moral, and female nature was without moral sense. In his widely circulated volume, Weininger argues that men and women exist in varying mixtures of masculine and feminine platonic ideals, which correspond to Aryan and Jewish types. He intuits that the problem is much greater than race or sex, however, and ends his chapter on "Judaism" with this ultimatum:

> The decision must be made between Judaism and Christianity, between business and culture, between female and male, between race and the individual, between unworthiness and worth, between the earthly and the higher life, between negation and the God-like. Mankind has the choice to make. There are only two poles, and there is no middle way. (330)[19]

In this passage, Weininger sums up his disdain for Judaism's feminine focus on the "earthly" materiality of business and the constraints of its communal aspect in favor of what he saw as Christianity's congruity with divinity, masculinity, individuality, and culture. Like Arnold, who he does not cite, and Nietzsche, who he does, Weininger's work continues the evocative use of "Judaism" as a potent yet abstract social force.[20]

Weininger's radical assumptions about the sexual and psychological mixtures of all people were extremely suggestive to Gertrude Stein. She heartily recommended his book to friends,[21] and yet in her private notebooks she categorized Weininger as a "fanatic," a worrisome character type she also used to describe her Harvard collaborator Leon Solomons (37.764.[8a]).[22] She differed from Weininger, too, in her largely positive valuation of Jewish nature. Although her thinking would later accommodate Weininger's florid and passionate convictions about abstracted human categories, Stein's early writings and her ambivalent racialism preceded Weininger. It was Arnold, then, whose Jewish abstractions were formative for Stein (and perhaps for Weininger too).

Contemporaries dubbed Arnold the "prophet" and "apostle of culture" for his spirited advocacy of "culture" as the remedy for an English society besieged by what he considered to be the Hebraic traditions of the middle class.[23] As part of the middle class that he was criticizing, Arnold claimed, "for the most part, [to have] broken with the ideas and the tea-meetings of [his] own class," and found himself, like "a certain number of *aliens*," regarded more often "as elegant or spurious Jeremiahs than as friends and benefactors" (*C&A* 144, 146, 95).[24] Arnold's position as an unheeded middle-class prophet certainly resonated with Stein, who, from the start of her writing career, likewise cast a critique of the middle class along Jewishly imagined racial-historical lines.

Arnold hoped his inward and ideational notion of "culture" would deliver the English populace to perfection. His volume *Culture and Anarchy* and several other works celebrate both Hebraism and Hellenism as epic forces admirably aiming for human perfection, if by radically different means. Continuing what he dubbed Renan's "science" of reading ancient textual sources ethnographically, Arnold's Hebraism derived from the character of Biblical Jews and his Hellenism from ancient Greeks (*C&A* 173).[25] "Our world," he explains, moves between "two points of influence . . . Hebraism and Hellenism," which take their "names from the two races of men who have supplied the most signal and splendid manifestations of them" (163–164). Arnold's Hellenes, desiring the apprehension of truth, conduct themselves with a *"spontaneity of consciousness"* and an "unimpeded play of thought" in contrast to the *"strictness of conscience"* and "moral impulses" of Hebrews (165, 171). Hebraism was known for its deeds and was responsible, according to Arnold, for the Protestant Reformation, Victorian religious dogmatism, the mighty mercantilist thrust of the British Empire, and the political ascendancy of England on the world stage. Respecting the enormous productivity of Hebraism, Arnold nonetheless feared that an overarching emphasis on action had sublimated intellectual pursuits, reasoning, and the arts—the gems of Hellenistic "culture"—precisely for their lack of practical utility. To temper the Hebraic "preference of doing to thinking" (163), Arnold hoped to encourage a devotion to "culture" that would, he thought, bring the English closer to the force he considered more "naturally" theirs in terms of racial make-up, since the "English, a nation of Indo-European stock, seem to belong naturally to the movement of Hellenism" (173).

Arnold's goals for the attainment of "culture" are broadly social. And yet, befitting his job as a school inspector, he is attentive to individual cultivation or *bildung*. Every person should, he instructs, aim for self-understanding, akin to "the old Socratic commonplace, *Know thyself*" ("My Countrymen" 28). This imperative was in common use among Stein's friends at Harvard, keen to reconcile their philosophical ideals with lived experiences.[26] For Arnold, such knowledge should be "disinterested" and not made to serve practical purposes (FC 268). He rejects "political and practical" pursuits in favor of "*curiosity* . . . [the] disinterested love of a free play of the mind on all subjects, for its own sake" (268). Instead of politicization, Arnold aestheticizes the pursuit of knowledge by asserting that, with Hellenism, one aims "To get rid of one's ignorance, to see things as they are, and by seeing them as they are to see them in their beauty" (*C&A* 167). For Arnold (as for Keats), beauty was truth and truth beauty; the Hellenic striving to "see things as they are" in truth, would be to see the beauty in things—or what he referred to as their "sweetness and light" (167). These two phrases, "seeing things as they are" and "sweetness and light," quickly became touchstones for Arnold's thinking about Hellenism and culture and were foundational to Stein's literary investigations into human character.[27]

Arnold's writing on religion, meanwhile, informed Stein's understanding of Judaism. In *Literature and Dogma* (1873), Arnold promotes the pursuit of "culture" by reading the Bible as a literary text rich with the wisdom of human experience rather than as a book to be heeded as dogma. And because he thought it impossible to prove God's existence, he preferred to consider the deity as an inspirational "force that makes for righteousness" (*L&D* 200).[28] While the pious T. S. Eliot would later complain that Arnold had abandoned religion for culture,[29] Stein, as I discuss below, refers to Arnold's ethical notion of a deity when listing the varieties of Jewish religious experience in a college essay.

Arnold's imperative to "see things as they are" appears ultimately to depend on empirical methods of observation, or *literal* seeing. And yet his potent abstractions of English character suggest there might be other, metaphorical means to arrive at the truth through *figurative* seeing. In his vision for a modern, rational, and nonetheless *transcendent* Christianity, for example, scriptural accounts of miracles were to be read not literally or prescriptively but poetically, as literature. Arnold's science, too, accommodated poetry. As we saw in the introduction, Arnold claimed that scientific notions of race had "made visible to everybody the great and pregnant elements of difference" between "Semitic" and "Indo-European" peoples (*C&A* 173). If "race" was an attempt to differentiate the insides of people, what racialists "got right" is that "to see things as they are," one must ascertain internal differences despite minimal outward signs. It is through Arnold's theory, I argue, that Stein engaged with the idea of a reading practice that "makes visible" elements of abstract value that are otherwise hidden—a practice at the root of both a tantalizing literary ideal and, as wielded by race scientists, a terrifying cultural reality.

Stein and Arnold

Arnold's broad-reaching dualisms are imperative for understanding the Jewish types, tradition, and history that invigorate Stein's experimental literary style. Stein seized upon Arnold's Hellenic creed from *Culture and Anarchy*, "To see thing as they are," and placed it with irony, frustration, and desire in the mouths and minds of her earliest protagonists.[30] One biographer attributes Stein's use of the phrase to Henry James's "metaphor of vision and its necessary emphasis on perceptive intelligence" (Wineapple 205). Given that James himself was perhaps the premier Arnoldian among American writers, the attribution is incomplete. Others suggest that Stein uses the phrase to describe a literal appearance of the truth in Cézanne's abstractions, but Stein's first use of it predates by a year her 1904 acquaintance with Cézanne's painting.[31]

In her first fictions from 1903, Stein establishes an experimental typology rooted in Arnold: she bases her characterizations of the dueling protagonists in these early compositions on his Hebraism and Hellenism, oppositions that remain vital as she reworks them in *Three Lives* (completed 1906) and then again in *The Making of Americans* (completed 1911). In her notebooks for the latter, Stein's ethnographic studies include bifurcated classifications of Jews and Anglo-Saxons who embody Arnold's epic forces. These classifications eventually seed the accounts of differing psychological types that make up the final draft of *The Making of Americans*, though Stein dropped her use of "Jew" and "Anglo-Saxon" for a nomenclature that described character traits and behaviors. In that novel, the narrator explains his own experimental method of writing typology as the culminating development of like-minded "Brother Singulars," figures uniting Arnoldian Hebraism and Hellenism.

Stein is not alone in her use of Arnold. Numerous references to Arnold are found in the work of Stein's forebears and contemporaries George Eliot, Thomas Hardy, Henry James, Joyce, Woolf, Ford, Forster, T. S. Eliot, Sarah Orne Jewett, and Wyndham Lewis.[32] Arnold's Hellenic notion of "culture" costumed the work of most modern writers, either explicitly, like Joyce's "deaf gardener, aproned, masked with Matthew Arnold's face," or implicitly, like Buck Mulligan's suggestion that he and Stephen Dedalus do something for Ireland, "Hellenise it" (*Ulysses* 1.173, 1.158).

Among Arnoldians, Henry James most directly shaped Stein's first fictional endeavors. As the unofficial American ambassador for Arnold, James was a correspondent, sometime acquaintance, and mostly supportive critic of Arnold and Arnoldianisms appear throughout his work.[33] Stein read and admired James throughout her life, but his literary influence surfaces most directly in the 1903 composition of her novella *Q.E.D.* In her manuscript notes for that first piece of fiction, Stein copied out several passages of James's 1902 novel *Wings of the Dove*.[34] The trio of main characters in James's novel provided a literary framework for casting her own romantic disappointments in the lesbian love triangle of her novella, and her protagonist explicitly compares another character to "Kate Croy," after James's heroine (*Q.E.D.* 121). The allusions to *Wings of the Dove* in *Q.E.D.* demonstrate that Stein's interest in James was Arnoldian. In many parallels, Stein plays up James's use of Hebraism and Hellenism in his characters. She adapts his use of Arnold's ideological debate by casting her Kate Croy as a gentile American "Helen" and Kate Croy's suitor, Merton Densher, as the stalwart Adele, a characteristically Arnoldian Hebrew.

Despite the abundant textual and contextual evidence, critics have overlooked Stein's serious and sustained interest in Arnold. As I will detail, Stein attended Harvard at a time when Arnold was in ascendance; as a voracious reader, she surely encountered Arnold at many a turn. During her years as a university and medical student, both she and her brother Leo cite Arnold by name and quote him in essays about modern Jewish life and literature.

At Harvard, Stein's curricular exposure to Arnold was split firmly along disciplinary lines: the faculty of letters were enthusiastic Arnoldians, but scientists were skeptical. The scientific curriculum at Harvard immersed Stein in a positivist empiricism, which, as described above, was rife with a non-empirical racialism. Like Disraeli, Stein was proud of her racial origins: she firmly believed in Jewish genius and was troubled by the possibility of an inherently Jewish degeneracy.[35] In 1896, as a student of William James at a time when he was steeped in degeneration literature, Stein would have been immersed in studies of degeneration theory and its critics.[36] In a forensics class that same year, Stein united her fervent interest in Jewish continuity with the ideology of racial degeneration in a composition that also bears the marks of her reading of Arnold.[37]

Stein's philosophy professor George Santayana had been a student at Harvard in the 1880s, and later mused, "Perhaps Matthew Arnold moved in the background and inspired us" (qtd. in Raleigh 155).[38] Literature scholar Ludwig Lewisohn, Stein's slightly younger contemporary, observed, "We all talk Arnold, think Arnold, preach and propagate Arnold" (qtd. in Raleigh 145). Arnold had become "*the* preëminent academic critic" in America, as literary historian John Henry Raleigh asserts:

> All the great Victorian authors had become standard subjects for study in college curricula in the late nineteenth century. Arnold, however, was not only a subject to be studied but a prophet to be heeded, and the professor himself was more likely than not an "Arnoldian." (140)

This certainly held true for Stein, who studied English with Professor Lewis E. Gates when he was editing a volume of Arnold's prose that he prefaced with a long appreciation.[39] And William James had been reading

Arnold for at least three decades by the time Stein was his student. Although his brother Henry was Arnold's primary advocate and promoter in America, William read Arnold with muted enthusiasm: he thought his literary manner "priggish" and was extremely skeptical of his pretensions to scientific method (*CWJ* 2: 86).[40]

Outside of the classroom, Stein would have encountered Arnold's ideas in discussions among Harvard's Jewish students, many of whom were striving to assimilate into the gentile American intelligentsia. Arnold's dualistic view of civilization struck a chord with American Jews in the midst of what Stein described as a nativist "fever to be an Anglo-Saxon and a gentleman" (MA 137).[41] These Jews struggled to maintain a connection to Jewish tradition and yet immerse themselves sufficiently in the majority to contribute in meaningful ways to American culture. "Western Jews," opined a writer in Harvard's *Menorah Journal* in 1924, "whether they have read Arnold or not, look at Judaism through his bi-focal glasses" (qtd. in Fredman 97).

Almost thirty years earlier, Stein herself observed that these opposing cultural forces exerted an inescapable pull on the Jewish student at Harvard:

> One part of them [the Jews] are attempting to identify themselves entirely with the Christians and turning their backs on their own people. Instances of this sort are numerous in the German universities and are also to be found in our land. Even here in Harvard we have had at least three such instances, here where to be a Jew is the least burden on the individual of any spot on earth. (TMJ 424)

Stein considered herself to be Jewish but also fully assimilated into university life, even if her classmates did not see it that way. Biographer Wineapple notes, "A Radcliffe student close to Stein in the years just after graduation recalled that 'before I had become liberated in regard to racial questions I had never known a Jew; thought they were something different. I remember [Gertrude Stein] saying, "I'm the top of the heap," and I said, "The top of your heap." She was much offended'" (56).

Horace Meyer Kallen, the German Jew who would later coin the term "cultural pluralism," arrived at Harvard as an undergraduate in 1899, a year after Stein left, and yet his experience there sounds like one of the "instances" of Jews trying to pass as gentiles that Stein had observed. Kallen's Jewish identity was affirmed by English professor Barrett Wendell, a gentile known to affect an English accent. Wendell encouraged Kallen to give up his posture of non-Jewishness, by lauding what he saw as the major "role of the Hebraic tradition in the development of the American character" (qtd. in Fredman 110). Wendell was not the only one to hear in Arnold's Hebraism a means to ratify the Jewish presence in Christendom.[42]

Despite Arnold's foreboding about the Jewish spirit in modernity, his inclusion of Hebraism as a major force in civilization was foundational to an entire generation of modern Jewish writers, including Stein, who took the mention of Hebraism as an invitation to Judaize Arnold's "culture" and to appropriate his Hellenism for the Jews. In the 1890s, American Jews described themselves using the interchangeable terms "Jew," "Israelite," and "Hebrew," the last of which chimes linguistically with Arnold's Hebraism.[43] As the sociologist John Cuddihy writes, "Hebraism as ideology gave meaning to Jewish civilizational inferiority and moral superiority at one stroke," leading modern Jews to reinterpret dialectically Arnold's characterization of "culture" to include themselves (184). Literary historian Stephen Fredman suggests that Kallen, perhaps inspired by Wendell's affirmation of Jewish identity, "invent[ed] cultural pluralism as a means of fighting off the assimilation of Jewish ethnicity to an Anglo-Saxon ideal" (111).[44] Indeed, cultural pluralism, Jewish continuity, and transnationalism were some of the ideas introduced among members of the Menorah Society "for Hebraic Culture and Ideals," founded at Harvard in 1906, and in the *Menorah Journal*, begun in 1915, by the likes of Kallen, Charles Reznikoff, and Randolph Bourne (Kessner 192). Like Felix Adler's "Ethical Culture," these explicitly not-Jewish theories of "culture" were a Jewish response to the nominal non-Jewishness of Arnold's Hellenistic "culture."

The Radcliffe Essay

Though Stein's time in Cambridge preceded the Menorah Society by ten years and the *Menorah Journal* by twenty, her polemical essay about "the Jewish problem in its modern aspect" similarly attempts to reconcile Jewish and American identities (TMJ 423). Writing in 1896, her third year at Harvard, Stein celebrates Jewish contributions to American society but instructs that such boons depend on the maintenance of a discrete Jewish community. The essay's title plainly states Stein's thesis that nonbelieving "modern" Jews should avoid intermarriage with gentiles: "The Modern Jew Who Has Given Up the Faith of His Fathers Can Reasonably and

Consistently Believe in Isolation." In the essay, she reasons that a vibrant familial separatism or "isolation" is imperative to preserve a racially conceived Jewish "brain-power" from threats of dissolution (424). To those concerned that isolation would distance Jews from being Americans, Stein firmly replies that "Judaism" is a family connection and "does not interfere with their citizenship" (426).

Stein's focus on non-intermarriage to healthily sustain American Jewish integration was prompted by her pained awareness of the often precarious status of Jews domestically and internationally. Even those Jews fully participating in gentile society were, she noted, "admitted on sufferance only" (427). She saw foreboding signs of antisemitism in the Dreyfus Affair, "the spirit prevalent in Germany, the recent anti-semitic riot in Paris and the not so very distant exodus in Russia" (424). In the wake of these events, she observed two divergent responses of Jews at Harvard. In some Jews she saw a complete denial of Jewish identity, which prompted her plea to limit assimilation to the public sphere by avoiding intermarriage. In other Jews she saw "a strong revival of Jewish feeling," which affirmed for her the idea that the Jews were a chosen people (424). She deemed it necessary, however, to refine the import of Jewish chosen-ness through the modern lens of religious skepticism.

Like Arnold, Stein's conception of Jewish character embodies the driving forces of modernity tout court. Innovation, progress, and skepticism were, according to Stein, era-changing Jewish inclinations to be preserved by isolation. Jews were predisposed to "embrace . . . the general skeptical spirit prevalent at this period of the world's history" (424). Stein's own skepticism leads her to defend non-intermarriage by using "nineteenth century interpretations of the Scriptures" (425). Stein here refers to German scholars, involved in what we now call Higher Criticism, who sought to historicize biblical texts by determining their human authorship. This movement inspired Renan's historical *Life of Jesus* (1863) and his ethnographic readings of the Bible to determine Jewish character. Arnold, too, tried his hand at it in *Literature and Dogma*, a work Stein refers to in her Radcliffe essay. Like Renan's ethnographic interpretation of the Bible and Arnold's salvaging of the Bible as literature, Stein asserts that most religious observances in Judaism have outlived their historical necessity and are merely commemorative.

The prohibition of intermarriage, however, is not an obsolete practice, since, according to Stein, it preserves the Jewish people as a race. Jewish identity is, in her eyes, a bond that is a "race-feeling, an enlargement of the family tie," and "the feeling of kinsfolk" (426). Within this racial family, she recognizes a diversity of forms of Judaic expression, from the belief in "a personal God" to the belief in a more metaphorical divinity described in *Literature and Dogma*, what she refers to as "a Matthew Arnold sort of 'force that makes for righteousness'" (423).[45] Despite the variety in Jewish belief, she saw unity in Jewish opposition to racial mixing: "Non-inter-marriage," she writes, is "the sine qua non of Judaism . . . for inter-mar-riage would be the death-blow of the race" (423).

The methodology of Higher Criticism buttresses her argument about the racial basis for Jewish identification, especially against those who would deny her claim that even nonbelievers can be Jews. Stein reads the Pentateuch as a "poetical description of the rise of a race" and reinterprets the Covenant, that mythical marker of Jewish singularity, along racial lines:

> Let us remember that in answer to this we may plead nineteenth century interpretations of the Scriptures and yet not have them lose their meaning for us. The covenant with God described in the Old Testament may well be a poetical description of the rise of a race, strong in a hereditary clan feeling, standing by each other as brothers and thus by the strength of their union, remaining uncrushed in the clash of nations round about them and having thus truly a covenant with God which has made them endure. The spiritual meaning of the Chosen People may well signify a race having inborn a strongly ethical and spiritual nature ever fostered and increased among themselves, thus making them in the very highest meaning of the words, a Chosen People chosen for high purposes. (425)

Stein's Jews endured because of heredity rather than divine action. For her, Jewish chosen-ness was a "poetical" allusion to an "inborn" clannishness that disposed Jews to "stand by each other as brothers" (425). Similarly, in a preceding passage, she argues that the Jews were a "race [that] had become a nation" before many of the fundamentals of the religion were established or the law given at Sinai (425). She believed that the basis of the covenant was an "ethical ideal . . . without any reference to a religious mis-sion" and that the Jews' ethical origin predated the religion and remained a racial characteristic (425). For Stein, Jewish clannishness and ethics are positive qualities vulnerable to racial mixing.

Despite their hereditary origins, Jewish communal ties are ideological and elective in Stein's thinking. Modern Jews should, she proposes, form a familial bond with other Jews united around ideals of ethics and action: "let the modern Jew . . . still be a Jew although his Judaism is no longer a creed, but a religion of endeavor. Let Judaism mean a banding together of a people making of themselves a brotherhood devoted to noble aims and great deeds" (427). Her Jewish "brotherhood" aligns with Arnold's Hebraism in its ethics and in its emphasis on action, what Arnold described as a "preference of doing to thinking" (C&A 163). Dependent upon a racial understanding of Jewish nature, Stein's modern Judaism, stripped of laws or "creed," becomes solely a "religion of endeavor," an Arnoldian notion that echoes Felix Adler's motto for his Ethical Culture Society: "Not by the creed but by the deed" (Adler 1). Stein differs from the apostate Adler, however, by insisting that the Jew will "still be a Jew" (427).[46]

Stein ends her essay by underscoring the racial "instinct" for those ethical acts that distinguish Jew from non-Jew:

> A feeling that has become so strong that it is a well-spring of action and is so deeply ingrained in the soul that a departure from it makes one feel a dastard and a renegade and that the most advanced opinions cannot root out, such a feeling is too great, to be wantonly cast away. (427)

Despite her modern abandonment of Jewish creed, Stein romantically holds fast to a racial feeling "ingrained in the soul" that is resistant to "the most advanced opinions" (427). Like racialists of the era, Stein blurs empirical and nonempirical understandings of human nature when describing as instinctual characteristics that are indistinguishable from behavior and religious belief.

A pseudo-empirical racialism shapes the contradictory portrait of what Stein sees as the familial and *unfamiliar* bonds uniting modern Jews—a dynamic of collectivity she later dubs "Brother Singulars." In the Radcliffe essay, Stein seizes on the trope of brotherhood to represent the ties of Jewish communal unity, and yet this brotherhood is largely estranged. Stein claims that because of racial instinct, the bond of Jewish brotherhood, even among those who are "perfect strangers," would trump the tie to an "intimate Christian friend" (426). Stein's modern Jews are thus an iconic if isolated fraternity.

In international relations, Stein grants Jews membership among the avant-garde of other world-historic nations, though their membership has fiercely guarded boundaries. Jews fruitfully contribute their modern outlook to world culture through a delicate balance of integration and segregation. For Stein, the Jews are "a nation to stand apart, to be with nations but not of them" (425). She nonetheless prides modern Jews on the sustaining powers of their estranged brotherhood and on the boon it provides to the larger "brotherhood of man" (427). For Stein, Judaism and Christianity, Hebraism and Hellenism, modernity and tradition, brothers and singulars are not irreconcilable, if distinct. Invoking a messianic sensibility, Stein defends racial separatism to incur universal benefits. She predicts its eventual good for gentiles as well as Jews, pointing to socialist leaders and charitable men, who "show that the strength and power that is the heritage of the race has not been devoted to their own to the exclusion of others" (426). The Jews are, she claims, "to be ever in the fore-front of progress and enlightenment but not to mingle with others" (425). Thus, fulfilling the Covenant, Stein grandiosely envisions Jewish racial isolation as a force for modernity.

In the Radcliffe essay, the estranged fraternal bond and the socially limited internationalism highlight the acutely *singular* character of Stein's modern Jews. Unlike Weininger, who later insisted "there is no middle way" between the race and the individual, Stein combines the strengths of each for the modern Jew, whose fraternity is an admirable example of both clannishness and individuality (330). Like Weininger, however, Stein associates Jewish nature with the collective race and associates non-Jewish nature with individuality, a dichotomy with Arnoldian resonances. Stein's modern Jews, as a people, exhibit a utilitarianism, activity, and ethics that hearken back to Arnold's Hebraism. The singularity of Stein's ideological brotherhood, however, emphasizes a freedom from collective social bonds that enables the "free play of the mind" so crucial to Arnold's Hellenic ideal (FC 268). Thus, we see in Stein's modern Jew an embodiment of Arnold's competing forces: the cohesiveness and ethics of Jewish familial tradition and the more free-wheeling independence of modern culture.

Less than a decade later, the isolated fraternity characterizing Jewish racial identity in Stein's college essay serves as a model for her modern writerly ideal, figures she calls "Brother Singulars" (MA 153). With its Jewish roots, the fraternity of Brother Singulars was likely something she discussed with her brother Leo, and she may have contributed to his thinking (or vice versa) about how questions of Jewish nature were to be answered in modern fiction. After leaving Harvard for medical school at Johns Hopkins, Stein shared an apartment with Leo in Baltimore where he penned two essays for the weekly *Jewish Comment* outlining his ideals for modern Jewish writers. Leo proposed that the "modern" Jewish writer must write "realistic fiction" as a truthful "corrective" to stereotypical portraits of Jews ("Society and Art" 3). In concert with his sister's Arnoldianisms, Leo argues that this literary truthfulness "is what Matthew Arnold had in mind when he made 'the criticism of life' the distinguishing quality of literature" (3).[47] And like the isolated fraternity with which Gertrude bound modern Jews to one another, Leo's modern Jewish writer balances communal identity with individuality. His exemplar was Abraham Cahan, whose discerning fiction, Leo thought, derived from an immersion in immigrant Jewish life counterpoised with an isolation from that life. The Brother Singulars featured in Stein's first fictions are, like Leo's explanation for Cahan's greatness, solitary figures born of tight-knit communities whose innovations derive from their source tradition. They are Jewish and share the modern Jews' contradictory dynamic of association and estrangement. Ultimately, Stein's Jews are Jewish by association, as a familial society of strangers with shared ideals.

Stein's proposal in "The Modern Jew" for public assimilation and private Jewishness illuminates the choices she made later about how and when to write about Jews. Early on, she wrote explicitly about Jews and Jewish nature only in personal, private writings and manuscript drafts: she did not intermarry open statements about Jews with publication. Instead, beginning with her Radcliffe essay and developed in her first fictions, she keeps Jewish tradition hidden in allusion and abstraction. In the middle and later parts of her career, her references to Jews and Jewish nature surface more publicly and yet remain comparatively private due to puzzling contexts that keep the references hidden. Stein establishes a Jewish grammar in her writing that is modern and Jewish by its association with Arnoldian ideals of Hebraism and Hellenism and with fin-de-siècle racialist notions of Jewish character.

2

Brother Singulars

The "Hidden Tradition" of Jewish Culture in Stein's First Fictions

> underneath her very American face body and clothes were seen now and then flashes of passionate insight that lit up an older and a hidden tradition
>
> (Gertrude Stein, "The Making of Americans: Being the History of a Family's Progress" 146)

> From Maine to Florida, and back again, all America Hebraises.
>
> (Matthew Arnold, *Culture and Anarchy* 243)

Gertrude Stein had little patience for traditional synagogues with dividers between the sexes. As an American Jew from a reformed congregation, she experienced great discomfort when visiting two synagogues in Amsterdam in 1896. She wrote:

> I am at present engaged in giving thanks that I was not born a female Israelite in ye older time or even in Amsterdam to-day . . . I don't like to sit behind galleries with a fence around it even if they are considerate enough to leave peep holes in it. (Gertrude Stein postscript, Leo Stein to Fred Stein, July [20], 1896, YCAL)

Stein's complaint affirms her allegiance to the more egalitarian practices of modern Judaism in contrast to the sex segregation of "ye older time." While distancing herself from the limitations of orthodox practice, her ironic thanks-giving nonetheless shows a familiarity with the traditional morning prayer's petition, "Thank God I was not born a woman."[1] With this comment, Stein conceptually jumps the gallery fence and speaks in the voice of a male Jew reciting the morning prayer, an identification with the male voice that, as critics have noted, recurs in much of her writing, particularly when describing herself.[2]

An overlooked though significant feature of Stein's masculine identification is that it is inextricably tied to her Jewish identity, a topic this chapter will explore as a formative feature of her earliest writings. Stein's masculine identity is a *Jewish* masculine identity, and her play with gender stems from her gendered experiences in Jewish communities. Gendered and queer readings of her early works like *Q.E.D.* and the first draft of "The Making of Americans" depend on understanding their Jewish contexts.

In the novella *Q.E.D.* from 1903, Stein ironically reiterates the Jewish morning prayer's petition in the female protagonist's exclamation: "I always did thank God I wasn't born a woman" (58). Maria Damon argues that with this line Stein "exposes the misogynistic traditions of her own culture," which the letter above corroborates ("Gertrude Stein's Doggerel 'Yiddish': Women, Dogs, and Jews" 231). But the character in question, Adele, makes this masculinist Jewish allusion to express an ironic and exasperated dis-identification with her gentile female companions. One must therefore complicate Damon's reading of Adele's assertion of "difference" at "the intersection of gender *and* 'race'" (232). By "thanking God," Adele affiliates herself among Jewish men and implicitly embraces what Stein had previously described as the "noblest brotherhood" of the Jewish people. She may resent the gendered isolations of Jewish practice, but nonetheless affirms the associations integral to Jewish identity, however masculine.

Adele thus fashions herself as an outcast communitarian—a figure in the model of the Brother Singular, Stein's obliquely Jewish figure for the modernist writer. The "Brother Singular" appears implicitly in *Q.E.D.*'s Adele and explicitly in the narrator and other male characters in the first draft of Stein's novel "The Making of Americans" (1903) as well as in the final draft of *The Making of Americans* (completed 1911 and published 1925).[3] These characters are not only nominally male (or, in Adele's case, male-identifying), but also modern and middle class. In them, masculinity is linked to innovation (the modern) and convention (the middle class), a paradox that occasions a major departure from the cluster of feminist and queer associations that critics have made about Stein's Jewish identity, her Singulars, and her other early protagonists.[4]

Stein's protagonists are queer only because they are Jewish. For although Stein infuses her Brother Singulars with an oddity that sometimes covers for sexual queerness, and even dubs them "queer people," her oblique use of Jewish identity in these characters more often emphasizes the state of being at odds with oddity itself, that is, they are odd and yet oddly conventional, too (MA 152). Stein traces a Jewish genealogy of atypicality through her Brother Singulars by asking: Where do interesting people come from? How is singularity born of tradition? How are apostles born? The answer, in Stein's first fictions, appears to be that the modern singular derives from the stability and comforts of explicitly middle-class and implicitly Jewish foundations. These individuals (her Singulars) maintain a firm foothold in tradition while innovatively breaking from it. This apparent contradiction renders the Brother Singular one of the earliest icons of the modernist writer's complex relation to tradition, something later engaged by T. S. Eliot, Virginia Woolf, and James Joyce.

In his 1919 essay "Tradition and the Individual Talent," Eliot would assert a similar generational paradox—that "not only the best, but the most individual parts of [a poet's] work may be those in which the dead poets, his ancestors, assert their immortality most vigorously" (*Selected* 4). And, in *A Room of One's Own* from 1929, Woolf argues that "master-pieces are not single and solitary births; they are the outcome of many years of thinking in common, of thinking by the body of the people, so that the experience of the mass is behind the single voice" (65). Stein's Singular—like Eliot's Talented Individual and Woolf's "single voice"—importantly figures the relationship of the individual writer to tradition as familial and communal in his brotherhood. And yet, as a figure of the modern writer, the Brother Singular repeats the moral, hereditary, and cultural influences of Jewish ancestors while, in abstracted kinship, taking up the "impersonality" of Eliot's modern poet and choosing the isolation of Woolf's single room.[5]

In her first mature literary writings, Stein portrays the role of the Jew in modern fiction as both tradition and the individual talent. Taking the best of Matthew Arnold's ideals of "Hebraism" and "Hellenism," Stein has her first protagonists, raised with the values of German-American middle-class Jews, cast off their anti-intellectual Philistinism to "see things as they are" and embrace a "Hellenic" ideal of culture. Stein literalizes the implied Jewishness of Arnold's metaphorical Hebraism to reveal an "older and a hidden" Jewish tradition within the Philistine middle class (MA 146).

Stein's conception of Jewish character thus negotiates a generational and incomplete progression from Arnold's ethical, action-oriented Hebraism to the Hellenic drive for culture and truth, arriving at a modern and Jewish cultural ideal that blends Arnold's types.

Stein's formal expression of tradition and the individual talent, too, is Jewish. She formulates a theory of the modern literary aesthetic from a dialectical and Jewish reinterpretation of Arnold's abstract forces. Stein takes Arnold's Hellenic credo, "seeing things as they are," as an imperative to see the "hidden traditions" in modern character (MA 146). Being attuned to "hidden traditions" involves reading traces of Jewishness in repetition and abstraction, the experimental "literary effects" that Stein would use throughout her career (142). Repetition and abstraction also served as a means by which her characters understand the truth about human nature. Specifically, Stein manifests what she saw as a Hellenic emphasis on *thinking* in her use of abstraction, which maintains a more intellectual relationship to the past. And she manifests what she saw as a Hebraic emphasis on *doing* in her use of repetition, to insist on the past's relationship to the present. Even the formal realism of her early prose, such as the quip derived from the morning prayer, engages in this type of Hebraic repetition as a means of calling forth past Jewish tradition. Above all, in these fictions, Stein suggests that repetition is Jewish because it represents the monotony of middle-class life.

The Hellenizing of a Jewish Singular in *Q.E.D.*

Stein's first Singular is Adele, the autobiographical protagonist of *Q.E.D.* Stein signals Adele's Jewish identity by indicating her background as middle class and by imbuing her with the signature trait of Arnold's stalwart Hebraism as a staunchly ethical thinker. Adele's implicit role as a Brother Singular, however, exemplifies a merging of Arnold's forces that Stein figures in terms of Adele's outcast communitarianism. Adele's devotion to a Hellenic self-knowledge and "seeing things as they are" alienates her from her clan and peers, establishing her as a burgeoning Singular still devoted to her middle-class origins.

In the novella, Stein charts Adele's oscillations between the conventions of middle-class communal identity and the innovations of the Singular. Adele begins as a dutiful Arnoldian Hebraist fiercely loyal to her middle-class upbringing, and she gradually abandons her positivistic approach to human relations in a literal and figurative romance of Arnoldian Hellenism. She falls in love with a "blooming Anglo-Saxon," aptly named Helen, whose tie to another woman, Mabel, is eventually revealed to be more of an obstacle than Adele had assumed (Q.E.D. 80).

Adele's name may be German for noble, good hearted, and pleasant, but Adele combines these laudatory characteristics with an unintentionally cruel dogmatism. She declares:

> I believe strongly that one should do things either for the sake of the thing done or because of definite future power which is the legitimate result of all education. Experience for the paltry purpose of having had it is to me both trivial and immoral. (59)

Adele's cool positivism positions her as an Arnoldian Hebrew in valuing experience for its utility, a devotion to doing over thinking, which, for Stein, renders Adele a Philistine in matters of love.

Although her mind may be "attuned to experiment," Adele's strict "moral sense" limits any impulses she may have toward Arnoldian Hellenism's "free play of the mind," impulses crucial, Stein suggests, to the fluctuations of any relationship (Q.E.D. 62, 63; FC 268). As Helen complains, "You are so afraid of losing your moral sense that you are not willing to take it through anything more dangerous than a mud-puddle" (Q.E.D. 63). And indeed, once Adele avails herself of Helen's amorous tutelage, she begins to feel that "her moral sense had lost its importance" and she no longer gleans any "definite future power" from experience (64, 59). By the end of the novella, Adele drops some of her utilitarianism, and Stein begins to construct a new ideal of Jewish culture associated with the "free play" of Arnoldian Hellenism by casting Adele as a Brother Singular.

In Q.E.D., allusion and metaphor veil Adele's Jewish identity. Most critics have pointed to the novella's lesbianism as a forbidden topic but, within the narrative, female lovers openly discuss passion and love, kiss, and meet for romantic trysts.[6] However, the hidden Jewishness is significant in a work that explicitly specifies the old-world roots of other modern American identities. The narrator observes that all three women in the story are "distinctly American" and yet "bore definitely the stamp of one of the older civilisations, incomplete and frustrated in this American version but still always insistent" (54). Helen Thomas is "the American version of the English handsome girl," and Mabel Neath is the "vulgarised" and "weakened" version of "Italian greatness" (54, 55). The narrator deprives

Adele of a family name, however, and makes no mention of the older civilization from which she derives. In a draft of the novella, Stein describes Adele as "distinctly Oriental in type," but, in the end, she drops this euphemistic racial allusion to Jewish identity (Collection of notes and quotations, ca. 1890s, YCAL MSS 76 [139.3274.5]).

Though unnamed, Adele's Jewish nature is "still always insistent," and the repetitiveness of insistence takes on racial, ideological, and formal meaning in the novella. Stein introduces "insistence" as a form of repetition, akin to the "flashes of passionate insight" had by another Steinian protagonist, "that lit up an older and a hidden tradition" of Jewish identity (MA 146). An insistence on what is only implied forms a methodology of indirection and abstraction in the novella, what Damon terms Stein's "metaphoricity of Jewishness" ("Women, Dogs, and Jews" 234).[7]

Stein's "insistent" portrait of Jewish nature encompasses the "noble" significance of Adele's German name, her warm feelings of tribal affiliation, the Jewish characteristics of racial scientism, and, with a nod to Arnoldian Hebraism, the purported righteousness and honesty of her middle-class roots. Adele alludes to her Jewish membership in one of the biblical tribes of Israel, for example, when she admits that talkativeness is a characteristic "failing of [her] tribe" and yet, ironically, her Jewish identity goes unspoken (57). Her Jewish affiliation is, nonetheless, an alienated sense of community, since, as she sardonically declares, "I believe in the sacred rites of conversation even when it is a monologue" (57).[8]

In the heavy physicality of Adele's body, Stein portrays Jewish identity as a racial characteristic with ideological import. She suggests a primitive Hebraism in Adele's heft that is a dark and weighty counter to Hellenism's "sweetness and light," though Adele exudes plenty of sweetness (Arnold C&A 167). The narrator first introduces Adele lying on the deck of a ship, "with the freedom of movement and the simple instinct for comfort that suggested a land of laziness and sunshine. . . . as if accustomed to make the hard earth soft by loving it" (Q.E.D. 55–56). Jaime Hovey rightly reads Adele's earthy and exoticized sprawl as a "Sapphic" primitivist fantasy: "the white American lesbian's 'discovery' of the sexual and racial 'other' buried within her" (557). Hovey's reading nonetheless elides Stein's tendency to racialize both blacks and Jews. Adele's Jewish earthiness differentiates her whiteness from the whiteness of the other women, Stein's narrator indicates, by "suggest[ing]" the stereotypical laziness of blacks in the American South (Q.E.D. 55).[9] In a fictional Radcliffe theme from 1895, Stein had similarly infused a white speaker's reclining posture with a rosy yet racist portrayal of happy-go-lucky blacks in Baltimore, "where no one is in a hurry and [one hears] the voices of the negroes singing as their carts go lazily by" ("Radcliffe Manuscripts" 139). The iterations of Adele's posture in *Q.E.D.* behaviorally identify her lesbian sexuality as "other" while emphasizing the physiological racialism of her German-Jewish Americanism.

Adele is an American version of the German Jew combining racial qualities associated with German and Jewish identities of the era. Adele's "noble" German given name echoes the adjective Stein uses repeatedly to characterize the Jewish people in her collegiate essay (second only to "great"). In another Radcliffe composition, Stein describes a young woman named Hortense Sänger, whose family name is German for "singer," indicating her kinship with the "negroes singing" ("Radcliffe Manuscripts" 142). Sänger's name also contains the French word for "blood," confirming her physiological difference from her classmates as "a dark-skinned girl" (141). Sänger's first name, Hortense—German for "Hydrangea"—literalizes the female metaphor of flowering sexuality that Stein employs when describing her "in the full sensuous development of budding woman-hood" (141). Months earlier, Stein had described a similar protagonist as "fair" but with a nose that "just escapes being beautiful for at the last moment it drooped and spoiled its perfect shape" (123). If these protagonists were merely German Americans, their Teutonic racial identity would render them kissing cousins to the dominant white Anglo-Saxons of late nineteenth-century American racial mythology. Instead, the behavioral and physiological differentiation, marked by a dark complexion, a disappointing Jewish nose, or the characteristic habits of "negroes singing," demonstrates that these young women are German-American Jews and have what Matthew Frye Jacobson would call a "whiteness of a different color."

Stein inflects Adele's racial Jewish difference with an Arnoldian idealism that isolates Adele from her companions. The "sensuous" flowering of Adele's precursors in Stein's college fiction alludes not only to primitivist ideas of black licentiousness, but also the perceived crassness and Philistinism of bourgeois Jewish parvenus. In *Q.E.D.*, Mabel's prudish, "angular body" is seasoned by the "tropics," but she returns to her steamer chair after losing patience with Adele's sun-worshipping sprawl on the "bare boards" of the ship's deck (55–56). Her departure is a warning signal to Helen that she disapproves of Adele's flirtatious posture as a breach of respectable comportment. The narrator ironically notes that Adele's apparent composure belies a mind suffused with "an almost puritanic horror" of "the cultivation" of "physical passion" (59). So, despite her suggestively sprawling body, Adele's mind, like Mabel's, rebels against unrespectable comportment to reveal her proudly middle-class mores.

Adele's proud pose and Mabel's recoil are opposite sides of the same coin: the fin-de-siècle association of Jews with the American middle class. Jews were commonly thought to have business acumen. In her Radcliffe essay, Stein had trumpeted the "financial ability and . . . great clannishness" that made the Jews "a great power" (424). Historians confirm the notable association between the characterization of Jews as good businessmen with upstanding values and the ideals of the American middle class, hence Arnold's late nineteenth-century Judaizing of the American middle class's ascendancy, "all America Hebraises" (C&A 243).[10] As Eric Goldstein argues, Jews and non-Jews alike in the 1880s and 1890s held this perception (37). This might be why, looking back on their lives in 1952, Alice Toklas responded to a query about whether Stein had felt part of a cultural or religious minority by protesting, "We never had any feeling of any minority. We weren't the minority. We represented America" (qtd. in Janet Malcolm 196).

In *Q.E.D.*, Stein associates American middle-class ideals with Jewish clannishness, ethics, and business acumen. She has Adele pontificate on the "affectionate family life" of her middle-class community:

> I simply contend that the middle-class ideal which demands that people be affectionate, respectable, honest and content, that they avoid excitements and cultivate serenity is the ideal that appeals to me, it is in short the ideal of affectionate family life, of honorable business methods. (59)

Defending the middle class against attacks of materialism, Adele characterizes them with an abiding "honor" and "respect." When she was in medical school just a few years before, Stein had praised the healthful effects of the "home of a tradition that stands for honesty and right living" ("Degeneration in American Women" 413). Adele adds the purposeful avoidance of "excitement" to her praise of honest professionalism and affectionate family life, anchoring her ideals in a monotonous "serenity." Such an unexciting backdrop serves, as Adele often protests, as the best soil to cultivate those who must separate themselves from their roots to exercise their singularly "individual imagination" (*Q.E.D.* 117). For Stein, both the stability of middle-class tradition and the singularity of one who ventures from it are Jewish by association.

Drawn to the ethics and close-knit family ties of middle-class tradition, Adele nonetheless shares Arnold's criticism of her class and ironically casts herself as an "apostle" on an unpopular mission. When Helen coyly baits her, stating that "surely to understand others and even to understand oneself is the last thing a middle-class person cares to do," Adele agrees with Helen's—and Arnold's—view that a Philistine middle class was mindlessly dogmatic and had an aversion to self-understanding (58–59).[11] As a true American cousin to the "apostle of culture," Adele replies, "I never claimed to be middle-class in my intellect and in truth. . . . I probably have the experience of all apostles, I am rejected by the class whose cause I preach" (59).

Stein associates Adele's middle-class lamentations with those of characteristically Jewish apostles. Manuscript notes for the novella reveal the Jewish roots of Adele's apostolic posture in four aphoristic statements (spoken by Adele or the narrator) that echo *The Book of Lamentations*, a work ascribed to the prophet Jeremiah.[12] The Hebrew title for *The Book of Lamentations* is *Eikhah*, or "How," after the plaintive question traditionally commencing a lamentation. Stein's first two notes begin by asking "How":

How often do we find ourselves prostrate before the wall of lamentation beating it with our impotent hands praying to a God that will not hear. Our faith is stronger [because we know that it is the wall of Jerusalem and] and our life weaker than ever before.

How difficult when we want to pour one simple drop from a bottle, we incline ever so patiently and gently until the feat is almost accomplished and then with a quick movement we destroy it all. . . .

They say that old people do find themselves at last face to face with a solid blank wall. It sounds it seems to have something beyond it but it won't move.

At the end of our powers we are like the exiled Jews before the wall of lamentations. Our faith is stronger than it ever was but we are hopelessly stopped. (139.3274.9–10. Brackets indicate words that Stein wrote and then crossed out.)

Stein's aphoristic laments play hide-and-seek with Jewish topics while maintaining the repetition and themes of Jeremiah's lamentations about failures of strength, lovers' deceptions, and the lack of comfort from anyone including God (Lam. 1.14, 1.19, 3.8). The speaker compares her frustration to "the exiled Jews" impeded by "the wall of lamentations . . . the wall of Jerusalem." These walls echo an address in *Lamentations* to "the wall of the daughter of Zion," which scholars claim is a metaphor for the city of Jerusalem (370). Stein drops the entire reference to "Jerusalem," however, and her remaining image of a "solid blank wall" reminds us of the process of erasure in the composition of *Q.E.D.*, where Jewish allusions come and go. As these omitted passages from her notes indicate, Stein maintains an Arnoldian association between singularity and a Jewish apostolic biblical tradition, even while she rejects some of the narrowly racial implications of Arnold's types.

Stein figuratively erases allusions to Hebraism's Jerusalem in the novella by concluding her drama in Rome, a city seen as Jerusalem's opposite and, as such, the modern site of Hellenic greatness.[13] Adele's compatriots begin the novella as Hellenic archetypes, as American offspring of England and Italy, but they end up where Adele began, as icons of the Philistinism of the American middle class. Stein's Roman setting ironically highlights the stultifying Hebraism of Mabel and Helen: they represent the "conformity" of the "general American sisterhood" known for a "lack [of] individual imagination" (117) and have an "intensely serious but unenthusiastic interest in the things to be observed" (118). Their blasé attitude costumes them with blinders of duty that prevent them from seeing the "sweetness and light" that Arnold might have imagined to be suffusing their Hellenic Roman surroundings; instead, "aloof from the life about them," they become E. M. Forster–like anti-heroes who fail to connect (118).

In contrast, Stein grafts Adele's waning, if vital Hebraism, onto an Arnoldian ideal of an ethical and revitalizing Hellenism that the Roman setting emphasizes. Adele possesses the "individual imagination" that her compatriots lack and embodies the ideal of a *Sister* Singular. Although clothed in an American style, Adele appears a breed apart from her "national sisterhood" (117), as "Large, abundant, full-busted and joyous, she seemed a part of the rich Roman life" (118). Adele personifies Mabel and Helen's view of Roman life as "an alien mass of earthy spontaneity whose ideal expression is enthusiasm," a description that combines a Jewish "earthiness" with the "spontaneity" of the Roman environs (118). Ironically, Stein's Jew embraces the "free play" of Arnold's Hellenic ideal, while those who should "belong naturally to the movement of Hellenism"— as Arnold imagined the English (and the Italians)—are straitjacketed by American middle-class duty (FC 268, C&A 173).

Stein further dramatizes the triumph of "culture" in her Jewish protagonist by creating a "spectacle" of Arnold's Hellenistic mantra "to see things as they are." In a scene of triangulated glances, Adele witnesses the moment when the truth about Helen's love for Adele becomes apparent to Mabel. The narrator describes the action of crossed gazes: "Adele saw Mabel's eyes grow large and absorbent. They took in all of Helen's weariness, her look of longing and all the meanings of it all. The drama of the eyes was so complete that for the moment Adele lost herself in the spectacle" (*Q.E.D.* 123). Seeing Mabel's seeing is transportive for Adele as she realizes that seeing the truth involves seeing what is hidden. To Adele, Helen's relationship with Mabel is nothing more than prostitution, but she suddenly understands that Helen will not leave Mabel, whose holding power, like her name—Mabel Neathe—lies underneath the surface of things.[14] Helen, meanwhile, now plays the Philistine: she no longer knows herself and is unaware of the revelations going on around her. The scene dramatizes Adele's exasperated and Hellenic peroration about Helen: "Can't she see things as they are and not as she would make them if she were strong enough as she plainly isn't" (133).[15] *Q.E.D.* concludes with Adele and Helen lamentably in a "dead-lock," firmly set in behaviors that can only repeat their failure to connect with one another (133).

Despite Adele's maturation into a robust, nonconforming Singular, she ends up an ambivalent figure of progress. Powerless to force Helen into either Hebraic right-acting or Hellenic right-thinking, Adele is left with another Hellene: her own right-understanding, however useless such knowledge may be. In Stein's Arnoldian vision, Hellenic knowledge is almost by definition useless as a joyous escape from the practicalities and pragmatism of bourgeois Hebraism. Stein pairs the Hellenic ability to see what is hidden with the imagined insight of Jewish nature to produce an indirect literary style. She makes useless knowledge not only what one knows but what one does, in a practice that Arnold might consider a

Hellenized Hebraism and which Stein figures as the achievement of the Brother Singular, icon of a modern and composite Jewish culture.

Hidden Jewish Traditions in "The Making of Americans"

Stein composed the first draft of her novel "The Making of Americans" in 1903, the same year she wrote Q.E.D. The draft is similar to Q.E.D. in narrative voice, themes, and realist style, and the narrator presents the title family's Jewish identity, like Adele's, only through allusions to what he considers to be the racial difference of their middle-class living. Stein wants readers to see the family's implicit Jewish nature through their explicitly unassimilated differences from Anglo-Saxon Americans. Importantly, the five short chapters that make up this draft serve as touchstones crucial to the abstracted Jewish and Anglo-Saxon framework of the epic novel that Stein would complete in 1911.[16]

In this literary seedling, Stein again fictionalizes Arnold's dialectical forces by associating them with different characters. She investigates the tensions between the Dehning family's mercantilist immigrant roots and its rebellious progeny, which figure the relationship of Jewish tradition to the modern American individual. The tensions converge around Mr. Dehning's disapproval of his daughter's marriage to a young Hersland, who the narrator considers to be a fellow "Brother Singular" (MA 153). Here, the Brother Singular explicitly serves as a figure central to Stein's narrator's ruminations on the interrelation between generations: What do we owe to our parents and past tradition? How are "The new people made out of the old"? Of what significance is an "older and a hidden tradition"? From whence comes the freedom to stray and differ? These Brother Singulars represent, for Stein, the struggles of the modern Jewish writer torn between a thinly veiled Jewish tradition and individual talent.

In this early foray into long-form fiction, genealogical knowledge enables an understanding of the modern individual, especially when attempting to "know ourselves" in the present. The narrator's openly epistemological inquiry dissolves the surety of Arnold's cultural imperative to "see things as they are," so heralded by Adele in Q.E.D. As the narrator declares on the opening page of the novel:

> We need only realise our parents, remember our grandparents and know ourselves and our history is complete. The old people in a new

world, the new people made out of the old that is the story that I mean to tell for that is what really is and what I really know. (MA 137)

The narrator's proposed intellectual *Bildung*, a process of "knowing ourselves" and the Jewish past to realize "what really is," provides the foundation of narrative, or "the story that [the narrator] mean[s] to tell." In the first draft of "The Making of Americans," that story centers on a middle-class family in which the impulse to assimilate the new competes with the impulse to maintain the old. The paterfamilias dismisses as modern the inclinations of the young heroine and her fiancé toward the arts and other "literary effects" (156). The tensions between father and daughter, Stein's icons of Arnoldian Hebraism and Hellenism, establish the familial, class-conscious, and rebellious American literary concerns of the modern writer that become the crux of Stein's later and epic revisions of the novel and its inimitable use of repetition and abstraction.

For Stein, the making of Americans involves an incomplete estrangement from old-world tradition, with a repeated harking back to Jewish names, history, and traditions. The Dehning family struggles with the American "fever to be an Anglo Saxon and a gentleman," since they "sprang from peasant rather than gentle sources" and, it is implied, do not behave as either Anglo-Saxons or gentlemen (MA 137, 138). Their journey to the respectable ranks of the American middle class has been accomplished by mercantilist means thought to be characteristic of Jews.[17] The close-knit Dehnings exhibit the affectionate and clannish characteristics of Stein's modern Jews and likewise seem to heed her directive against intermarriage by "summer[ing] among their kind" at a country house when their daughters reach marriageable age (138). The country house—that symbol of English nobility and the setting for so many English novels—here ironically signals the Dehnings' isolation from the Anglo-Saxons and gentlemen who would normally inhabit it, as they sequester themselves "among their kind."[18]

In addition to distinguishing the Dehnings from Anglo-Saxon Americans, the narrator alludes to their Jewish identity by taking literally Arnold's imperative to "see things as they are." The narrator presents a "picture" of the family when describing them "standing together on the lawn," in front of the country house, as an "old peddler comes up the road" (MA 141). The peddler was a stock Jewish role in the popular theater of the day. Here, too, he brings to life the Dehning family's Jewish roots as immigrant peddlers.[19] The narrator muses that "The sight of the old peddler had roused in" Abe Dehning memories of his own past, prompting him to recall the industriousness of his mother, who made peppermint candy that he peddled to help support the family of nine children (142).

Once Dehning identifies with the Jewish peddler, the narrator confirms that "the picture is complete the picture you must understand if you are to rightly read the story that I mean to tell" (141). A self-made man, Dehning credits itinerant peddling for his later success as a stable member of the "bourgeois" "middle class" with its "certainty of place and means" (152). At thirteen, the age at which a Jewish boy is welcomed into the community as an adult, Dehning boasts that he was "already earning [his] living and giving [him]self an education" as a peddler (142). "Rightly reading" the story of the Dehning family's progress means recognizing their evolution, from "peasant sources" and racially marked Jewish peddling and mercantilism, to a more abstractly Jewish and assimilated position in the American middle class.[20]

The Dehning family's naming practices, too, mark their evolving relationship to Jewish tradition. In the beginning, the patriarch was a peddler named Abraham; the family tree transplanted in America nominally shares roots with the biblical forefather. Two elder daughters, "born while the old world was still a vital background," carry the names of their grandmothers, following the Ashkenazic Jewish tradition of naming a child after a recently deceased relative, often a grandparent (140–141).[21] The practice itself establishes an individual's relationship to family and tradition through repetition, and signals continuity by keeping the "vitality" of the "old world" alive across generations, if in name only. Later, with a "complete neglect of ancestry," the Dehnings submit to the American "fever to be Anglo Saxon" and name their third child George (141, 137). The narrator emphasizes the break with the unnamed Jewish tradition by mentioning a "christening" (145). Even with George, though, the Dehnings hold onto Jewish tradition with his middle name, Simon, where, as the narrator acknowledges, only "to be slightly held as an initial was there any harking back to sources" (141). Stein, whose middle brother was named Simon, may well have intended this as a pun on the Hebrew meaning of Simon, which is *hearkening*. The abbreviation of his middle name to "an initial" suggests both the diminishment and the persistence of a trace presence of the Dehning family's implicitly Jewish identity as they Americanize.

For Abe Dehning, the names of the "old world" had long provided a sense of familiarity and home amid the dispersals of migration.[22] In Dehning's account of his journey to America, for example, the mere sound of his father's name was a comfort:

> I was only a little chap when we came to America. We didn't all come together and I remember how lonely Brother Sam and I were when we left home. I remember too while we were waiting in a big bare room for them to give us our tickets that we heard some one mention our father's name. We didn't dare speak to any man and indeed we didn't know which man it was but it made us feel less lonely. (143)

The "lonely" brothers may have "heard some one mention [their] father's name," but Abe's listeners and Stein's readers do not hear it. Dehning maintains the fearful silence of the story—"we didn't dare speak"—by not naming the forebear even in his retelling. The identity of the speaker in the memory, too, remains unknown—"we didn't know which man it was"—and yet, the vitality of the utterance and its "harking back to sources" alleviates the brothers' loneliness and demonstrates that even a disembodied voice can meaningfully signify family, history, and identity. This off-stage voice prefigures the way that, for the next generation, the names and struggles of the old world become distanced, disembodied, and abstracted into family lore.

Despite his nostalgic loyalty to an otherwise hidden past Jewish tradition, Abe Dehning wants to see concrete evidence of his children's gains in the present. He may have attended the school of hard knocks as a peddler, but he has nurtured his children on luxuries and "modern improvements" that he hopes will develop their character. Surveying his children, he wonders aloud whether they will benefit other than materially from the progress made by his generation:

> You children have an easy time of it nowadays. . . . You have to have your horses and your teachers and your music and your tutors and all the modern improvements. . . . I am afraid there is too much education business and literary effects in all of you for you ever to amount to much. . . . Well it won't be long now before you will all have a chance to show me what you can do for yourselves and whether all these modern improvements and all this education

business will teach you as much as peddling through the country did to us. (141, 142, 143)

Skeptical of the life of the mind, Dehning is unable to imagine the learning process as other than a "business," even while using the term ironically to dismiss the educational endeavor as not productive enough in a business sense. He anticipates a practical and measurable outcome rather than any intellectual richness education may bring, which for Stein means he is the ultimate Arnoldian Hebrew—a Philistine.

It was typical among offspring of the European and American Jewish bourgeoisie for liberal education and cultural fluency to be the heirs of financial stability.[23] The narrator describes this generational change as one of "progress" for Jewish families of the American middle class, especially once liberal education, with its bent toward "culture," seems to materialize in Dehning's offspring in questions of courtship. The narrator warns of the approaching generational conflict likely when a "bourgeois mind," like that of Dehning's eldest daughter Julia, "long[s] for culture" and "for knowledge of made things, of works of art, of all the wonders that make a world for certain cultured people" (152, 154). This is another romance of Hellenism: Julia may be a born-and-bred bourgeoise, but, despite having an "eager palate," she has some "taste" for what Stein considers to be the apex of Arnoldian culture (154).

Stein's pointed and repeated use of the word "culture" unambiguously invokes Arnold's Hellenic ideal in implied opposition to the Philistinism of the elder Dehning's Hebraism. The object of Julia's affections, the young Henry Hersland, has an air that conveys "the world of art and things," which affirms their common Jewish genealogy and their common social trajectory: Hersland's people "were of the same community to which the Dehnings belonged but this family had acquired more culture in their progress. They had attained success a little earlier and had all of them by nature a pretty talent in the arts" (153). Julia is not so much in love with Hersland as desiring "that free, wide and cultured life to which for her young Hersland held the key" (161). Stein shows that Arnoldian culture is an ideal so powerfully desired by Julia that marriage becomes its foot soldier.

Ironically, in her intemperate desire to wed someone with "culture," Julia has all the failings of a parvenu. Hersland's look and manner suggest "culture" to Julia, but, as the narrator ominously suggests, it is a "world to her but vaguely known" even though "It was a real desire this longing for culture in Julia's breast" (153–154). The narrator conveys the "reality" of this craving by describing Julia's desire as a hunger: "And it was not strong meat that Hersland offered to her eager palate; still it had the flavor of the longed for dish and to her young eagerness it was plenty real enough" (154). Julia nonetheless mistakes Hersland's slightly more cultured heritage for what she imagines is a more potent character attribute. But, as the narrator notes, the trace presence of flavor marks an absence—what only an unrefined and "eager" palate might mistake for the real thing.

Under the spell of this mistaken promise of culture, Julia decides to marry Hersland and quickly abuts her father's criticism of "culture" as effeminate, unproductive, and immoral. Stein exposes the gendered valences popularly read into Arnold's oppositional types by depicting Dehning's dogmatically Hebraic sensibility as fiercely masculinist. Dehning dismisses any deviation from middle-class norms as effete Hellenism and disdains his daughter's interest in this "cultured" man as a useless romantic fiction gotten from books, protesting, "Yes those are your literary notions. . . . Literary effects and modern improvements are alright for women but Hersland is in business" (156).[24] Julia counters with a revised model of modern masculinity and Jewish identity—"surely it can't hurt a man to be interesting even if he is in business" (156). Her plea reiterates Arnold's complaint that without culture, businessmen are mere Philistines.[25]

Julia's idealizations about the decency of her middle-class community, however, falsely reassure her of the morality of her "interesting" fiancé. She discovers that Hersland is not the man she imagined, when, a few weeks before the wedding, he confesses to having "big" schemes that rely on her father's wealth and reputation (166). The discovery forcibly awakens her to the truth of his character: "He[rsland] was in no wise different in his ways or in his talk than he had always been only she seemed to see now as dying men are said to see, clearly and freely things as they were and not as she had wished them" (167).[26] For a moment she sees a reality—a previously hidden truth—that fundamentally challenges her beliefs, and she begins to "sense that perhaps the world had meanings in it that would be hard for her to understand and judge" (167). Julia's potentially revolutionary realization about Hersland echoes Adele's about Helen at the end of *Q.E.D.* Unlike Helen, though, who (according to Adele) would rather remain content with fiction, Julia gets a glimpse of the facts about her situation, but stays the course and marries Hersland.

Julia's somewhat cloudy moment of clarity is something that Stein's narrator codes as a combination of "Hebraic" tradition and "Hellenic" insight. Unlike Arnold, Stein redeems what she considers to be Jewish aspects of middle-class convention. She takes the combination of Dehning's fears and Julia's folly as a Jewish model of progress for an American middle-class tradition that reconciles Arnoldian Hebraism with Hellenism, masculine with feminine, the practical with the poetical, and the individualistic interest with the interesting individual. The "modern Jew" may have "given up the faith of his fathers," but, as Stein had earlier argued, he must still hold clannishly to their endogamous traditions (TMJ 416). Even though Hersland may be a "poor" specimen of an interesting person, the narrator defends the liberatory possibilities of those singular Jews like Hersland who strive to break away from the conventions of the Jewish bourgeoisie (153).

Even before her courtship with Hersland becomes the source of intergenerational strife, Julia imperfectly represents American modernity because she is forever trying to "live down her mother in her" (147):

> Perhaps she was born too near the old world to attain quite the completeness of crude virginity for underneath her very American face body and clothes were seen now and then flashes of passionate insight that lit up an older and a hidden tradition. (146)

Like the serendipitous appearance of the peddler in the Dehning family portrait, the truth about Julia includes what is only "seen now and then." The sporadic bursts of "passionate insight"—what Stein considered Hellenic cerebration—are in fact part of Julia's own temper. The narrator illuminates the "sweetness and light" of Julia's Jewish heritage by suggesting that Julia's rebellious desire for culture was inherited from her mother.

Hebraic Heredity: The Middle-Class Roots of a "Queer People"

Stein had earlier Judaized the spirit of revolt in her college essay, arguing that members of "the Jewish community . . . naturally have a strong tendency to embrace revolutionary ideas and skepticism in all its forms"

(TMJ 424). The narrator in this first draft of "The Making of Americans" satirizes the dramatic irony of discovering the hereditary roots of filial rebellion by telling "an old story"—drawn from Aristotle's *Nicomachean Ethics*—about an old man and his son:

> There is an old story of a man who mercilessly and in his anger drags his father along the ground through his own orchard. "Stop," groans out the broken old man at last "Stop! I did not drag my father beyond this tree." (MA 147)

In Aristotle's telling of the story, the man explains his behavior through heredity: "He'll beat me when he becomes a man—it's something we're born with in our family" (198). Stein's narrator also points to the hereditary nature of the son's "anger," playing with the paradoxical notion of rebellion as an unwitting maintenance of tradition.[27]

Stein combines Hebraic and Hellenic symbolism with satire in her re-telling of the Aristotelian tale of the "dreary business" of "living down the tempers we are born with" (147). The narrator satirizes the notion of progress itself in this story, since the newer generation's "merciless" progress in the old land must not surpass that of the older generation. Despite what Arnold and Stein might consider the story's Hellenic origins in antiquity, Stein's narrator's re-telling summons biblical images of the trees of life and knowledge, which give concreteness to the family tree implied in the narrator's earlier conviction that one arrives at true knowledge of oneself when one "realises [one's] parents and . . . grandparents" (137).

The narrator then jumps from the ancient to a more modern investigation of the changing "doctrines" for ascertaining "temper" (147). There had been a certain correlation between mind and body in the eighteenth century but now, the narrator reports, with "the science of heredity . . . it was discovered that generalisations must be as complicated as the facts and the problem of interrelation was not to be so simply solved" (147). A modern indeterminacy, the narrator muses, seems to result in a purely subjective sense of heredity: what we attribute to our parents in ourselves changes as we age and reckon with our intolerance for "our own sins writ large in others" (147).[28] The narrator implies that learning "to see things as they are" in the present involves acquiring greater knowledge of our relationship to the past, however elusive it may be. It also demands an attention to systems of representation and to developing an eye for "rightly reading" "literary effects" and other nonexplicit means of uncovering "hidden tradition."

In addition to recounting a marriage plot and mulling over the ironies of heredity, Stein's narrator declaims the wonders of middle-class character despite the discontents of its descendants. Like Adele's forthright announcement of allegiance to her middle-class origins, the narrator in "The Making of Americans" identifies middle-class American living as the necessary parent to the modern "interesting" individual:

> I believe in middle class tradition and in honest business methods. Middle-class, middle-class—I know that in America we are to have none of you for bourgeois life is sordid material unaspiring and traditional and yet I am strong to declare even here in the heart of individualistic America that a material middle class with its straightened bond of family is the one thing always healthy, human, vital and from which has always sprung the best the world can know. (144–145)

By affirming the "straightened bond of family" that Stein had previously praised for sustaining the "great clannishness" of the Jews, the narrator casts the American middle class as a metaphorically Jewish antidote to the Anglo-Saxon ills of "individualistic America." In this passage, the narrator heartily "declares" a belief in the sovereignty of the middle class for its role as the generator of "the best the world can know," which, as the narrator goes on to discuss, are those "brother Americans" (145) who he will shortly dub "Brother Singulars" (153).[29]

Stein defends American middle-class life for its clannish, mercantilist Hebraism and defends—as Jewish—those interesting individuals who, however incompletely, break away from its conventional molds. In the following apologia, the narrator speaks for and apostrophizes the singularly "queer people" who had been so recently expendable by their middle-class community:

> Singularity that is neither crazy, faddist or low class is as yet an unknown product with ourselves. It takes time to make queer people time and certainty of place and means. Custom, passion and a feel for mother earth are needed to breed vital singularity in any man and alas how poor we are in all these three.
>
> Brother Singulars we are misplaced into a generation that knows not Joseph. We flee before the disapproval of our cousins, the courageous condescension of our friends who gallantly agree to sometimes

walk the streets with us, we fly to the kindly comfort of an older world accustomed to take all manner of strange forms into its bosom and we leave our noble order to be known under such forms as that of Henry Hersland, a poor thing and hardly even then our own. (152–153)

To defend the alienated "Brother Singulars," the narrator once again relies on Jewish tradition. Like the biblical Joseph, spurned by his brothers and yet esteemed by Pharaoh, these singular people must seek out "an older world" for acceptance. In the manner of Stein's collegiate writings on the "noblest brotherhood" of modern Jews whose feeling of connection unites "perfect strangers" (TMJ 426), these Singulars coalesce in a "queer" challenge to the "conventional respectability" of the middle class from which they have "sprung" (MA 152, 145). Like "the modern Jew" who remains a Jew, despite having "departed from the faith of his fathers" and, like Adele's self-appointed role as an apostle "rejected by the class whose cause [she] preach[es]," Stein's Brother Singulars may be "queer people," but they are respectable rebels (TMJ 424; *Q.E.D.* 59).

Stein identifies these singular Jewish subjects as "queer" in the sense that critic Anne Herrmann describes as "less about object choice than about the recognition on the part of others that one is not like others" (6). Damon finds an "almost explicit" linking of "Jewishness and gayness" in Stein's Brother Singulars ("Women, Dogs, and Jews" 229). The difference between "almost explicit" and "explicit" is very much to the point here, however. The "queerness" of these figures is a general oddity that confuses gender and generation: they are feminized by the "condescending" "gallantry" of their friends and infantilized by their "feel for mother earth" and flight to the "bosom" of "an older world."

Above all, Brother Singulars represent the embattled relationship of a writer to his readers and to literary tradition, especially a writer with a growing interest in "strange forms." With these isolated figures of authorship, Stein inculcates herself into the "classic writers" of American tradition, such as Emerson, Thoreau, Melville, Whitman, and early orators, who, as Sacvan Bercovitch describes them, "have tended to see themselves as outcasts and isolates, prophets crying in the wilderness" (180).[30] Bercovitch dubs these writers American Jeremiahs, a classification that fits neatly with Adele's lamentations as an outcast apostle and the transmutation of her laments into the voice of Stein's narrator in "The Making of Americans." Bercovitch notes that "To declare oneself the symbol of America is by definition to retain one's allegiance to a middle-class culture," which is precisely the combination Stein depicts in her Brother Singulars (181). She portrays American Jeremiahs who maintain their allegiance to a Hebraic middle class and to a Judaic version of Arnold's Hellenic culture. Stein affirms the importance of Jewish culture for the development of the modern American writer through the outcast Brother Singular in his roles as a Joseph and a Jeremiah, his repeated if hidden roots in the Jewish middle class, and his abstracted Jewish fraternity.

The repetition and abstraction at the heart of this Jewish cultural endeavor spark the development of Stein's modern style and "literary effects." In an early passage in the final version of *The Making of Americans*, for example, Stein increasingly uses repetition and abstraction to convey the hidden Jewish aesthetics of the "middle-class ideal" from which modernist writing springs. By 1911, Stein had revised the narrator's praise of middle-class tradition, more than doubling the number of words from the 1903 draft.[31] The expansion demonstrates the novel's iconic "insistence" style that expresses the mundane "monotony" of middle-class living. The style finds its ideological forebear in Stein's interest in tracing the past's influence on the present, especially, as in *Q.E.D.*, when the narrator remarks that the "stamp of . . . older civilisations [is] incomplete and frustrated in this American version but still always insistent" (54). In this style, form and subject matter coalesce in the repetitive expression of the "ordinariness" of middle-class living:

> Yes it is a misfortune we have inside us, some few of us, I cannot deny it to you, all you others, it is true the simple interest I take in my family's progress. I have it, this interest in ordinary middle class existence, in simple firm ordinary middle class traditions, in sordid material unaspiring visions, in a repeating, common, decent enough kind of living, with no fine kind of fancy ways inside us, no excitements to surprise us, no new ways of being bad or good to win us.
>
> You see, it is just an ordinary middle class tradition we must use to understand this family's progress. There must be no aspiring thoughts inside us, there must be a feeling always in us of being in a kind of way in business always honest, there must be in a kind of ordinary way always there inside us the sense of decent enough ways of living for us. Yes I am strong to declare that I have it, here in the

heart of this high, aspiring, excitement loving people who despise it,—I throw myself open to the public,—I take a simple interest in the ordinary kind of families, histories, I believe in simple middle class monotonous tradition, in a way in honest enough business methods.

Middle-class, middle-class, I know no one of my friends who will admit it, one can find no one among you all to belong to it, I know that here we are to be democratic and aristocratic and not have it, for middle class is sordid material unillusioned unaspiring and always monotonous for it is always there and to be always repeated, and yet I am strong, and I am right, and I know it, and I say it to you and you are to listen to it, yes here in the heart of a people who despise it, that a material middle class who know they are it, with their straightened bond of family to control it, is the one thing always human, vital, and worthy it—worthy that all monotonously shall repeat it,—and from which has always sprung, and all who really look can see it, the very best the world can ever know, and everywhere we always need it. (*MA* 34)

In this passage, Stein's narrator aestheticizes the repetitiousness of middle-class tradition, which he characterizes as "a repeating . . . kind of living" that is "to be always repeated." He repeats the pronoun "it" to refer, abstractly, to membership in and the values of middle-class living as well as middle-class living itself: "I know no one of my friends who will admit it, one can find no one among you all to belong to it." The repetition indicates the continual presence of the past as it progressively moves the narrative forward. Yet the unconventional excesses of Stein's insistence on past tradition by the combined use of repetition and abstraction break from that tradition.[32]

Stein's repetitious invocation of the monotony of bourgeois life is strikingly similar to Joyce's mockery of middle-class prose style in the "Eumaeus" episode of *Ulysses*. Joyce's process of composition, too, involved constantly increasing and magnifying these qualities as he revised the episode, a process Sam Slote dubs "Eumaeification" (23). And while Joyce may mock middle-class aesthetics in "Eumaeus," he, like Stein, presents an earnest version of the middle-class singular and Jew in Leopold Bloom, whose monotony provides the ground for Joyce's portrayal of an avant-garde aesthetic.[33]

Stein had once recognized Joyce as her literary compatriot, with Proust, in the innovative abandonment of story in the novel (*LA* 184).[34] And it is not hard to see the similarities between the Hebraic-Hellenism of Joyce's Jewish Odysseus—an aesthetic-minded middle-class peddler of newspapers ads—and Stein's Brother Singulars who usher in the future of modern literature and human relations. However, in an interview a decade later, near the end of her life, Stein differentiates her work from Joyce's regarding their orientations to the past:

> You see it is the people who generally smell of the museums who are accepted, and it is the new who are not accepted. You have got to accept a complete difference. It is hard to accept that, it is much easier to have one hand in the past. That is why James Joyce was accepted and I was not. He leaned toward the past, in my work the newness and difference is fundamental. (*A Transatlantic Interview* 29)

This strategic statement of difference obscures the hand Stein had in the past, however hidden. A flagrant if Hebraized fusion with Arnoldian Hellenism imbues Stein's work, like Joyce's, with the smell of the museums. Taken with Bercovitch's "Hebraising" of the apostolic vein of early American writing and, in the context of Stein's explicit collegiate writing about Jews, Stein's ethos of progress and her iconic Brother Singular are inextricably tied to a middle-class Jewish past of conventional thinkers, whose ethical and aesthetic concerns have nonetheless shaped the stylistic experiments of literary modernism.

3

"So much like a yid"

An Associative Genealogy of "Jewish Types" in the Notebooks for *The Making of Americans*

> ... the mistress of a hundred cases or categories, receptacles of the mind, subdivisions for convenience, in which, from a full experience, she pigeonholed her fellow mortals with a hand as free as that of a compositor scattering type.
>
> (Henry James, *The Ambassadors* 7)

Stein kept her first fictions very much alive by drawing on them directly in the writings to follow. Most significantly, in 1906, when she resumed writing "The Making of Americans," Stein altered the first draft of the novel and, over the next four and a half years, appended another nine hundred pages to it.[1] For the second foray, Stein wrote preliminary notations in dozens of small notebooks that she drew on when composing her "long book" in large manuscript notebooks (38.791.[32]). In the smaller notebooks, written concurrently as she drafted the novel, Stein outlined her plans for the novel's characters and plot. Eventually, she left behind the characters and used the notebooks to describe the character of all kinds of people in elaborate detail. In step with the notebooks, the novel's story of two families would evolve into the narrator's epic studies of character.[2] Stein writes openly about Jews and "Jewish types" in the notebooks, in stark contrast to the oblique nods to Jewish identity in her first fictions and the wholly abstracted character types in the finished novel. Stein's notes on Jewish character nonetheless preserve her earlier interests in Matthew Arnold's Hebraism and Hellenism. By reading the unpublished notebooks for *The Making of Americans*, we discover an explicitly Jewish genealogy for the typological investigations conducted by the novel's narrator.

Held at the Beinecke Rare Book and Manuscript Library at Yale, the notebooks reveal Stein, a Jamesian heroine, as "the mistress of a hundred cases or categories" culled from scientific observations of those around her. On dozens of French notepads (*carnets*), one finds a cache of classifications of the people, literary characters, and celebrated figures of Stein's social and imagined worlds. She mined the *carnets* when drafting the novel in larger manuscript notebooks (*cahiers*) by grounding the narrator's characterological endeavors in her own.[3] These studies were not meant for publication, however. They contain Stein's frank estimations of herself, her family, and her soon-to-be-famous circle of friends. They mention Picasso, Matisse, Hutchins Hapgood, Bernard Berenson, her parents, cousins, uncles, aunts, her siblings Bertha, Leo, Simon, and Michael, as well as Michael's wife Sarah (called Sally) and son Allan. The notebooks also contain psychological studies of members of Sally Stein's entourage of young Jewish women from San Francisco, notably Annette Rosenshine, Harriet Levy, and, Gertrude's future life-partner, Alice Toklas.

The notebooks demonstrate Stein's intentions to make science one of the novel's concerns. She writes herself instructions for assembling her characters (again the Dehning and Hersland families) from real-life people, such as the note that instructs, "Make George a doctor like Leo Friedman. . . . Use all my doctoring experience" (37.760.[21–23]). Her years as a student of psychology, zoology, and then medicine provided Stein with ample material. In the same notebook passage, for example, she refers to one character's "scientific ways," which she plans to depict using memories of the "Different kinds of science" practiced by people she had known (37.760.[24]). Another note describes the "reclaim of scientific methods and hygiene" that will enter the story following a character's illness (37.760.[25]).

In later notations the emphasis shifts from the *depiction* of scientific characters to the *practice* of the science of character. Detailed notes about the Dehning and Hersland families give way to more general notes on character types such as the charts, tables, family tree diagrams, and lists of interrelated character types found in a large "Diagram book" (37.761. [Front Cover]). In that notebook, Stein recorded her plans for the novel underway as a lengthy characterology: "In this book (the long book) describe all the kinds of women and the way the men are like them" (37.761. [Front Cover]). The plans were ever changing, even regarding which character types would appear in the novel. An early page of the Diagram book asserts: "The long book. For this book use all the diagram people plus the complete lady & servant girl list + prostitute. Earth group, not" (37.761. [3]). And yet, in a later notebook, Stein commits herself to including studies of the "earth group" that she had previously planned to omit: "In long book must go at great length into earthy and non-earthy practical type and their relation to sentimentality and babies, aunt hearts mother hearts, Matisse and Pablo and everything" (38.791.[32]).

In the notebooks, despite designating numerous people explicitly as Jewish types, Stein's typing of people as Jewish is still largely associative. Stein uses terms such as "ethical . . . earthy," and "resisting" to describe types that are "so much like a yid" (37.761.[28], 38.798, 38.788). When applying these mantles, Stein uses admixtures that combine such characteristics with their opposites in varying amounts. This resembles Arnold's recipe for England, whose Hebraism he thought was in dire need of a good dose of Hellenism. And indeed, as I will demonstrate, Stein's nomenclatures have Arnoldian ancestors: for example, in one instance, Stein calls her modern Jewish type a "Hellenising Jew" (37.761.[97]). At the end of this chapter, I will show how Arnold's thinking also undergirds Stein's categorizing of experiential Calibans—her modern Jewish types—in terms of their perception of things: how they see objects plainly and disinterestedly, in the manner of Arnold's Hellenic ideal.

By retooling Arnold's types for her notes on modern Jewish character, Stein redeems Jewish identity and the modern writer. And in fact, a major subject Stein treats in the notebooks is conventional narrative and the type of person it takes to make modern, unconventional works of art. She analyzes one Jewish type called the "moral Caliban," whose remove from life's experiences makes him unable to "unconventionalize," which is, for Stein, the key to modern creating (37.761.[110], 39.814). She contrasts the "moral Caliban" with a second type of Caliban who is more "earthy" or experiential: the latter Jewish type fully experiences the world and thus "think[s] originally" (39.814). Stein's examples of this "earthy" Jewish type include herself, Picasso, Cézanne, Matisse, Flaubert, and Darwin. In this way, Stein codes modernism as Jewish, because it is the output of the typologically Jewish people in her characterology.

"Yid & Anglo-Saxon": Transforming Types

The characterology in the notes for *The Making of Americans* continues studies of character Stein had begun while in college in the 1890s.[4] When she left medical school and neuroscience research in 1904, Stein settled in Paris with her brother Leo and reinvigorated her study of the character of the people around her. The siblings often summered in Florence, where Mary Berenson, the wife of art historian Bernard Berenson, observed of Gertrude and Leo: "They are people who are above all interested in character . . . & as they have good minds they arrive at a closeness of observation—especially Gertrude—that we know nothing of" (qtd. in Wineapple 257). Later, Mary came to despise their "pretended omniscience as to character!" a complaint their friend, journalist Hutchins Hapgood, echoed (qtd. in Wineapple 319). Hapgood found it "very striking" that Gertrude and Leo were "capable of absolute esthetic and moral condemnation of human beings, and are also incapable of close human association" (219). He continued: "Coming in contact with only a few elements of personality, which fit in with their *a priori* ideas, they never get the full personality of anyone" (219). Hapgood nonetheless distinguished between the siblings and admitted that at least Gertrude had had contact with the "eccentricities of art and the human being," while Leo had had none (219).

One eccentric human being Stein knew was Annette Rosenshine, who later described herself as a "human guinea pig" that had fallen into Stein's lap (qtd. in Wineapple 261). Rosenshine had come to Paris from San Francisco for an extended stay with Stein's sister-in-law Sally, and at some point in 1906 she began sitting for daily psychotherapeutic sessions with Stein. This arrangement, perhaps fraught with sexual tension, was powerful enough that Rosenshine turned over all her correspondence to Stein, including letters from another of Sally's protégés, Alice Toklas, who was shortly to arrive in Paris with her friend Harriet Levy. All three women would end up as "psychological models" of Stein's "analysis" and part of a network of character studies that Stein committed to paper in the notes for her novel (Leo Stein, *Journey Into the Self* 28; Katz, "The First Making" 236).[5]

Stein's characterology spans numerous volumes and, in an unsystematic fashion, enumerates many subtypes, varieties, and sides of people, such as "fanatic," "practical," "disinterested," and "genius," and groups identified by a specific role or station in life, such as "man of the world," "prostitute," and "servant girl" (37.763.[1], 38.791.[32], 37.761.[13], 38.788, 37.763.[2 (verso)], 37.761.[26], 37.774).[6] Stein studied people through the formal and informal interactions afforded by her Parisian and Florentine social circles.[7] She drew, too, on literary, artistic, and historical figures from Kipling and Michelangelo to Frederick the Great as reference points for character types or as subjects. And, like Freud and other scientists of the psyche drawn to fictional characters as archetypes, Stein included her share of literary creations as prototypes, such as Shakespeare's primitive Caliban and Turgenev's nihilist Bazarof.

Jewish and Anglo-Saxon types provide an overarching framework to the sprawling menagerie of characters and character types in the notebooks. Stein maps opposing "Jewish" and "Anglo-Saxon" types on separate diagrams and on opposite ends of one diagram (37.764[3b, 4a]). She refers to the types in colloquial or dialect-inflected shorthands, such as "Scotchmen and jews," "Yid & Anglo-saxon," and "The Jew and de Chlistian" (37.752, 39.819, 39.816). She also establishes a series of abstract nomenclatures for Jewish and Anglo-Saxon types that are by turns racial, behavioral, psychological, and the stuff of popular stereotype. I have organized the major correspondences in Stein's characterology for Jewish and Anglo-Saxon types in table 1. Stein's opposed Jewish and Anglo-Saxon types correspond to the "earthy" versus "beauty" and "ethical" versus "faith" groupings.[8] She lays out the Jewish type's correspondences in the Diagram book, stating, "May call Jewish type ethical & earthy" (37.761.[28]). In another note, Stein describes the connection between earthy and ethical types: "Earthy—more apt to be ethical until you come to the primitive souls who are religious or pagan" (37.761.[58]). Such direct statements of correspondence are rare, however. As I show here, readers of the notebooks and the novel must carefully piece together Stein's evolving nomenclature for these dueling character types.

Stein also describes her Jewish and Anglo-Saxon types as the kinds of people who win fights by resisting or attacking, a dyad that exhibits qualities similar to contemporary notions of passive-aggressiveness and active-aggressiveness.[9] The Anglo-Saxon type's "attacking" quality had begun to germinate for Stein as early as 1903 in *Q.E.D.*, where Adele addresses Helen, the "blooming Anglo-Saxon," quite literally as an attacking kind of person: "If you want to stick a knife into a man you just naturally go and stick straight and hard" (*Q.E.D.* 80).[10] Stein also abstracts the Jewish

TABLE 1. Major Correspondences in Stein's Characterology for Jewish and Anglo-Saxon Types

Jewish (Jew, jew, Yid, yid)	**Anglo-Saxon** (Christian, Chlistian, chlichen, Scotchman, non-Jewish person)
Ethical (or Bazarofian)	Faith
Earthy (or servant girl)	Beauty (or lady-flavor)
Dirty (or *sale*, in French)	Clean
[wins a fight by] Resisting	[wins a fight by] Attacking
Dependent-independent	Independent-dependent
Intellectual (or "free soul")	Idealist
Running oneself by the mind	Running oneself by conventions or training
"real experiencing" and seeing the "object as object" (Cézanne, Caliban, Picasso, and Gertrude Stein)	"Moral Calibans" are not really experiencing and not seeing the "object as object" (Leo Stein, Claribel Cone, and Harriet Levy)

and Anglo-Saxon terminologies with the more psychological designations of "independent dependent" for the "attacking" Anglo-Saxon kind and "dependent independent" for the "resisting attacking" Jewish kind (38.792.[43]).[11] In *The Making of Americans*, however, Stein assiduously avoids mentioning Jewish and Anglo-Saxon types explicitly. Instead, the behavioral rubrics serve as the primary means for classifying those types in the novel.

Many characteristics of the Jewish and Anglo-Saxon pairings across the different nomenclatures reflect their Arnoldian source. With the Anglo-Saxon "beauty group," for example, who are "beauty lovers" (37.761.[59]), Stein gestures to Arnold's definition of "culture" as the Hellenistic striving "to see things as they are, and by seeing them as they are to see them in their beauty" (*C&A* 167). Stein's Jewish type, in contrast, has "no instinct for culture" (37.761.[62]). Instead one finds a Hebraic morality and materiality in the Jewish type's correspondences when she suggests, "May call Jewish type ethical & earthy" (37.761.[28]). Like Arnold's avowed appreciation for both of his epic forces, Stein, too, esteems aspects of both Jewish and Anglo-Saxon types: "The earth admixture makes for justice and having his way, the beauty admixture makes for quality" (37.761.[32]). It

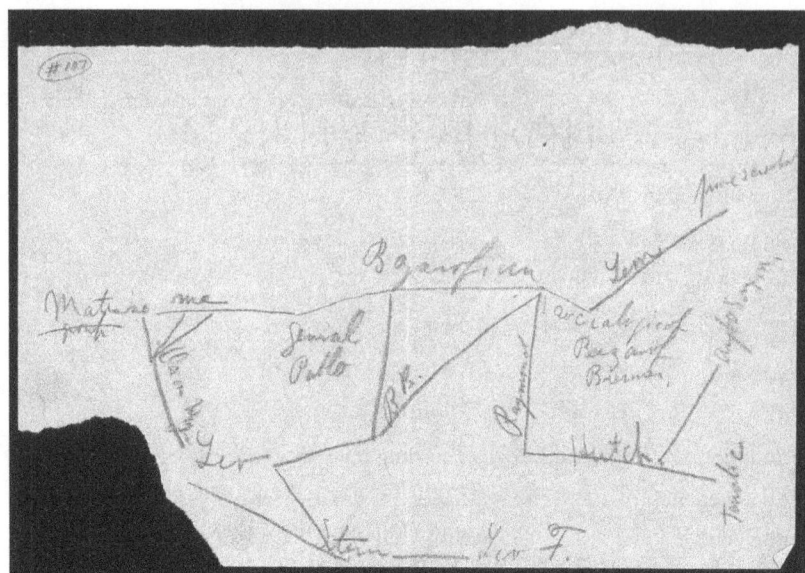

FIGURE 1. Untitled diagram that includes "me" (Gertrude Stein) at one end, near the "Matisse group," and the "Anglo Saxon" group at the other end. Studies for *The Making of Americans*, YCAL MSS 76, 37.766.

is not surprising, then, that she celebrates the creators of modern art and literature as earthy and ethical Jewish types who also have an ability to "see things as they are . . . in their beauty."

Indeed, as these often-hybrid nomenclatures suggest, Stein considered Jewish and Anglo-Saxon to be two poles between which people fall in a spectrum of intermediate types or "admixtures" (37.761.[32]). In one diagram, for example, Stein positions herself at one end, alongside other Jewish types she dubs the "Matisse group" near the "Oscar Mayer" types. In the middle close to the "Bazarofian" type there is "Pablo" Picasso and, separately, Bernard Berenson ("B.B."), who links to her brother Leo and others. At the other end, a branch with Harvard Psychology Laboratory collaborator Leon Solomons leads to the "pure scientist" and a branch with childhood friend Raymond Duncan leads to "Hutch" Hapgood, who splits into "Anglo Saxon" and "Fanatic" sides (37.766). See figure 1. Stein divides her own family along such typological lines and often finds both Jewish and Anglo-Saxon characteristics in a single person, much like the protagonists of her first fictions who combined Hebraic and Hellenic qualities.

"Stains necessary to the deepest understanding": Stein's Earthy Jewish Type

Stein's use of predominantly abstract admixtures of Jewish and Anglo-Saxon character types in the notebooks follows directly from the first revisions she made to her early fictions. In the 1905–1906 writing of "Melanctha" in *Three Lives*, for example, Stein recasts the ill-fated love affair from *Q.E.D.* using Arnold's implicitly racialized typology of Hebraism and Hellenism in the romantic travails of two black Baltimoreans, Jeff Campbell and Melanctha Herbert. As part of Stein's first published literary work—*Three Lives* was published in 1909—"Melanctha" impressed readers with its psychological acuity. Edmund Wilson observed that "Behind the limpid and slightly monotonous simplicity of Gertrude Stein's sentences, one becomes aware of her masterly grasp of the organisms, contradictory and indissoluble, which human personalities are" (238). In the lengthy and repetitious sentences of "Melanctha," however, Stein questions the very ethics and interpersonal dynamics of classification.

Stein presents a critical portrait of American Hebraism in the scientifically minded doctor Jeff Campbell, who is determined to understand his beloved Melanctha according to fixed categories.[12] He is unable, however, to reconcile his categorical judgments of Melanctha—a woman with a reputation for wandering—with his changing impressions of her character. He confesses, "I certainly after all this time I know you, I certainly do know little, real about you" (*TL* 138). Because he seeks a static and monolithic sense of Melanctha's character, Jeff has trouble understanding the fluid mixture of kinds yielded by his observations.

Stein suggests that Jeff's narrow if earnest Hebraism needs to broaden to include a more finely textured and changing reality. His mode of inquiry needs to resemble a robust curiosity—one that Melanctha's wandering references. Such curiosity would recall the Hellenic mode of criticism or what Arnold called the "free play of the mind" (FC 268). Melanctha's criticisms of Jeff suggest that a meandering methodology that exhibits a "strong . . . sense for real experience" leads to a more empirically sound truth about people (*TL* 116). This is what Stein champions in the novella and, shortly thereafter, what her narrator strives to convey in *The Making of Americans*.

As mentioned above, in her notebooks for *The Making of Americans*, Stein focuses on two varieties of the Jewish type, moral and experiential

Calibans, spun off from Jeff and Melanctha. Stein types people with Melanctha's "strong . . . sense for real experience" as "earthy" Jewish types. They exhibit a vaunted Hellenic curiosity that leads them to view the world critically, as Arnold hoped, "see[ing] the object as in itself it really is" (FC 258). Stein's terminology echoes Arnold's when she describes the earthy Jewish type's tendency to see the "object as object" or "the object itself" (38.788). She names Cézanne, Picasso, and herself as examples of this Jewish type poised to create modern art, since they have what she calls the ability to "unconventionalize" (39.814). In contrast, Stein observes that there is another Jewish type—like Jeff—whom the strictures of convention rule. He simply cannot acknowledge his experiential realities. In the notebooks, Stein labels these brilliant but blindered seekers as "moral Calibans" (37.761.[110]).[13] Her brother Leo and friends Claribel Cone and Harriet Levy are good examples of this second Jewish type. These two Jewish types, the experiential and moral Calibans, combine Arnoldian notions of Hebraism and Hellenism. With the former, especially, Stein seeks to celebrate, encourage, and preserve the moral and earthy Hebraic qualities that could, she thinks, if improved with Hellenic curiosity and disinterestedness, serve as a potent force for the creation of modern art and literature.

Stein deploys her Jewish category as a platonic force that anyone might inhabit, no matter their origins or religious beliefs. This does not, however, prevent her from insisting on the verity of racial differences, largely indistinguishable from popular antisemitic stereotype, when describing swindling salesmen, misers, capitalists, musicians, theater managers, and her own family and friends as Jewish types.[14] She notes, for example, that one of her subjects has the kind of "big thick vulgar Jewishness that runs theaters and trains ballet girls" (39.809). Likewise she refers to certain physiological traits as Jewish, including hair color, "eyes, jaw and mouth" (38.797).[15] And, like the race scientists who thought that Jewish genius tended toward degeneracy, Stein's Jews typically suffer from neuroses, such as hypochondria, paranoia, and melancholia.[16] These unpleasant characteristics show the extent to which Stein saw Jewish types as needing improvement: her characterology was both descriptive and diagnostic.

This scientific and pseudoscientific outlook extends to Stein's gendering of the Jewish type as masculine. According to Maria Farland, a major debate over sexual dimorphism had raged during Stein's time in medical school and Stein's interest in the topic continues into her characterological studies. For Jewish and Anglo-Saxon types, Stein identifies male and female versions and subsets.[17] Her menagerie has gendered "sides" of men, such as "boy," "adolescent," "man of the world," "purely intellectual," and "idealistic," and sides of women such as "servant girl," "mistress," "prostitute," "spinster," and "lady." Like the protagonists of her first fictions, Stein, in the notebooks, identifies herself as both masculine and Jewish, declaring, "I am masculine type" and "Me, not passionate adolescent [but rather] earthy boy" (37.761.[36, 33]). She also describes herself as someone influenced by maleness and exerting a "male influence" on others (38.790). In contrast, Stein designates in servant girls a feminine counterpart to the masculine Jewish earth type, noting "Servant class particularly earthy" (37.774).

The diagram of the "Jewish group," however, consists largely of men, Jewish and gentile. She includes the non-Jewish painters Hans Purrmann and André Derain alongside Jewish family members, such as her brothers Leo and Mike and cousin Fred Stein, and friends Maurice Stern[e], Leo Friedman, and Leon Solomons. She further categorizes Solomons as "Persian, Bazarof, Fanatic" (37.764.[3a-verso]). See figure 2. The diagram of the largely non-Jewish "Anglo Saxon" group, meanwhile, includes Oscar Wilde, writer Henri-Pièrre Roché, artist and art historian Walter Pach, art critic and writer Félix Fénéon, and the fictional detective, Dr. Thorndyke (37.764.[4a]). See figure 3.

For both men and women, Stein dubbed Jewish character "earthy" to emphasize the racial qualities of the Jewish type and the material immediacy of its experiencing. In one note, Stein references her classification of Cézanne as a "resisting" Jewish type with the abbreviated notation "Cezanne-earthy resis" (38.798). The shorthand recalls a lengthy earlier explanation of the tactile-seeming immediacy the painter had for his subjects: "Cezanne is the great master of the realisation of the object itself" (38.788). Likewise, the feminine Jewish type—the servant girl—maintains an earthy quality due to her occupational proximity to household dirt, but she is not the only type Stein associates with literal and figurative dirtiness. Using the French word *sale*, meaning "dirty," Stein describes one group as "more saleté in the liver" and notes that "Hortense & Jane nearer earthy, saler type" (37.761.[147, 148]).

Stein's paired notebook classification of the Jewish type as "earthy" and "ethical" suggests her sense of the redemptive quality of Jewish character's earthiness. Stein had described the Jewish type this way in her collegiate

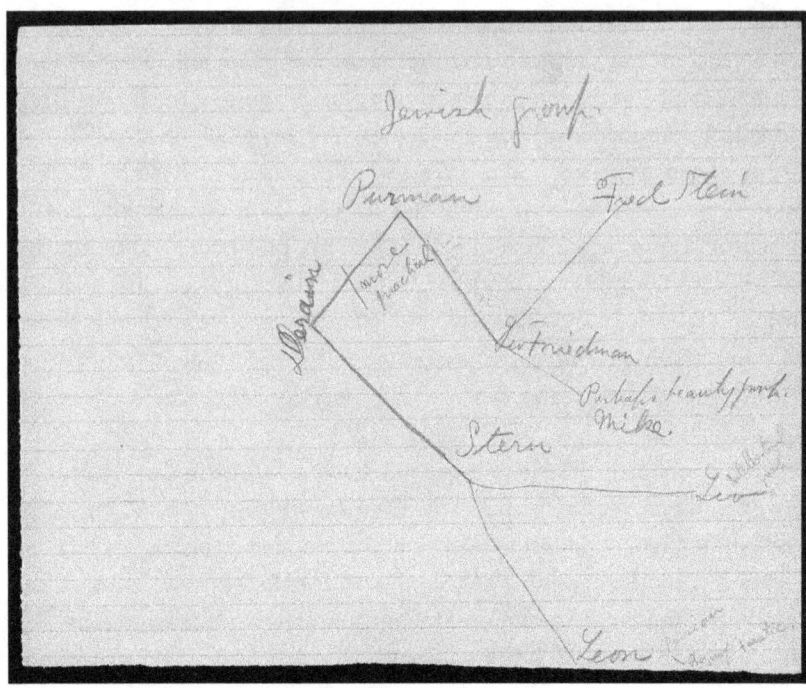

FIGURE 2. The Jewish group. With "Perhaps beauty" and "intellectual" subgroups and branches tending toward the "more practical" and toward the "Bazarof" or "Fanatic" sides. Studies for *The Making of Americans,* YCAL MSS 76, 37.764. [3a-verso].

writings and first fictions when writing about modern Jews who have "noble aims" and Brother Singulars who have a "feel for mother earth" (TMJ 427; MA 152). Earthiness, in particular, recalls a dirtiness in the American character that Adele values in *Q.E.D.* After returning from London, Adele reflects that in the Anglo-Saxon enclave of Boston, where one found "the very essence of clear eyed Americanism," there was a

> cleanliness that began far inside of these people and was kept persistently washed by a constant current of clean cold water. Perhaps the weight of stains necessary to the deepest understanding might be washed away, it might well be that it was not earthy enough to be completely satisfying, but it was a delicious draught to a throat choked with soot and fog. (101)

Adele prefers the metaphorically "earthy" "stains," a welcome flavor in the current of American character, over the literal dirt of Anglo-Saxon

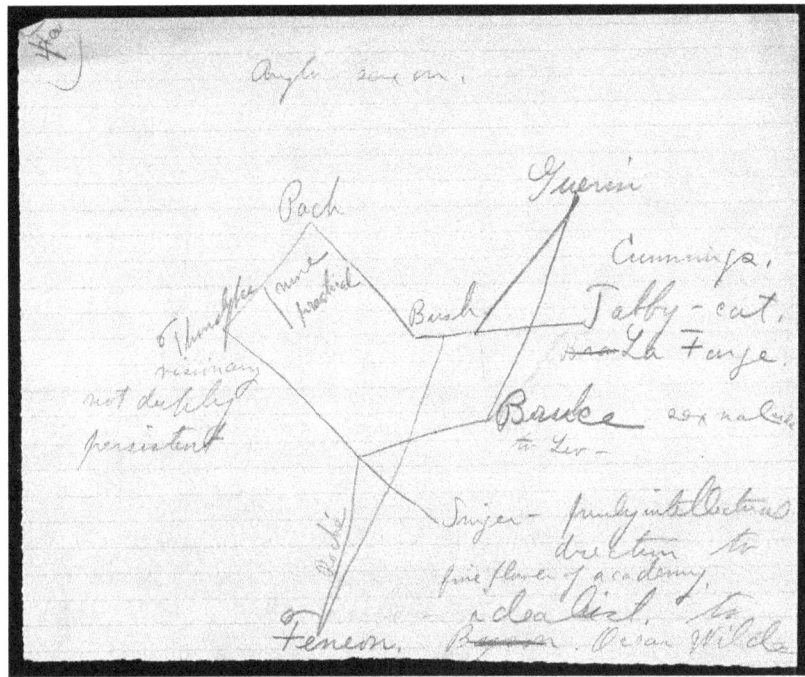

FIGURE 3. The Anglo Saxon group. With a "more practical," a "visionary," and a "sexual side," as well as a "purely intellectual direction" that tends to a "fine flower of academy" flavor and an "idealist" that may have an "Oscar Wilde" flavor. Studies for *The Making of Americans*, YCAL MSS 76, 37.764. [4a].

London's soot.[18] This earthiness provides the first fictional hint of Stein's recuperation and revaluation of Arnold's Hebraism as against the broader degradation of Jewish character by racial scientism, something she continues to make explicit in the notebooks. Stein redeems Jewish character as a hybrid type, however, a Jewish nature whose Hebraism is tempered and inspired by Hellenic criticism and culture.

Over the last half-century, critics have avoided mentioning Stein's use of a Jewish type in the notebooks and disregarded the role of Jewish nature in her thinking about the avant-garde. Wineapple, Ruddick, and Walker refer to the "earthy" variety, "earth feeling," and Cézanne's "earthiness" as keys to Stein's modernist development without noting that "earthy" is synonymous with "Jewish" in the notebooks (Wineapple 264; Ruddick 56–57, 99–102, 123; Walker 4, 62, 156).[19] The oversight is not inconceivable, given the unsystematic characterology penned in Stein's notoriously illegible handwriting across dozens of small notebooks. Critics may also have shied away from exposing what might have seemed to be racist and antisemitic references to Jews.

A significant factor in this critical lacuna has been a reliance on two documents by Leon Katz: his pioneering 1963 dissertation about the notebooks and his partial typescript of them housed alongside Stein's own papers in the archive. The latter document apparently provided researchers with quick and legible access to Stein's notebooks, a relief for hands painstakingly paging through crumbling notepads or eyes wearily glued to microfilm readers. But the typescript is incomplete and its accuracy unverified. In the dissertation, meanwhile, Katz argues that Stein progressively hid the Jewish identity of her characters when drafting *The Making of Americans*. He claims that Stein used the word "Jewish" in her earliest notes and drafts, replaced "Jewish" with "German" in secondary drafts, and then replaced "German" with "middle class" in the final version of the novel ("First Making" 207).[20] Katz explains this apparent erasure of Jewish identity as an expression of Stein's "own inverted anti-semitism," which he thinks had been encouraged by her reading of Otto Weininger (204).[21]

Citing Katz, many critics have mistakenly concluded that Stein's allusions to Jews as "middle class" were the culmination of her personal and literary assimilation to Anglo-Saxon American culture.[22] As I discuss in the previous chapter, however, "middle class" and "earthy" were among the *first* of several thinly veiled references to Jewish nature in Stein's fiction. There was no progressive hiding: from the start, even though Stein avoided explicitly mentioning Jews and Jewish character, she was centering her fictions on the moral journeying of Jewish characters and character types.

Although he is dismissive, Katz correctly links Stein's thinking about Jews—what he perceives to be her antisemitism—with her formal experimentation. Katz blames Stein's reading of Weininger for the innovative "characterological" writing in *The Making of Americans* ("First Making" 273).[23] Similarly, it is the argument of this chapter and the next that Stein associates the modernism of characterology writing with her ideas about Jewish types.

Jewish Truth-Tellers and Hellenism's Empirical Corrective

Stein's notebooks reveal how she ascribes Jewish qualities to the making of avant-gardists and prophets. As her typology indicates, Stein believed that the earthy Jewish quality of human nature lends itself to an ability to see things for what they are, grafting Arnold's Hellenic ideal of culture onto a Hebraic character type. Stein personally dons the mantle of these iconoclastic figures by portraying herself "au fond" (literally *at bottom*) as a Jewish truth-teller. In a note describing her intellectual development, she cryptically reflects that she is "au fond like the Jew in Auctioneer, but I did see him" (37.773). The remark alludes to Charles Klein's 1901 play, *The Auctioneer*, whose Jew is Simon Levi, the play's titular protagonist. Levi is believed to have lost his wits when he is, in fact, perfectly sane and telling the truth. Levi comes home and announces that he has seen and caught the thief who had framed his future son-in-law, but no one believes him, causing him to protest, as Stein recalls, "but I did see him."[24]

The role of the Jewish truth-teller who is disbelieved—a role that recalls the prophetic tradition of Jeremiahs echoing through Stein's first fictions—is one that she embraces for herself as well as for the narrator of her long novel. Like Simon Levi in *The Auctioneer*, Stein's narrator in *The Making of Americans* has trouble finding a receptive audience and announces, "I write for myself and strangers" (289). Stein's conjoined feelings of import and alienation—her Jeremiah posture—reflected her dissatisfaction with conventional scientific methods of studying human character. In order to have classifications reflect how she saw people's natures—independent of their socially recognized backgrounds—she turned to abstracted notions of Jewish nature.

It is here that Stein may have found a kindred spirit in Otto Weininger, rather than in his antisemitism. In *Sex and Character*, Weininger assumes the posture of a scientific rebel who doubts positivism. He considers "Aryan" and "Jewish" as platonic designations between which lie an array of "intermediate forms" (53). These mixtures accommodate what he sees as indisputable similarities and differences between Jews and gentiles and, relatedly, between men and women. Like Weininger, racial scientists studying the psyche were trying to prove that differences not always visible could be substantiated through glimpses of certain gradually discerned behaviors, habits, or other characterological "symptoms."

Stein admired Weininger's ability to craft a comprehensive psychological system not straitjacketed by positivism. Within her admixtures, various typological components compete for dominance of one's essential or "bottom" nature (37.761.[48]). The bottom nature, "bottom layer," or "the below," might remain hidden and give no indication of its presence, while, as Stein notes, the active or more apparent "top" nature "flavors and interrupts but does not govern" (37.761.[47–48], 38.791). Stein felt these "two depths" acutely, despite their nonempirical basis, and listed them for numerous people in the notebooks (37.761.[46]). Her nephew Allan, for example, is "Sally on top—Mike below," and she deems herself as her mother's family, the Keysers, "on top" with "daddy below" (37.761.[46–47]). Stein's discernment of these layers was ever-changing, however, as she remarks: "Note the way two depths in most people. first resemblance least important in great moments they coalesce" (37.761.[46]).[25] Such dynamism made it difficult to firmly identify a person's character type. As she notes, with accomplishment and trepidation, "Types are getting clear. Still still remains a puzzle" (38.798). Stein eventually abandons top and bottom natures, and the terms are absent from the latter notebooks and later portions of the novel. She determines, nonetheless, that only close and lengthy observation can solve the puzzle of human character.

In any estimation of character, Stein suggests, the necessary proximity of observer to subject might come to resemble a love relationship. "To know surely in these cases one has to know the complete history and weigh it carefully, almost one has to love them," she muses (38.788). While in *Q.E.D.* and "Melanctha," scientifically minded lovers unwittingly torment their romantic objects of study, in the notebooks Stein records a more satisfactory union. In her study of Alice Toklas, she describes how her subject had, to Stein's satisfaction, wrested control over her:

> the last thing noticed is the way she can make you talk like one of her old gentlemen to whom she loves to listen and be docile to and so she makes a poor thing of one because one talks badly then, she listens, she is docile, stupid but she owns you, you are then hers. (37.761.[109])

Stein goes on to note that Toklas's subtle strength has a "pride" that gets expressed "in whore clothes" (37.761.[154, 155]). Barbara Will aptly sums up Stein's classification of Toklas as a version of Weininger's "prostitute type," which was the closest female equivalent to the male genius on his character spectrum (at the sexual and intellectual end), making Toklas the perfect match for Stein's classification of herself as a masculine genius (Will, *Gertrude Stein* 74–75). Her esteem for Toklas's psyche, furthermore, has import for Stein's broader investigations of Jewish nature as a quality of mind.

In college, Stein identified "brain-power" as a Jewish racial characteristic to be preserved by avoiding intermarriage (TMJ 424). A decade later, Stein more widely applies this characteristic, which she still deems Jewish. Specifically, Toklas's intelligence is something that Stein classifies as dynamically Jewish. Toklas has

> the practical intelligence of the Hellenising Jew, but not the practical instinct as Stern has it. . . . The mental xpression is practical and concrete the emotion is subtle, instinctive beautiful. (37.761. [97, 100–101])

With the gerundial phrase, "Hellenising Jew," Stein indicates that Toklas's Jewish mind, with its Hebraic practicality and concreteness of "mental xpression," strives for a Hellenic emotion that is "subtle, instinctive beautiful." This admixture achieves something different from what Katz saw in Weininger's antisemitic stance, since Stein values the Jewish type (of mind) but values an adulterated rather than an absolute Jewishness. Indeed, a fuller excerpt shows the extent to which Stein prizes the fusing of Hebraism and Hellenism in Toklas's character: "Along with this is not a moral purpose or intention but an exquisite and keen moral sensibility" (37.761.[97–98]). For Stein, Toklas exhibits the moral character of the "ethical" Jewish type, and yet Stein celebrates this Hebraic attribute in Toklas for its Hellenic disinterestedness, its lack of "purpose or intention."

Stein and Weininger shared the widespread notion that Jewish character was, in Weininger's words, a "tendency of the mind" (303). For Stein, the intellect was the "Jewish group's" most marked characteristic, and her notes and diagrams of Jewish types frequently include the words "intellect" or "intelligence."[26] And she repeatedly classifies *as Jewish* an intellectually headstrong way of life, noting, "Jews mostly run themselves by their minds" (38.788). To explain this classification, she writes, "I think of Goethe and Frederick the Great as Jewish because they persistently and consciously educated themselves, consciously ran themselves by their minds. They had great minds and used themselves to the full" (38.796).[27] Here Stein holds up Jewish nature for its intellectual acumen and fierce personal drive. As she enumerates what she sees as quite varied qualities of mind, however, her investigations begin to sound like pages from the Social Darwinian genius books.

Like the genius books, Stein identifies a Jewish root to genius, though unlike those books she does not necessarily condemn Jewish genius as degenerate. Under a Jewish umbrella—"all this may be called Jewish"—Stein distinguishes several varieties of intellectual types who run themselves by their minds (38.791). She lumps together writers, statesmen, artistic innovators, industrialists, and members of her own "peasant group" (38.785). Toklas and her typological sibling Bernard Berenson, for example, "run themselves by their intellect" (37.761.[101]). And in a more wide-ranging investigation of minds and intellectual motors, Stein notes:

> Chalfin don't run himself by his mind, he just set himself in motion by it but thats because he hasn't mind enough to go around, Edstrom does that is the reason he is so much like a yid, He don't run his emotions by it and they are sometimes great but he runs himself by it, his mind is good but not great. Dougherty thinks he runs himself by his mind but he don't.... Leo and James run themselves by their minds but they have pretty great minds[.] (38.788)

She identifies these men—a sculptor (David Edstrom), painters (Paul Dougherty and Paul Chalfin), and William James and her brother Leo—as Jewish subtypes who have "good but not great" minds while remaining Jew-ish, or "so much like a yid." Stein admires the Jewish behavior of "running oneself by the mind" for its productivity and continues to use this characteristic in the published novel (without mentioning that it "may be called Jewish"). And yet, in the notebooks, she observes, in Arnoldian fashion, that many of these Jewish types exhibit a powerful Hebraic drive and productivity (in their almost dogmatic practicality and automaticity) which, untempered by Hellenic qualities, show no attentiveness to experience. Stein determines that "great minds" combine a powerful Jewish intellect with what I am playfully referring to as Hellenism's empiricism, that "strong sense of reality."

Like the Hellenic Melanctha, who "always had strong the sense for real experience," Stein's classification of herself in the notebooks as Jewish confirms her high estimations of her own intellectual powers and empirical sensitivity (*TL* 116). She asserts: "Mine the peasant group, earthy, patient, real intellect, strong sense of reality" (38.785). She locates herself on the Jewish side of several diagrams by classifying herself as an "earthy successful" type with a "quickness of mind" (37.761.[28, 30]. See figure 1 above).

Stein distinguishes herself—and Picasso—from those Jewish types with "pretty great minds" (such as Leo and William James) because she creates original work in lieu of criticizing or philosophizing about ideas or things

(38.788). For Stein, the distinguishing Jewish-Hellenic tendency that she and Picasso share is "the power of xperiencing" or fully engaging with the concrete experiences of life (39.814). "Pablo and I," she declares, "refuse to run ourselves by our minds" (38.788). She and Picasso are, she suggests, a variety of the Jewish type—the modern artist and truth-teller—that benefits from a Hellenic ability to see things as they are. Their way of "seeing," being truly alive to "real experience," puts them on par with "great thinkers" of the caliber of Darwin, who she considered to be "the real rationalist" (39.815).[28] As I discuss below, she pits Darwin's strengths against those of her brother Leo, who, because of his "lack" of "experiencing" is "not a real thinker in philosophical matters" (39.814).

Moral Calibans: Disconnected Jewish Types

Stein elects herself and Picasso, as Jewish types, to the pinnacle of the genius category: the avant-garde artist seeing so truly and yet so differently from others. Her creative, modern Jewish type connects Hebraism and Hellenism, unlike the disconnect exhibited by those she calls "moral Calibans." Like E. M. Forster's imperative to "only connect," written when Stein was writing notebooks for *The Making of Americans*, she strongly criticizes those Jewish types who are "not in any way connect[ing]" their intellects to their experience (39.815.[28]).[29] She dubs these types of people "moral Calibans" because instead of residing in the muddy milieu of Shakespeare's Caliban, they are at a remove from experience and function only in the "moral" or ideological realm (37.768.[1a]). "Moral Calibans," she writes, have "good heads but it don't connect with their xperience," they exist, instead, in the "cotton-wool" of their idealism (37.768.[1a,1c]).

Stein's moral Calibans have the genius of a Jewish type but also its degeneracy. In the notebooks, Stein describes at great length the failings of her archetypal "moral Caliban," Harriet Levy (37.768.[1a]).[30] In Stein's analysis, Harriet is "brilliant," has an "intellect [which is] purely academic," and "a wonderful power of emptying out your words as [she] quote[s] them" (37.768.[1a]). Despite her radical way with language, Harriet suffers from the "sordid," "miser quality" of the "earth type," and is "cold-hearted" and chronically neurasthenic, like the physically degenerate Jew of racial scientism (37.768.[1a, 5a, 3b, 3b]).

The moral Calibans, as flawed Jewish types, recall Adele and Jeff Campbell from Stein's first fictions and preview the flaws of David Hersland, the doomed "hero" of *The Making of Americans*. Their pathological tendencies explain why Stein asserts of moral Calibans that "These are not Tomlinsons, they are Calibans with just the same quality of vice each one of them in their different ways that Caliban had" (37.768.[2a]). Unlike Kipling's amoral Tomlinson, who is denied entry to heaven and hell because of his inability to commit deeds either good or bad, Stein's moral Calibans have a natural tendency toward vice.[31] But the distinction is only necessary for Stein to remark on because of the otherwise close association of moral Calibans with Tomlinsons as types of people who keep their distance from life's experiences. Harriet, in Stein's metaphor, eschews experience by locking her mind in a "triple-lined double back action automatic safe" with its key in another safe that is guarded day and night by a cadre of police officers (37.768.[2a]). By insulating herself so absolutely from experience, Harriet lacks a nuanced understanding of the world. Stein complains that "her conclusion was always too simple it had not in it the quality of xperience. it did not enlarge the subject, it made it too plain, too simple" (37.768.[3b–4b]). In the modern post–Darwinian era, as Stein had previously argued, generalizations must not be simple, but rather "as complicated as the facts" (MA 147).

The moralizing of the moral Caliban renders Harriet, in Stein's cosmology, a Hebraic Philistine. The secured separation of mind and body leaves Harriet with a "fake-idealism" and prompts her to consider those who commit "daring" acts to be "immoral" (37.768.[1c,2b,2b]). Stein exasperatedly concludes that daring "was almost immoral to [Harriet] as Matisse paintings are immoral to Americans" (37.768.[2b]). Here, Stein conflates the art of living dangerously with Matisse's paintings in order to condemn Harriet for the moralistic Philistinism for which the American public was notorious.[32]

Stein did not reserve Philistinism for the Jewish types in her characterology—quite the opposite. Holding fast to convention was something she considered a particularly "non-jewish" trait. As she notes: "the non-jewish person runs themselves apparently by their conventions and their training but they don't do it themselves to themselves therefor they are freer than the more intelligent yid" (38.788). Although ruled by social conventions, this mode of living seems "freer," in Stein's thinking, than that of Jewish types beholden to an internal motor or morality and running themselves by their minds. And yet both the "non-jewish person" who dares not stray from convention and the Jewish moral Caliban are typologically unfit for creating modern art.

For Stein, the freedom to "unconventionalize" and act against social norms derives from a Jewish keenness for experience. She explains, for example, how her brother Leo's moral Calibanism thwarts original thinking:

> The xplanation of why L. is to me not a real thinker in philosophical matters is on account of the lack of richness of internal general xperience. He thinks away the conventional part of thinking as Raymond principles them away and really the only way to unconventionalize is by the power of xperiencing. He has the power of thinking that Pablo has but much greater paucity of internal xperience about everything but the art created by others. It is that that he can really xperience and really originally meditate upon and that is the solution of why he don't think originally upon anything but art products. (39.814)

According to Stein, Leo's primary fault is his inability to fully register inside what is happening around him. She applauds his gifts as a critic of art—he would later pen two volumes of art criticism—but she pinpoints his remove from experience as the reason he cannot create his own works of art.[33] Stein sees Leo and childhood friend Raymond Duncan (the brother of Isadora) as examples of people who use ideological means such as "thinking" and "principles" to disarm convention. They are too intellectual to create. Stein herself, in contrast, stands firm in thinking that "the only way to unconventionalize is by the power of xperiencing." Her modern Jew "think[s] originally" thanks to the Hellenic corrective of experience.

Object Relations: Modern Authorship and the Jewish Type

Stein's modern author embodies a new ideal of "culture" that is Hebraic in its earthy proximity to experience. And yet, like the "Hellenising Jew," the authorial type in Stein's characterology strives for Hellenic ideals in relating to objects. For Stein, experience is necessary for just estimations of character and the "esthetic quality" of narrative description (39.813.[22]).

This perspective is evident in Stein's analysis of Kipling and Flaubert in the notebooks. She criticizes Kipling as a writer who has lost his feeling for the things he describes, even though he maintains an emotional connection to the names of things, which "still makes him an artist" (39.813.[19]).[34] For Stein, the exactitude that Kipling's naming demonstrates gives the impression of experience, much like "the way people like to hear medical jargon etc, . . . [because] it presupposes so very much xperience" (39.813.[16–17]). She determines, however, that the vividness of Kipling's depictions lack the truly substantive element that experience provides.

Stein is more admiring of Flaubert, instead, who "has no emotion about his material but complete emotion about his xperience" (39.813. [24]). Flaubert seems to have what Leo lacks, that "richness of internal general xperience," hence the unconventional and "esthetic quality" of Flaubert's prose, as Stein reads it (39.814, 39.813.[22]). (And read it and emulate it, she did: his *Trois Contes* [1877] served as the model for her *Three Lives*.) Stein associates Flaubert's genius with her most vaunted Jewish type, a character she believes combines the best of Arnold's Hebraism and Hellenism.

The modern artistic fraternity that Flaubert represents in Stein's notebooks are singular Jewish types who strive to "see things as they are." As we saw earlier in the chapter, Arnold deemed "Hellenic" a quality of curiosity that he believed led to "seeing the object as in itself it really is" (FC 258). It is this "Hellenic" kind of "seeing" that Stein sees in her Jewish artistic cohort. They also model curiosity, a trait prized by Arnold for what he deemed the "Hellenic" disinterestedness at the basis of good criticism. Curiosity was the "disinterested love of a free play of the mind on all subjects, for its own sake" (FC 268). He thus promoted a Kantian disinterestedness that engages directly with experience to appreciate (or criticize) *what really is*, but without a utilitarian purpose like political engagement or practical instruction. "Disinterested" serves as a characteristic for some of Stein's types, whether she notes someone behaving "disinterestedly" or having "a gleam of disinterestedness," or lacking such a quality, such as the "Napoleonic type [who is] not disinterested" or her friend Mabel Haynes, who is certainly "not disinterested. no disinterestedness" (37.761.[57, 13, 34, 35]).

In Stein's reformulation of Arnold, Jewish types exhibit these ideal characteristics of Hellenism. They constantly enrich themselves with experience, such that "the object" is not just present but repeatedly represented to their thinking. They see an "object as object," to be considered "for its own sake." For Stein, the vision of these Hellenising Jews contrasts with the outlook of a moral Caliban like Leo, who is at a remove from life and "does not present the object to his thought not having the xperience" (39.814).

Stein specifically associates modern artistic production with Jewish character by putting herself in league with Cézanne and Picasso, both of whom she considered to be typologically Jewish—as "earthy" and "resisting" types at "bottom" (38.791).[35] She also aligns herself artistically with Matisse, who she thinks expresses his "daring" encounter with experience in unconventional ways. In Stein's eyes, these characteristically Jewish artists, imbued with the gifts of Arnoldian culture, see objects as they are.

Stein unabashedly names Cézanne as the archetypal "great master" of seeing "the object itself" and then explains how she and others follow in his footsteps:

> Now Cezanne is the great master of the realisation of the object itself, Pablo connects on to him. . . . Bruner is on our side, he is of these who have an affection for the object not an emotion started by the object. I think this is the basis of the different methods of attack. Pablo and Braque and I and Cezanne and Mike are all of the other kind, object as object. (38.788)

To Stein, Cézanne's way of seeing is characterological as "the basis of the different methods of attack." These artists (and her brother Mike) collectively form one "side" or character type, and, like Cézanne, they are interested in capturing the "object itself" unobscured by emotion.[36] In Stein's system of classification, this type may have "an affection for the object" but such feeling is not integral to the object. Too many artists mistake "an emotion started by the object" for the object itself because, according to Stein, they are not in touch with experience.[37]

Stein cements the notion that aesthetics betray a typological difference—in this case the Jewish roots of modern art—by racializing that difference as Calibanesque.[38] For Stein, Caliban's aesthetic sense expresses his connection to experience, in contrast to moral Calibans. She introduces the association between Caliban and Cézanne in a passage that announces her own "belief in reality":

> When Leo said that all classification is teleological I knew I was not a pragmatist I do not believe that, I believe in reality as Cezanne or Caliban believe in it. I believe in repetition. Yes. Always and always, Must write the hymn of repetition. (38.797)

In this passage, Stein embraces a Calibanesque sense of reality linked to repetition. The parallel phrasing suggests that her belief in reality *is* a belief in repetition. She thereby dissociates herself from Pragmatism as understood through Leo's report of its teleological nature. As I discuss above, Stein had explained her approach to reality as seeing the "object as object," which, in its repetitive phrasing, conveys the nonteleological sense of Stein's aesthetic. If an object is just an object, then meaning is present in the thing itself. Only the object can express that meaning, which must be presented repeatedly for the understanding to be conveyed. Stein's determination to "write the hymn of repetition" is, like Joyce's secular "epiphany" in *A Portrait of the Artist*, a song of lasting praise to the creation of modern art.

Repetition is at the heart of Stein's means of "unconventionalizing" and, through its association with Cézanne and Caliban, Stein's repetition becomes, in her eyes, Jewish. She thinks that ideas are born from a direct engagement with reality, which constantly needs to be repeated. As she mentions elsewhere in the notebooks, "Real thinking is conceptions aiming and aiming again and again always getting fuller that is the difference between creative thinking and theorising" (39.815). Here we get a sense of how nonteleological classification and the belief in repetition coalesce for Stein. She privileges "creative thinking" as an empirical practice of experiencing the world: it is the inherently repetitive process of having "conceptions" that constantly strive toward the fullness of truth. When one is burdened with a piecemeal endeavor, Stein advocates engaging with that repetitious reality, instead of "theorizing" it, which is how Leo and others "think . . . or principle . . . away" the immediacy of life (39.814). Empirical methods, then, underlie Stein's characterological practices as she determines a person's type "through experience" (38.792).[39] Despite the concreteness of her experiences, understanding is not immediate, but a slow process of "growing into realisation" (38.792).

The making of Stein's aesthetic self and, more specifically, the making of herself as a writer is, she recalls in the notebooks, a repetitious sequence of "realisations." Stein considers that she began in a Caliban-like state— "early just being of the earth"—and later realized that "aesthetic has become the whole of me" (37.773). She recalls her

> xperience in Spain when got the awful depression of repetition in history, then realisation much later that I did not believe in progress,

that I was in that sense not an optimist, then realising that I was not a pragmatist just recently do not believe all classification is teleological, then realise, that aesthetic has become the whole of me[.] (37.773)

Here we see the formal and ideological importance of repetition to Stein's authorial development. Early on she had been dispirited by the "repetition in history" and yet, once she determines her incompatibility with pragmatism's utilitarian teleology, art and self merge for Stein, as she avers, "aesthetic has become the whole of me." She rejects the teleological derivation of meaning from use-value, as suggested by Leo's understanding of pragmatism, to embrace meaning in the object itself.[40] In the vein of Arnold's notion of criticism, Stein revalues the seemingly primitivist and abstractly Jewish "belief in reality" for concretely "seeing things as they are." With her celebration of aesthetic Calibans and her excoriation of moral Calibans, she rehabilitates the failings and recuperates the strengths of nineteenth-century Jewish stereotypes and abstractions—including Arnoldian Hebraism—as the means to producing an ethical, Jewish aesthetics for the twentieth century.

The Rise and Fall of Characterology

Stein believed in her characterological system of classification in the notebooks and believed that it evinced her typologically Jewish genius. In notes that narrate characterology, she earnestly focuses on how to convey the "experiences" and "realisations" involved in ascertaining the essence of people. She also believed that characterology was the force behind her epic novel, *The Making of Americans*. We hear her determination to incorporate her own studies "explaining" the people she knows into the *bildung* of the novel's protagonist. She reassuringly notes, "I need not be in a hurry to give birth to my hero because it will be an enormous task to struggle his development. I want to make him realise everybody in the book the way I am" (38.789). Following from the notebooks, Stein codes the writing and narrating of characterology as a typologically "Jewish" endeavor in the novel.

In writing the notebooks and in composing the novel, Stein was, nonetheless, struck by doubts as to the feasibility of the endeavor despite full-hearted ambitions. The lengthy period of composition—between six and nine years—revealed to Stein the limitations of her painstaking methods. As the narrator in *The Making of Americans* discovers, "Categories that once to some one had real meaning can later to that same one be all empty. It is queer that words that meant something in our thinking and our feeling can later come to have in them in us not at all any meaning" (440).

4

Pariah Modernism

Estranging Narration in *The Making of Americans*

In the summer of 1925, Stein was at last reading the page proofs for *The Making of Americans*. Struck by its youthful hubris in grappling with "large thoughts," she remarked to a friend, "You know it is rather funny and youthful there are moments when I think I should prune it but then after all it was done as much done as it could be and after all these years I guess it will do" (*GS/CVV* 118). She was not alone in questioning the excessive size of the thousand-page book: E. E. Cummings called it "a hugely fat hyperopus stuffed-to-bursting with repetitions," Edmund Wilson "balked" at "her soporific rigmaroles, her echolaliac incantations," Wyndham Lewis sketched its style as "a gargantuan mental stutter," and T. S. Eliot complained of the crude and barbaric vulgarity its style "*ominously*" foretold (*Selected Letters* 267; E. Wilson 252; *The Art of Being Ruled* 400; "Charleston, Hey! Hey!" 595).

Stein may have had these criticisms in mind when she observed that people do not see the beauty in "modern" unconventional writing. In her 1926 lecture "Composition as Explanation," she admits that "outlaw" creations may be harder to appreciate and yet reproaches readers: "If every one were not so indolent they would realise that beauty is beauty even when it is irritating and stimulating not only when it is accepted and classic" (496, 497). With this instruction, Stein ratifies the categorically "irritating annoying stimulating," and, as she had done in the long novel, casts the writing and appreciation of avant-garde literature as respectable rather than reprehensible endeavors (496).

The Making of Americans is about turning outlaws into classics in the social and artistic senses. In the book, Stein aims to replace Matthew Arnold's ideal of beauty with a beauty that may not immediately be recognizable:

she makes it Jewish. Her narrator enumerates types of character in a lengthy classification narrative that formally disrupts literary convention. Stein implicitly racializes this novelistic method as Jewish, re-interpreting Arnold's Hellenistic ideal of "sweetness and light" as an aesthetic that is both unconventional and Hebraic. Stein differs from much of the racial scientism of her era, however, in her positive valuation of the Jewish race; she found beauty in the essence thought to be most irritating, annoying, and stimulating in modern European society.[1] The novel demonstrates that some aesthetic judgments are arrived at, like racialist estimations of character, according to conventional terms and considerations that are not just indolent but immoral.

The narrator champions the expression of vitality by unconventional individuals, even when society disdains it. With the oft-quoted declaration, "I am writing for myself and strangers," the narrator explains that he purposefully alienates himself from his familiars to write the book he feels he must write, though he knows they will not appreciate it (*MA* 289). This makes him a "conscious pariah" in what Hannah Arendt considered to be a hidden Jewish tradition (Arendt 66). Although Stein's novel may not be self-consciously political, as is Arendt's writing on Jewish pariahs, Stein's alienated narrator is nonetheless engaged in an ideological battle over freedom of expression by advocating the importance of minority or "outlaw" points of view.

The narrator positions himself as an authorial *pariah*, but his desire for acceptance positions him socially as a *parvenu*. Over the course of the last century, these two figures, pariah and parvenu, have come to represent the modern Jewish *and* the modern American experience. Literary modernism's most famous parvenu, Jay Gatsby, for example, was the working-class son of German-American gentiles. And yet Meredith Goldsmith argues that he is figuratively a Jew whose identity Fitzgerald conveys through a "series of ethnic and racial analogies" (443). Likewise, in *The Making of Americans*, Stein does not refer to Jews or Jewish types by name, but by wholly indirect means. Stein builds meaning associatively in the novel by referring to the explicitly Jewish character types from her preliminary notebooks and the implicitly Jewish figures, both pariahs and parvenus, from her first fictions.[2] The Jewish figurations in these earlier writings appear in modified or abstracted form in the novel. They are as crucial to finding meaning in the novel as, over the course of the "long book," earlier passages are to the later ones. Lisa Ruddick aptly describes *The Making of Americans* as "a genealogy of modern writing" (127).

Several thematic and stylistic changes evince the many stages of the novel's composition and its changing iterations of Jewish character.[3] The beginning of the novel, largely a revised and repetitiously expanded version of the 1903 draft, maintains the coded Jewishness of Stein's previous fiction as it follows the emigration and settlement of the middle-class Dehning family through three generations in America. The narrator again recounts the fraught courtship of Julia Dehning and Alfred Hersland and again *interrupts* the recounting of their courtship to address his outcast community of Brother Singulars.[4] Subsequently, the narrator widens his scope from the 1903 draft's focus on the Dehning family to tell the history of the Hersland family, whose three children, Martha, Alfred, and David, provide the nominal focus of the long novel and the names of its latter chapters.

Scholars have long considered the story of the Herslands and the Dehnings a thinly veiled family memoir. They read the two families as German Jews who, like Stein's grandparents, immigrated to America in the 1860s.[5] Literary critics who make claims about the Jewish identity of these families provide important first steps in our understanding of the novel. Since the narrator's attention and most of the book steer away from the Herslands and Dehnings as conventional narrative subjects, however, we need likewise to turn our attention away from Jewish characters and toward Jewish character types.

The Making of Americans draws extensively on the character studies from Stein's notebooks.[6] The narrator makes good on a promise from the 1903 draft to eschew "a simple novel with a plot and conversations" in favor of "hearing more" about "the character" of its characters (MA 144). Like Stein, the narrator turns to classification and situates the members of the Hersland and Dehning families within an epic enumeration of character types, kinds, subkinds, groups, sides, and admixtures. As Jessica Berman writes, "Stein's narrative comes to present the compendium as narrative alternative" (174). In massive, repetitious sentences, the narrator moves beyond the familial realm into a more generalized framework of character study, which, as another critic notes, resolves that in *The Making of Americans*, "the question of character becomes largely a question of composition" (Meyer, "Introduction" xxxiii).

In the lengthy classification narrative, the narrator gives characteristics precedence over specific characters. The named Hersland and Dehning characters often recede, becoming merely "one" among many elaborately enumerated varieties of a type. The sentences shift from a strictly familial genealogy, such as, "The children had many ways of having the father and the mother mixed up to make them," to large extrapolations from known people, such as, "There have been always many millions made just like the mother" (*MA* 64, 81). Eventually, characterological claims become wholly general statements about character types, such as, "There are many kinds of men, there are many kinds of women there are many kinds of ways of mixing them in the children that come out of them. There are many kinds of men and many millions made of each kind of them" (116).

Jewish nature remains important in the narrator's classification endeavors, albeit in a coded manner. The designation of Jewish nature is one of two major kinds of people in Stein's notebooks. The novelization of the characterology likewise presents Jewish nature as a central determinant in the narrator's schema. Stein abandons the explicit naming of the Jewish and Anglo-Saxon categories, however, substituting their corresponding nomenclatures from the notebooks.[7] In lieu of "Jewish" nature, the narrator describes types that are "earthy," "resisting," and "dependent independent" (348–349). In lieu of the Jew's "Anglo-Saxon" counterpart, the narrator describes types that are "clear," "white and vibrant" (though sometimes "slimy, gelatinous, gluey"), "attacking," and "independent dependent" (349). In the notebooks, Stein had designated herself as a Jewish type, and the novel's narrator also classifies himself Jewishly as an earthy, resisting, "dependent independent" kind. He even classifies his characteristic classifying of people as Jewish, suggesting that the characterology itself is a typologically Jewish endeavor.

Despite autobiographical parallels, Stein was consciously writing the novel as a literary creation. As a result, the narrator is a persona who is not necessarily Gertrude Stein. As Steven Meyer observes, this "author-narrator," Stein's "alter-ego," is one of Stein's "remarkable achievements" ("Introduction" xxvii; *Irresistible Dictation* 242; "Introduction" xxvii). Certainly, the narrator is closer to representing Stein than any other known person, something the narrator's Jewish nature seems to confirm. This is why many critics simply equate Stein with the narrator.[8] The purposeful construction of an "I" in the novel who shares numerous characteristics with the "me" of Stein's notebooks cannot be said to embody Stein, however, since the notebooks often announce ways in which Stein incorporates her experiences into *several* of the novel's characters.

As is fitting for a book about the difficulty of knowing human beings, the narrator's identity remains anonymous and the narrator's gender indiscernible. I use the masculine pronoun to refer to the narrator as a means of acknowledging the narrator's stated affiliation with Brother Singulars and Stein's classification of herself as a masculine type in the notebooks for *The Making of Americans*. By using a masculine pronoun for a woman writer's narrator, I further hope to maintain throughout my narrative an awareness of the differences between Stein and her fictional narrator, despite their many similarities.

This chapter aims to shift critical study of the novel in general and of the locus of Jewish interest in particular away from the story of German-Jewish immigration and assimilation and toward the characterological Jewish tradition established by the narrator.[9] According to the narrator, his own Jewish nature finds particular expression in his passion for classifying people and in his narration of that classifying. To consider *things as they are* in *The Making of Americans* means focusing on the narrator's adventures in writing people's character. Such an approach deals with the novel as it really is and not with the remnants of the conventional novel that many readers seek.

Despite the novel's decisive turn from conventional plot to classification narrative, Stein's narrator repeatedly questions the viability and ethics of the classification process itself. As Stefanie Hawkins explains,

> Stein's critique of empirical methods [in *The Making of Americans*], particularly realist description, not only deconstructs the narrative conventions of the nineteenth-century novel, but also calls into question the systematic authority of nineteenth-century science upon which narrative realism was based. (70)

The narrator realizes that you can't watch all of the people all of the time and determines that the aimed-for truths of characterology are flawed truths. This resembles William James's idea of the scientific endeavor, as Stein later recalled it: "he said science is not a solution and not a problem it is a statement of the observation of things observed and perhaps therefore not interesting perhaps therefore only abjectly true" (*EA* 242).[10] Stein follows James's dictum by centering her novel on the narrator's struggle to explain human nature and subsequently write that explanation. Stein presents the science of character as an experiential account of the narrator perceiving people. Thus, the novel in its entirety becomes a statement of the ever-changing and contingent processes of observing, ascertaining, and writing an understanding of human nature. As a science made ethical, accurate, humane, and original by narrative, quite literally a narrated science of human kinds, the novel's "unconventionalized" empirical psychology embraces modernity (39.814). And yet, it is a process that the narrator is only able to pursue by being a pariah, or as he says, by "writing for myself and strangers" (*MA* 289). The novel's raison d'être, the characterology and its discontents, are thus categorically Jewish and modern.

Brother Singulars as Exemplars of Arendt's Jewish Pariahs

If, as historian John Higham claims, "In an age of parvenus the Jew provided a symbol of the parvenu spirit," such symbolism was not wholly critical (27). Like the narrator's portrayal of the "decent family's progress" made by the Dehnings and the Herslands, the parvenu was often admired in America at a time when new fortunes were thought to evince entrepreneurial savvy (*MA* 34). And such approval might extend to Jews. Historian Hasia Diner points to robust stereotypes about the "commercial integrity" of Jews in the latter part of the nineteenth century (196). However, Diner also notes, "Another pervasive American idea maintained that Jews used their money crudely and flaunted their riches" (191). Such ostentation made them exemplars of the practice Thorstein Veblen, in criticizing the turn-of-the-century American parvenu, called "conspicuous consumption." In the 1870s, for example, those bent on excluding Jews from hotels and vacation places called Jews "pretentious," "vulgar," and "crude" to distinguish them from Protestants who evidently spent money "with grace" (Diner 193).

At midcentury, looking back on the "age of parvenus," Hannah Arendt sought to revive modern interest in another Jewish figure—the pariah—as an important but less remarked spirit of the age. In several essays, Arendt considers the pariah as a Jewish type and a "trend of Jewish tradition" running counter to the more prevalent parvenu or "upstart" (65).[11] Arendt figures parvenus and pariahs as brothers, but in the worst sense, almost as Cain and Abel. Unlike the well-remarked ostentation of the parvenu, the Jewish pariah is part of a "hidden tradition" that Arendt sees subtly expressed by "tacit and latent" means (67, 68). Not deprived of judgment by the parvenu's class-conscious materialism, pariahs have, according to Arendt, a "humane attitude" and a "natural insight into reality" (66). She suggests that these Jewish visionaries have chosen a righteous if difficult path and that they are, in the coinage of Bernard Lazare, "conscious pariahs" (qtd. in Arendt 66).[12]

In Arendt's view, the pariah's self-consciousness as an outsider becomes a tool for social criticism, helpful in considering the marginalized and useful in the "evaluation of mankind in our day" (68). She finds the iconography of pariah "types" in Lazare's fin-de-siècle writing on Jewish nationalism and in Heine's *Hebrew Melodies* (69). She also finds it in works by Chaplin and Kafka that make no explicit reference to Jews or Judaism, but where she thinks the "hidden" pariah tradition is not so hidden. In Arendt's analysis, Chaplin's tramp "betrays what are clearly Jewish traits" and Kafka's K. in *The Castle* is "plainly a Jew," recognized through his involvement "in situations and perplexities distinctive of Jewish life" (82, 84). Though these characters are wholly without conventional Jewish markers, Arendt names them as Jews. She casts the tramp and K. as representative speakers for the Jewish people: their miserable status makes visible the problematic structures of modern society and, thereby, critically "evaluates mankind" (68). Here we get a sense of Arendt's overarching interest in human rights and how, for her, the Jewish question figures what is, essentially, a humanitarian crisis.

For Arendt, abstraction is a tool for communicating interconnectedness and universal humanity. "Jewish poets, writers and artists," she writes, "have evolved the concept of the specifically Jewish pariah as a generalized "human type" (68). She argues, for example, that Kafka's K. is a pariah whose attempts to work his way into the life of the townspeople near the Castle represent the striving of every Jew for acceptance "as a human being" (85). She especially admires K.'s ethical drive:

> This is the Jew who chooses the alternative way—the way of goodwill, who construes the conventional parlance of assimilation literally. What Kafka depicts is the real drama of assimilation, not its distorted counterpart. He speaks for the average small-time Jew who really wants no more than his rights as a human being: home, work, family and citizenship. (84–85)

For Arendt, the parvenu's masquerade of respectability is not assimilation, but a monstrously "distorted counterpart" of a social ideal that does not afford everyone basic rights. The pariah, in contrast, chooses to reject the conventions of that society and, in Arendt's reading, this becomes the "real drama of assimilation." According to Arendt, in K.'s search to become what Kafka's narrator describes as an "indistinguishable" member of humanity, Kafka seeks to awaken others to society's inhumane ways (qtd. in Arendt 84). Arendt thereby revalues the socially undistinguished and the aesthetically indistinguishable for their purposeful postures of estrangement.

Arendt's analysis of parvenu and pariah *forms of expression* highlights the abstraction of Kafka's depictions. Like Chaplin's anonymous tramp, Kafka's confident stranger, nameless except for his initial, is textually "indistinguishable." Arendt suggests, perhaps unwittingly, that abstract and estranging avant-garde modes of expression—the iconic modes of the pariah tradition—are the "vaunted" and ideal "culture for Jews" (72, 93).

Following from Arendt's reading of the Jewish pariah tradition, I explore Stein's Jewish practice of estranging narration in *The Making of Americans*. I trace the evolution of the pariah figure in a series of social misfits and others who the narrator designates as "queer things like us" (*MA* 47). I do this by extrapolating from the portrayal of the Brother Singular to figures whose hygiene, occupation, taste, or class alienates them from respectability. These pariahs include a "virtuous poor woman" with a dirty daughter, lonesome servant girls and others with unsophisticated taste, and those who write unconventionally (16). In these, the novel's stalwart figures of difference, Stein shapes the ethical and earthy Jewish qualities from her notebooks into an implicitly Jewish nexus of morality, dirt, and aesthetics, thereby embedding the Jewish identity of these figures in the alienating characteristics of the pariah type.

Just as Arendt considered the pariahs in Heine and Lazare to have been "conceived essentially as Jews," Stein "conceives" the narrator and his abstracted Brother Singulars "essentially as Jews," even though such figures appear metaphorically Jewish, like Chaplin and Kafka's outcasts (Arendt 81). As *The Making of Americans* becomes the story of telling the story of characterology-writing, the narrator ceases to address his Brother Singulars *by name* but, instead, as an abstracted community of "strangers" with "queer ways." Stein's narrator himself heads the procession of pariahs with his pronouncement, "I am writing for myself and strangers" (*MA* 289). His address cements the central characteristic of *strangeness* with its *estranging* function: strange characteristics, be they racial, sexual, aesthetic, or behavioral, may have a social impact by alienating the odd fellow from others.

The narrator further estranges narration in the novel's final chapters. He uses indefinite pronouns to insist on the presence of singularity in *some* people, if not *many* people or *any* people. Referenced by indefinite pronouns, the odd, the queer, and the different become supremely abstract iterations of the narrator's Brother Singulars, a Jewish pariah people become, even more than Kafka's K., textually indistinguishable. At the end of the novel, Stein uses abstraction to convey the connectedness of the uncommon in the very uniformity of difference. With this experimental gesture, Stein paradoxically reveals the proximity of relatedness, or what the narrator calls, in another sense, "family living" (913). Stein ultimately reconceives the notion of family, moving away from the biological and toward the characterological as the primary means to connect people.

"Conscious Pariahs": An Array of Jewish Types at the Beginning of the Novel

In 1906, when Stein returned to *The Making of Americans*, her interest in estranged identities found expression in strange narrative forms. At first, this meant expanding her sentences from the 1903 draft and taking up writing as an explicit subject of her work. In the earliest, more conventionally written pages of the novel, for example, the narrator depicts writing as a metaphor for an estranging and earthy Jewish individuality. He favors the "scribbled and dirty and lined paper that is really to be to me always my receiver" in lieu of a typewriter's "metallic clicking" (*MA* 33, 47). Regularizing constraints are not conducive to cultivating the "queer," "eccentric," and "vital singularity" that he associates with fundamental human freedoms (47).[13] "Machine making," the narrator complains to his fellow "brother singulars," "does not turn out queer things like us" (47). Typewriters, in rendering letters as uniform "type," obscure the irregularities of handwritten manuscript, so self-expression in the machine age needs a new means of irregularity: for Stein's narrator, this means style.

Stein's characterological narration uses long and repetitive sentences, a style she had begun to use in the recently completed novellas of *Three Lives*. The result was prose that critics describe as "intensive," "generalizing," "combinative," and "insistent" (Pondrom lvi and DeKoven [pace Stein] in *A Different Language* 46). The peculiar combination of repetition and irregularity in Stein's sentences became the novel's primary innovation.[14] As Stein has Toklas reflect in *The Autobiography of Alice B. Toklas*, "those long sentences . . . were to change the literary ideas of a great many people" (57).

The aberrant form of the sentences in *The Making of Americans* reflects their characterological content: they evince the narrator's own queerness—or "vital singularity"—as he ascertains the precise singularity of others (47). He aims to accumulate a "completed understanding" of people through observation to classify "the whole of them" (322).[15] Unlike the obtuse scientific companions of Helen and Melanctha in Stein's first fictions, the narrator in *The Making of Americans* is duly aware of the inevitable resistance to his classifying project. His social circle does not want to know his ideas about them, and he concludes that truthfulness is prone to offend. Though his endeavors and their irregular means leave the narrator a pariah, he nonetheless finds that singularity is imperative for the unconventional writer.

Like Lazare and Arendt, Stein casts her pariah narrator as a Jewish type, a distinct part of Jewish tradition. From her earliest writings, Stein depicted Jews as pariahs. She had begun writing about Jews at Radcliffe, for example, by defending their volitional pariahdom. Jews derived from "sturdy independent forefathers" and had been chosen by God, and so they must, she urged, continue to self-segregate by "embrac[ing] isolation" and ennobling a segregated position that is only ignoble when not chosen (TMJ 427). In her college essay against intermarriage, she depicts this segregated Jewish collectivity with the trope of an estranged fraternity. Among Jews, the young Stein claimed, "A bond of love and of duty exists between perfect strangers . . . [who] are as brothers" (426). While in that essay Stein advocates a specifically conjugal isolation in arguing for endogamy among Jews, the grandiose rationales for preserving the "brain-power" of the Jewish "race" suggest a broader embrace of Jewish isolation (424).

In the novel, Stein's narrator is a "conscious pariah" much like Arendt's outcast Jewish observers. At the beginning of the Martha Hersland chapter, almost a third of the way into the novel, the narrator addresses the inevitable alienation caused by his uncharacteristic need to do and say characterology, with a manifesto of pariahdom:

> I am writing for myself and strangers. This is the only way that I can do it. Everybody is a real one to me, everybody is like some one else too to me. No one of them that I know can want to know it and so I write for myself and strangers.
>
> Every one is always busy with it, no one of them then ever want to know it that every one looks like some one else and they see it. Mostly every one dislikes to hear it. It is very important to me to always know it, to always see it which one looks like others and to tell it. I write for myself and strangers. I do this for my own sake and for the sake of those who know I know it that they look like other ones, that they are separate and yet always repeated. There are some who like it that I know they are like many others and repeat it, there are many who never can really like it.
>
> There are many that I know and they know it. They are all of them repeating and I hear it. I love it and I tell it, I love it and now I will write it. This is now the history of the way some of them are it. (*MA* 289)

In a coincidence of scientific and avant-garde methods, repetition formally structures the telling of the narrator's observations. Repetition is his means of understanding people and inimical to the process of determining each person's kind. He sees the uniqueness in each person ("everybody is a real one") and sees their similarities to other individuals ("everybody is like some one else too"). Despite popular discontents, his classifying furthers the project of human understanding, and so he persists.

The narrator portrays his alienation as a necessary estrangement that is Jewish only by association. As a classifier, he is the type of person whose "love" for "repeating" catalyzes oral and written narrative: "I love it and I tell it . . . and now I will write it" (289). In his gerundial phrasing, he types himself as someone "loving repeating being" (301). These types, in turn, he describes as "earthy," "slow-minded resisting," and "dependent independent," all Jewish qualities from the characterology in Stein's notebooks (298). This constellation of material and behavioral characteristics comprises—with pariahdom—the coded Jewish lexicon of the novel.

Critics rightfully recognize the manifesto of pariahdom as a dramatic break in the narrator's address and methods. And yet, looking back over the nearly three hundred pages that precede it, we can see that the narrator's declaration, "I am writing for myself and strangers," is the culmination of several studies of "queer" individuals who choose pariahdom.[16] In the pages leading up to the manifesto, the narrator introduces a fraternity that includes a "virtuous poor woman," Brother Singulars, and servant girls (16). Following the manifesto, he continues to invoke these characters as a courageous fraternity willing to risk social pariahdom by following their unconventional natures. Eventually, he links their ways of being with avant-garde writers. Alienated by class, occupation, race, or nation, these "queer" characters, purposeful outcasts like Arendt's "conscious pariahs," form the major Jewish characterizations of the novel and establish the moral basis for the narrator's endeavor.

The first of the narrator's singular brethren is a "virtuous poor woman" whose rebellion he champions (16). This woman feels insulted when the doctor of a charitable health clinic refuses to treat her child who he insists is not clean:

> and the woman cries out in her indignation, what you think I am poor like a beggar, I got money enough to pay for a doctor, I show you I can hire a real doctor, and she slams the door and rushes out with her daughter. Yes it certainly is very queer in her. All this washing business is certainly most peculiar. Surely it is true that even little fleas have always littler ones to bite them. (16)

The narrator marvels that the woman exercises agency in a disempowering situation and shares the woman's nonstandard English voicing of "indignation."[17] For the narrator, the woman's refusal to accept the moral condemnation accorded someone of little means ennobles her choice to exit the clinic, hence his dubbing her "virtuous." His focus on the "poor woman's" dirt as a social divider suggests, further, that "queerness," like dirtiness, depends on context, convention, and subjectivity.[18] By seeing virtue and purposefulness where others see dirt and degradation, the narrator suggests the moral importance of this singular type.

The case of the virtuous poor woman illuminates the ramifications of iconoclastic tendencies for potential pariahs, such as a middle-class person drawn to someone who shows a "strain of singularity" (21). If a singular maintains the respect of his class while departing from behavioral norms, the narrator suggests that a woman might reasonably pursue such a man. If, however, such singularity goes too far, it loses its legibility of *purposefulness*, and the singular risks being taken "for the lowest, those who are simply poor or because they have no other way to do it" (21). The "conscious pariah" might then be taken for a parvenu or poor person and thus not make a good middle-class match.

A second Jewish type that dances a fine line between rebellion and tradition is the narrator's Brother Singulars. Like the virtuous poor woman, this isolated fraternity comprises Jewish types in the mold of the "conscious pariah," but with biblical roots. In a vestige of the 1903 draft, the narrator addresses his "Brother Singulars" directly and, as in Stein's first fictions, they echo the isolation of the explicitly Jewish strangers from Stein's college essay and the earthy characteristics directly linked to the Jewish type in Stein's notebooks. The narrator rallies these "queer people" as "earthy" types who have "a feel for mother earth," calling:

> Brother Singulars, we are misplaced in a generation that knows not Joseph. We flee before the disapproval of our cousins, the courageous condescension of our friends who gallantly sometimes agree to walk the streets with us[.] (21)

This address alludes to the biblical Joseph to suggest that the plight of the singular is part of a prophetic Jewish tradition. Joseph persists in his visions even when family (his brothers) or friends (Pharaoh) do not welcome them. Like Joseph, the narrator exchanges a biological family for a figurative one, as an archetypal "Brother Singular." Members of this fraternity alienate themselves from friends, cousins, and the criticisms of conventional society in a flight that prefigures the narrator's later determination to write for himself and strangers. Through purposeful alienation, Stein associates the narrator and his Brother Singulars with Jewish tradition and Jewish narrative.[19]

Stein extends the characterologically Jewish pairing of the virtuous poor woman's "queerness" and the narrator's "vital singularity" to include servant girls who exhibit "servant queerness" (171). He depicts servant girls as people whose occupation alienates them and imbues them with "this queerness," making them implicitly female cousins to the narrator's Brother Singulars (170).[20] In the characterological schemas of Stein's notebooks, she presents the servant girl as a female counterpart to the male Jewish "earthy" type.[21] This helps explain why servant girl is one of the first character types to be examined at length in the narrator's characterology in *The Making of Americans*: The narrator breaks off his vaguely conventional description of the Hersland family's servants to relate their odd behaviors as characteristics had by "[m]any servants" (168). The narrator classifies this "servant girl being" as a characteristic "kind of being" had by "many millions" of women, which he carefully differentiates from related types, such as "just servant being" and "little girl being" (172). Despite this type's diminutive aspects, which derive from a kinship with "little girl being," the servant girl type is very "much" a force with which to reckon, which explains why the narrator associates it with his courageous pariahs in the middle of the novel (172).

The narrator's interest in servant girl nature echoes nineteenth-century discussions of the "servant girl question," one of many social "questions" of Stein's day. As the subject of newspaper articles and pamphlets beginning in the 1880s, the servant girl question was the concern of wealthy women who had difficulty managing their serving women.[22] Stein was certainly aware of these debates and made the relationship between serving women and their mistresses the subject of "The Good Anna" and "The Gentle Lena," two of the stories in *Three Lives*. In *The Making of Americans*, the servant girl question becomes a touchstone for examining class, race, nation, morality, aesthetics, and hygiene. It also stands in for the Jewish question.

The servant girl's dirt is an important Jewish marker. Dirt associates the servant girl with the female variety of the "earthy" Jewish type in Stein's notebooks, suggesting the servant girl's kinship with the narrator's Brother Singulars, who have a "feel for mother earth" (*MA* 21). Marked by their milieu, those with "servant girl being" have, according to the narrator, an occupational type that stains them, so that, like Lady Macbeth, they find "their hands so grimy nothing can clean them" (172). And yet, much like the brash exit of the "virtuous poor woman" with a dirty daughter, those with "servant girl being" have "a little grimy defiance in them" when quitting their jobs, a comparison that implicitly takes the crime out of the servant girl's grime (173). The narrator explains that this type of woman is also considered by most people to be figuratively dirty, or unrespectable, a difference compounded by class and perceptions of racial-national difference.[23] In the eyes of the narrator, however, the grime is a sign of the servant girl's virtuous Jewish nature, for the same reason that *Q.E.D.*'s singular Adele finds an implicitly Jewish dirt "necessary to the deepest understanding" (*Q.E.D.* 101). This combination of dirt and singularity combine to produce what Stein considers, *pace* William James, the necessarily abject and Jewish quality of truth conveyed by avant-garde writing.

Servant Girls and Avant-Garde Writers: Jewish Types in the Middle of the Novel

The narrator makes avant-garde writing Jewish by associating the denigrated taste of a servant girl with the denigrated aesthetics of the avant-garde writer. Like Stephen Dedalus's bitter quip about that "symbol of Irish art"—"The cracked lookingglass of a servant"—Stein's narrator presents an array of desires and behaviors that link servant girls to avant-garde writers (*Ulysses* 1.146). In a series of long repeated passages from the middle of the novel, two of which I discuss in detail, the narrator considers the social repercussions of deviance. Using repetition, contrast, and accretion, the narrator compares servant girls to avant-garde writers as people whose nonnormative tastes are perceived to be bad taste—like that of a parvenu. In these passages, the narrator, in contrast to conventional judgments, redeems the avant-garde writer's chosen difference as a courageous expression of self and implicitly presents the acceptance of avant-garde writing as analogous to the revaluation of Jewish character.

In the first passage, the narrator praises the strength of character it takes to admit liking something that others denigrate. The narrator writes:

> It is a wonderful thing how much courage it takes even to buy a clock you are very much liking when it is a kind of one every one thinks only a servant should be owning. . . . It is very hard to have the courage of your being in you, in clocks, in handkerchiefs, in aspirations, in liking things that are low, in anything. . . . It is a very difficult thing to have courage for something no one is thinking is a serious thing. (*MA* 463–464)

As the narrator implies, the well-to-do condescendingly criticize servants' tastes to enforce their standards about aesthetics or, really, "anything." The narrator suggests that no one generally wants to be mistaken for a servant, since servant taste presumably indicates a meager means or an ostentatious desire to imitate the well-to-do. In other words, when a servant deigns to express human desires, she is nothing more than a parvenu. Such comparisons echo a common mockery of the parvenu in fin-de-siècle fiction as someone known for having servant girl taste. Henry James, for example, has a character who describes the showy decor of a parvenu as including "gimcracks that might have been keepsakes for maid-servants" (*Spoils* 7).[24]

In Stein's novel, the "wonderful" courage it takes to express idiosyncratic tastes registers the distances between "you" and a servant and between "you" and upholders of social convention. As the narrator later complains, "It is a hard thing to be loving something with a serious feeling and every one is thinking that only a servant girl could be loving such a thing" (487). The narrator points out the painful irony that what should be *natural* for a person ends up a point of agony. "It is very hard," the narrator earlier avows, to embrace one's nature when it goes against convention, since some narrow-minded people "can never understand the queer ways in another one" (453). Such judgmental stances indicate the subjective nature of our judgments, for, as he notes, "mostly every one" tends to judge other people's ways as "foolish" (453).

In presenting this series of actions, behaviors, and desires, the narrator reveals the fraternal relationship between parvenu and pariah. Unlike Arendt's embattled class-climbing parvenus and culture-making "conscious pariahs," Stein's narrator merges the types, redeeming parvenus as courageous people whose taste subjects them to ridicule. When the courageous singular is a buyer, for example, he risks being mistaken for a servant by buying something inexpensive, even though, as the narrator later notes, he has "plenty of money for the buying" (487). The consciously chosen pariahdom of the parvenu celebrates the importance of minority forms of expression. His uninhibited freedom of expression is, the narrator goes on to suggest, a crucial ingredient for the creation of modern art.

Stein's narrator Judaizes the pariah by associating him with the parvenu. As part of this series of linked passages in the middle of the novel, the narrator demonstrates the common concern over self-expression by writers and buyers. He repeats his meditation on the courageous deviance of those with "queer ways" and, notably, adds book writing to the list of things that one does seriously even if others take it for a joke.[25] He writes:

> It is a very strange feeling when one is loving a clock that is to every one of your class of living an ugly and a foolish one and one really likes such a thing and likes it very much and liking it is a serious thing, or one likes a colored handkerchief that is very gay and every one of your kind of living thinks it a very ugly or a foolish thing and thinks you like it because it is a funny thing to like it and you like it with a serious feeling, or you like eating something and liking it is a childish thing to every one or you like something that is a dirty thing

and no one can really like that thing or you write a book and while you write it you are ashamed for every one must think you are a silly or a crazy one and yet you write it and you are ashamed, you know you will be laughed at or pitied by every one and you have a queer feeling and you are not very certain and you go on writing. (485)

The parallel structure of this long sentence links various people with queer feelings. The grammatical structure of the passage links the personal pronoun "you," who "likes something that is a dirty thing," with the "you," who feels ashamed writing a book.[26] Writing a book becomes part of a series of things that "no one" who considers him- or herself morally upstanding can abide unless that morality itself is upended, which is precisely what the narrator does.

Despite the denigrated taste of servant girls and the snobbish dis-esteem for a servant's occupational provenance, Stein's narrator valorizes the writing that is like a "dirty thing." Previously he had referred to convention as something upheld by "every one having good taste" (463), but here he implies that "good taste" is merely the convention followed by "every one" of a particular "class" or "kind" (485). Over the next few passages, when describing the "masters and schools in living and in working, and in painting and in writing and in everything," the narrator marvels over the courage of a pioneering "first one . . . [who does] something no one is thinking is a serious thing," suggesting that this figuratively Jewish writer is in the avant-garde and part of a fraternity of deviants at the forefront of taste-making (486, 487).

Stein's experimental narration of characterology in long repetitious sequences slowly builds associations between singulars and their audiences by repeatedly using pronouns. Berman claims that the narrator's use of the impersonal pronoun "one," for example, "always bridges the gap between the particular and the general" and becomes "a name for the plural subject . . . and a new basis for constructing community" (174–175). I agree with Berman in large part, but her analysis waivers when we consider this series of long repeated passages. Here, the narrator's use of "one" affirms that even in community we remain individuals and possibly strangers to one another. For just as the narrator's address to a sequence of "yous" in the passage above creates a fraternity of pariahs, likewise the repetition of the impersonal pronoun "one" creates a fraternity of all "ones," ironically linking the singular person with deviant tastes ("a silly one") to the majority perspective policing such deviance ("every one") and thereby suggesting the importance of "outlaw" contributions to modernism. As I discuss below, Berman's claim becomes more apt toward the end of the novel when Stein's narrator increasingly uses pronouns to generalize about types of people in writing characterology and to suggest community.

These passages from the middle of the book suggest the inherently relational roots of avant-garde writing, even when it is the product of a solitary someone "making it new." The narrator punctuates the long sentence above with an admirer's ratification of purportedly deviant "writing or liking," which confirms the revaluation of unconventional actions or desires. He adds:

> Then some one says yes to it, to something you are liking, or doing or making and then never again can you have completely such a feeling of being afraid and ashamed that you had then when you were writing or liking the thing and not any one had said yes about the thing. (485)

The acceptance of even one "yes-sayer" releases the odd author from absolute alienation and affirms the value of his "queer ways." The narrator asserts that aesthetic pioneers eventually find an appreciative audience.

Several critics have rightfully pointed to the implied comparison between avant-garde writing and homosexuality in these passages due to the odd person's preference for "very gay" handkerchiefs and the "queer feeling" that others will not approve of the writer's work.[27] This interpretation dovetails with a romantic reading of these outcast desires and their eventual ratification by a consummate yes-saying. Queerness may, in the words of Anne Herrmann, "serve as a cover" for other differences, such as gender ambiguity and homosexuality (6). I would add that queerness, as the stated difference being explored here, serves as cover for the narrator's Jewish difference. The narrator figures these pariah writings or buyings or likings as Jewish by association and then notes that "some one" affirms them with a yes-saying, much like Joyce's yes-saying Penelope, who concludes *Ulysses* by affirming her love for Dublin's outcast Jewish Odysseus.

Abstracting the Avant-Garde: Something Jewish at the End of the Novel

For the remainder of this chapter I turn to the narrator's increasingly prevalent use of abstractions. The latter portions of *The Making of Americans* bring to the fore Stein's associative means of conveying the typologically Jewish qualities of the novel. This occurs in three stages, roughly coinciding with the book's last two chapters and epilogue. First, in the penultimate chapter, the narrator establishes the Jewish qualities of feeling words when writing and makes clear the linguistic determinacy central to his composition process. He repeatedly revises his methods, however, by "beginning again and again" using ever greater abstraction, despite, and sometimes to increase, textual indeterminacy. Second, in the novel's last chapter, the narrator contrasts the plasticity of his increasingly abstract methods with those of David Hersland, a fatally flawed Jewish singular with more static ideals. Finally, in the epilogue, the narrator estranges narration by using only impersonal pronouns, which abstract the fraternity of Brother Singulars and their characterological subjects into modern, textual indistinguishability, while nonetheless distinguishing them in the context of "family living."

Beginning Again in the Alfred Hersland and Julia Dehning Chapter

During medical school, Stein asked a Jewish colleague about a "special tendency toward melancholia among our people" (as referenced by Leon Solomons. Letter to Gertrude Stein. YCAL). The narrator's thinking in the penultimate Alfred Hersland and Julia Dehning chapter echoes this theory. Like the fear and shame that afflict the narrator in the middle of the novel, constantly emerging doubt about his characterological endeavor is, for him, a symptomatic Jewish trough. In the Martha Hersland chapter, for example, he complains, "I am all unhappy in this writing" (348). But the complaints seem to grow exponentially in the 250-page Alfred Hersland and Julia Dehning chapter, where the narrator worries, "I think it is all foolishness this I am writing" (587). Like servant girls, the narrator's isolation sometimes makes him miserable, and he complains of "much lonely feeling" and being "almost all alone" (593, 601). And, like the eponymous malady of Melanctha, the narrator feels "desolate . . . almost sulking," and reflects, "I am sometimes quite a melancholy one" (611, 646). The narrator diagnoses his melancholy as a particularly Jewish plaint. Using the novel's veiled Jewish terminology of "dependent" and "resisting" types, he admits that "in me there is quite a good deal always of dependent despairing" and "I was a sad resisting depressed jealous one" (595, 609). The writer's pathologically Jewish melancholy bears beneficial fruit, however.

In a cycle repeated throughout the novel, the degenerate trough of Jewish doubt prompts the narrator to persevere, regain confidence, and "begin again," attaining a characteristically Jewish peak. Doubt turns out to be "a nicely disturbing feeling" for the narrator, especially when the palliative of a writing cure is applied (663). The narrator repeatedly recovers his narrative momentum and makes his overcoming of potential obstacles a formal characteristic of the novel, often straightforwardly stating, "I will now begin again" (574). Akin to the narrator's revaluation of dirt as virtuous and necessary to the deepest understanding, Jewish melancholy becomes a catalyst for his cheerful, Jewish "Beginning again," which ushers in the novel's modernist repetitions. The Jewish pariah figure passes the baton to the Jewish parvenu, who continually arrives, unfazed by the pessimism of his narrative surroundings.

In the Alfred Hersland and Julia Dehning chapter, the narrator modifies his diction, purpose, and audience, making it more modern and Jewish, as he begins again and again. For the narrator, an abstract diction and repetitive syntax are crucial to accurately narrating an empirical truth. The somewhat indeterminate precision of an abstract pronoun, he wagers, may be more accurate than an absolute generalization. The narrator marks the evolution of his thinking by stating, "Every one was a whole one in me and now a little every one is in fragments inside me" (519). His inability to understand people wholly does not invalidate his surety about knowing them partially. On the contrary, the narrator's partial knowledge reflects a constantly modified field of observations. Instead of doubtfully claiming to know "all," he can confidently claim to know something about "many" or "some": "There are a great many men and women always living. This is to be now some history of some of them" (612). He also modifies his characterological claims, using adverbial phrases, to admit that he is "almost certain" that he will know "pretty nearly all the kinds there are in men and women" (598, 620).

The narrator's "progress" in the novel is thus one of adaptation and accretion. He rejects classification as a method for determining "a complete thing" (791). Instead, as the project's means, scope, feasibility, and audience change, the narrator begins anew, with changing and abstracted diction, in order to practice what he deems an experimental, empirically sound narrative method. The method stymies some critics. Priscilla Wald, for example, complains, "The continual definition and redefinition of the project counteracts comprehension" (275). In William Jamesian fashion, however, the narrator's revisions *comprise* his comprehension. He comes to define classification as an ever-renewed process of understanding gradations of experience.

The Jewish character of the narrator's writing practice appears when he contrasts it with its Anglo-Saxon opposite. The act of beginning again is Jewish because it allows him to attend to the concrete parts of experience. Anglo-Saxons, in contrast, tend to ignore the concrete in favor of an abstract "generalised conception," in a process the narrator calls "equilibration" (499).[28] Equilibrating means that not all the observed pieces of a person's character fit the mold they have fashioned for themselves, such as, "A man having it in him to have the generalised conviction of good being as completely him and the concrete acting of being a mean spirited and tyrannical man in living" (500). In the narrator's schema, Anglo-Saxon types lie about themselves in a logic of overgeneralization where one's theory about who one is takes precedence over one's empirical practices.

Determined to avoid equilibration, the narrator holds fast to Jewish ways of categorizing. He struggles to categorize people, and so he begins again and again. As he ruefully observes in an earlier chapter, however, his problem is not just methodological (trying to balance partial observation with holistic measures of character type), but semantic. He writes: "Categories that once to some one had real meaning can later to that same one be all empty" (440). He continues, "It is queer that words that meant something in our thinking and our feeling can later come to have in them in us not at all any meaning" (440). Writing evinces past states of mind, marking the temporal and existential differences between our present and past selves. The words do not later maintain their meaning even to the classifier, hence his constantly renewed imperative to begin again.

The process of naming is an elusive, imperfect task. Early in the novel, when discussing the attacking (or independent dependent Anglo-Saxon) and resisting (or dependent independent Jewish) kinds, the narrator admits, "As I was saying this is not always easy to know about them, it is not always easy to know which kind of these two kinds of being are in any one, it is hard to know it about them, it is hard to describe what I mean by the names I give to them" (192). Stein, in a later lecture, disdains regular nouns as stale, dead words, since "A noun has been the name of something for such a very long time" (*LA* 214). And she posits that renaming is one way to enliven nouns, like the way people give nicknames. Characterology-writing provided Stein, in the notebooks, and her narrator, in the novel, the opportunity to enliven the names of longstanding Jewish and Anglo-Saxon character types by renaming them. The names change frequently to denote the shifting, repeating, and not-always-apparent qualities of human character that Stein and her narrator were observing and classifying. The renamings reflect constant and deterministic attempts to make names mean something particular.

The narrator describes his commitment to linguistic determinacy, despite the temporal weathering of semantic stability, as a typologically Jewish way of relating to words. Like the Jewish melancholy that prompts a modern repetition of beginning again and again, he associates another Jewish feeling—a feeling for words—with his commitment to linguistic determinism and with its corollary, a carefully curated indeterminacy. In this Jewish semantics, he uses words that he knows well, not just words he can define. In the Alfred Hersland and Julia Dehning chapter, for example, the narrator returns to the subject of his relationship to words and their meanings by explaining:

> Every word I am ever using in writing has for me very existing being. . . . I may know very well the meaning of a word and yet it has not for me completely weight and form and really existing being. There are only a few words and with these mostly always I am writing that have for me completely entirely existing being[.] (539–540)

The narrator's deep acquaintance with words manifests as a way of feeling a word's "existing being," as if words were living people. Using the behavioral schema of resisting types, he establishes this way of feeling words as a characteristically Jewish tendency to feel "everything" with a lively and palpable sense of its "existing" (544). He continues:

> Mostly then these the resisting kind in men and women have it in them to feel very strongly the completely existing of everything, they have it in them to be certain that everything in a way is made out of real earth the way it was done to make Adam that is to say the resisting kind of them in their feeling have it to be certain that

a thing is existing more than that a thing has a use and can give to them an emotion. (544)

Stein's narrator characterizes the "resisting" Jewish type's aesthetic as one that marshals a robust sense of concreteness. With an allusion to Genesis that emphasizes the primacy of this Jewish feeling, the narrator describes a feeling imbued with a tactile, earthy quality characteristic of the Jewish-resisting kind. This contrasts with the Anglo-Saxon-attacking way of feeling objects, as having "a use," which the narrator describes as a pragmatic, secondary experience.

This oppositional schema of Jewish and Anglo-Saxon semantics is part of a larger Jewish aesthetics the narrator describes in the first half of the novel. There, the Jewish type's direct experience of feeling "objects as real things" derives from feeling the "earthy meaning" of the object itself "as a real thing." This is a contrast to the Anglo-Saxon type's more metaphysical ways of seeing objects "as beauty, as symbolism" (348). The Jewish type's direct experience also contrasts with the Anglo-Saxon practice, described above, of "equilibration" where people deny concrete experience to assert an abstract truth (499). The narrator's characterizations draw directly on Stein's notebook characterology, which suggests that Jewish types see objects solely as objects, rather than as truths.

As I discuss in chapter 3, Stein associates the Jewish resisting quality explicitly with artistic innovators. In the notebooks, she claimed to have this characterologically Jewish vision herself and classified Cézanne, Picasso, Braque, and her eldest brother Michael in a similar vein. The distinguishing characteristic of this cohort is that "the reality of the object count[s]" for them (38.788–38.790). She explains her categorization further by imbuing that reality with a Jewish "earthy" quality, "the actual earthyness of the object the object for the object's sake" (38.790). Stein considered Cézanne's and Picasso's way of seeing objects to be typologically Jewish by association and considered their "earthy" sense for objects as indicative of the kind of realism that her narrator aims to practice. Given its similarity to Cézanne's and Picasso's way of feeling the "earthy" "reality of the object," the narrator's way of feeling words in the second half of the novel is both Jewish and modern.

In the Alfred Hersland and Julia Dehning chapter, the narrator's Jewish modernism shows itself in the repetitious characterological practice of "beginning again." The narrator pledges an allegiance to repetition to describe his experiences of the world in contrast with the untruthful abstraction of experience at the heart of Anglo-Saxon "equilibration." His earthy Jewish repetitions nonetheless require abstraction—often pronouns—to best convey his controversial realizations. He begins again and again with an ever more abstract diction and, in continuing the passage above about his feeling for words, explicitly associates characterologically Jewish feelings with modernist abstraction.

The Hersland-Dehning courtship had first launched the novel, but the marriage dissolves as the novel progresses. In synchrony with this uncoupling, the narrator finds that abstraction may uncouple an author's intended meaning from a reader's reach for signification. Although he is unwavering in asserting that he "always" has a specific referent in mind when writing—"Always in writing it, it is in me only one thing" (539)—the narrator nonetheless enjoys gaining an awareness of other meanings that a word may hold. He writes:

> Sometimes I am using a new one, sometimes I feel new meanings in an old one, sometimes I like one I am very fond of that one one that has many meanings many ways of being used to make different meanings to every one. Sometimes I like it, almost always I like it when I am feeling many ways of using one word in writing. Sometimes I like it that different ways of emphasising can make very different meanings in a phrase or sentence I have made and am rereading. Always in writing it, it is in me only one thing, a little I like it sometimes that there can be very different ways of reading the thing I have been writing with only one feeling of a meaning. This is a pleasant thing, sometimes I am very well pleased with this thing, very often then I am liking a word that can have many ways of feeling in it, it is really a very difficult thing to me to be using a word I have not yet been using in writing. I may know very well the meaning of a word and yet it has not for me completely weight and form and really existing being. There are only a few words and with these mostly always I am writing that have for me completely entirely existing being[.] (539–540)

Experience gives the narrator a feeling for all facets of a word. He intends words to have a single meaning when composing and yet is aware of and enjoys it when a word signifies "different meanings to every one." He illustrates this semiotic fluidity in his very discussion of it by using temporally—or numerically—indeterminate abstractions like "sometimes" or "many," and by using impersonal pronouns such as "one," "it," and "thing." Over the course of the passage, these abstractions show off their semantic versatility. "One," for example, appears as a pronoun referring to "word," then as a numerical adjective, and finally as a reference to individual people. The variable nature of abstract pronouns highlights the plurality of linguistic signification pleasing to Stein's narrator and which he happily employs when he has enough experience with a word.

For Stein, pronouns, like nicknames, enliven nouns by renaming them, and the active, referential function of pronouns is likewise enlivening. As she had lectured, pronouns (and other non-nouns) are "lively because they all do something and as long as anything does something it keeps alive" (*LA* 214). In referring, pronouns "posses[s] the whole of the active life of writing" in Stein's poetics (220). This was especially true, she recalled, when composing "those long sentences of *The Making of Americans*" (220).

Many critics have pointed to what they claim is Stein's "commitment to linguistic indeterminacy as an aesthetic value and principal of composition" (Ashton 581). As Jennifer Ashton points out, however, especially when considering Stein's extremely repetitive use of pronouns, some critics mistakenly conflate differing significations with complete indeterminacy. Ashton reminds us that a pronoun's variability is not the same as its indeterminacy or lack of meaning. She argues that "for Stein the essential function of names" (or nouns) is that of a "stipulated reference" (591). Following that theory, Ashton sees Stein's use of pronouns as aiming to delimit the possibility of ambiguity, since the pronoun generally is "essentially defined by its referential function," much like "the mathematical variable *x*" (597). Ashton's thinking is an important corrective to earlier readings of Stein's diction in *The Making of Americans*. The novel's narrator has firmly committed to linguistic determinacy as a principle of composition. In the Alfred Hersland and Julia Dehning chapter, the narrator, in his characterologically Jewish endeavor, turns more and more toward abstraction with impersonal and indeterminate pronouns that yet maintain a "stipulated reference" that is vast, hopeful, and nonspecific.

The story of determinacy, variability, and ambiguity gets more complicated, however, as the novel develops. The narrator enjoys the potential for different meanings, but sometimes uses impersonal pronouns strategically to encourage slippage in signification. In the passage below, for example, he embraces the anonymity of abstraction to trick readers into enjoying his characterology. Impersonal pronouns enable the narrator to write for familiars by masking his subjects' identities, making it possible for them to like his work because they don't recognize themselves in it. He explains:

> It is a very interesting thing the history of this one. The complete family living of this one is a thing I could make a remarkably interesting thing to any one, that is certain. I have been telling that to this one. This one did not like very much to hear me say that thing, it is a certain thing that it is an interesting thing to me and I could tell it so to every one, I have been telling it to this one that I can make it a completely interesting thing. This one was not liking it very well then. Sometime I will be feeling completely the telling of it and then I will be telling it, I have told this one that I will tell it then. This one will not know then it is this one. That is the very nice thing in this writing. (566–567)

As he concludes, the narrator's determination and openness to methodological change unite in an unnamed "very nice" means of altering his telling of characterology. He elaborates his plan by repeatedly using the phrase "this one" to refer to one auditor. The abstract mask of a deictic "this" and the neutral pronoun "one," however, estrange the auditor from recognizing him- or herself in the characterology. Through the estranging anonymity of abstract pronouns, the narrator fosters connections between himself and readers who are unwittingly reading about themselves.

Despite his optimism about using pronouns to sway readers, the narrator eventually claims to free himself from the tyranny of trying to please readers at all. By the end of the Alfred Hersland and Julia Dehning chapter, as Steven Meyer notes, the narrator "reject[s] *in toto*" the original "credo of disengagement" to write for himself and strangers ("Introduction" xxix, xxviii). The narrator announces:

> so then I will go on writing, and not for myself and not for any other one but because it is a thing I certainly can be earnestly doing with sometimes excited feeling and sometimes happy feeling and sometimes longing feeling and sometimes almost indifferent feeling and always with a little dubious feeling. (708)

The narrator liberates himself by realizing the importance of being earnest and expressing it. To write sincerely emboldens him with "happy" and "excited" feelings, and yet it also leaves him vulnerable, with "longing," "indifferent," and "dubious" feelings. Once again, a Jewish melancholy prompts a Jewish salve of beginning again, so he "will go on writing." Like the Brother Singulars, the narrator is a "rare one" who feels the meaning of words in a concrete way and, uncowed by solitude, emboldens himself to write another chapter, this time about Alfred's younger brother David (565).

David Hersland's Moral Calibanism

In the final chapter, David Hersland serves as an anti-hero whose doomed presence highlights, through negative association, the narrator's Jewish and modernist methods. In *The Autobiography of Alice B. Toklas*, Stein (in Toklas's voice) retrospectively advertises Herland's entry into the plot as follows:

> Gertrude Stein was at that time writing The Making of Americans. It had changed from being a history of a family to being a history of everybody the family knew and then it became the history of every kind and every individual human being. But in spite of all this there was a hero and he was to die. (113)

Although Toklas protests that this traditional plot twist interrupts the characterology, Hersland's ill-fated presence is not at odds with the narrator's telling of "the history of every kind and every individual human being." Instead, the David Hersland chapter continues the characterology, giving the history of David Hersland in the context of other people. As the narrator does this, he weans the narration of named categories, proper nouns, and personal pronouns, using ever-more abstract methods that showcase the narrator's Jewish modernism.

Most significantly, in the David Hersland chapter (and subsequent epilogue), the narrator abandons his use of behavioral terms to describe Jewish and Anglo-Saxon types of people. He announces the change, obliquely, at the end of the penultimate chapter, reflecting, "This is the ending of just this way of going on telling about being being in some men and in some women" (719). Though the stipulated reference of "this way" remains implicit, the narrator ceases mentioning dependent independent and independent dependent kinds of people. He drops the hidden Jewish and Anglo-Saxon category names of "resisting" and "attacking" to simply describe David Hersland in comparison to other people.

The demise of named characters accompanies the demise of named behavioral categories. The narrator increasingly abstracts his subjects, making the text more general and anonymous, with declarative statements about characters as either "David Hersland" or as "he," "each kind," "one," "she," "some," "many," and "they." Likewise, first-person narration and the narrator's metanarratives dwindle in the opening pages of the David Hersland chapter. The narrator limits his "I" almost exclusively to the punctuating phrase "as I was saying" and, by the latter half of the chapter, he drops the first-person voice altogether. Writing solely in the third person, his statements gain pith and authority, ringing axiomatically in the grammar of the plural and the universal.

Although he no longer writes in the first person, the narrator remains vitally present in the chapter through his resemblance to Hersland. Hersland shares the narrator's interest in classifying people by kinds and in disseminating those classifications. The narrator observes, for example, that "David Hersland was interested in ones being living" and "He was one certainly very much an interested one in experiencing, in thinking, in meaning, in telling being in men and in women" (748, 785). It seems, moreover, that Hersland was very nearly one of the narrator's Brother Singulars, since Stein refers to him in her notebooks as "David the singular the man not of talent but a certain genius in him" (37.756.[25]). Early in the novel, too, the narrator yearns for David to be one of "us" and lists the ways that he is what Arendt might call a "conscious pariah": "David who is different from the people all around us, in him who always was seeking to be free inside him, to know it in him, and no one could ever understand him, what it was inside him that made it right that he should go on with his living" (48). Hersland thus resembles the narrator as a student of character and as someone living unconventionally. More striking, however, are David Hersland's crucial differences from the narrator and most other people.

Hersland's marked differences from the narrator indicate his failures as a Jewish singular and pariah type. At the beginning of the novel, the narrator reveals that Hersland is "not really" the possessor of a "vital steadfast singularity," despite being alienated from those around him (48). A Singular manqué, who resembles the problematic and Jewish "moral Caliban" discussed in the notebooks, Hersland avoids reckoning with the particularity of concrete experiences and, like the Anglo-Saxon type, prefers a more generalized sense of completeness (37.768.[1a]). He also resists change, echoing Stein's theory that moral Calibans "have good heads but it don't connect with their experience" and that they lack any "principle of growth" (37.768.[1a]). Like Harriet, Stein's exemplar "moral Caliban," who "is in the very essence of her nature damned," the narrator presents Hersland as irredeemably different from the Brother Singulars (37.768.[2c]).

Across the Alfred Hersland and Julia Dehning chapter, the narrator announces the failures of David Hersland and his differences from the narrator as fatal character flaws.[29] He asserts that "Some love themselves so much immortality can have no meaning for them, the younger David Hersland was such a one" (505). Hersland's disaffection for immortality does not, however, inspire gusto in living: he "was always in his living . . . trying to be certain from day to day in his living what there was in living that could make it for him a completely necessary thing" (484–485). His lackluster view of life follows from the "disillusionment" of learning the extent to which every person is an individual or "the finding out nobody agrees with you" (485). And while the narrator survives such disillusionment, reconciling himself to a lonely maturity and writing "not for any other one," Hersland does not (708).

In the final chapter, the narrator elaborates on David Hersland's failed strivings, such as his desire for meaning to be absolute and comprehensive. Unlike the narrator who learns to settle for partial understandings, Hersland needs to feel everything completely:

> Hersland was certainly sometimes in his being one being living almost needing to be thinking something out to be a complete thing, he certainly was in his younger living, he certainly was sometimes in his older living needing to be sometimes thinking everything out to be a complete thing. He was not in his living ever completely wanting to be needing to be thinking everything out to be a complete thing, he was certainly in his living, in his younger living certainly and perhaps in his later living almost completely wanting to

be needing to be thinking something out as a complete thing.... He was one in a way needing to be thinking out a thing to be a complete thing. (791)

The narrator reveals his own limitations as an observer by qualifying what he knows about Hersland using abstract pronouns and other modifiers, a lexical adaptation that heightens the contrast between them. The narrator's modifiers indicate Hersland's dogged adherence to "completeness" despite a palpable reluctance to "needing" it. Hersland is "almost," "sometimes," "not . . . ever completely wanting to be," "almost completely wanting to be," and "in a way" needing to be thinking things out completely. The narrator's suppleness in modifying his diction demonstrates a willingness to accommodate the changes over the course of a person's life to maintain a truthful certainty, in contrast to Hersland's desire for a generalized completeness. Hersland's cerebral interest in "thinking things out" also keeps him at a remove, in the style of a moral Caliban, rather than directly immersed in living.

Though Hersland suffers only "sometimes" from his need to be completely feeling things, he is plagued by a constant and perhaps fatal need to find meaning in life. As the narrator observes, "He was one needing to be understanding every minute in being living what meaning there was to him in his needing to be to him one being being living" (743). The narrator suggests that the very doggedness of Hersland's unchanging mind, his desire to understand the meaning of life, and his determination to feel fully alive lead, ironically, to his demise. He does not live beyond his middle years, and his death contrasts with the narrator's perseverance in "Beginning again and again." The end of Hersland's life is explicitly a moment of *not* starting over, as the narrator forecasts: "He would not be one commencing again and again to be one being living. He would not be one commencing being living" (879). Hersland dies, the narrator indicates, because he refuses to modify his demands for a fixed sense of other people and because he cannot relinquish his need for completeness in his sense of self. He is finally and fatally unable to embrace the necessarily uncertain, imperfect, and incomplete nature of modern identity and thought, as embodied by the shifting textual practices of a characterologically Jewish narrator.

Given Stein's belief in the vitality of pronouns, it is an ironic epitaph that Hersland becomes a pronoun once he dies. The narrator stops using proper nouns five pages before the end of the David Hersland chapter and, as Berman aptly describes it, "pronouns have taken over" (174). The narrator buries Hersland's proper noun in the winding sheet of a personal pronoun: "He had come to be a dead one" (904). A page later, when the narrator begins the book's epilogue, he repeats Hersland's death sentence, further loosening the referent, by stating, "Any one has come to be a dead one" (907). With a shift in tenses, from past perfect to present perfect, Hersland lives a strikingly modernist afterlife as a ghostly referent in the narrator's embrace of abstraction. In death, Hersland embodies the vital means of lexical change used by the narrator, who begins again by shifting wholly from personal to impersonal pronouns as he narrates the epilogue. In that chapter, the switch to impersonal pronouns pivots away from Hersland's specific demise toward more general notions of mortality and singularity.

"That One Is the One": Jewish Pariah Types in the Epilogue

The twenty-page epilogue features a Jewish abstraction of the narrator's subjects and subjectivity. The narrator cloaks himself and the kinds he is classifying with an estranging grammar of the impersonal and indefinite pronouns "some," "some one," "any," "any one," "each one," "every one," "one," "others," "many," "very many," and "they all." The narrowing of the novel's diction signifies a widening, though not a universalizing, of subject and subjectivity.[30] While Hersland and others may be dead, many others survive, although no single character is specified. Instead, the narrator has "some one" or "some others" making claims about "kinds in men and women" and how "some of each kind" age and die (910). He also enumerates the changing make-up of families, the "kinds of them doing something in a family living," as people marry, bear children, age, and die (921). In this final classification sequence of the novel, the narrator deracinates families into categories and yet familiarizes kinds into families. In the context of "family living," the Jewish pariah maintains ambivalent ties to tradition and convention in the epilogue.[31]

Like his subject matter, Stein's narrator abstracts his own subjectivity (and that of his Brother Singulars) using impersonal and indefinite pronouns, primarily the singular and plural terms "some one" and "some" (909). These pronouns distinguish the narrator socially and textually. They also suggest his brotherhood with potential successors in writing characterology. For, while abstract pronouns may betray his uncertainty about precisely *who* will take over his project, they enable him to confidently predict that some one or another *will* continue it: "It is certain that some will come to be realising differences in kinds in men and women and will come to make lists of them and long lists of them" (909). The narrator delights in reminding readers of the procedurals involved in realizing, noting, narrating, and disseminating characterology and echoes the emphatic declarations from the Martha Hersland chapter to tell and write the repeating of others. In the epilogue, however, the emphasis is on the eventual remembering of such tellings. He expects that "some one" will grow to "some others" so that the greatest possible pool of people will hear the wisdom of kinds and characterology and "any one will then be one having heard something of some such thing" (910). With the comforting assurance of continuity, the narrator in the epilogue resumes the posture of an ethical Jewish type when he "begins again" by classifying family structures of difference and alienation.

In the middle of *The Making of Americans*, the Jewish pariah figure courageously breaks from others of his class or kind, but at the end of the novel, the narrator locates this breech within the family to suggest the power and value of bourgeois Jewish family traditions. Family traditions, the narrator observes, are established and upheld by what is done, said, heard, and remembered by that family "doing what any one is doing that is living in any family living" (914). As odd-family-members-out, the epilogue's singulars recall the Jeremiahs and other Jewish truth-tellers in Stein's notebooks and first fictions who are disbelieved and spurned by their own people and nonetheless value the "middle-class ideal . . . of affectionate family life" (*Q.E.D.* 59).

The narrator's use of abstract pronouns is central to his description of the singular's pariah status in the traditional family. The indeterminately referential phrase "any one" launches the epilogue; the narrator frequently repeats it to describe individuals, singulars, or nonsingular others. Berman identifies a dramatic shift from the narrator's use of "one" to "any one," which she argues is a shift from "how specific characters exemplify Americanness to the ways that all Americans exist" (174). This reading accurately pinpoints the opening-up of the narrator's possible referents, but it overgeneralizes his use of "any one," which does not designate "all," but instead refers to one indeterminate individual, distinct from "some" or "many" or "Every one being living" (*MA* 916). "One" is less frequently used, but does not disappear from the epilogue, nor does "any one" reign there. In fact, "one" remains as a presence to be singled out—"that one is the one"—and "any one" is frequently used in tandem with "some" to illuminate actions that distinguish particular family members from the rest (920). The narrator observes, "Any one in a family living is certain that some in the family living are not doing something" (923). Here the "some" may be singulars who distinguish themselves from a specific "family living" by "not doing" whatever behavior is characteristic of that family. Using the counterpoint and repetition of indeterminate pronouns, the narrator presents pariah alienation as both kinship-breaking (inside the family) and kinship-finding (inside and outside the family).

The narrator describes the fraying of family bonds when behavioral differences are not accepted or understood. He notes, for example, instances of individuals who do things differently or say things or refrain from speaking freely in family living by "not completely mentioning something" (915). Some, if they are behaving in the way characteristic of their family, may not be doing what is "natural for them" (921). People are aware of nonconformity within a family, as the narrator observes, "Every one . . . is knowing that any one in the family living is not doing something" (923). Nonconformity can still be mystifyingly misunderstood, as the narrator complains, "Some are not understanding any one not understanding something" (916). The constituency of a family, too, varies due to death, birth, marriage, and people who "are ones not going on being in the family living in which they are being" (917).

Like the Jewish pariah type from the middle of the novel, who prefers clocks and handkerchiefs that others disdain, some of the epilogue's singulars distinguish themselves through preferences. The narrator observes that some preferences may determine a person's opinion of "being in a family living":

> Any one in any family living is certainly not one liking everything. Any one in any family living is one not liking anything. Any one liking that something is being something and is then liking anything being anything and is then not liking everything being everything is one being in a family living and being one liking and not liking being in a family living. (917)

Unlike in the middle of the novel where the singular feels shame and expects mockery for liking something "no one can really like," the focus here is on the feelings that the epilogue's singular has toward his cohort (485). The singular's ambivalence *about* "being in a family living" shows the narrator's interest in giving weight and legitimacy to singular preferences. These preferences may even lead the singular to find another family, since, after all, "There are very many family livings being existing" (922).

Another way that the narrator affirms the behavior of the epilogue's singulars is to note the kinship they find in "some other one." In an echo of the yes-saying companion to the Jewish pariah figures from the middle of the novel, the narrator observes a kinship based on similar actions:

> When some one has done something and some other one has then done something and it is a similar thing and they both then have not been doing something, they have similarly not been doing something then, they might be doing something and not doing something together. (917)

The repeated act of "doing something together" joins these Brother Singulars, whether as members of the same family or not. Though his actions may alienate the singular or his similar from "any family living," "family living" is contingent and changeable, as the narrator makes clear. He notes, "They may. . . . [or] may not be in the family living they are *then* having," which underscores the potential mobility of the singular—Jewishly—to begin again by joining a different family (917, emphasis added).

In the epilogue, the narrator asserts what is knowable and how. He writes, "All that some one knows about some one is what is true of that one as being one doing what that one is doing when something is happening" (908). That we know others contingently based on a momentary action suggests the radical potential for change in individuals and groups. Using the characteristically Jewish practice of "beginning again," an individual maintains a wide horizon of possibilities: "Any one can begin again doing anything, any one can begin again not doing something" (914). Likewise, as people can change their behaviors, so can groups, as the narrator notes of families: "Sometimes then that family is going on in that way of existing. Sometimes that family living is going on into another way of being existing" (922). One catalyst for changing family traditions is, in fact, the singular, when his differences gather momentum among other family members. The narrator expresses only a muted optimism about this possibility, however, presenting it as something that does not happen, even when it is clear that "every one" in a family is aware of the singular's different behaviors. Change is possible, if unlikely, since it takes more than one person to enact change:

> Some one in a family living does a thing and not any other one in that family living is doing *enough* of that thing to make it that thing the thing one in that family living is doing. Some one in a family living is doing something, and is doing it and every one in the family living is knowing that that one is the one who is doing that thing. (920, emphasis added)

Singularity can be recognized but only has the potential to change tradition if it does not remain the actions of one individual.

The novel closes by confirming the courageousness and certain plurality of a queer, singular fraternity of Jewish classifiers, whose knowledge about people no one had previously wanted to hear. The novel maintains tradition in a radical fashion by proffering the vaunted position of Brother Singulars to those unnamed individuals who embrace the task of remembering what has been understood and recorded by the narrator. The final sentences of the epilogue affirm that even when families die out, "some" remain who "can remember":

> Every one in a family living having come to be dead ones some are remembering something of some such thing. Some being living not having come to be dead ones can be ones being in a family living. Some being living and having come to be old ones can come then to be dead ones. Some being living and being in a family living and coming then to be old ones can come then to be dead ones. Any one can be certain that some can remember such a thing. Any family living can be one being existing and some can remember something of some such thing. (925)

The narrator emphasizes the remembering of "family living" by echoing the word "some" three times through the last sentence, each time with a different referent: the first "some" points to those singulars who remember, the second to the partial "something" that they remember, and the third to "some such thing" that they remember about family living or a similar topic. Scientific values of specificity and exactness have lost their meaning. Instead, the narrator affirms the value of his project in its anonymous, partial, and approximate future, showing off the unconventional beauty of modernist practices of repetition and abstraction, which here are Jewish by association with their pariah purposefulness. His project thus continues to epitomize James's radical empiricism, which presumed that an object could not be understood apart from the human context of the observer. The outlaw at last becomes a classic, since even with the death of "every one," in the contexts of familiars, "some" will carry on the story.

In her writings on the Jew as pariah, Hannah Arendt looks to Kafka's K. as an example of a character striving for social indistinguishability. In her eyes, K. is a pariah assimilating to the humblest of human conditions. Kafka has K. approach textual indistinguishability by giving him a mere initial for a moniker. In *The Making of Americans*, the pariah figure is part of a specifically Jewish tradition that is purposefully abstracted, as in Chaplin and Kafka, to illuminate greater social and psychological truths about the interconnectedness of human beings. Across the novel, the narrator's Brother Singulars include a virtuous poor woman, servant girls, dandies, and other queer folk—including avant-garde writers—who play with bourgeois respectability.

At the beginning of the epilogue, these and the novel's named characters become as anonymous and textually indistinguishable as "any one" who "has come to be a dead one." By the end of the epilogue, the narrator, too, has subsumed himself into the nonspecific "any one" who "can be certain that some can remember such a thing," as well as the larger cohort of "some" who "can remember something of some such thing." As part of an ever-more anonymous group of singulars, this narrator's estranged narration touts human similarities and human differences as truths that may result in an alienated model of communitarianism, which for Stein exemplified a Jewish modernism. The Jew is a figure validated for its particular indistinguishability in Stein's first fictions up to and including *The Making of Americans*, but this abstract method changes dramatically in the next chapter of Stein's oeuvre. The later poetry and prose names Jews openly and reinvents modernist writing by revealing the abstraction present in seemingly nonmetaphorical language.

5

"Can a Jew be wild"

A Radical Jewish Grammar in the Voices Poems

> He was terribly deceived about the Jews about Napoleon and about everything else.
>
> If you do not know the meaning of such things do not use them. That is all. Such phrases.
>
> **(Gertrude Stein, "Geography" 240)**

Gertrude Stein purposefully omitted the word "Jew" from her early fiction, even though Jewish characters and character were central to those texts. In 1910, while still completing *The Making of Americans*, Stein began to experiment with a new style of writing that abandoned scientific racialism. Characterology was gone, as was a recognizable narrative voice of any sort. Stein veered away from kinds of people as perceived from the outside and from sentences and paragraphs as basic syntactical units. She composed *Tender Buttons* in a style that she called "simply different" ("Composition as Explanation" 500).[1] After that, Stein combined the strange and the familiar in a poetic style that consisted of conversational excerpts by unattributed voices.[2] These "voices" poems often seem habitually unmoored from any static context save the human voice: short statements with varying degrees of sense follow one another creating "voice-montages" that make it difficult to ascertain where sense-continuity begins and ends (Moad 1). Successive voicings may indicate semantic breaks, and one puzzles over the juxtaposition. Or they may indicate continuity, and one attempts to make meaning between them. Strikingly, once Stein's writing shifted toward a more contextual abstraction, she wrote openly if still cryptically about Jews and Jewish topics.

If a primary concern is arguably identifiable in the voices compositions, it is not, by and large, with things Jewish. Stein peppered these writings with the names of locales, newsworthy figures, and events both domestic and international. From time to time, she included a Jewish lexicon predominated by the words "Jew" and "Jewish." These words appear as abruptly as lightning striking, or in the illumination of "see[ing] to the lighting," as the speaker does before mentioning "a Jew" in the poem quoted in my title, "Have They Attacked Mary. He Giggled. (A Political Caricature)":

PAGE IX

Lighting.
We can see to the lighting.

PAGE X

Can a Jew be wild. (534)

As in this example, Stein's Jewish lexicon in the voices poems maintains a surprising degree of abstraction due to the strange fabric of the texts in which it appears. Such explicit references to Jews and Jewishness resonate with the gradually accumulated if often enigmatic meanings about Jews and Jewish identity that had appeared in Stein's earlier writing in a more veiled form. Stein's "Jew" allows the word's long history as a racial epithet to be heard while also blithely ignoring it. Later, Stein affirms this reappropriation, insisting that Jews should be called Jews: "I dislike it when instead of saying Jew they say Hebrew or Israelite or Semite, I do not like it. . . . Well its name is Negro if it is a Negro and Jew if it is a Jew and both of them are nice strong solid names and so let us keep them" (*EA* 200).

Despite her later insistence on fixed naming practices, Stein asks readers of the voices poems to *choose* between sound and sense and among various significations, by punning on the sound of the word *Jews* and the notion of Jews as a chosen people, in what seems to be persistently indeterminate writing: "I choose Christmas and I choose an education. And I choose a robust jew. And I choose, I choose mending glasses" ("As Fine as Melanctha" 267). Such choices emphasize the methodological determinacy of the voices poems in maintaining simultaneous and multiple significations that frustrate the possibility of choosing a single meaning. DeKoven sees such semantic openness as forming a "comic contrast" with the "absolute assurance of th[e] tone" of such declarations (*A Different Language* 86). The following examples, culled from several poems, demonstrate how this contrast functions with Stein's use of the word "Jew." Whether Jews are superstitious ("A horse shoe soothes a Jew"), a people to be bothered en masse ("she annoys every Jew"), or the subject of trickery ("He was terribly deceived about the Jews"), Stein registers uncertainty over the nature of Jewish difference and whether "Jew" or "Jewish" have real meaning in describing cultural, racial, national, or biological character ("Reread Another. A Play" 352; "Saints and Singing: A Play" 393; "Geography" 240). In *The Poetics of Indeterminacy: Rimbaud to Cage*, Marjorie Perloff sees in Cubist painting a "peculiar tension between conventional symbols . . . and [more] stylized images of reality" (72). Similarly, in Stein's voices poems, the Jewish lexicon reveals a peculiar tension between the conventional cluster of associations about the word "jew" and a resistance to such conventional or singular signification.

When, in 1915, Stein makes her first direct references to Jewish people, ideas, and history in writing that was aimed at publication, her references find little context in early modernist writing.[3] At that moment, the closest comparable Jewish presence would have been Ezra Pound's prosaically demonized Jews in *BLAST*, "Let us be done with Jews and Jobbery, / Let us SPIT upon those who fawn on the JEWS for their money"("Salutation the Third" 45), or the handful of Jews scattered about Joyce's *Dubliners*, both from 1914. By 1919, one could have read of "Rachel née Rabinovitch" with her "murderous paws," who inaugurates the London publication of T. S. Eliot's *Poems* and is joined in 1920 by the "spawned" and "squatting" Jews of the New York edition (*Poems* 13). Only in the twenties and thirties would Stein's references to Jews coincide with the more notable and varied semitic presence in many of the seminal works of the modernist era.[4]

The conventional critical reading of Stein's voices texts argues that their purposeful openness to interpretation forms a liberatory and "thoroughly democratic" language practice (Quartermain 43).[5] Such claims, however, often rely on assumptions regarding Stein's marginalized and queer "Jewomanish" subject position, which stereotype Stein's sense of her identity as a lesbian, a woman, and a Jew (Damon, "Gertrude Stein's Jewishness" 502). When Maria Damon argues, for example, that "Stein creates makeshift homelands in books comprised of language that itself is not stable, but. . . . enacts the instability that necessarily informs a Jewish notion of home," her thinking dovetails with the general narrative of displacement in modern Jewish history and with Stein's biography (499). Stein had lived in three countries by the age of five and lost both of her parents in her teens. While instability may have permeated her youth, Stein consistently figured the middle-class Jewish home as an ideal of domestic stability, worthwhile because of the strictures of conventionality it engendered. Even if she did partake in an early twentieth-century Jewish *gestalt*, the evidence from her early writing is at best contradictory: at times she endorses fin-de-siècle theories of Jewish primitivism, dogmatism, and deviance, and at times she reappropriates such associations to bolster notions of Jewish chosen-ness, superiority, and genius. In any case, critical assumptions about Stein's identity that draw conclusions about her metaphorically Jewish textual practice have tended to overlook the explicit, nonmetaphorical Jewish content that appears in her voices writing.

Stein's explicitly Jewish lexicon in the voices writing functions in three ways. First, as seen in the examples above, Stein asks qualitative questions about Jewish nature, such as "Can a Jew be wild," which in turn suggest ontological questions about Jews individually and as a group. Second, she merges private and public discourses by writing about a love relationship whose language of affection has a familial Jewish accent, affirming her sense of the clannish comfort and support of the conventional bourgeois Jewish family. This romantic Jewish lexicon focuses on the possession of a Jewish noun, the love-object, in domestic relations. In contrast, her third use of a Jewish lexicon focuses on the international relations concerning the proper nouns "Zionist" and "Palestine" in the aftermath of World War I. Grammatically, speakers in these poems exploit the diplomatic personification of nations as individuals inhabiting relationships of independence and possession, and semantically, these voices call into question the very nature of nations and national identities. In each of these lexical uses, Stein's "Jew" becomes a wildcard of modern identity, remaking romantic, diplomatic, and nationalistic discourses, while also confirming conservative poetic, political, and social traditions.

This chapter builds on the previous one where I argue that in *The Making of Americans* Stein figures a Jewish narrator desirous of determinacy yet content to strategically employ indeterminacy. Perloff argues for a "poetics of indeterminacy" in *Three Lives* and *Tender Buttons*, a notion that must be considered in tandem with my argument, here, that Stein's use of the word "Jew" makes clear her continued (if complicated) commitment to linguistic determinacy in the voices poems. Stein's Jewish references point to disparate meanings and her puns pull at differentiating between the sound and the sense of the very word "Jew." As Lorna Smedman argues, however, "not all indeterminacy is created equal" and, in her study of the Africanist lexicon in the "simply different" texts of the early teens, she observes that Stein tried and failed "to defuse this [racialized] language, to disempower it. . . . [which] shows how deeply rooted these linguistic formulations are in American speech and writing" (582, 585). This is a useful model for thinking about the steadfastness of Stein's racial terminology, especially racial epithets, which Smedman describes (pace Aldon Nielsen) as "frozen metaphors" (575). For Stein's use of a Jewish lexicon, too, exhibits a measure of fixity in the voices texts, despite seemingly ephemeral and indeterminate contexts. Against the desires of critics to read Stein's Jewish identity as a solely revolutionary impulse, I argue that, like the paradoxical use of Stein's previous ideas about Jews and Jewish nature as icons of both convention and singularity, Stein's Jewish lexicon in the voices poems figures both fixity and indeterminacy in experimental texts that trace the possibilities and limits of modernist writing.

"My Little Hebrew": The Romantic Jewish Lexicon

In the first voices poems, written in what she later referred to as her "romanticism" era, Stein names the love of her life, Alice B. Toklas, sometimes using a Jewish lexicon ("Composition as Explanation" 501). On or about 1910, Stein and her brother Leo were joined in their Paris apartment by Alice Toklas. Once Leo departed in the summer of 1913, Stein and Toklas began a domestic arrangement they considered a marriage, which lasted until Stein's death thirty-three years later.[6] Julie Abraham argues that Stein's love life and her writing life were intimately intertwined (87). Ulla Dydo claims that "Stein likens the creative act to the sexual act" (*Gertrude Stein* 28). As these critics have observed, one finds ample evidence of a metaphorical merging of writing and loving throughout Stein's career, which she herself theorized in her lecture, "Poetry and Grammar." In that lecture, Stein states that "Poetry is doing nothing but using losing refusing and pleasing and betraying and caressing nouns. . . . really loving the name of anything" (*LA* 231–232). Stein wrote frequent love notes to Toklas, such as one addressing her as "my little Hebrew" (qtd. in Dydo 27).[7] In numerous voices poems, Stein transformed these private love letters into public, publishable language within the poems themselves. References to pearls, rosebuds, weddings, and honeymoons, as well as constant "cooing," declaim the romantic and often connubial context of the poems

("A Sonatina Followed By Another" 4). One voice observes outright that the poem is made up of "Eighty pages of love and blandishment and small hand writing" (4). That voice reveals its romantic methods to be those of traditional love poetry whose function, as blandishment, was a persuading or cajoling flattery. But critics have ignored the Jewish character of Stein's celebratory amorous and domestic writing.

In poems whose voices are by turns epic, choral, epithalamial, lyrical, doggerel, and sexual, Jewish nature serves as a kinship marker of the marital bond between Stein and Toklas, typically with Stein as husband or baby to Toklas's wife or mother.[8] "Lifting Belly" (composed 1915–1917), one of the earliest and longest of the romantic poems, includes the exchange: "Say how do you do to the lady. Which lady. The jew lady. How do you do. She is my wife" (100). And in another long voices poem, "A Sonatina Followed By Another" (composed 1921), one hears that "Little Alice B. is the wife for me" from a speaker who repeatedly exclaims, "I love her too my little jew" (12, 31). "Jew" serves here as a possessive endearment that evokes the idealized cohesiveness and affection of the middle-class Jewish family.[9] Stein thus articulates her relationship, as husband to Toklas's wife, in Jewish terms of endearment that invoke traditional poetic methods of blandishment, while radically departing from traditional poetic forms and objects.

Some feminist critics frown on Stein's frequent use of this conventional and often chivalric poetic husbandry. Others interpret it as a transgressive reinterpretation of gender roles.[10] Gender transgressions (or lack thereof) seem secondary, however, to the transgressive allusions to Jewish household traditions in "A Sonatina Followed By Another":

> I took a piece of pork and I stuck it on a fork and I gave it to a curly headed jew jew jew. I want my little jew to be round like a pork, a young round pork with a cork for his tail. A young round pork. I want my little jew to be round like a young round pork. I do. (13–14)

Although it sounds like a parody of Mother Goose, this passage repeats, verbatim, a common nineteenth-century schoolyard taunt.[11] In the broadly romantic context of the poem, however, the epithetic invective, stripped of the schoolyard locale, takes on affectionate significance. The speaker feeds her "little jew" with loving attentions that parody the fattening of Hansel and Gretel by the witch.[12] Such nurturing here transgresses Jewish dietary laws, juxtaposing the speaker's role as the best kind of Jewish mother with the worst (or witchiest), by having the caregiver feed pork to a Jew. And yet the passage concludes with a rhyme that affirms traditional family ties by binding "my little jew" to the speaker with the wedding vow "I do." The following year, Stein corroborates the connubial context of this poem by writing in another poem that "A sonatina followed by another is a honeymoon" ("Mildred's Thoughts" 364).

The amatory context of these Jewish references highlights the peculiarity of "Jew" as a name that had not before been dared to be spoken as an object of affection in English poetry. The main speaker in "A Sonatina Followed By Another," for example, repeatedly refers to the very recital of her love, prompted apparently by her Jewish lover, as revealed in an exchange of voices in the poem's opening lines: "And what would you have me do. / I would have you sing songs to your little Jew" (4). The voice serenading this "little Jew" sustains the vocalization of the word "Jew" through rhyme (with "do") and repetition (the "jew jew jew" above). Near the end of the poem, the speaker reprises the annunciatory framework:

> I say it to you and I say it to you I say it to you how I love my little jew. I say it to you and I say it to you. I say it to you and I say it to you. I say it to you.
>
> How I can I have the air of here and there and I say it to you I say it to you I love my own little jew. How can I have the air and I do care I care for her hair and there for the rest of her too my little jew. I love her too my little jew. (31)

The repetition of the phrase "I say it to you" advertises to both a general audience and the specific love-object "how" the speaker "loves my little jew," and demonstrates the ease of rhyming "you" with "jew," perhaps suggesting synonymity in this context. Further, the speaker's interest in the sound of the voice ("I say it") recalls the poem's titular form, the musical composition "A Sonatina," which shares its root in the word for *sound* with the sonnet, a traditional poetic form for avowals of love. The vocal sounding of a Jewish noun punctuates this and other voices poems with a radical grammar: the "little jew" addressed by the speaker is not a traditional love-object in English poetry. The romantic lexicon of the voices poems radically breaks from tradition by "unfreeze-ing" the word "jew" from its history as an epithet in English literature. Instead, "jew" is positioned as a harmonic counterpoint to the serenades and blandishments of traditional love poems.

The "Jew"-ish presence in these poems affirms the peculiarity of Jewish difference by harmoniously disrupting the comfortable monotony of the romantic and familial fabric encompassing Stein's newly joined life with Toklas. In the quotidian, ephemeral, and mundane montage of the voices style, Stein often conveys the domestic space as a place of convention and continuity. Her speakers in the long poem "Look At Us," for example, note the arrival of holidays, such as the Jewish New Year, and other temporal markers disruptive to daily routine. The poem was written in 1916 when Stein and Toklas were in Mallorca; the two speakers converse with one another and may also speak jointly in the first-person plural.[13]

> Look at us. Yes I say.
> I say look at us.
> We are here.
> Yes we are here.
> Look at us. Commence to look at us.
> I said it to-day.
> We did.
> We are worthy of it all we are not ashamed of each other we know how to place wood.
> We often discuss about the paper.
> I don't mean to read it you know I don't mean to read it.
> What.
> We have said it every day. We say it to-day.
> In two days look at us.
> That is the Jewish new year.
> How do you know. Everybody knows about birthdays.
> Oh yes indeed.
> Look at us. (263–264)

In the detached voices style which here announces attachments, Stein's designation "Jewish" insists on Jewish difference as remarkable and yet as routine as celebrating birthdays.[14] One speaker remembers the "Jewish new year," traditionally considered the birthday of the world, just like any other birthday: when one of the speakers asks, "How do you know," perhaps wondering if "That is the Jewish new year," the other replies, "Everybody knows about birthdays." And yet the first speaker may have thought of "the Jewish new year," traditionally celebrated for "two days," because "to-day" is practically a homonym to "two days": "We say it to-day. / In two days look at us."[15] The uncertainty that may surround the Jewish holiday, "How do you know," raises questions of Jewish difference as questions of grammar: How do adjectives describe? What does "Jewish" signify?

In the poem, the descriptive possibilities of Jewish differences shift from the private and secure affirmations of "my little jew" to the public and uncertain attention of readers and others. Speakers in "Look At Us" muse over the necessity for an audience beyond the domestic sphere, for example. In "Home Truths: Gertrude Stein, 27 Rue de Fleurus, and the Place of the Avant-Garde," Sara Blair argues that Stein's domestic space was markedly unconventional as home to her avant-garde labors. With that in mind, we can read "Look At Us" with an ear to its dual-purposed and Jewish setting, a place of pleasant monotony and stimulating creativity. The poem's voices invite readers in for a "look" at a Jewishly colored domestic partnership and a Jewishly singular body of writing. Within the poetic function of many of the voices poems, which publicly announce Stein's love to her lover, rests the question of Stein's relationship to audiences large and small: Is an audience of one enough for the writer-lover? Will her "little jew"'s reassurances suffice, or are "a great many" readers necessary?

The wider recognition of print publication largely eluded Stein for years, although, as Karen Leick argues, Stein was famous in America for being a modern writer. In the oft-repeated titular invitation to "Look At Us," one hears the quotidian concerns of Stein's efforts to publish and Toklas's quotidian encouragement: "When I ask you to look at us I want you to mean that you will be critical not of us nor of our publications but earnest and encouraging. Do you think they will publish us. / I do" (260). The culminating matrimonial affirmation weds Toklas's support to more general support: Toklas's affirmation becomes indicative of those who will assuredly publish, read, or appreciate Stein's work.

Despite Stein's frustrated attempts to get her work in print and acquire a serious readership, she succeeded in having a handful of poems published each year. In the nine years spanning the publications of *Tender Buttons* (1914) and *Geography and Plays* (1922), twenty pieces of Stein's appeared in newspapers and magazines.[16] One of these, "Have They Attacked Mary. He Giggled," was the poem containing the question "Can a jew be wild." When it appeared on page 55 of the June 1917 issue of *Vanity Fair*, the editor, Frank Crowninshield, cut thirty-three lines from Stein's original and yet left in the line with the word "jew."[17] Perhaps concerned that readers might accuse him of publishing an obscenity, or at least something impolite, he remarks in his headnote to the poem that "Miss Stein, who is immensely famous in France, is a Jewess, once of San Francisco, but now of Paris" (55). Crowninshield also guides readers on the poem's subject, reporting the poem "is said, by all who know Miss Stein, to be a portrait of Henry McBride, the New York writer and art critic" (55). McBride and Stein had been corresponding since 1913, and he is mentioned—inconclusively—in the poem: "Page XVI / It is wonderful the way I am not interested. // Page XVII / What can you do. / I can answer any question. / Very well answer this. / Who is Mr. McBride" (55). Instead of a portrait of McBride, Stein may be using the name for its play on the idea of a man named "bride." Along with the possible pun on "Mary" in the poem's title, "McBride" is part of the connubial diction of Mary-ing or marrying so prevalent in this and other voices poems. The portrait might not be of Henry McBride but of one or both of the speakers *as brides*.[18]

Near the beginning of the uncut version of the poem published in Stein's *Selected Writings*, the voices claim to have "the reasonableness of a woman" and announce, "We wish we were married" (533). The voices in the poem may be two women who may be marrying each other. They later state, "We marry," although given the ambiguities of Stein's punctuation, which omitted question marks, they could be asking, "Do we marry?" (534). What seems plainly to be wished for, in any case, is the desired domestication of a lesbian sexuality in a marriage. In this poem, unlike other voices poems in which the Jew plays a role in staging lesbian sexuality, it is the lesbian sexuality, the brides and their Mr. McBrides, that plays a role in domesticating the otherwise semantically wild Jew.

In the forty-six short stanzaic "pages" of "Have They Attacked Mary. He Giggled. (A Political Caricature)," voices refer to quotidian events such as what kinds of matches to use and questions like "Why am I so sleepy" (538). Voices also refer to the not-so-quotidien, such as the sale of a Matisse painting from Stein to her brother Michael, the anticipated arrival of a Ford that Stein and Toklas had ordered from the States so they could assist with war relief, and several references to the war itself (Dydo 44). What does Stein mean to say, then, when using the word "Jew" in this poem? Unlike other voices poems in which the Jew transparently refers to a love-object, this Jew is almost opaque in appearance. Like the voice that asks, "Who is Mr. McBride," it seems natural to ask, "Who is a Jew?" when reading the line "Can a Jew be wild" (534). "Can a Jew be wild" seems to suggest a Jew could be *almost anything*. But the query also assumes a Jewish tameness, a solid assurance of sedateness that *presupposes* the possibility of a Jew ever being wild. One would be forced, quite honestly, to ask if it is *really* possible, "Can a Jew be *wild*?" Perhaps there is a concern, as was common in racialist thinking, for a possible primitivism lurking beneath the peaceful and apparently domesticated traditions of bourgeois Jewish family life. As the narrator had declared in the beginning of *The Making of Americans*, "I throw myself open to the public,—I take a simple interest in the ordinary kind of families, histories, I believe in simple middle class monotonous tradition" (34). If a Jew can be wild in these circumstances, it is a reminder that the domestic spaces and conjugal conversations suggested by these voices may not be safe from or uninterested in the war.

"The Revery of the Zionist" and a Nationalist Jewish Lexicon

Following the Paris Peace Conference of 1919, where a treaty for Palestine was signed and where discussions of the formation of The League of Nations began, Stein wrote what she called her "World Series," consisting of the poems "Land of Nations," "IRELAND," and "The Revery of the Zionist." The series may also have included the poems "A League," "More League," and "Land Rising."[19] These works express a titular concern with current international affairs, however various or indeterminate their topical foci. Stein's interest in international affairs may have been an accident of history, rather than an intrinsic interest, as she suggests in a poem about discovering one's natural gifts: "indeed gifts may be said to be chosen rather from the occasion offered by the passage of a chinese or perhaps a Korean stranger than from the desire to study colonisation" ("Yes You Do" 121). Nonetheless, amidst explicit references to the continuing Irish War of Independence and the diplomatic negotiations concerning British colonial possessions in Africa, Asia Minor, and the Levant, several voices poems mention Jews and Palestine and, in the case of "The Revery of the Zionist," consider the question of Jewish nationalism.

As Barbara Will notes in "Gertrude Stein and Zionism," Stein later recalls the politics of the moment in *The Autobiography of Alice B. Toklas*, where she writes about the Paris Peace Conference with a familiarity gleaned from Alfred Whitehead's daughter, Jessie, who "had come over with the peace commission as secretary to one of the delegations" (*ABT* 189). Stein continues:

of course we were very interested in knowing all about the peace. It was then that Gertrude Stein described one of the young men of the peace commission who was holding forth, as one who knew all about the war, he had been here ever since the peace. (189–190)

This reference—"it was then that Gertrude Stein described"—alludes to the 1919 poem "The Revery of the Zionist," which begins with one voice's account of this young man's speech. Despite the poem's titular reference to a Zionist (the only work in Stein's oeuvre to mention a Jewish topic in its title), firmly establishing who or what in the poem expresses the Zionist's reverie is difficult. Here is the poem as it appears in Stein's bound volumes of typescripts:

> The Revery of the Zionist
>
> I know all about the war I have been in France ever since the peace. Remember what was said yesterday.
>
> We can think and we know that we love our country so.
>
> Can we believe that all Jews are these.
>
> Let us remember that the little bird of all is not the one that has the singing doll. It sings and it sings and a great many people say it is not pleasant. Is it likely that there is real grief. Anywhere there are beards and everywhere there are girls and all about there is a wealth of imagery.
>
> I saw all this to prove that Judaism should be a question of religion.
>
> Don't talk about race. Race is disgusting if you don't love your country.
>
> I don't want to go to Zion.
>
> This is an expression of Shem.[20]

The voices style makes it difficult to distinguish between the knowing "I" of the first line, likely "one of the young men of the peace commission who was holding forth," and the voices that follow. While Will is convinced this man speaks from a Zionist point of view, no evidence supports such a claim. The first speaker may be Jewish and a Zionist or merely an example of someone "holding forth" in a provocative manner. Either way, the voice unwittingly provokes mistrust of his "know-all" claims to authority about a war from which he has been absent.

After all, Stein expresses a similar concern over claims to expertise in the short voices poem "A Radical Expert," quoted below in its entirety, where one voice calls into question the idea of expertise and where, for another voice, authority ambiguously rests on the "saying-so" of "a great many Jews":

> A Radical Expert
> Can you please by asking what is expert. And then we met one another. I do not think it right. Marksman. Expert. Loaf. Potato bread. Sugar Card. Leaf. And mortar. What is the meaning of white wash. The upper walls.
> That sounds well.
> And then we sinned.
> A great many jews say so. (198)

In this poem, written in 1918, the opening questioner challenges the expert's authority and the very idea of expertise, implying it might not be "pleasing" to the so-called expert for others to ask, "what is expert."[21] As is typical in the voices poems, sequential lines are indeterminately related by sense, disarming even the expert reader, and making it difficult to determine the semantic context for the mention of Jews in the poem's final line. The concluding triplet first expresses an affirming judgment ("That sounds well"), then a confession ("And then we sinned"), and then perhaps a justification for the judgment, an attribution for the confession, an attribution of the authority according to which "we sinned," or merely the unrelated observation that "A great many jews say so." The final line implies that large numbers may authorize expertise and, in the case of large numbers of Jews, this may allude to biblical authority in which, Genesis-like, the saying makes it so. Jewish declarations may be considered suspect, however, if one considers the literary reputation of Shylock's merciless steadfastness or the popular reputation of the alleged degeneracy plaguing the genius of fin-de-siècle Jews. The last line may thus call into question the validity of these judgments or confessions, not just as hearsay, but untrustworthy precisely because "a great many jews say so."

Likewise, in another "World Series" poem, "Land of Nations," Jews once again have their say in the final line. In this case, the plural reference masks the voice of a character penned by Jewish writer and English politician Benjamin Disraeli. Stein alludes abstractly to a passage from Disraeli's

1870 novel *Lothair*, in which the heroine is asked if she is conventional, and she answers, "Well, I live only for climate and the affections" (105).[22] Stein concludes "Land of Nations" with the lines, "What do you live for. / Climate and the affections. Jews quote that" (408). By abstracting the famed Jewish source of the quotation, Stein renders the voice anonymous. It maintains its authority, however, as part of a Jewish plurality. Both "A Radical Expert" and "Land of Nations" present an ambiguous relationship between an unidentified speaker ("And then we sinned" and "What do you live for") and the third-person-plural Jewish speakers. Whether by "saying so" or "quoting that," Stein highlights the plural articulations of Jewish expression to assert Jewish authority as a broadly unified voice.

"The Revery of the Zionist," in contrast, disperses Jewish expression, as Damon and Will have observed.[23] Although the poem concludes with a reference to the thoughts of a single Jewish speaker, "This is an expression of Shem," not only does "this" remain indeterminate as the referent for Shem's expression, but who Shem is and his relationship to other voices in the poem remain indeterminate as well. Syntactically, Shem's "expression" might refer to the titular "Revery," perhaps embodied by the entire poem, or merely to the desire not to go to Zion voiced by the speaker of the penultimate line. Shem, the Hebrew word for "name," is commonly used in Jewish tradition to refer to God without using the name for God. If the poem's contents in whole or in part are "an expression of Shem," the name of the one who, according to the Bible, named and created, then Shem's authority is authorial, and it follows that poetry assumes a divine function for Stein as it names and "caress[es] nouns," something Stein may allude to with the two definite articles in the poem's title.

Or, by way of the Bible, Shem's "expression" might refer semantically to the nature of Judaism and the Jewish people as a race, nation, or religion, topics debated by voices in the poem. In Genesis, Shem was one of Noah's sons who, with his brothers Ham and Japheth, was considered to be one of the progenitors of world peoples, differentiated, as later commentators understood it, by racial phenotype: Ham as progenitor of those with black skin, Japheth with white, and Shem with the yellow-brown or red of those people from the Levant now called "Semitic" after him.[24] An "expression of Shem" might therefore indicate more colloquially a "Semitic expression," not unlike "Jews quote that," and thereby affirm, through allusion to the story of Noah, a Jewish racial difference.

Years before, in the essay she wrote at Harvard, Stein argued that Jews were a race whose spiritual foundation was a morally purposeful religion of endeavor. She suggested that Jews should remain racially distinct to preserve their strength of moral purpose and other beneficial Jewish character traits, since the familial bond of race "does not in any sense clash with the loyalty of a man to his nation" (TMJ 426). Although the Jews may have been a nation in ancient times, Stein reassured her collegiate readers that the Jews were no longer a nationality: "the Jew's loyalty to Judaism is not that of obedience to any temporal power, not to a formation of any kind of government" (426).

Some of the voices in "The Revery" seem to echo Stein's collegiate urgings for Jews to maintain a racial separatism through endogamous marriage and to avoid Jewish nationalism. These voices insist on a differentiable if interdependent notion of race and nation and may mock the Zionist's reverie by disavowing Zionism in lieu of diasporic patriotism.[25] Once Zionism is equated with racialism, it becomes a nationalism gone awry, something expressed by the three negative imperatives "don't" near the end of the poem: "Don't talk about race. Race is disgusting if you don't love your country. / I don't want to go to Zion."[26] Similarly, the patriotic sing-song of the third line may be diasporic or Zionist—"We can think and we know that we love our country so"—although, if this *is* the song of the Zionist rallying a unified Jewish citizenry, the next line inverts the "we can" surety of the previous by asking, "Can we believe that all Jews are these." This question emphasizes the grammatical abuse of power when someone purports to speak for "all" by using the first-person-plural "we," even if the questioner uses it, perhaps ironically, to suggest that there might be more than one "we." In this vein, the young man unpleasantly "holding forth," who claims to "know *all* about the war," may likewise be mocked when another voice tells of "the little bird of *all*" whose singing "a great many people say is not pleasant" (emphases added). Despite a "wealth of imagery" and one speaker's "all"-encompassing empirical proofs—"I saw all this to prove that Judaism should be a question of religion"—the nature of Judaism and Jewish identity remain indeterminate in "The Revery of the Zionist," even as various voices affirm separable racial, national, and religious Jewish identities. Given the heterogeneous voices in the poem, "all" Jews may not be Zionists interested in tying Jewish identity to the land of Palestine.

The opening lines of the 1920 voices poem "Coal and Wood," which describe "a ridiculous authority" (3), may be referring, like "The Revery of the Zionist," to a dubious voice "holding forth" at the Paris Peace Conference. Unlike the voice in "The Revery," however, this one plausibly sounds like a Zionist despite the lack of specificity in his proclamation, since he expresses interest in an unspecified "land." The first voice we hear in "Coal and Wood" states, "This is an introduction to a description of an incident which will interest all of us in the land which interests all of us and where we all would like to be" (4). If the "we" in question refers to Jews, this voice sounds like a Zionist, who energetically if undiplomatically exhibits what a voice in another poem calls "this ever rising tide of national enthusiasm" ("Painted Lace" 2). When the voice in "Coal and Wood" imagines a place where, in the perfect future, "we all would like to be," the pronounced use of "all" insists that his listeners are of one mind, a rhetorical tic that unintentionally implies that Zionism (or any nationalist fervor) may *not* "interest all of us," even if "a great many" "Jews *are* these." Instead, the call for a Jewish state in Palestine, a specifically Zionist reverie, ironically provides Stein with the opportunity to cement her understanding of a heterogeneous racial and religious Jewish identity exclusive of nationality. With these voices, she affirms the idea that Zionism or any nationalist movement could not exist without rhetorical or diplomatic "enthusiasms."

What then is the significance of Stein's references to Palestine in these and other voices poems?[27] The wider scope of the much longer poem "Coal and Wood" gives a clearer sense of Stein's thinking of Palestine as part of Britain's imperial endeavors, which were decidedly on the upswing in the wake of the Paris Peace Conference of 1919. Britain may have been losing Ireland to independence but maintained its sway as a great power, winning territories through diplomatic proceedings at the Peace Conference and in the League of Nations.[28] Political historians recount that in order to provide fuel for its immense navy, Britain was determined to ensure its access to oil concessions in the lands of the former Ottoman Empire, from Baku to Mosul.[29] As the war ended, Britain quickly moved armed forces to maintain and establish colonial administrations in several newly mandated lands in Asia Minor, Palestine, Mesopotamia, and even portions of the former German Cameroon (to be administered as part of Nigeria). Bülent Gökay explains that resistance to the occupying British-led Allied forces helped spark Turkish nationalist movements "all over Anatolia," which "reached a crisis stage by late 1919" (51). The formal make-up of Stein's voices poems domesticates (and pacifies) international affairs to the level of salon conversation—the point of intersection between the public and private realms—and confirms Stein's attention to both the diplomatic proceedings in Paris and to news of events taking place outside the diplomatic arena. The often-indeterminate voices in the poems also convey her sensitivity to the limitations and oft-masked purposes of diplomacy. As one voice says, "I can exist in conversation. So can the Turk" ("Coal and Wood" 7).

The politesse of the diplomatic rhetoric rehearsed by many voices in "Coal and Wood" veils a greed for the natural resources to be procured in British colonies and protectorates, including Palestine.[30] Implicitly and explicitly, the poem is concerned in large part with natural resources (such as those named in the title) and the often-fraught international dynamics of acquiring and maintaining those resources in the face of national struggles for possession and independence. Voices in the poem debate, for example, whether "We need to conquer the British Empire" or "The British Empire conquers" (8). Voices also question the merits of independence struggles like the one in Ireland. One asks, "And what do you believe should be done by independence" (4), and another, "Can you tell me how to protect possessions" (7), and another, "But why should Ireland be free" (7), and another, "He feels it necessary to offend Ireland" (7). These and other questions, such as "How many nations make a country," openly trouble "country" and "nation" as names for people and places in order to suggest the constructed and often consolidated nature of empire (5). Examples of such consolidation and acquisition—through a conquest thinly veiled as diplomacy—may have been in the news reports Stein read about the Paris Peace conference.[31]

The following voice-montage from "Coal and Wood" sounds as though countries are conducting diplomacy at a tea party, rather than a meeting of the League of Nations:

> Let us call countries.
> The first one. How do you like one another.
> Very well. Does it astonish you. Not very much. How willing are you. We are very nearly willing.
> Let us call countries.

> How often are you exasperated. We are exasperated very often.
> A great many meanings are respected.
> We respect the other.
> Thank you politely.
> Let us call their countries.
> Little country to a big country. Split in two you. You split in two.
> I excuse you.
> Let us regret Sylvia.
> I dare not use another name.
> How many nations make a country.
> A country is tall.
> Very tall. Not small.
> Let us call a country. (5)

Like the lover in Stein's romantic poems who likes to mention having things said aloud, one of the above voices repeatedly refers to the "calling" of countries by name, even though no country names are mentioned in the first third of the poem and none are mentioned in this country-calling section. Instead, when "calling countries," a voice names "Sylvia," a name that looks and sounds like Syria and echoes through other place names like Transylvania or Pennsylvania, exposing the artificiality of diplomatic conventions of personification, according to which things may not necessarily be called by their real names. Indeed, the very next voice asserts, "I dare not use another name," an allusion to the famous concluding line, "I am the love that dare not speak its name," of Lord Alfred Douglas's poem "Two Loves" (25). Stein's line ironically couches the ceremonious discourses of diplomacy's calling of countries in the romantic lexicon of desire. The nature of the allusion is ambiguous, however, for the voice may "use" a name not dared to be spoken, or, like the speaker in Douglas's poem, the voice may not dare to "use another name" than the one allowed by convention or propriety.

The conversational diplomacy in "Coal and Wood" nonetheless maintains copasetic relations through semiotic openness, as when "A great many meanings are respected" and "We respect the other" (5). Perhaps this openness even encourages the bluntness of directives that might "exasperate" or "offend," such as "Split in two you. You split in two. I excuse you" (5). Later, another voice in the poem calls on Palestine and a series of colonial lands plagued by diplomatic and personal offenses. Echoing an earlier call to "Come together colonies" (6), a speaker rallies these "dear" and "offended" lands into a kind of colonial counterpart to the League of Nations:

> He feels it necessary to offend Ireland. Defend Ireland. Offend Arabia. And Palestine. Dear Palestine. Arouse yourself dear Nigeria. Arouse yourself dear Southerland. Arouse yourself you are dormant. Arouse yourself land of promise. Be proud of oil, olive oil, wood oil, ground oil, cotton seed oil, ginger oil, palm oil, and gushing oil. Be proud of yourselves all of you together and sing peaceably. Gather yourselves together for an education. Read the notices. Decide the parts. And be gracious. If you must do it do it graciously. (7)

By including Palestine in a litany of English colonial possessions in Europe, Africa, and the Levant, Stein confirms her sense that Palestine was part of larger diplomatic conversations about international relations, rather than solely a question of Jewish nationalism. A voice with a hint of divine authority nonetheless distinguishes Palestine from the others with the biblical allusion to the "land of promise." And yet, the context of the passage frustrates attempts to fix the referent and renders the significance of the allusion indeterminate. The voice may allude to the Promised Land to signify not just Palestine but, more broadly, the "promise" that Nigeria, Southerland, *and* Palestine have as British protectorates rich in natural resources. In this passage the rhetorical caresses of a condescending blandishment (the repeated use of "dear") seem to sooth the "offenses" of empire (enacted by a representative "he"). But it is impossible to determine whether the addresses to these colonies are examples of offensive remarks (by "he") or rebuttals to such offenses. However ambiguous, the rules of this vocal game follow the thinly veiled imperialism of European diplomacy and suggest a reading of Stein's interest in Palestine as a land among other lands "chosen" for exploitation by Europe.

The voices poems remain one of the most enigmatic works of modernist writing, and their use of a Jewish lexicon reveals the abstraction present in seemingly nonmetaphorical language. Persistent ambiguity and abstraction would seem to tend toward the asemantic and hermetic, but the voices poems are fascinating for their plain-spoken voicing of quotidian concerns. For Stein, there may be something Jewish about the modernist determination to frustrate the surety of interpretation while persistently encouraging it. In the poem "Geography" from 1923, she associates such resistance to semantic fixity and surety with "the Jews":

> He was terribly deceived about the Jews about Napoleon and about everything else.
> If you do not know the meaning of such things do not use them. That is all. Such phrases. (240)

The first voice clearly states that an unspecified "he" had not realized how much he misunderstood "the Jews," "Napoleon," and "everything else." It is not clear, however, whether the deception was caused by his own reluctance to accept the truth about "the Jews" (or "Napoleon" and "everything else") or if someone else had deceived him "terribly" about them. The subsequent lines complain about someone's dubious usage of "such things," the meaning of which one may not know. The "things" in this case might be words, since there is a voice earlier in the poem that seems to be looking up a word in the dictionary—"Looking up under fairly see fairly looking up under as to movement" (239)—or groups of words, since a voice says with possible exasperation, "Such phrases." "The Jews" in the passage, possibly indicated by one of "such phrases," are elusively meaningful as a group of people who are as imperiously and singularly evocative as Napoleon and yet as diffusely identifiable as "everything else."[32]

Stein's Jewish lexicon figures both indeterminacy and fixity in these poems that trace the possibilities and limits of modern poetry. "The Jews" might inhabit a concretely geographic place or verifiable dictionary definition and also be "terribly deceiving." Jewish identity, for Stein, thus inhabits a "meaning" that may individually name Jewish history, tradition, place, ideology, and people, while also affirming a multiplicity that renders abstract, ambiguous, and anonymous the words and phrases "Jew," "Jewish," "a Jew," and "the Jews." By summoning the wild heterogeneity of modern Jewish identity, Stein expresses a paradoxical marriage of convention and singularity. For Stein, Jews are wild. Whether as frozen metaphors for stranger, lover, religious tradition, or semantic apostasy, they remain abstract, representative pretenders and symbolize the ever-separating but never absolutely distinct nature of words and meaning.

6

"Everybody can persecute anybody"
What's Funny about Jewish Identity in *Wars I Have Seen*

Gertrude Stein and Alice Toklas lived in the south of France during World War II and somehow, as Jews, survived. In *Wars I Have Seen*, a memoir written during the Nazi occupation, Stein warily reported that the reality of "what it is to live in an occupied country" meant carrying on with everyday life as much as possible, while keeping "quiet until the Germans are gone just naturally play[ing] possum just as long as one can" (200). Despite some limited freedoms, Stein and Toklas's position during the Occupation was ultimately one of vulnerability. They inhabited a France where it seemed "Anything can happen" and "Everything is dangerous" (120, 121).

In *Wars I Have Seen*, Stein reflects that she and Toklas were "rather favored strangers" in France, and yet the story of their survival, however favored, was not unique (114). Like three-fourths of the Jews in France, they survived the war through personal connections or as the beneficiaries of inconsistent enforcement of anti-Jewish directives.[1] Stein's protection or offers of protection, sometimes tacit, came from French friends, neighbors, gendarmes, resistance fighters, lawyers, industrialists, mayors, and journal editors.[2] The diversity of her support spanned the political and ideological spectrum, reflecting on one hand Stein's heterogeneous social ties and, on the other, an affirmation of her claim that "the French people take care of me" (*WIHS* 119).[3]

Though Stein did not elaborate on the precise arrangements of her protection, she had a very powerful friend in Bernard Faÿ, the Vichy-appointed director of the Bibliothèque Nationale.[4] Faÿ had been a prominent professor of American literature with "monarchist" politics and had a long and complicated friendship with Stein.[5] In his memoirs, Faÿ claims that he personally ensured Stein's survival by insisting that the Maréchal Philippe Pétain, head of the Vichy government, contact the subprefect of Stein's region on her behalf.[6]

Given Stein's longstanding political conservatism and her likely protected status during the Occupation, many readers have wondered whether we should see her relationship to the Vichy regime as one of collaboration. Wanda Van Dusen piqued interest in this question with her 1996 publication of Stein's "Introduction" to a planned volume of wartime translations of Pétain's speeches.[7] Scholars have looked closely at Stein's translations of Pétain as one means to document "the delicacy of Stein's situation" (Will, "Lost" 664).[8] Barbara Will assesses the culminating years of Stein and Faÿ's friendship, asserting that "Faÿ was fully aware of the importance of Stein's reputation and understood that Stein's wartime vulnerability could be leveraged to serve the Vichy regime" ("Gertrude Stein, Bernard Faÿ" 658). Stein had become "a pawn in the power game of her friend," which, as Will explains, is likely the reason that Stein began translating Pétain's speeches in the middle of the war (657). Stein's survival may have depended on her preparation of this never-completed piece of propaganda.

In her 2011 book *Unlikely Collaboration: Gertrude Stein, Bernard Faÿ, and the Vichy Dilemma*, Will amplifies her earlier studies to anoint Stein Vichy's "unlikely collaborator" (138). In the book, Will argues that "Stein's support for Pétain was authentic," and suggests that "Stein's own words portray her as a 'propagandist' for the 'new France'" (143, 135). Given the volume and variety of Stein's written wartime output, however, Stein's wartime politics—as gleaned through her writings of the era—are not so simply parsed.[9] Stein's numerous publications throughout the war in anti-Vichy literary reviews, for example, might show Stein as an unlikely resister instead. (In my conclusion, I briefly discuss Stein's publications with several major outlets of the intellectual resistance.) While Will omits any mention of these resistance publications, she nonetheless acknowledges that Stein's Vichy-era novel *Mrs. Reynolds* and other "literary texts clearly run counter to the pro-Pétainist tendencies" Will sees elsewhere (144). And although Will reads *Wars I Have Seen* as evidence of Stein's "unrepentant Pétainism," she admits to some political ambiguity in the memoir as it "dances through" the "gray zone of her collaboration" (116, 144).

As a literary text that includes important reportage of Stein's and her neighbors' wartime experiences, *Wars I Have Seen* is crucial to understanding Stein's wartime life, lived and literary, as well as her personal and political concerns as an American and a Jew in Nazi-occupied France. Stein began the memoir in January 1943, after the Germans occupied all of France. Another look at the memoir with an eye to its historical, biographical, and literary contexts is necessary. It must be read in relation to Stein's other major wartime writings: "The Winner Loses" (written September 1939 to August 1940), *Mrs. Reynolds* (written December 1940 to August 1942), Stein's "Introduction to the Speeches of Maréchal Pétain" (written December 1941 or January 1942), and the play *Yes Is for a Very Young Man* (August 1944). Stein's formal experimentation in the memoir once again reveals something Jewish about Stein's modernism, as she subverts support for Vichy and criticizes Pétain while recording her life under the Occupation.

"It was so awful that it became funny"

In the "Introduction" Stein wrote to accompany her translations of Pétain's speeches, she undercuts an otherwise heroic portrait of Pétain, who she considers to be cut from the same cloth as George Washington and Benjamin Franklin. Like many of her adopted countrymen, Stein admired Pétain's heroism in World War I and his signing of the armistice that brought an end to French fighting in World War II. Her narrative in the "Introduction" is, however, riddled with the skepticism she and others—"the most critical and the most violent of us"—have had about Pétain's leadership (95). She professes, for example, "We have not all of us, and I too have been of that number, over here in France always had faith in the Marechal but in the end we have all come to have faith" (93).[10] Although Stein purports to put all doubts and contradictions to rest, she goes on to report a French friend's quip that every Frenchman has "four points of view" about Pétain, as they try to reconcile competing familial, business, and political interests (94).[11] She also proceeds to relate long-held concerns about Pétain's tendency to capitulate to German demands by noting ruefully, "this time the Marechal has given in," though in the end, she says with relief, he does not give in (95). And she punctuates her unrest by recounting the egoistical story that Pétain, when asked who would win the war, the English or the Germans, "touched his breast and answered Moi" (95). In *Wars I Have Seen*, as I discuss below, Stein again recalls her conflicted feelings about Pétain, and yet frankly expresses disgust for his egotism: "I did not like his way of saying I Philippe Petain, that bothered me" (87).

As if to quiet the internal contradictions of the translation project and the compromised standing of its maker, Stein, in the penultimate paragraph of the "Introduction," recounts an anecdote, which she admits "has nothing to do with this [story of Pétain's winning of hearts and minds] but which is a story that I like" (95). The story describes Pétain curtly quieting young officers who are "excited and laughing and shouting" in the lead-up to World War I by asking them, "and do you think war is always funny, toujours drole" (95). Stein's translation of the punch line "always funny" back into French, "toujours drole," suggests that the anecdote speaks in more than one language and in more than one register as well. It is a passage in which Stein plays with the word "funny" to write at her most serious. Her punchline refers to France's ill-preparedness and inactivity in the 1939–1940 war with Germany, dubbed by many the "*drôle de guerre*"— meaning phony or funny war. For Stein, the story also underscores the gravity of war despite what seems to be the grotesque levity of its makers.[12] She repeats the story in her two major wartime literary endeavors, *Mrs. Reynolds* (the novel whose composition overlapped with the translation project) and the later memoir *Wars I Have Seen*.[13]

The anecdote about Pétain's retort suggests that, though war is not to be laughed at, Stein finds it funny as a situation that has turned her world— and that of most of France—upside down while maintaining pretenses of normality. "Funny" had long been a key word in Stein's lexicon for incongruous situations.[14] In her wartime writings, Stein uses the word to alert her readers to the painful peculiarity of her life in France under Vichy, and then under German occupation.[15] In the memoir, she describes one afternoon in December 1943, for example, when she was in a train station where "there were a good many Germans about" and where she spies a French copy of *The Autobiography of Alice B. Toklas* for sale at a newsstand (*WIHS* 119). She runs back to tell Toklas about the book, and the ticket seller in the station, hearing her speak excitedly in English, asks whether the Germans are giving her any trouble. Stein replies that she and Toklas "are women and past the age to be bothered and beside . . . I am a writer and so the French people take care of me" (119). Then the ticket seller asks what Stein writes, and Stein tells him that one of her books is for sale at the newsstand, whereupon a "young woman ticket seller" goes out to the newstand and buys the book and has Stein sign it. Stein concludes, "we were all very pleased and Alice Toklas thought it was all very funny, with all the Germans coming in and out and all about. Anything can happen in France and that makes it what it is, just that makes it what it is" (120). Stein reports that Toklas finds the harrowing experience "funny," in the sense of incongruous, belying Stein's explanation to the ticket seller that the Germans have no cause to bother her and Toklas.

From the very beginning of France's defeat, moreover, Stein registers—as "funny"—the shocking peculiarity of events including the bizarre situation that will shortly turn the name of a mineral water into a provisional government. In "The Winner Loses," she recalls hearing the painful news of continued German invasion, "We had a drink in a café, Vichy for me and pineapple juice for Alice Toklas, and we heard the radio going. 'What's the news?' we asked mechanically. 'Amiens has fallen,' said the girl." And Stein reflects, "It was so awful that it became funny" (619).

In the memoir, Stein makes explicit her frequent use of the word "funny" to convey a haunting experience of a reality that is "so awful" that it seems unreal and not wholly comprehensible, saying, "It is funny funny in the sense of strange and peculiar and unrealisable" (*WIHS* 47). The aggressive persecutions of the Vichy government, its complicity with the Nazis, and the eventual occupation of all of France by the Axis powers in November of 1942 had turned the provincial home front inhabited by Stein into a surreal theater of war. Near the end of the war, feeling completely cut off from the outside world due to blockades and severed telephone lines, she concludes, "Is life real is life earnest, no I do not think so, it certainly is not real. This kind of war is funny it is awful but it does make it all unreal, really unreal" (201).

The "funny" feeling that the war is "unreal" also conveys Stein's concerns about antisemitism under the Occupation, as I detail in this chapter. With her retelling of Pétain's sobering admonition that war is no joke, Stein expresses her own reckoning—amidst the necessary exaggerations and falsehoods of political propaganda—of the seriousness of the present war and of her own precarious situation as a Jew. Given her persistent contrariness in the "Introduction," a work that should unhesitatingly applaud Pétain, it is not surprising that, in the memoir she begins on the heels of the translations and continues writing through the end of the war, her ambivalence develops into disapproval for Pétain's persecution of Jews, freemasons, and communists. In *Wars I Have Seen*, Stein gives a diaristic account of her life in the south of France amidst occupying forces, refugees, and a divided and disgruntled citizenry. In this politically volatile milieu, without any mention of her position as a protected Jew, she testifies to the persecutions, deprivations, and curtailment of civil liberties afflicting those around her, Jew and gentile.

Too many critics have mistaken Stein's impersonal approach to Jewish topics and her tendency to draw grave parallels between antisemitism and other persecutions as a dismissal of rather than an engagement with Jewish topics.[16] Her purpose in the memoir, I argue, is to suggest—through parallels and associations—that the Jewish experience of persecution epitomizes the persecutions experienced by the French under Vichy and German occupation. Throughout the memoir, Stein Judaizes the experience of occupation by associating the displacements, imprisonments, and refugee situations of the occupied French with the experiences of Jews past and present. She considers Jews to be icons of twentieth-century modernity and progress and condemns the antisemitisms of Hitler and Pétain as atavistic clingings to nineteenth-century medievalism. At the end of the memoir, as the culmination of Stein's many associations of the Jewish with the modern, she again champions the singular and Jewish figure of the modern writer, this time as an active resister of the Occupation.

Stein's Home Front in Literary and Historical Context

Stein and Toklas spent the beginning of the war in the summer home they had rented for over a decade in the hamlet of Bilignin near the town of Belley not far from Lyon. When the owner of the home resumed occupancy, Stein and Toklas moved twelve miles away to Culoz, a picturesque railway town in the shadow of a mountain. In *Wars I Have Seen*, Stein narrates her thoughts about the war as it was happening in the conversational style of *The Autobiography of Alice B. Toklas* (1933) and *Everybody's Autobiography* (1937). She writes during and about the period from early 1943 until the arrival of American forces in her town on September 1, 1944. Random House published the book in 1945, and this immediacy gives the memoir what one critic has called its "unique, documentary quality" (Lesinska 48).[17]

Like *Mrs. Reynolds*, which Steven Gould Axelrod astutely compares to *Waiting for Godot*, as a "text of patient and impatient waiting," where characters "mak[e] conversation to fill the voids," *Wars I Have Seen* largely consists of Stein's conversations with friends, neighbors, and the people she meets when out walking her dog or on excursions to nearby towns (259, 269). Stein juxtaposes these quotidian conversations with the terrifying not-so-everyday events conveyed therein, namely imprisonments, denunciations, desertions, deportations, and refugee situations. The juxtaposition suggests to Stein the ways that the Occupation has estranged modern life—as detainment and displacement become everyday events—such that her daily reality feels "funny" and "unreal."[18] In trying to understand the overwhelmingly painful feelings of oddity in the present war, furthermore, Stein peppers the memoir with her titular experiences of other wars, both lived and literary.

Critics of *Wars I Have Seen* still, by and large, mistakenly read the seemingly artless style and the provincial purview of the book as an exhibition of Stein's inexcusable myopia regarding the war and the deaths of Jews in France and across Europe.[19] For example, critic Jean Gallagher derides Stein's account of everyday life for its "discursive neutrality" (140). She argues that Stein inhabits an "occupation [that] seems to suspend the act of interpretation" (137). In a similar vein, Liesl Olson criticizes Stein's focus on domestic habits, which she thinks allows Stein to avoid actively protesting or truly engaging the reality of the war.[20] As I show, however, Stein's attention to daily life was typical and comprehensible according to literary and historical accounts of the era.

Stein was, of course, not alone in underscoring the way that the situation of occupation magnified connections between home front and warfront. The French-Jewish novelist Irène Némirovsky, in notes for her never-completed wartime epic, asserts: "The most important and most interesting thing here is the following: the historical, revolutionary facts etc. must be only lightly touched upon, while daily life, the emotional life and especially the comedy it provides must be described in detail" (*Suite Française*, Appendix 1, 389). Stein wrote similar notes when composing her play *Yes Is for a Very Young Man* in the autumn of 1944, reminding herself how instructive and revelatory it would be to show how life was "lived by most of the ordinary people": "I think we could use a lot more detail, little stuff about daily life under the Nazi occupation . . . all the things that are really interesting to people who have not been occupied" (YCAL qtd. in Bay-Cheng 104).

Many Stein critics defend Stein's recording of "daily life under the Nazi occupation" as realistic and ethical wartime testimony. Phoebe Stein Davis, for example, takes Stein's predilection for "daily living" as both feminist and realist means to "repeatedly underscore[e] the inherent connection between the personal and the political, between the everyday life on the home front and 'the larger political scene' of the international theater of war" (598–599). Madelyn Detloff takes Stein's "valuation of the non-momentous" and the "non-heroic" as "a sign of resiliency and resistance to the dehumanizing purpose of war" (77–78). And Dana Cairns Watson argues that Stein uses "everyday conversation" as a form of resistance to the "pressure of the political situation" under the "cloud" of "Hitler" (153, 155). Karen Lawrence, meanwhile, defends Stein's reportage of her neighbors' wartime struggles as testament to Stein's ethical response to suffering. For Lawrence, "How suffering . . . is made real through stories is fundamental to the question of ethical response. . . . How close does the suffering need to be for us to imagine it vividly enough to care?" (23). Indeed, as I describe below, Stein's stories of her neighbors' sufferings show her utmost concern and often her horror as the war turns suffering into the stuff of everyday conversation.

In *Wars I Have Seen*, Stein's conversations with "ordinary people" suggest the peculiarity of living under occupation. Although one may be at home, home is no longer safe, and the home front comes to resemble a warfront. In *This Land Is Mine*, Jean Renoir's propagandistic 1943 film about occupied France, the protagonist declares, "Even an occupied town like this can be a fighting front." For Stein in Culoz, the political reality of occupation becomes a domestic unreality when "first the German officers and then later on the Italians" lodge in her house (69). In her several reports of having "enemies in the house and in the barn," she is struck by how "strange [it is] just as strange as it can be" (62, 59). She concludes by again acknowledging the fearful absurdity of the situation: "It is funny to be Americans and to be here in France and to have that" (69).[21]

Near the end of *Wars I Have Seen*, Stein notes the kinds of precautions she had taken in the writing of the memoir because of such uninvited guests. "Alice Toklas has just commenced typewriting this book, [for] as long as there were Germans around we left it in manuscript as my handwriting is so bad it was not likely that any German would be able to read it" (229). The close German presence underscores John Whittier-Ferguson's rejoinder that the expectation many critics have that Stein would take a "risky, public, political stand" or announce her Jewish identity in an occupied country that was deporting Jews would have been foolhardy as well as uncharacteristic of Stein's peacetime writing persona ("Stein in

Time" 119). Indeed, Stein's wartime writings are no exception to her lifelong practice of not naming herself as a Jew when writing for publication. Stein never denied her Jewish identity and yet, as I have shown, when Stein wrote openly about and with great concern for Jews, she wrote about them impersonally.

The precariousness of life for Jews in France forcefully colors Stein's sense of what's funny—or unreal—about life under the Occupation, most notably when a Vichy official suggests that she and Toklas leave the country or risk internment in a concentration camp. At the time of Stein's writing, "concentration camps" denoted domestic detainment centers where France had recently interned refugees and enemy aliens and were now interning Jews, Romani peoples (gypsies), and communists and other antifascists. In addition to the violence of being veritably imprisoned, many people died in French concentration camps due to unsanitary conditions and poor access to food and medical attention. Though trains would begin deporting Jews from these French internment camps to Nazi death camps in March 1942, Stein and the French population she lived among did not know about the genocide of European Jewry in Nazi extermination camps.[22]

Historian Renée Poznanski describes the changing situation of Jews in France as a context in which "new types of normality were becoming standard: in certain cases persecution was central, in others it was buried under other worries" (xviii). Roundups of Jews into French camps began in May 1941 and deportations east, we now know to Auschwitz, began in March 1942. The plight of Jews in France was, however, competing for space in the national imaginary with more general news of the war and the subsequent Occupation. It was not until July of 1942, with the roundup of thirteen thousand Jews at the Vél d'Hiv in Paris, that the roundups provoked widespread popular outrage.[23] After a few months of respite, moreover, France resumed deporting Jews to Auschwitz and continued to do so through August of 1944 to comparatively little protest. Historian Annette Wieviorka reminds us that Jews made up 54 percent of the 138,806 persons deported from France, making "deportation a concern not only for Jews" (20).[24] The deportations were, for example, overshadowed in large part by the announcement, in February of 1943, of the indenture of close to 700,000 French men and women to forced labor in Germany as part of Vichy's tribute agreement, the Service du Travail Obligatoire (STO), which "then came to seem the real deportation" (Marrus and Paxton

184).[25] As Zofia Lesinska argues, any "perceptible evasions" in Stein's writing may realistically share a broader inattention on the part of the general population to the deportations of Jews from France (43).

And although Stein is quiet about the Jewish aspect of her own situation, including the threatened internment, in the memoir she nonetheless makes her most extended and unambiguous statements about European Jewry and antisemitism since her Radcliffe essay of a half-century before. She writes openly of Jews and Jewish history and discusses what she deems the metaphorically Jewish character of people, culture, and epochs. She also takes a clear stand against German antisemitism and the injustices of France's puppet government, unequivocally protesting the specifically anti-Jewish persecutions by both Hitler and Pétain.

Stein's Semitic Landscapes and "The Orientalizing of Europe"

In *Wars I Have Seen*, Stein's Jewish concerns structure a narrative that otherwise feels formless. Unlike the earlier autobiographies, the memoir has no chapters: it is one long recital marked only by Stein's periodic references to the advancing calendar. The memoir's putative organization begins with an account of Stein's life in epochs, such as "between babyhood and fourteen" and "from fifteen to twenty-four," as remembered through the lens of somewhat-chronological reflections on past wars (26). She interrupts her retrospective account with anecdotes about the present war until the narrative becomes largely an account of Stein's everyday life during the war. There are, however, thematic refrains that form what Shirley Swartz describes as "a sort of semantic landscape, a space neither vigorously definitive nor linear, but multidimensional, revealing a movement and clustering of concepts" (227). For Swartz, these "semantic landscapes" bring together concepts lacking logical relation as an "indiscriminate . . . recording" of Stein's experience (232). I argue, however, that the "semantic landscapes" of *Wars I Have Seen* are deceptively disorderly and, in fact, document the relational nexus Stein observes during the Occupation between Jewish and other persecutions.

The associative logic of the memoir's "clustering of concepts" signals not only the importance of antisemitism in the present war but, allusively, the nightmarish banality of Stein's own experiences as a Jew in Vichy and German-occupied France. In her tendency to group the experience of Jews with refugees more generally, for example, *Wars I Have Seen* documents a political and social connection that historians have affirmed.²⁶ In another cluster, Stein recounts her threatened internment in a concentration camp followed by a passage that gives her thoughts on Dreyfus, imprisonment, and antisemitism. These two passages presage a handful of brief bulletins attesting to the apparent requisitioning of and lodging in Stein's house by German and Italian officers. Through this associative, clustering aesthetic, Stein conveys her understanding of Jewish experience and Jewish history as crucial lenses for understanding the modern condition of the era more generally.

Attitudes toward Jews play a key role in her characterization of historical periods and, in the memoir, they color her imagined trajectory of the current era. She characterizes antisemitism as the epitome of European retrogression and dates the most recent wave of antisemitism to the "Jew baiting" that had sprung up in England around the 1936 "abdication of Edward" (122).²⁷ The current revival of antisemitism, she warns, heralds "a new nineteenth century and a new plunge into mediaevalism" (122).

If the day's antisemitism is an accursed throwback to medieval times, Jews themselves, notes Stein, have been a modernizing force in recent European history. In a 1934 *New York Times Magazine* interview, Stein had pinpointed the treatment of Jews as pivotal to the politics and progress of modern nations, remarking ironically, "I say that Hitler ought to have the peace prize . . . because he is removing all elements of contest and of struggle from Germany. By driving out the Jews and the democratic and Left elements, he is driving out everything that conduces to activity. That means peace" ("Gertrude Stein Views Life and Politics." SM9).

Edward Burns and Ulla Dydo argue that Stein's remark about Hitler has too often been "taken literally and out of context" (414). They remind us that later in the *Times* interview, Stein "is quoted as asserting that what matters in a country is 'competition, struggle, interest, activity that keep the people alive and excited'—the very opposition that Hitler wishes to remove. The proposal about the peace prize, then, is ironic, a point of black humor" (414).²⁸

Stein saw Germany's antisemitic efforts to "drive out the Jews" within the larger context of nativist political discourses in Europe and the United States. The 1934 interview captures Stein's liberal, modernizing, and cosmopolitan enthusiasm for the "stimulation" brought by Jews and other immigrants, when she criticizes "the stringent immigration laws in America today," which "suppres[s] . . . natural activity and competition lead[ing] to dullness and stagnation" (*NYT* SM23). And though one hears racism in Stein's interest in "preserving the color line" and "bar[ring the immigration of] certain peoples" to the United States, she criticizes French xenophobia and favors France's more open immigration policy. According to historians Michael R. Marrus and Robert O. Paxton, by the beginning of the war, France "had become 'the leading country of immigration in the world,' with a greater proportion of foreigners than any other" (35). This proportion was much higher among Jews in France, where foreign-born people and refugees would make up half of the Jewish population.[29] Jews and other refugees figure for Stein as stimulating antidotes to "dullness and stagnation." As she explains in the *Times*, "The French may not like the competition of foreigners, but they let them in. They accept the challenge and derive the stimulus" (*NYT* SM23).

Stein continued to applaud the European tendency toward heterogeneity as a modern and Jewish phenomenon. Later in the 1930s, in her memoir *Everybody's Autobiography*, she articulates her sense of the increasingly and beneficially Jewish character of modern life. Harkening back to the early notes for *Q.E.D.*, where she dubs her Jewish protagonist "Oriental," she differentiates between a European West and a non-European East that encompasses Russia's Asian "Tartars," Spain's North African "Saracens," and "Oriental" Jews (Collection of notes and quotations, ca. 1890s, YCAL; *EA* 21). Such Orientalism builds once again on Matthew Arnold's broadly conceived designation of Hebraism as a modern social force in Europe. Unlike Arnold, who argued for the lessening of Judaic influences, Stein again appreciates the increased "mixing" of specifically Jewish forces into the European character as a sign of progress (*EA* 21).

The very modernity of twentieth-century culture is, for Stein, Jewish and "Oriental":

> And all this is very important with what I have been saying about the peaceful Oriental penetration into European culture or rather the tendency for this generation that is for the twentieth century to be no longer European because perhaps Europe is finished. (*EA* 21)

The archaic nature of antisemitism is plainly at odds with Stein's estimation that in the modern era "this generation" was increasingly, if metaphorically, Jewish. Later, when explaining the origins and present-day successes of capitalism and communism as Jewish, for example, she concludes, "The Jews and once more we have the orientalizing of Europe" (*EA*

41). She points to two Jews, Einstein and herself, as examples of "the same tendency" toward a European Orientalizing in the realms of "philosophy and literature" (*EA* 21). Further, Stein's characterization of the increasingly Judaic presence in Europe as "peaceful" may be an attempt to diffuse the increasingly bellicose antisemitic sensibilities stirring across Europe in the 1930s.

By 1943, writing in *Wars I Have Seen*, Stein positions the antisemitic persecutions of the current regimes as a bellwether of European decline and expresses her concern for the persecutions of almost "everybody" in the war. Stein sees Hitler as the "embodiment" of the nineteenth century's illogical spirit alongside Napoleon and Caesar (16). She sees Hitler's Germany, in turn, as a nation whose antisemitism reveals the extent to which it is "so desperately clinging to any past century" (56). The last century may have wrought "civilising" advances in literacy and science but, given the persistence of wars, persecution, and the banning of books, Stein decides that the nineteenth century did not make much "progress" after all: "although everybody is civilised there is no progress and everybody knows even though anybody flies higher and higher they cannot explain eternity any more than before, and everybody can persecute anybody just as much if not more than ever, it is rather ridiculous" (62). With the universalizing and nonparticularist pronouns "everybody" and "anybody," Stein linguistically extends the reach of her concern for persecuted peoples. This reflects her broader tendency in the wartime memoir to criticize the persecutions Vichy and Germany were perpetrating on Jews, refugees, and other minority populations, and to express solidarity with the disempowered French majority as well. As I show in what follows, the memoir's "semantic landscapes" often function as *semitic* landscapes, in which Stein casts the persecutions against Jews as representative of the strange persecutions plaguing Europe. For Stein, these are inseparable from the difficulties afflicting her and those around her, whether refugee, native-born, Jew, or gentile.

"It is funny about things being real": Stein's Acquaintance with Mass Displacements and Concentration Camps

Amidst the crosscurrents of modern Orientalisms and medieval antisemitisms, Stein remarks in *Wars I Have Seen* that the epoch's aesthetic has been veering away from realism toward the modern. In a portion of the memoir dated from July of 1943, she writes that, beginning with the Spanish-American War and continuing into the present, modern war has affected—and deformed—the contemporary sense of reality, such that "there is no realism now" (44). The reflection on realism calls to Stein's mind a shocking instance of unreality, when, months before, she and Toklas were threatened with internment in a concentration camp. She introduces the event, tellingly, as something "funny," cementing the connection in vocabulary and experience between the funny, the unreal, and, obliquely, her Jewish identity. "It is funny about things being real," she offers, "Something happened a few months ago like that, in February 1943" (48).

February 1943 marked the tail end of Stein's legal wrangling over the house in Bilignin she and Toklas had rented for fourteen years. Stein embeds the account of their threatened internment within a discussion of the resolution of her housing saga. The landlord of the Bilignin house had decided to resume occupancy once Stein's lease came to an end, and Stein unsuccessfully sued the landlord for continued occupancy. Friends found Stein and Toklas a house to rent in the nearby railway town of Culoz and, on the eve of their move, Stein stopped in Belley (the town closest to Bilignin) to thank her lawyer. He unexpectedly relayed the advice of Vichy official Maurice Sivain that Stein and Toklas flee immediately or risk being "put into a concentration camp" (50). This warning was likely a response to German orders in January and February of 1943 for concentrating and then deporting Jews from the southern zone.[30]

Stein begins to narrate the "curiously unreal" account of that ordeal as follows:

> We had recently quite a number of difficult moments. America had come into the war, our consul and vice-consul in Lyon with whom we had gotten very friendly because they had taken a summer home right near us and kept a white goat called Genevieve, and there we first found out that you could have goat's milk that did not taste of goat, had been interned first at Lourdes and then taken to Germany and now I went to Belley to say good-bye [to my lawyer] as we were moving. My lawyer said that everything was nicely arranged and we thanked each other and said what a pleasure it had all been, and then he said and now I have something rather serious to tell you. I was in Vichy yesterday, and I saw Maurice Sivain,

Here Stein makes the explanatory aside that

> Sivain had been sous-prefet at Belley and had been most kind and helpful in extending our privileges and our occupation of our house,

She then resumes reporting her lawyer's narration:

> and Maurice Sivain said to me, tell these ladies that they must leave at once for Switzerland, to-morrow if possible otherwise they will be put into a concentration camp. But I said we are just moving. I know he said. I felt very funny, quite completely funny. But how can we go, as the frontier is closed, I said. That he said could be arranged, I think that could be arranged. You mean pass by fraud I said, Yes he said, it could be arranged. I felt very funny. I said I think I will go home and will you telephone Madame d'Aiguy to meet me. He said shall I walk home with you, I did feel very funny, and I said no I will go home and Madame d'Aiguy will come down to see you and arrange and I went home. I came in, I felt a little less funny but I still did feel funny, and Alice Toklas and Madame d'Aiguy were there, and I said we are not moving to-morrow we are going to Switzerland. They did not understand that and I explained and then they did understand, and Madame d'Aiguy left to go and see the lawyer and arrange and Alice Toklas and I sat down to supper. We both felt funny and then I said. No, I am not going we are not going, it is better to go regularly wherever we are sent than to go irregularly where nobody can help us if we are in trouble, no I said, they are always trying to get us to leave France but here we are and here we stay. What do you think, I said, and we thought and I said we will walk down to Belley and see the lawyer and tell him no. We walked down to Belley it was night it was dark but I am always out walking at night, I like it, and I took Alice Toklas by the arm because she has not the habit of walking at night and we got to Belley, and climbed up the funny steps to the lawyer, and I said I have decided not to go. Madame d'Aiguy was still there and she said perhaps it was better so, and the lawyer said perhaps we had better go and then he said he had a house way up in the mountains and there nobody would know, and I said well perhaps later but now I said to-morrow we are going to move to Culoz, with our large comfortable new house with

two good servants and a nice big park with trees, and we all went home, and we did move the next day. It took us some weeks to get over it but we finally did.

But what was so curious in the whole affair was its unreality. . . . (49–51)

Stein's telling of the threatened internment comprises one of the longest paragraphs in the memoir. She broaches the "rather serious" events about to unfold by stating ominously that she and Toklas "had recently quite a number of difficult moments."[31] These events rattle Stein, and she tattoos the charged paragraph with the unsettling word "funny." Her persistently odd feelings may prompt her stated craving for "regular" comportment and the decision not to flee to Switzerland illegally.[32] The funny feelings cease, however, once she decides to stay in France, even if the path she has chosen involves taking some "funny steps" up to her lawyer's house.[33] Although the paragraph ends on a seemingly light-hearted note—"It took us some weeks to get over it but we finally did"—the next paragraph looks back on the "curious . . . unreality" of "the whole affair," underscoring its seriousness. Rather than a "cursory" treatment, as one critic claims, Stein amplifies the gravity of the event described in this passage by centering it in a trauma-laden "semantic landscape."[34] In the passages immediately preceding and following, and in passages a bit farther afield, she reflects on the "funny" or "unreal" nature of detainments, forced displacements, imprisonments, and the deaths of those around her near and far in occupied France.

Earlier in the memoir, for example, Stein uses the second-person point of view to write about the threatened internment in both personal and impersonal terms. Widespread uncertainty in France gives her "a funny feeling, that any time not only that you can be told to go and you go but also that you can be taken." And she concludes, "Nevertheless you stay, and if you stay you do not go away" (26–27).[35] The second-person phrasing makes Stein's own experience indistinguishable from those around her terrorized by the possibilities of either being "told to go" or being "taken." This undated passage, likely written between March and May of 1943, may have been Stein's first written attempt to reckon with the experience of threatened internment, something she returns to explicitly in the July recital of the "funny feelings" she had when she was "told to go" by her lawyer and Sivain the previous February.[36]

Today it is difficult to avoid reading the threat of internment as an event that marks Stein and Toklas as Jews, even though Stein does not mention her Jewish identity at all during the account. While acutely aware of her vulnerability to internment as a Jew under two regimes whose antisemitism she condemns, Stein's experience of present and past wars had not led her to consider concentration camps as the sole province of Jews—far from it. Rather, the roundups, mass displacements, and internments in France prompted her to recall news of the starvation and death suffered by Boer civilians in concentration camps decades earlier. So, while Stein knew of concentration camps as horrific places, given their history, they would not necessarily have signified to her a death penalty.[37] At the time of the incident, "in February 1943," as I must repeatedly underscore, it was almost impossible for Stein to have known that the Jews being concentrated—rounded up and placed in French internment camps—were then being deported east to near-certain death at Auschwitz or other extermination camps. Instead, Stein situated her own experience and the experience of Jews who were interned or deported, within a larger reign of terror experienced by French civilians, refugees, and other noncombatants.

Only weeks before Stein and Toklas were "told to go" from France, Stein had been stunned by the news that "they have sent forty thousand people out of their homes in Marseilles" (11). The news of this mass displacement is one of the first events in the present war that Stein directly writes about in the memoir.[38] From January 22 to 27 of 1943, the French police, assisted by the German military, went door to door evacuating the entirety of Marseilles' Old Port quarter, home to refugees, immigrants, bohemians, artists, and Jews. The evacuation of the Old Port and other simultaneous sweeps around the city resulted in six thousand detainments; among these were eight hundred Jews almost immediately put on trains we now know were headed to death camps.[39]

The mass evictions and expulsions in Marseilles must have seemed, at first, a surreal and ghastly parallel to Stein's own experience of being put out of her home by her landlord. And yet, within weeks, if not days, she too is threatened with internment and possibly deportation, like so many in Marseilles. Stein responds to the news of the Marseilles evacuation with disbelief, "it is so real to me that it is a dream, not that I know any of them" (11). What was once an unimaginable "dream"—the mass victimization of civilians—has now become "so real." The horrifying news casts a long shadow over the memoir as a magnification of her own "unreal" and "funny" experiences. The news from Marseilles is just days removed from the events of February 1943, and yet Stein waits six months to record them—a separation of forty pages in the memoir. In contrast, she immediately prefaces her recollected narration of Sivain's warning with her memories of the concentration camps in the Boer War, clustering her personal story amidst that of a historically distant mass displacement.

Despite its distance in time and place, the recollected "unreal" news of the Boer War, fought in South Africa from 1899 to 1902, serves Stein as a potent symbol of the horrifying deprivations wars visit upon civilians.[40] Contemporary responses echo her sense of the Boer War's unreality. In June of 1901, for example, the leader of the Liberal opposition party in Britain, replied to someone's question, "When is a war not a war?" with the answer, "When it is carried on by methods of barbarism in South Africa" (qtd. in Spies 9). According to historian S. B. Spies, the barbaric British methods the leader was referring to were "the devastation of the country and the [use of the] concentration camp system" (9). Like the complete evacuation of the Old Port and the roundups in Marseilles by the Franco-German regime, the British leaders Roberts and Kitchener cleared an entire civilian population by using concentration camps alongside their infamous "Scorched Earth" policy of burning farms.[41] Tens of thousands of Boer civilians were put in concentration camps by the British, and, in effect, the camps functioned as extermination camps due to meager rations, deplorable hygiene, and punitive policies of deprivation directed at the interned wives and children of Boer militants. Over 100,000 Black Africans, too, were interned and perished in the camps, even though they were not officially hostile enemies (Spies 256–266). In the end, tens of thousands of Boers, mostly women and children, died, sparking international outrage (Spies 215–216).

In the memoir, Stein connects these atrocities to her own contemporary wartime experience, as well as that of Europeans more broadly, by topical and textual association. "The concentration camps for the Boers excited us all, nobody knew then how everybody was finally that is everybody in Europe was finally not going to have anything to eat," she writes (44). Not only have concentration camps become a weapon in the current war, reminding her of the Boers' experience, but Stein is shocked that the Boer camps could ever have been thought to presage the current shortages faced outside of concentration camps.

As these passages suggest, Stein communicates her Jewish experience of persecution in the memoir by contextual and associative means. The "semantic landscape" situates the account of her threatened internment as inseparable from the internments, imprisonments, and deportations that now affect almost all sectors of France or Europe or had afflicted civilians in other wars during Stein's lifetime. And yet, paradoxically, in Stein's cosmology, the history of this kind of persecution is metaphorically Jewish. A few pages after narrating her threatened internment, Stein recalls the Dreyfus Affair as a seminal experience she had of fully understanding, however vicariously, the reality of imprisonment. Though Stein omits mention of her own Jewish identity in discussing internment, by referencing the Dreyfus Affair she suggests the specifically Jewish character of the uncertainty and persecutions afflicting almost everyone under the Occupation.

A Strange Delusion: Antisemitism, Dreyfus, and the Reality of Imprisonment

In *Wars I Have Seen*, Stein considers the Dreyfus Affair as a shorthand for antisemitism and unwarranted imprisonment in France. She reflects that the Dreyfus Affair had once prompted the same feelings of strangeness she feels now that she has been threatened with internment and now that imprisonment has become a reality for so many people around her.[42] Her memory of the Dreyfus Affair sparks a long disquisition on antisemitism and the *unreality* of its rationales, concatenating "unreality" and Jewish experience. In the passage, Stein roots the scapegoating and persecuting of Jews in economic theories of antisemitism. She dubs these theories "a strange delusion." Taking a polemical posture, she debunks the rationales for antisemitism as fictions publicized for political gain.

She begins her disquisition quixotically with an ironical thanksgiving for the persistence of antisemitism, whose staying power, like other outdated ideologies, Stein bemoans throughout the memoir. The passage reads:

> And then the next thing was the Dreyfus affair, that is anti-semitism, and that is a very strange thing in connection with mediaevalism and nineteenth century and how a century is so hard to kill, anything is so hard to kill, thank heaven.
> He can read acasias, hands and faces. Acasias are for the goat, and

the goat gives milk, very necessary these days and hands and faces are hands and faces, and dreams when one is dancing and falls asleep are real, and all this has this to do with anti-semitism that it is true and not real and real and not true.

Through and through.

There is a strange delusion.

Before industrialism Jews were international bankers and before that international money-lenders, but since industrialism, all the Jewish money in the world is only a drop in the bucket and all of it together could never buy anybody to make war or make peace, not a bit. The Rothschilds in the Napoleonic wars and just after, were the end of the Jewish financial houses. After that began industrialism and in that the Jews have never been an economical power as anybody knows who knows and as everybody knows who knows. But the European particularly the countries who like to delude their people do not want to know it, they must know it of course, anybody must know it, and the Jews do not want anybody to know it, although they know it perfectly well they must know it because it would make themselves to themselves feel less important and as they always as the chosen people have felt themselves to themselves to be important they do not want anybody to know it. But of course everybody must know it, the big names in industrialism and in the financing of industrialism are not in any modern country Jewish and everybody must know it but nobody wants to know it, because everybody likes it to be as it was supposed to be and not as it was because nobody likes anything to disappear, and as for so many hundreds of years it was so and of course religion does get mixed up with it but as it is not any longer possible to keep it strictly a religious question, and complicate life with Christianity, so it is inevitable that they all want to go on believing what they know is not so, and it was first made real for me by the Dreyfus trial and now from Germany who is so desperately clinging to any past century, any past century is a hope and a force any past century even any present century, they [like] to cling to a century and what that century stood for, they have thus to keep themselves together, and so anti-semitism which has been with us quite a few centuries is still something to cling to. . . . Anyway financially there is no sense in anti-semitism. That is what I say. (55–56)

In recalling the Dreyfus Affair, Stein reflects that nationalist political rhetoric has scapegoated Jews as economic parasites in Europe. Stein introduces the topic by abruptly mentioning a goat, which as Dydo suggests, may figure the biblical scapegoat (Malcolm 82). The material reality of the goat who "reads" only what is right in front of him, be it people's hands or faces or the acasias he is fed, contrasts with the more ethereal scapegoats of antisemitism that Stein probes in this passage. The Jews may have played a role in international finance, especially "before industrialism," but Stein insists that since then Jews have not been a significant power in the economy, and to think so is a "strange delusion." Like hearing news of the roundups in Marseilles, which are "so real to [Stein] that it is a dream" (11), the shocking revelation of antisemitic ideology resembles a surreal experience of when "dreams . . . are real" (55).

Stein imagines that despite its propagandistic sources, the "strange delusion" of antisemitism is a barely conscious motor driving European society. This unconscious morality, she observes, resembles having "dreams when one is dancing and falls asleep" (55). The comparison recalls the "walking marathon" Stein saw in Chicago during her 1934 lecture tour where contestants were "more clinging than moving" (*EA* 209).[43] Stein suggests that, like the couples able to walk in their sleep by clinging to one another, contemporary German antisemites "like to cling to a century and what that century stood for, they have thus to keep themselves together" (*WIHS* 56).[44] Above all, Stein seems keen on exposing antisemitism as a tool for governments who rule by deceit.

Stein suggests that economic rationales for antisemitism have served the propagandistic narratives of corrupt governments and the communal self-concept of Jews. In the tradition of her first protagonists who complain that others refuse to "see things as they are," she argues that both non-Jews and Jews have had a stake in perpetuating the fallacy of Jewish "economical power. . . . because everybody likes it to be as it was supposed to be and not as it was" (*WIHS* 56). She believes that Jews maintain antisemitic fallacies of their essential difference to sustain the notion that they are "the chosen people." Her mention of this iconic notion, furthermore, confirms the Jews' success in sustaining a reputation for singularity.[45]

The notability of the Jews as a people of repute may, however, be a worrisome source of admiration. Later in the memoir, Stein hypothesizes that German propagandists are envious of the Jews' success in creating and publicizing a lasting reputation for themselves. She writes:

> Publicity, that is what we hear them say publicity, and is not that the real meaning of persecution, publicity, it is not nearly as complicated as it seems. There always has been a great passion for publicity in the world the very greatest passion for publicity, and those who succeed best, who have the best instincts for publicity, do have a great tendency to be persecuted that is natural enough, and here I think is the real basis of the persecution of the chosen people and just now more than ever because as publicity is more and more a conscious process those who have the greatest instinct for publicity are naturally those of whom the others who would want to be masters of publicity are jealous, at least I do think so, and perhaps yes. (165)

In concert with her notion that Jews epitomize modernism, Stein arrives at the tragically ironic theory that Germany's antisemitic propaganda exposes their resentful indebtedness to Jews, who they consider to be paragons of publicity. Stein frequently heard German propaganda on the radio and deemed it hateful, childish, and heavy-handed.[46] She writes the passage on publicity during "Easter week," historically a time for pogroms, and views the current persecutions through the lens of this past violence (165). She does not blame Jews for antisemitism, as Janet Malcolm suggests, but strives to make sense of an otherwise nonsensical phenomenon (Malcolm 94). Stein had earlier wondered what else could explain such a "funny thing" as how "a nation that feels itself as strong as the Germans . . . [could] be afraid of a small handful of people like the Jews" (114). However, in her wavering conclusion—"at least I do think so, and perhaps yes"—we hear Stein's discomfort in her claim that publicity-envy is "the basis of the persecution" of Jews by Germans.

In Stein's semantic clusters, anti-Jewish persecutions join a larger German war of aggression, making "anybody" and "everybody" in Europe into a Jew. Around the long passages on Stein's threatened internment and "the Dreyfus affair, that is anti-semitism," she clusters anecdotes concerning the literal and figurative imprisonment of friends, neighbors, and other people she meets. Given Dreyfus's iconic status as wrongly imprisoned Frenchman and Jew, Stein implicitly characterizes *as Jewish* the widespread fears felt by French people vulnerable to imprisonments, denunciations, and retributions. By generalizing Dreyfus's imprisonment and, relatedly, the long history of Jewish vulnerability to persecution in Europe, Stein Judaizes her own threatened internment and the current French experience of being terrorized by deportations and imprisonments under the Occupation.

Like "the chosen people," Stein believes that "anybody" in France might be singled out and imprisoned. In the passages immediately preceding her disquisition on antisemitism and shortly following her account of threatened internment, she reflects: "And now in 1943 the large part of the men of a whole nation are in prison. Prisoners, prison. . . . Anybody can be a prisoner now" (54). The pronoun "anybody," in its liminal position between the plural referentiality of "any" and the singularity connoted by a "body," conveys the individual suffering felt during an occupation that blankets everyone with uncertainty. This pronoun, as an emotional barometer of the larger condition, echoes the finale of Joyce's "The Dead," when Gabriel pessimistically reflects on the paralytic state of his own heart and of his entire country by agreeing with "the newspapers" that "snow was general all over Ireland" (*Dubliners* 152). When a particular plight becomes "general," it is a surreal phenomenon and, for Stein, the shocking estrangement of the Occupation, its "funny" reality, seems no different than a mass imprisonment. Shortly before reporting her threatened internment, she remarks (in dialogue cited in part earlier in the chapter), "It is funny funny in the sense of strange and peculiar and unrealisable, the fact that so many are prisoners, prisoners, prisoners every where" (47). In the later play *Yes Is for a Very Young Man*, Stein has a character compare post-Armistice France to a national imprisonment, "we are all in prison, every Frenchman is in prison . . . every Frenchman in France is in prison" (3–4).

Stein's writings about imprisonment are not solely empathic perceptions but also documentary observations. At the time of the armistice, there were two million French prisoners of war in Germany, a statistic she has one of her characters recite in *Yes Is for a Very Young Man*. Though the number of POWs went down by a fourth during the Occupation, the number of non-Jewish people detained increased, whether sent to labor in Germany as part of the STO or as part of the Chantiers de la Jeunesse, a mandatory months-long training camp for young men of military age, which Stein refers to as the "camp de Jeunesse" (*WIHS* 47).[47] "Even those who are only in a training camp feel themselves to be prisoners," Stein notes, based on a letter from her young gardener (54). Those who refused to serve in these corps were imprisoned or, to avoid arrest, hid in the hills, where they were vulnerable to denunciation. Stein protectively expresses concern for these "young men of twenty-one," or "the mountain boys," who often joined up with the Resistance, or *maquis* as they were called, after the hill shrubs they hid among (42, 142).[48] She avers that seemingly without cause, people expose the hiding places of STO-resisters: "some of these people have told where young men of twenty-one were hidden, and it was not necessary to tell they just did tell" (42).

Stein sees those around her imprisoned by suspicion and petty hatreds. She notes that "every neighbor is denouncing every neighbor, for black traffic, for theft, for this and for that, and there are so many being put in prison" (37).[49] Denunciations in turn bring about retaliation, whether in the form of death threats, such as the "little coffins that are being sent to all pro-Germans," or in outright assassinations, as in the case of her neighbor's cousin who was shot for "denouncing his neighbors" (48, 92). Stein concludes, then, that Frenchmen are fighting an internecine war on the home front that complicates the already complicated process of determining friend from enemy under foreign occupation.

The general nature of suspicion and betrayal now reminds Stein of another seminal moment in her own history. At age fifteen, reading a James Fenimore Cooper revolutionary war novel, she realized that enemies could exist and might even be indistinguishable from friends. Cooper's book, she recalls, "made me understand that you could think that some one was devoted to you and loyal to you and really not at all they were opposed to you and would if such a thing were necessary denounce you. And now and again in June 1943 it is happening all around one" (41). The unknowable character of identity Stein had discovered when reading Cooper is common to her experience of the present Occupation where nobody reveals his true colors.

With his fiction, Cooper had awakened Stein to the unsettling possibility that "It is hard to know about enemies" (38). The present war confirms this notion, as when Stein later recalls encountering two German officers, one who resembles a friend (Hemingway) and another an enemy (Goering). She first sees a "good-looking" German officer in a café who looks strikingly like the young Hemingway (118). The resemblance suggests the betrayals possible with friends and the friendships possible with enemies since, in his youth, Hemingway had been Stein's great friend, while the older Hemingway had not been. Later in a tea shop, she sees a German officer who looks like Goering, and yet, since he is *not* Goering, his qualitative status as an enemy is called into question: either the officer is a terrible enemy, as the resemblance to Goering suggests, or he is not an enemy because the resemblance makes Stein aware of the fact that that officer cannot be Goering, since "surely he would not be there drinking chocolate too" (119). Cooper's fictional war is now her reality, for, as Stein observes, "now it is not certain that enemies are what they seem" (34).

Stein further exposes the unreal ambiguity between friend and enemy with a dramatic sighting of German soldiers, which she recalls in the cluster on imprisonment. She mourns the imprisonment of her adopted countrymen, and yet, it seems to her that the occupiers, too, suffer a kind of imprisonment. "Now we have a feeling" she notes, "that they who put everybody in prison are now in prison they feel themselves in prison, they feel imprisoned" (47). Stein sees, for example, an unreal show of debility by the German army at the train station at Aix-les-Bains. As a train moves slowly through the station, she and "all the French people" witness the passage of German soldiers, mostly unclothed, seated atop tanks and trucks, "which did not look very strong, as they were not armored" (47). The surreal quality of the scene, which directly precedes the account of Stein's threatened internment, is not, however, the revelation that the Germans are humanized by their near nakedness. The French onlookers shock Stein by studiously ignoring the beleaguered display: "and the train went on slowly and all the French people were as if they were at a theatre that was not interesting" (47). In Stein's vignette, the French desire uncomplicated beliefs about their enemies despite what passes directly before their eyes. Like those who believe the rationales for antisemitism, despite all evidence of fictitiousness, the French, Stein complains, refuse to see the humanity of their occupiers and "want to go on believing what they know is not so" (56).

The only exceptions to this purposeful avoidance are some young men of military age, "from the camp de Jeunesse," who laugh at the passing German soldiers (47). The image recalls Stein's anecdote about Pétain's curt remark to the joking young officers that war was not funny. She later underscores the horror of such passivity and frivolity by joining the fate of the young men of twenty-one with either "enemies"—or Jewish deportees—in another frightening scene of trains passing through stations.

In the later scene, Stein again expresses the painful uncertainty of knowing friend from enemy, amidst a pages-long cluster on the young men of twenty-one, or "mountain boys." It is early 1944, and hearing that the local police will be trying to force out of hiding the "mountain boys" who had become part of the *maquis* or Resistance, Stein reports that people mourn the loss of national unity that has put their children in mortal danger. "There is preparing an effort," she writes, "to round up the mountain boys and as everybody's boys are there it is rather horrible" (142). The townspeople anxiously await the arrival of the American forces to "save the boys" from being shot by their own countrymen (142). Stein sees that "Everybody is unhappy and ashamed, ashamed because French are arresting Frenchmen" (142). Her neighbors are in turmoil over the uncertain fate of their sons at the hands of their neighbors. Identity has become monstrously unstable; nobody is who they seemed.

Stein deepens the horror of an already grim event by the macabre mention of trains passing, which some critics read as referring to the deportations of Jews. The second part of the passage, quoted below, repeats the opening plaint about everybody being ashamed, except this time Frenchmen are betraying Frenchmen *who are not French*:

> Everybody is ashamed, everybody is crying, everybody is listening to everything and the trains go on, with Germans who are not Germans and French who are not French, oh dear me, there is no nineteenth century about this, hardly the twentieth century, it is terribly the middle ages. (142)

For the townspeople, there is the shame of national betrayal with the rounding up of the mountain boys, "because French are arresting Frenchmen." Here, Stein illuminates a further betrayal involving nationality by negating the initial formulation. She refers to the people on trains as "Germans who are not Germans and French who are not French." She may be continuing to report on the mountain boy roundups, which might cast the French police as "Germans who are not Germans" because they are rounding up "French who are not French" as deserters and resisters. As Lesinska suggests, however, Stein may be "cryptically" recording the deportations of Jews in this passage (47). "Germans who are not Germans" may refer to the thousands of recent Jewish refugees from German lands and "French who are not French" may refer to Jews who had been in France for decades but have recently been deemed "not French." Stein refers to French Jewish refugees in a similar manner, when describing the numerous refugees in Culoz, which included "lots of Jews French and every other kind," a phrasing that acknowledges their French nationality while also indicating their not-French-ness by naming them first as Jews (111). In this scenario, "the trains go on" with German and French Jews stripped of German and French identities. Such deportees have been betrayed by their adopted governments and countrymen, just like the "mountain boys" being hunted by their own countrymen.

Stein's bitter conclusion to the passage—"It is terribly the middle ages"—casts the deportations and roundups as akin to the medieval persecution of antisemitism, to which, in Stein's view, the Germans cling. More generally, she notes the impermanence and uncertainty of premodern European life that now "terribly" plagues everyone once more. As I discuss below, Stein had similarly lamented the drafting of young men of the STO in this vein: "it is just like the middle ages, they are carried off from them in their midst" (86). These medieval home front horrors afflict "everyone's boys" and "lots of Jews French and every other kind" and, ironically, they expose the painful modernity—with the traversing trains—of the war's reach even "here in a little town in France" (143).

Jews and Everybody: "Refugeed Anywhere in Any Small Place"

If Dreyfus represents the modern image of a singular and Jewish vulnerability to imprisonment, the refugee crises of the 1930s and the successive waves of Jewish roundups, deportations, and expulsions across Europe in the 1940s turns Jews into symbols of refugeeism.[50] Stein notes this conjoining of Jews and refugees in her memoir, but the idea was widespread. Samuel Beckett biographer James Knowlson describes how refugees from many nations were "known collectively as 'les Juifs'" in the small town of Roussillon, where Beckett sought refuge during the war (320). Beckett was living near Avignon, about two hundred miles south of Stein. Maren Linett, writing on Londoner Virginia Woolf, shows how Woolf's characters fuse Jews and refugees. In *Between the Acts* begun in April 1938 Woolf's audience members comment: "'And what about the Jews? The refugees . . . the Jews . . . People like ourselves, beginning life again . . . '" (qtd. in Linett 94).

With a cluster of writings about refugees in the memoir, Stein substantiates her impression that the singular has become generalized. Hence her quip in December 1943 that "There are so many refugees, roughly speaking one might say everybody is a refugee" (111). She suggests the Jewish character of being a refugee when she lists international refugees and internally displaced French people, both non-Jews and Jews:

> nearly everybody certainly every city, town village and hamlet has its refugees, and plenty of them, this Culoz, is a little town of two thousand inhabitants and there are lots of them, Alsatians and Lorrainers and Poles and Americans, several besides us, working people that somehow are Americans and any town is like that and French quite a few French and Belgians, and anything else and lots of Persians so the Swiss Consul told us. . . .

And twice, as the passage continues, she repeats her quip that "everybody is a refugee":

> anyway everybody is a refugee and it is a puzzle a considerable puzzle how everybody goes on living and spending money and looking fairly well fed and well clothed it is a puzzle, and then of course there are lots of Jews French and every other kind refugeed anywhere in any small place and then young men who do not want to go to forced labor and they change their town oh dear everybody is a refugee and how do they go on spending money and being fairly well dressed and well fed how do they. (111)

In Stein's account, Jewish refugees are particularly vulnerable to imprisonment and deportation, as the region is "of course" suffused with Jews precariously and perhaps not-so-clandestinely "refugeed anywhere in any small place."

Stein suggests, too, that refugee experiences have become commonplace.[51] She pairs refugeed Jews, for example, with gentiles who have had to relocate for fear of imprisonment, such as the STO-evaders "who do not want to go to forced labor and . . . change their town." H. R. Kedward, historian of the French Resistance, confirms the vital significance of this pairing, since STO resisters often found shelter in places that had reputations as "willing reception centres" for hiding Jews (20).

Inextricable from the widespread notion that being a refugee was a Jewish condition was the antisemitism of anti-refugee sentiment, something we also hear in Stein's account. She repeatedly asks about refugees, "how do they" seem to want for nothing, "spending money and looking fairly well fed and well clothed," perhaps insinuating that their means of sustenance may be ill-gotten. For Stein, this "puzzle" is particularly Jewish, and she sandwiches her mention of the Jewish refugees of Culoz between two iterations of her question, "how do they." As Marrus and Paxton report, among refugees in the Unoccupied Zone, "Jews were insistently singled out for particular suspicion and hostility" and, close to Stein's region, "Jews were considered 'synonymous' with the black market" (182, 183).[52]

While Stein may rehearse antisemitic sentiments in puzzling out how refugees survive, she may also be expressing awe and appreciation that so many refugees are somehow provided for. This latter interpretation is supported by her clustering of the paragraph on how "everybody is a refugee," beside an account of how she and Toklas were helped with their "trouble about money" by an unexpected source (111, 112). A discussion follows of the secret service, now the "resistance," and then her puzzling over the illogic of German antisemitism and her own position in France as a "favored stranger" (113, 114). Her "favored" status affords her the means to travel by train. The semantic cluster on being a refugee includes the episode quoted above, when the ticket sellers at the train station look out for Stein and Toklas and one buys her book, leading her to conclude, "I am a writer and so the French people take care of me" (119). Looking back, we can read Stein's "puzzle" over the Jewish refugees as a marveling that despite living under two antisemitic regimes, many French people unexpectedly took care of Jews.[53]

Stein explicitly casts her own lot as an American and not as a Jew in the passage about refugees.[54] She notes of American refugees that there were "several besides us." However, she may implicitly be suggesting that she is a Jewish refugee by testifying, in the next paragraph, to her own experience of getting by, explaining "Take our case." Her "case" reveals an underground economy of friendship, favor, and protection between French and refugee. When she faced financial hardship, cut off from her US-based income, a new neighbor, a young silk manufacturer from Lyon who "was interested in literature," insisted on loaning Stein money until she could find other resources (112).[55] "Life is funny," she offers once again, considering that the unreality of the situation is reflected in its illogic (112). Her "good-fortune" comes, funnily, from new acquaintances, not from old friends. Like the uncertainty of distinguishing friend from enemy, "You never can tell who is going to help you," she concludes: "that is a fact" (111).

Among refugees, however, Stein and Toklas are distinguished—and symbolically Jewish—as chosen people with a special allowance to move more freely than other "strangers" who "are supposed to stay more or less in [their] commune" (114). Borrowing from the French *étranger*, which means *foreigner*, Stein admits that she and Toklas are "rather favored strangers" (114).[56] The singularity of such "favor" (with no indication of its source) may distinguish Stein and Toklas as chosen people among "strangers" and, simultaneously, render them indistinguishable from the nonrefugeed French, at least in terms of regional mobility.[57]

The apparent indistinguishability of Jews or other refugees may have been utilized by some Vichy officials to protect Jews. Stein tells the story of a Parisian Jew whose life was spared by a Vichy official who refused to mark the woman's papers without "proof" of her Jewishness. In Stein's telling, the official appears to relish protecting a famous "Parisienne" by flouting Vichy regulations about Jewish identity.[58] She writes:

> Speaking of all this there is this about a Jewish woman, a Parisienne, well known in the Paris world. She and her family took refuge in Chambery when the persecutions against the Jews began in Paris. And then later, when there was no southern zone, all the Jews were supposed to have the fact put on their carte d'identité and their food card, she went to the prefecture to do so and the official whom she saw looked at her severely Madame he said, have you any proof with you that you are a Jewess, why no she said, well he said if you have no actual proof that you are a Jewess, why do you come and bother me, why she said I beg your pardon, no he said I am not interested unless you can prove you are a Jewess, good day he said and she left. It was she who told the story. Most of the French officials were like that really like that. (243–244)

As suggested by the official's repetition of the phrase, "you are a Jewess," the woman's ability to hide in plain sight requires his "official" cooperation. Although earlier in the memoir Stein pessimistically decries government officials for persecuting people by mindlessly carrying out orders, now, perhaps feeling hopeful about the end of the war, she deems this official's behavior exemplary.

Maquis as Metaphor: Jewish by Association

Some critics note the biographical parallels between Stein and the Jewish "Parisienne" refugeed in Chambery.[59] And yet, with the self-portrait she sketches in the memoir, Stein links herself more closely to the *maquis*.

Near the end of the war when the German occupiers retreat, she reports that the "maquis or mountain boys" come down from the hills to be honored by the townspeople for their efforts in the Resistance (209). Also honored are those who, like the rule-bending Vichy official in Chambery, covertly supported the Resistance in their everyday jobs. Stein admiringly dubs these people *maquis*, too, as she explains:

> there were another lot of affiliated but not fighting maquis. I like to call them maquis, that was what they were, when every moment was a danger, they had to receive arms they had to transport them and they had to hide them and they had to do sabotage and all the time a very considerable part of their countrymen did not at all believe in them, and there they were workmen, station masters, civil servants, tailors, barbers, anything, nobody knew but they naturally[.] (237–238)

As a writer, Stein identifies herself with these *maquis* hiding in plain sight, working alone, and suffering the skepticism of "a very considerable part of their countrymen." The hidden *maquis* sound like a clandestine version of Adele's frustrated experience in *Q.E.D.*, as an "apostl[e] . . . rejected by the class whose cause I preach" (59). And, in fact, Stein's depiction of the "affiliated but not fighting maquis" echoes her depiction of the modern Jewish writer, the Brother Singular, also a solitary actor in a larger fraternity, making Stein's portrait of the solitary *maquis* Jewish by association.

In the memoir, Stein casts herself as a Jeremiah: She depicts herself as a rhetorical *maquis* fighting Pétain's and Hitler's antisemitisms. She portrays herself battling Pétain's persecutions in the voices of scientists, prophets, and Americans. She also takes up literary arms against Hitler's antisemitism in the role of a gangster-like assassin. And yet she depicts her resistance as having broader, modernizing aims, since she sees Hitler's medieval antisemitism as slowing the progress of European civilization.

In a cluster of several conversations about Pétain (pp. 81 to 93), Stein depicts herself as an opponent of an illogical Pétainism. When countering the "mixed up" ideas of her former hero's adherents, however, manners sometimes mute Stein's rage, or she brings in surrogates to speak her mind (92). She nonetheless plainly shows herself countering Pétain's view that order and discipline are much needed in France. That claim, she notes, was shared by a "crazy man" in the previous war (81).[60]

She argues instead that the French desire order in theory but not in practice. For example, when "pleasantly" greeting a "nice" retired civil servant spraying his potato plants with disinfectant, something she notes "everybody" does, she is met with the complaint that more people would disinfect their potato plants "if there was more order in the country" (82). Stein is quietly indignant: "I was polite but I wanted to say oh Hell, you all feel you are in prison because you are always being ordered" (82). For Stein, the potato planter's rhetoric of order is completely divorced from reality and serves as a pretext for persecution. With this internal retort Stein suggests that the Pétainists hold up orderliness as a national characteristic to be maintained by disinfecting or weeding out foreigners from France, a subtle criticism of Pétain's persecutions.[61]

While manners—or fear—rein in her rhetoric on the road, Stein shows herself freely criticizing Pétain among neighbors. She recounts trying to reason with one neighbor, who is a "mixed up" Pétainist (92). Stein admonishes her: "I always say you can have any government you like but those who take to the sword will perish by the sword and if you persecute you will be persecuted" (92). Stein adapts a syllogistic line from the New Testament to expose the illogic of hatreds like antisemitism.[62] She later makes it explicit that her epigram articulates a Newtonian social order where "action and reaction are equal and opposite, [so] that when you persecute people you always rouse them to be strong and stronger, as the French say, sugar attracts bees more quickly than vinegar" (162). The blend of religious, scientific, and folk rhetoric affirms Stein's portrayal of herself as an anti-Pétainist prophet. She spouts a *logical* gospel of disorder to a citizenry that needs constant reminders ("I always say") of the dangers of persecution. Stein punctuates the exchange with her neighbor by burying Pétain in obscurity. She reflects: "And all the time there is Petain, an old man a very old man and mostly nowadays everybody has forgotten all about him" (92).[63]

As a member of a famously persecuted people, Stein is "roused" to fight the persecutors, further Judaizing her role as a resister (162). In the last conversation in this anti-Pétainist cluster, Stein, with a kind of ventriloquism, "speaks" out against his antisemitism through the voices of Americans critical of Pétain's "persecuting." She retells the account of a visitor who had recently been to America: "it was in the end of '40, and they said they had just come from America and they had just seen Marechal Petain and Petain had wanted to know how they felt about him over there and the man answered and said they did not like his persecuting" (93). The visitor reported that Pétain protested, "as for free-masons I hate them, as for communists I am afraid of them, as for the Jews it is not my fault" (93). Pétain's alleged denial of blame for persecuting Jews points to an area of weakness that puts the lie to his sovereignty: he is only faultless if someone else is in charge. With this explicit mention of Pétain's antisemitism, Stein condemns his persecution of Jews. Pétain's petulant attempt to exculpate himself for persecuting Jews may confirm his withered stature, but France's statutory antisemitism and the related persecutions of Freemasons and communists remained very much alive through the end of the war.

As part of her rhetorical resistance, Stein records the many voices of those around her recounting familial experiences of displacement, imprisonment, and death to keep Pétain's persecutions of Freemasons, communists, and Jews palpably present by association. Like the "mediaeval misery" of "Jew baiting" that sprouted in England in the 1930s and Germany's current antisemitic "clinging to any past century," France's deportations and forced displacements of Jews and political targets are part of what Stein deems the medieval character of the war (122, 56). Stein rues the fact that now, in addition to Jews, Freemasons, and communists, "Anybody can be taken away. . . . anybody can be taken away . . . and perhaps never to come home again at any age and in any place" (84).

Like most of the memoir, the cluster on Pétain is peppered with lengthy anecdotes of forced displacement concerning the relatives of people Stein knows. Here Stein mentions someone's son who is a German prisoner (81), a son who goes into hiding on the mountain to escape military service (84), and a grandson sent to Germany as a forced laborer, about which Stein despairingly reports, "they do not even say oh dear, it is just like the middle ages, they are carried off from them in their midst, and that is what is happening" (86). She also reports the large desertions by those sent to forced labor in Germany (89) and the assassination of her "neighbor's cousin," who was an escaped prisoner (91). Near the beginning of the memoir, Stein mourns the deportations in Marseilles, which were "so real to me that it is a dream, *not that I know any of them*" (11, emphasis added). In the cluster of conversations about Pétain, in contrast, Stein condemns Pétain by exposing the nightmarishly quotidian violence of deportation and desertion striking *French people she knew*.

In the cluster on Pétain, Stein depicts herself as a victorious debater pithily illuminating the irrationality of supporting German aggression.

By showing herself in conversations criticizing Germany, Stein makes it clear to readers that her opposition to Hitler was longstanding, logical, and passionately held. In late 1943, for example, Stein recalls her habit, from the beginning of the Occupation, of "pretty violently and pretty often" questioning the pro-German sentiments of her adopted countrymen (81). In another conversation, she challenges those who claim to welcome German-wrought "misery and oppression" over Russian or English rule (82). She goes on to ask whether they would fight side by side with the Germans but "that conversation ended" because, as Stein implies, they have recognized the foolishness of where such positions would lead them (82).

In addition to Stein's anti-Pétainist and anti-Hitlerian conversational combat, she enlists more "violent" means of voicing dissent when fighting Hitler's antisemitism and occupation (81). She portrays herself as a modern Jewish literary assassin of Hitler. As described above, in 1934 Stein condemned Hitler for "driving out the Jews" from Germany (*NYT* SM9). By 1943, in *Wars I Have Seen*, she refers to his Germany's antisemitism as a "desperat[e] clinging to any past century" and calls Hitler the "embodiment [and] the most persistent end of" that century (56, 16). As a modern writer, Stein asserts, "I so naturally had my part in killing the nineteenth century and killing it dead, quite like a gangster with a mitraillette, if that is the same as a tommy gun" (91). Comparing herself to an American gangster toting an automatic rifle, Stein boasts that her writing has contributed to the historical succession of Hitler and the nineteenth century.[64] She depicts herself as Hitler's assassin, using her writing metaphorically to eliminate his antisemitic persecutions and end the war.

To be clear, I am not trying to portray Stein as a war hero, but I am showing that she portrays herself this way. Stein portrays her lethal literary efforts as those of a *maquisard*, boyishly playing her part as a modern writer against the Germans, much like "the little boys in the villages," who, as the Germans retreat, mimic their weaponry with "what they called tommy guns in gangster stories" (217). Gangsters, bandits, outlaws, and terrorists were all part of the popular imagery (often accusatory) given the *maquis*, so it is no surprise that, as Stein observes, French boys would fantasize and play out "gangster stories" against the Germans. One such "gangster," interviewed in Marcel Ophüls's 1969 documentary, *The Sorrow and the Pity*, remembered that being in the resistance meant being castigated as "terrorists . . . ['Or bandits,' adds his friend.] Yes, bandits. . . . Some even called us profiteers." Stein expresses fierce criticism of those who denigrate the *maquis*. She condemns as collaborators those "who say they are gangsters" and uses her rhetorical weaponry to portray the *maquis*—and her own writing efforts on their behalf—as heroic (133).[65]

Early in the war, Stein may have honored Pétain by translating his speeches and portraying him as George Washington. But as the memoir details, she replaces the old general with young bandits, Robin Hood and his Merry Men, switching her allegiance from Pétain to the *maquis* as icons of freedom. "Around here it is getting to be just like Robin Hood," she offers, admiringly casting the *maquis* as outlaws working for the common people (133). Stein and "everybody" support these "young men in the mountains" who, even as they steal great quantities of butter and pigs from local farms, "are so young so gay so disciplined and they have so much money, presumably English and American gold and everybody is pleased" (133). By January 1944, the brazen trespasses of the *maquis* seem a sign of imminent liberation and, as Stein recalls, collectively inspire—or are excused—as the necessary thefts of national heroes.

As a memoirist, Stein portrays herself heroically by associating herself with the *maquis*.[66] And, by portraying herself as an intellectual resister, a pen-wielding, modernism-writing, nonfighting *maquis*, she also portrays herself as a Jew. Her ongoing concern with antisemitism in the memoir conveys her experience of the Jewish question as inextricably linked to other pressing concerns in occupied France and wartime Europe. In her own cosmology, her modern writing about Jews and non-Jews in the war heroically contributes to the process of making European culture more Jewish. She had long considered herself to be writing the latest chapter in the "peaceful Oriental penetration into European culture" (*EA* 21).

The word "peaceful" in Stein's phrase is not to be dismissed as merely playful alliteration. Despite her deployment of metaphorical weaponry as Hitler's assassin, Stein's ideal heroes are the "affiliated but *not fighting* maquis" (*WIHS* 237, emphasis added). Above all, she wants the war to end. She wants peace. And while she wants the *maquis* to be successful in battling the Germans and acknowledges the necessity of many of their trespasses, she grimly reports on the gravity—and violence—of the *maquis*' labors as soldiers of the resistance. She mourns the deadly cycle of denunciation and retaliation that has torn apart small towns and recognizes the culpability of the *maquis* for theft, threats of violence, and even murder ("the little coffins that are being sent to all pro-Germans"

[48]). The uncertain social fabric of the Occupation has violently trapped civilians between occupiers and resisters, and Stein narrates their sense of helplessness:

> Everybody says and that too does sound so like the middle ages, we are between two armed forces, the mountain boys shoot if you do not do what they say, and the Germans shoot if you do not do what they say, and what can you do, each side blames us if we do what the other side tells us to do but what can we do. And indeed what can they do. (147)

Stein's exasperated rejoinder, "what can they do," expresses her shared sense of frustration. Like the nonfighting hidden *maquis*, Stein as a memoirist has been trying to bury a Pétain whose peace through armistice has not been peaceful. She has been trying write an end to Hitler and to the war. The unreality of the Occupation, where international conflict has turned intranational, again strikes her as primitive, and she complains again that it is "so like the middle ages." But maybe medieval problems require medieval solutions.

Stein portrays herself as hopeful about the war's end, thanks to her readings of the prophesies of Saint Odile, who lived from 662 to 720. The Alsatian Odile described a violent world war and the rise and fall of a German invader in France.[67] Stein's Odile-studying self-portrait in the memoir continues from the protagonist of *Mrs. Reynolds*, who was also a devotee of Saint Odile.[68] One character in the novel asserts: "The Jews . . . are good prophets," perhaps referring to Mrs. Reynolds's prophecy-backed certainty about the imminent demise of the Hitleresque antagonist Angel Harper (313). This statement stands in contrast to the narrator's portrayal of Harper as someone who "knew he was no Jew" (97). Stein's Hitler in *Mrs. Reynolds* is not just anti-Jewish but is the opposite of a Jew. Stein's Hitler in *Wars I Have Seen* is also the opposite of a Jew. He is antimodern, as evinced by his medieval antisemitism and his mortal vulnerability to Stein's modern Jewish writing.

Stein cements the depiction of Hitler as the opposite of a Jew by also showing him to be the opposite of a "good prophet." Here we see Stein come full circle: she portrays Hitler as a leader believed by his people, though they shouldn't. That makes him the opposite of a Jeremiah. In the memoir, Stein recalls a Parisian dinner party in 1935 when she proclaimed that as an Austrian, "it was Hitler's intention to destroy Germany" (*WIHS*

231). She remembers that her audience "all thought that I was only trying to be bright but not at all,"—and here Stein returns to the present moment, sadly vindicated, to report—"it is true" (231).[69] Stein thus portrays herself as truth-teller who was disbelieved. Now, a decade later, her vision tragically has become reality. Her retelling of the story, in August 1944, appears toward the end of the memoir and toward the end of the war. With the Allies closing in and "the German army . . . beginning to mutiny," Stein hears that Hitler still refuses to surrender because "the civilian population still stupidly believes in victory" (230). Ruefully, Stein writes that her prophecy has come true as the Austrian Hitler, "the foreign monster," leads Germany to destruction:

> It is the judgment of Solomon over again, there is the call of the blood, but funnily enough the foreign monster has a glamor for the nation he is destroying that a home grown monster could not have. And so Hitler is quite comfortably waiting for the last battalion to fight and win or be killed, presumably killed but he has made them all feel like that because he is a foreigner and not a German, it is the other way to of a prophet not being recognised in his own country. (231)

With the allusion to the fabled judgment of King Solomon, Stein levies her own Jewish judgment and casts Hitler's abandonment of German troops as akin to infanticide. To Stein, it is ironic that this murderous Hitler is heeded by those he sacrifices because of his "glamor" as a "foreign monster." Hitler appears to Stein as the antithesis of Adele and her Brother Singulars, the Jewish outcasts from Stein's first fictions, whose experiences are like "a prophet not being recognised in his own country." Her condemnation of Hitler's popularity as an antisemitic leader, as someone received "the other way to" of a prophet, reaffirms his medieval immorality and, in contrast, affirms the Jewishness of the modern in Stein's semiotics.

In presenting herself as a modern Jewish literary hero attacking German and French antisemitism, Stein reveals her associative methods of making meaning in the memoir. An elaborate network of associations (like the one she imagines connects the hidden *maquis*) conveys her concern for the plight of Jews in the war. This semantic clustering intertwines Stein's Jewish and non-Jewish concerns, reflecting her sense of the inseparability of Jewish and other persecutions. Her quotidian accounts document the uncertainty among French provincials, prisoners, refugees, Jews, Americans, enlisted men, forced laborers, and *maquis*, portraying an occupation that has turned the particularity of antisemitism into a general experience of persecution. By Judaizing the situation of occupation, Stein extrapolates from the experience of a famously persecuted people to indict the human rights violations suffered by so many during the war.

Conclusion

Making Sense of a Sensationally Jewish Stein

It's rare for the *New York Daily News* and Alan Dershowitz to weigh in on Gertrude Stein. But in 2012, the *Daily News* denounced Stein as a "Nazi Collaborator" when New York's Metropolitan Museum of Art presented "The Steins Collect: Matisse, Picasso, and the Parisian Avant-Garde," a combined exhibition of the art collections of Gertrude Stein and her siblings (Chesnoff). The tabloid demanded that the museum tell visitors that Stein had planted her feet "on the wrong side of history." On the heels of the denunciation, Dershowitz, a polemical Jewish chauvinist who is an emeritus law professor at Harvard, published in the *Huffington Post* his outrage concerning what he deemed the museum's gross omission of "the ugly truth" of Stein's "collaboration with Nazism during the German occupation of France." The author of *Chutzpah*, Dershowitz likes brash statements. He boiled Stein's survival down to "one simple reason": she was "a major collaborator with the Vichy regime and a supporter of its pro-Nazi leadership." Dershowitz pointed "a finger of blame" at Stein, declaring that she "made [the Holocaust] possible." He blamed her for surviving while "dozens of Jewish children were deported to death camps" from her town. Dershowitz cited Stein critic Barbara Will as his source for the shocking information that "Stein publicly proclaimed her admiration for Hitler during the 1930s, proposing him for a Nobel Peace Prize." Like Dershowitz, popular media outlets weighed in, similarly describing Stein's wartime affairs with hyperbole, insinuation, and provocation.[1] After a week, the *Daily News* was happy to report that the "Gertrude Stein Exhibit at the Met Will Now Allude to Her Hitler-loving Past and Collaboration with Vichy Regime" (Nazaryan).[2]

Stein's Jewish identity was at the center of the sensational debate over "The Steins Collect" exhibition.[3] Specifically, Stein's apparent antisemitism as an admirer and translator of Pétain and an alleged admirer of Hitler were taken as evidence of Stein's Nazism.[4] As Emily Greenhouse confessed in *The New Yorker*, "The fact that Gertrude Stein was a Jew herself likely makes it trickier to lambaste her efforts in support of the Vichy regime" ("Gertrude Stein and Vichy").[5] Critic Rachel Galvin warns against this all-too-common rhetorical "slippage between the concepts of fascism, Nazism, and Pétainism" regarding wartime cultural production in France ("Gertrude Stein, Pétain" 264). To fully understand Gertrude Stein as a Jewish writer, then, means correcting the depictions of Stein as a Nazi-loving Jew, depictions that inevitably suggest (or, in Dershowitz's case, state outright) that Stein was complicit in or supportive of the extermination of the Jews of Europe in Nazi death camps.

Stein did not know about the Final Solution extermination camps.[6] She lived through the war, wrote through the war and yet, like the majority of Jews in France, was spared deportation without being aware that she had been spared extermination in Nazi death camps. She and her French contemporaries did, of course, know that Jews were a persecuted and vulnerable population in Vichy and occupied France. Stein's writing about Jews during the war shows her concern about French, German, and English antisemitism and the subsequent surge of Jewish and other refugees in her small corner of France. She knew about roundups of Jews into French concentration camps and may have known about deportations to the East. But by December 15, 1944, when she returned to Paris from the south of France, Auschwitz was still not known—to Stein or the general public—as an extermination camp and part of Hitler's "Final Solution."[7] In what Susan Suleiman describes as "backshadowing . . . expecting a person in the past to have known what we know later," Auschwitz mistakenly colors our reading of Stein's wartime utterances (262). Stein is a "before Auschwitz" writer who is too often read by "after Auschwitz" audiences unaware that she did not know about Nazi death camps.

No Nobel for Hitler

Allegations about Stein's "Hitler-loving past" nonetheless fortified the uproar surrounding "The Steins Collect" exhibition as well as other exhibitions and moments of public discussion about Stein. Such allegations have no sound basis, but many of them draw on Will's *Unlikely Collaboration: Gertrude Stein, Bernard Faÿ, and the Vichy Dilemma*, published in 2011. Will colors her study of Stein's war years and writings with the claim that Stein admired Hitler. In her much-cited book and in interviews and articles about it, Will frames her argument for Stein's collaboration with the 1934 interview in which Stein told the *New York Times Magazine* that "Hitler should have received the Nobel Peace Prize" (qtd. in Will 71).[8] Will characterizes Stein's remarks about Hitler as "delivered bluntly" and complains that they "remain unexplained, unapologetic, and elliptical" (71). But while *Times* reporter Lansing Warren initially presents Stein's statement "bluntly," he goes on to report Stein's explanations of her comment about Hitler at great length, and it becomes clear that Stein's remark about Hitler is ironic.[9] As Charles Bernstein aptly quips, "Saying that Stein endorsed Hitler for the Nobel Prize in the 1934 interview is like saying that Mel Brooks includes a tribute to Hitler in *The Producers*" ("Gertrude Stein Taunts Hitler in 1934 and 1945").

Misreadings of Stein's 1934 pseudo-statement that "Hitler should have received the Nobel Peace Prize" may derive from Warren's opening gambit, which is reminiscent of our own era's "clickbait." In its first iteration, Stein's comment on Hitler is decontextualized and, juxtaposed with six other statements, made to seem nonsensical, since they are, as Warren explains, "culled from an hour's conversation with Miss Stein" (SM9). Warren assures *Times* readers that Stein is "ready to elucidate" and, after extensive scene setting and descriptions of Stein's dress and demeanor, he shares the first of her elucidations:

> "I say that Hitler ought to have the peace prize," she says, "because he is removing all elements of contest and of struggle from Germany. By driving out the Jews and the democratic and Left elements, he is driving out everything that conduces to activity. That means peace." (SM9)

Warren then quotes Stein's lengthy appreciation for American "activity" and her criticism of the inactivity of French theorizing and "Saxon" German obedience, criticisms that further contextualize her censure of Hitler:

> Intellectual fireworks are what excite [the French] and what they enjoy. They don't think ever of putting their ideas into practical life as we [Americans] are continually doing. . . .

The Saxon element is always destined to be dominated. The Germans have no gift at organizing. They can only obey. And obedience is not organization. Organization comes from community of will as well as community of action. And in America our democracy has been based on community of will and effort.

When I say government does not matter, I do not mean that it cannot have bad effects. I mean that any form of government may be good, and any form of government may be bad. What matters is competition, struggle, interest, activity that keeps a people alive and excited in accordance with the instincts which best provide excitement for the individual people.

. . . . It is true in politics, in literature, in art. Everything in life needs constant stimulation. It needs activity, new blood. (SM9, SM23)

Stein's criticism of the Germans asserts that their "destiny" to be "dominated" drives them to accept Hitler's leadership, however ruinous.[10] Like her complaint that by expelling "Jews and the democratic and Left elements," Hitler is removing the "contest and . . . struggle" vital to Germany, she again insists that "what matters is competition, struggle, interest, [and] activity." She attacks Hitler's "peace" as the equivalent of "death," since he is removing the "new blood" aroused by "activity" that "keeps a people alive." In this way, Stein condemns Hitler's antisemitism as notoriously antidemocratic and worthy of international condemnation. Her suggestion that Hitler should have received the Nobel Peace Prize uses irony to suggest that his policies should be recognized as historically barbarous.

Stein consistently and enthusiastically criticizes Hitler in her writings. In 1935, she again attacks the inactivity of "Hitlerism," which is "so dull and so unfertile" ("A Political Series" 76).[11] In *Everybody's Autobiography*, written in 1936 and published in 1937, Stein describes Hitler, in the words of her Austrian cook, as "a crazy Austrian," and includes him with Mussolini, Roosevelt, Stalin, Franco, American labor leader John L. Lewis, and French Prime Minister Léon Blum, as evidence of the era's painfully "depressing" penchant for "fathering" (303, 133). In *Paris France*, written in 1939 and published in 1940, Stein reprises the pathological language of the 1934 interview by suggesting, again with dark humor, that under Hitler, things in Germany persist in an "[un]healthy state":

> As always art is the pulse of a nation. I was just thinking of a good title for an art book. From Bismark [sic] to Hitler, any one can see that since 1870 and to 1939 Germany has had no art. When a country is in such a state that people who like to buy things can find nothing to buy there is something wrong. (63)

Finally, as I demonstrate in chapter 6, Stein, in her major wartime writings *Mrs. Reynolds* and *Wars I Have Seen*, depicts Hitler as a bloodthirsty monster whose death is eagerly anticipated, and compares him unfavorably to Napoleon in his attempt to conquer Europe.

Only one piece of questionable hearsay evidence suggests that Stein thought Hitler was a great man: the 1988 recollection by James Laughlin of a 1934 conversation Stein was alleged to have had with Faÿ celebrating Hitler. Laughlin would go on to become an important literary figure as a poet and the founder of New Directions Press. But in July of 1934, he was a nineteen-year-old college student—with serious interests in Stein and Pound—taking a European hiatus. He met Stein through a chance encounter with Faÿ, who finagled him an invitation to stay with her in Bilignin for a week. None of Laughlin's plentiful letters from the time of his visit to Stein mention this conversation, but fifty-four years later Laughlin recalled:

> When Bernard Faÿ came down for weekends from Paris there really was conversation. The two old friends knew each other so well they could play off each other's interests and eccentricities. It was like hearing a duet, and Alice and I just listened.
>
> An exchange I heard one night troubled me deeply, though. They got on the subject of Hitler, speaking of him as a great man, one perhaps to be compared with Napoleon. I was stunned. Hitler's persecution of the Jews was well publicized in France by that time, and Miss Stein was a Jew. Faÿ, in his turn, had nearly gotten himself killed fighting the Germans in World War I. I couldn't forget that strange exchange, but later it came into sharper focus, at least in respect to Faÿ. (535)

The young Laughlin may have easily misconstrued what he heard, since, as the old Laughlin recalls, Stein and Faÿ "could play off each other's interests." As the Warren interview suggests, Stein tended to juxtapose provocative statements with long-winded explanations. Laughlin, at the time, was trying to write a book about Stein's work and would likely have read Warren's *New York Times* interview of two months prior, which may have colored his experience or even merged with his recollection of the "strange exchange." The most recent biography of Laughlin notes several misremembrances from that era in his life.[12]

If Stein and Faÿ did indeed compare Hitler to Napoleon as a great or notable figure, it may not have been the compliment that Laughlin heard it to be. Faÿ was no fan of Napoleon: he had recently written a hagiography of George Washington as a "republican hero" who differed markedly from contemporaries like Napoleon who were merely "enlightened Despots" (*George Washington, Republican Aristocrat*, xiv). Long before meeting Faÿ, Stein, too, had considered Napoleon to have been brutally successful—a despot, in other words. In her notebooks for *The Making of Americans*, circa 1908, she remarks cynically, "Can well believe Napoleon thought himself working for the glory of France" (37.761.[105–106]).[13] And such criticisms continued in her amusing-yet-wry satire of Picasso as a pompously Napoleonesque figure in "Portrait of Picasso" (1923) or her not-so-humorous comparisons of Hitler to Napoleon and Caesar as despots who must die for the next page of history to be written in *Wars I Have Seen* (written 1943–1944, published 1945).[14] As critic Annalisa Zox-Weaver quips, Napoleon was Stein's "suprahistorical anti-hero" (90).

Preferring Pétain's Peace

While Stein was certainly anti-Hitler, she admired Pétain well into the war, as did many of her adopted countryfolk. She also maintained close ties to her longtime friend Bernard Faÿ, as he became a Vichy appointee and an advisor to Pétain. As residents of the Unoccupied Zone, she and her neighbors were, to some extent, spared Nazi rule for two and a half years. Galvin plots Stein's "shifting views" between "maréchalisme"—"the admiration for or attachment to the person of Maréchal Pétain"—and "*pétainisme*," "the support for the Vichy government" ("Gertrude Stein, Pétain" 262, 288–289). And Václav Paris suggests that "Stein's enthusiasm for Pétain in th[e] introduction [to her translation of his speeches] appears to have had much more to do with his personal aura than the specificities of his policy" ("'Gertrude Stein's Translations of Speeches' by Philippe Petain"). This kind of enthusiasm was widely felt and, as historian Robert

O. Paxton reminds us, the rise of the battle-proven Pétain to head of state may have been especially reassuring to those fearful of Hitler:

> The Maréchal had formidable attractions: he stood for escape from an unpopular war, rejection of a loathed Third Republic, an appealing new start, and the capacity—as the victor of Verdun—to look Hitler in the eye. Long after the Vichy regime had lost credibility, the Maréchal himself possessed an authority and an apparent autonomy in which even some resisters believed for a time. ("Preface: From the Bottom of the Abyss" 11)

Victor Hell, who as a young man became a wartime acquaintance of Stein's in Bilignin, recalls being shocked to hear Stein speak of her admiration for and translations of Pétain in 1942. Stein explained to him, however, that her support rested largely on her interest in peace: she liked that Pétain, a former general, was not interested in fighting (Hell 428–429).[15]

The idea that Stein preferred Pétain's peace—though not without reservations—is confirmed in Stein's writings of the era, as I discuss in chapter 6 and will elaborate on here. In the January 1942 "Introduction" to her translations of Pétain's speeches, Stein admiringly recalls Pétain's World War I–era admonition that war was not something to be laughed about, a clear condemnation of what was popularly called the "drôle de guerre," the "Phony" or "Funny War" of 1939–1940. In 1943, in *Wars I Have Seen*, Stein not only reprises the war-is-not-funny anecdote to shore up the "retired" general's pragmatic military sense, but also to remind readers of Pétain's warnings in the 1930s and then again in 1939 that the French army was woefully unprepared for war "without sufficient armament . . . organiz[ation] . . . and . . . allies" against Germany (86–87). And, as in "The Winner Loses" (1940), her account of the Phony War and the armistice that ended it, Stein, in late 1943, shares the general ambivalence concerning Pétain's signing of an armistice:

> Well anyway there was the armistice Petain made it and we were all glad in a way and completely sad in a way and we had so many opinions. I did not like his way of saying I Philippe Petain, that bothered me and we were in the unoccupied area and that was a comfort. . . . no Petain was right to stay in France and he was right to make the armistice and little by little I understood it. I always thought he was right to make the armistice, in the first place it was

more comfortable for us who were here [in the Unoccupied Zone] and in the second place it was an important element in the ultimate defeat of the Germans. To me it remained a miracle. . . . but the thing we all talked about over and over again was whether France should have gone on fighting when she couldn't. (*WIHS* 87–89)

Stein here underscores Pétain's role in ending the war for France, assuring her own "comfort" in the Unoccupied Zone, and ensuring "the ultimate defeat of the Germans." And yet she asserts her approbation, once again, in the context of voicing her discomfort with and her reservations about Pétain. She returns to the story told in the "Introduction" to her translations of Pétain about the French having "so many opinions" about Pétain and the ongoing debates about France's role.

At the opening of this section of the memoir, Stein provides an important framework for doubting wartime attachments when she explains what's "funny about honey" (83). Stein recalls how with wartime sugar shortages, "you find honey so much better than sugar" and use more of it than you normally would, but once "peace is upon us . . . no one eats honey any more, they find it too sweet and too cloying and too heavy" (83). The constraints of war, she suggests, can distort our tastes. So, it is not surprising that, in the memoir, Stein recounts her eventual appreciation of the armistice and yet criticizes Pétain's antisemitism and "persecuting," compares his desire for order to that of a "crazy man," condemns his supporters as insane, and dismisses him as a "forgotten" and "very old man" (93, 81, 92).

As Stein mentioned to Victor Hell in 1942, she was translating most of a book of speeches by Pétain. She began about December 1941 and abandoned the project in perhaps February 1943. Some think that these translations indicate Stein's support for Pétain's antisemitic Jewish statutes and the eventual roundups and deportation of a quarter of France's Jewish population to death camps. Generally, however, since Pétain's stated goals were to unify and uplift a defeated nation, his speeches do not openly touch on his xenophobic and antisemitic policies and persecutions. This is true for the specific speeches that Stein translated, as Paris shows ("'Gertrude Stein's Translations of Speeches' by Philippe Petain"). Paris argues that Stein's choices of which speeches to translate broadly show her differences with Pétain. He also suggests that Stein might have reasonably taken as philosemitic both Pétain's approval of her as his translator and Pétain's advocacy (in a German-banned speech) on behalf of refugees from Alsace-Lorraine, many of whom were Jewish.

Stein's translations of Pétain's speeches diminish and discredit Pétain, according to Galvin's assiduous study of Stein's word choices and tonal modifications. In contrast to what Will reads as the "compositional submissiveness" of "incongruous, even inept" translations, Galvin finds that Stein's semantic decisions and the "Steined" quality of the translations show the ways that Stein "took ownership of Pétain's text and placed her own stamp on it," even if she otherwise may have had little agency in pursuing the project (*Unlikely* 140, 139; "Gertrude Stein, Pétain" 261). Galvin nonetheless sees the translations as "a particularly reactionary moment" in which Stein, as a translator, promoted Pétain's policies by helping to make his writings available to English readers ("Gertrude Stein, Pétain" 263). The contingency of this potentially reactionary moment is made abundantly clear, however, in a postwar exchange between Stein and Bennett Cerf, the head of Random House. In 1946, Cerf received an undated letter from Stein asking him to publish a volume of translations of Pétain's speeches she was just beginning.[16] Cerf quickly replied in outrage, and Stein cabled back, "KEEP YOUR SHIRT ON BENNETT DEAR LETTER RE PETAIN WAS WRITTEN IN 1941" (qtd. in Burns and Dydo 414).

Galvin's recent estimation of Stein's adroitly critical translations of Pétain affirms Will's earlier and persistent doubts about the "strength of Stein's commitments" to the Vichy regime (*Unlikely* 117). As Will acknowledges, "ultimately there was little to show for [Stein's] efforts," since the translation project was neither completed nor published after "a series of delays, deferrals, and postponements [as] Plans were changed, rescheduled, 'forgotten' in the midst of the privations of everyday life" (117). Though Stein abandoned the translations, we are beginning to learn the importance of those compositions and she did not abandon, works that she persisted in writing and publishing throughout the war.

The Wartime Publications of an American Jewess

In an era that might be considered Stein's heyday as a writer, publication remained as challenging a feat as it had been earlier in her career.[17] For those in France, the war presented numerous impediments to publication, with the occupation of Paris—the center of French cultural life, press, and publishing houses—the Jewish statutes, OTTO lists,[18] paper shortages, and interruption of mail service, but it also opened up other possibilities for Stein as a Jewish and American avant-garde writer. Like so many writers and artists during the Occupation,[19] Stein continued to pursue her vocation, writing new pieces, getting others translated, and ceaselessly attempting to find venues for publication. We know that over the course of the war Stein composed four book-length manuscripts: the novel *Mrs. Reynolds*; the poems, prose, and plays collected in *The Gertrude Stein First Reader*; the translation of a volume of Pétain's speeches; and the occupation memoir *Wars I Have Seen*. Virtually absent from recent critical and popular debates is mention of Stein's eleven contributions to four anti-Vichy resistance journals—primarily *Fontaine* and *Confluences*—and the printing of two French translations of her books by a "resistant" publisher.[20] These wartime publications were, however, in no way overlooked by her contemporaries—quite the opposite.

In the middle of the war, in December 1942, one of the leading "openly pro-Nazi intellectual" collaborators, Pierre Drieu la Rochelle, held up Gertrude Stein as the epitome—and nadir—of anti-Vichy literary publishing in the "southern" or Unoccupied Zone (Paxton, "Preface: From the Bottom of the Abyss" 14):

> The literary magazines of the southern zone have always manifested, more or less slyly, the greatest tenderness for the defunct Third Republic, its Jews, pederasts, and Freemasons.
>
> Among these magazines, *Confluences*, which is published in Lyon . . . has always distinguished itself by its zeal in opposing new ideas. To write for this magazine it is sufficient to be an American Jewess, without talent, like Gertrude Stein.
>
> A writer is interned? At once his name appears in the table of contents of the next issue of *Confluences*. . . . (qtd. in Lottman 209)

Drieu la Rochelle disparages Stein for contributing to a controversial July 1942 issue of *Confluences*. Stein's poem "Ballade," a thinly veiled anti-Occupation allegory, followed poems by Jewish-born Catholic Max Jacob and the Communist Louis Aragon. That August, the Vichy Ministre de l'Information issued a two-month suspension to *Confluences* because of the "winks at knowing readers" in Aragon's poem.[21]

During the war, French literateurs had a common interest in Gertrude Stein as an "American Jewess." As I argue throughout this book, Stein associated—in a mostly positive vein—notions of Jewish identity with qualities and practices of modernity. Vichy, the Nazis, and collaborators like Drieu la Rochelle demonized those very practices as degenerate, while those opposed to Vichy and the Nazi occupation championed Jewish and American writers and members of the avant-garde in acts of intellectual resistance. Stein's perceived identity as a Jewish American avant-garde writer gained importance for partisans of all political stripes in Vichy and then in occupied France.[22]

For collaborator Bernard Faÿ, Stein could corral American support for the Vichy regime while proving, as a Jew, that Vichy was no mere Nazi pawn expelling Jews. According to Will, Stein's friendship with Faÿ developed into a political tutelage that led Stein to celebrate the armistice with Germany, had Faÿ personally enlist Stein in translating Pétain's speeches, and brought her to write an essay—in French—on the French language for the propagandistic Vichy magazine *Patrie*.

For the intellectual resistance, Stein's Jewish-American identity and experimental style "more or less slyly" conveyed dissent and promoted an international avant-garde of arts and letters. Stein's numerous publications by resistance journals reveal a concerted effort by a far-flung yet closely knit group of leftist writers, editors, and publishers in Lyon, Marseilles, Algiers, Casablanca, and Tunis to promote and publish Stein for anti-Vichy and anti-Occupation ends.[23] Even Stein's August 1941 article for *Patrie*, a magazine inaugurated by Pétain himself, put her shoulder to shoulder with writers who were or would become prominent figures in the intellectual resistance.[24] A stately 1945 photograph of Stein posing with issues of *Confluences* and *Fontaine*, two of the most influential and resistance-oriented literary reviews, shows her interest in portraying herself as a partisan by virtue of her many contributions to those journals during the war.[25]

Stein's wartime writings, translations, and publications are important for understanding how Stein survived the war. They reveal what it was like for her to live and write in Vichy and occupied France and testify to what she considered to be the role and responsibility of a writer in wartime. They also reflect the contradictions and ambiguities of the war as it proceeded in France, where there were abrupt shifts of alliances and authority. And they teach us about how French writers, editors, and publishers marshalled her Jewish-American modernism for political and cultural ends. Further, as they address Jewish issues, themes, and figures, Stein's wartime writings serve as the culmination of her lifelong interest in the Jewish question.

The 2012 debates over Stein's alleged Nazism largely omitted her wartime writings other than condemning her for translating Pétain. They condemned Stein for her friendship with the rightist Bernard Faÿ but ignored her friendships with leftists, such as the "so-called red, communist duchess Elisabeth de Gramont, Madame de Clermont-Tonnerre," a relationship with striking parallels to Faÿ's, as Birgit Van Puymbroeck has shown (85). Commentators also tried to bolster claims that Stein was a collaborator and antisemite by criticizing Stein for not writing about Jews.[26] *The New Republic*'s Christopher Benfey, for example, dismisses Stein, saying that an "erasure of Jewish themes in Stein's books remained a pattern throughout her career" (June 7, 2012).

The present study corrects mistaken ideas of Stein's Jewish antisemitism, apathy, and erasure.[27] Stein's writing about Jews and Jewish topics remained constant or increased over the course of her writing life—including during World War II. As one might expect from fifty years of writing unconventionally, her Jewish writings took a variety of forms and approaches, sometimes looking back to ancient Hebrew textual traditions and sometimes forward to the modern era and modernists as Jewish phenomena.

Stein's Recipe for Jewish Modernism

Stein never let go of the idea that tradition nourished modernism. But her reiteration of it at the beginning of World War II has since been heard as an affirmation of the social and political conservatism that fed the antisemitism, xenophobia, and fascism of that war. In her 1940 essayistic and memoirish *Paris France*, Stein asserts, "I cannot write too much upon how necessary it is to be completely conservative that is particularly traditional in order to be free" (38). To "after Auschwitz" ears, Stein's avowal sounds terrifyingly Orwellian. And yet, such a reading is not only ahistorical but acontextual, reading against the grain of Stein's intertwined and Jewish notions about modernism and tradition.[28]

As I have shown in this book, Stein long cherished an ideal of the conventions of a traditional middle-class Jewish home as the foundation for an unconventional artistic fraternity of Jewish Singulars. With this in mind, we hear Stein's paean to conservative-born freedom as a reminder that modernism's epoch-defining experimentation was born of—and indebted to—a "particularly traditional" Paris and France in the first half of the twentieth century. Earlier in *Paris France*, Stein explains, "The reason why all of us naturally began to live in France is because France has scientific methods, machines and electricity, but does not really believe that these things have anything to do with the real business of living. Life is tradition and human nature" (8). Those like Stein and Picasso seeking "a new way . . . needed France," she insists, for its unwavering belief in tradition and in the unchanging nature of human beings (8).

Reading the exhortation to be "traditional in order to be free" in the immediate context of its *Paris France* chapter, it becomes clear that Stein was not promoting conservative politics. Instead, Stein was explaining why Paris had, as she recalled, so "suited those of us that were to create the twentieth century art and literature" (12). In the chapter, Stein illuminates this paradoxical tradition of fostering change with tradition, by turning to French cooking. Like French cuisine, she proposes, whose history involves "the provinces . . . giv[ing] the fashion to Paris," the changes wrought by avant-garde movements in Paris from 1900 to 1939 were only possible because of the conventions and stability of French tradition (53). Looking back on the era of innovation, Stein reflects, "the world in general needs a different imagination at different times and so there is the Paris France from 1900 to 1939, where everybody had to be to be free" (36–37).[29] She marvels that all the newness came about in a place where chefs go by familial honorifics like "Mère," "Père," or "Fils," meaning *mother, father*, or *son*, and where "they call a painter who is old cher maitre," meaning *dear master* (37–38). Then Stein reiterates,

> I cannot write too much upon how necessary it is to be completely conservative that is particularly traditional in order to be free. And so France is and was. Sometimes it is important and sometimes it is not, but from 1900 to 1939, it certainly was. (38)

Without the context of Stein's analysis of Paris as an avant-garde hub in the preceding decades, it is easy to misinterpret Stein's championing of conservatism as politically reactionary. Without her analogy to the art of French cuisine, one overlooks the affectionate accents of the French tradition that had given bosom to those breaking free from tradition. And we may not hear in this repeated remark Stein's sense that European culture—as epitomized by the Parisian creation of "twentieth century art and literature"—was Judaizing, without hearkening back to the context of Stein's first fictions, where her alienated and Jewish "Brother Singular" takes refuge in "the kindly comfort of an older world accustomed to take all manner of strange forms into its bosom" (*Paris France* 12; MA 153; *MA* 21).

Stein's Singular, her Jewish avatar for the modern writer, was always making a virtue of convention. In her notebooks from the beginning of the century, Stein identified herself as an innovator able to "unconventionalize" like those she deemed typologically Jewish kinds of people, namely Picasso, Cézanne, Matisse, Flaubert, and Darwin (39.814). And yet, such unconventionalizing was, in Stein's thinking, born from convention. "Queer people," she affirmed early on, derive from the constancy of "time and certainty of place and means" (MA 152; *MA* 21). This was not a minor thematic thread in Stein's oeuvre. She concludes her epic novel *The Making of Americans* with the notion that such singulars, the novel's Jewish pariahs, were part of traditional "family living," even if that membership was ambivalent, contingent, or impermanent. Hence, the narrator's description of "one being in a family living and being one liking and not liking being in a family living" (917). And the novel's final sentence asserts that "some" Jewish singulars will, however incompletely, pay homage to their familial roots, since "Any family living can be one being existing and some can remember something of some such thing" (925).

Stein's insistence "upon how necessary it is to be completely conservative . . . to be free" confirms, as well, the lasting influence of Matthew Arnold. While Arnold criticized a dutiful notion of Hebraism for being at odds with his ideal of a Hellenism that allowed for the "free play of the mind," Stein, here, looks back on her Paris years, and again conjoins his oppositions as necessary ingredients for the artistic flowering of that time, by celebrating the traditional Judaic nurturing of the modern. For the era from 1900 to 1939, tradition and conservatism were, she contends, fundamental to the creation of culture.

Given Stein's practice of "beginning again," within and between texts, interpreting her writings carefully and fairly entails reading her as fully and historically as possible. Stein's oeuvre, her reputation as a Jewish writer, and her critical legacy as a modernist suffer, ironically, from quoting pithy and powerful utterances whose meanings crucially depend on context. As I show above, Stein announces this reading practice in her first fictions, where, when pointing to the iconic Jewish figure of the peddler as the key to understanding the history of the American family being depicted, she affirms that now "the picture is complete the picture you must understand if you are to rightly read the story that I mean to tell" (MA 141). Gaining an ear for the Jewish ideas that undergird so many of Stein's repeated idioms and formulations is crucial for "rightly reading" modernism.

NOTES

Introduction: The Stein Era

1. As reported by Alice Toklas to Leon Katz ("First Making" 208).

2. While the editors of the *Norton Anthology of Jewish American Literature* (2001) included Stein, many critics still dismiss the notion of Stein as a Jewish writer. Ruth Wisse remarks that a skeptical colleague asked if she was going to include Paul Celan and Bruno Schultz in her *Modern Jewish Canon*, and if not, "Who then—Gertrude Stein?" (18). Gary Levine resists the "tempt[ation]" to analyze "Stein's Jewish cultural identity" (159). In contrast, Charles Bernstein argues that Stein "takes her place in that line of what Isaac Deutscher calls 'non-Jewish Jews,' going back at least to Spinoza, and, in this, her most immediate company in American poetry includes Louis Zukofsky (who incorporates Spinoza and Stein into "*A*") and Laura Riding (her onetime protégé)" ("Stein's Identity" 487). For Bernstein, "Stein is one of the least assimilationist of American modernist writers and, in this, one of the most American, if, following Stanley Cavell's reading of Emerson, we take America to be a movement away from given identities and toward something new, unapproachable, unrepresentable, and unattainable" (487).

3. Target Margin Theater Company followed their *Three Sisters Who Are Not Sisters* (2009) with an entire season inspired by Stein texts (2014–2015). Mark Morris Dance Troupe has performed *Four Saints in Three Acts* (2000/2006), The Wooster Group adapted *Doctor Faustus Lights the Lights* into *House/Lights* (1998/2005), and Heiner Goebbel's *Hashirigaki* (2000/2003) included portions of *The Making of Americans*. See also Appendix B of Sarah Bay-Cheng's *Mama Dada: Gertrude Stein's Avant-Garde Theater* for a listing of productions based on Stein's work through 2004.

4. Matt Miller suggests that "Stein's formidable skills at self-promotion" have dissuaded critics from looking for her literary influences and, instead, they "preserve for Stein an idealized autonomy from her peers and antecedents" (39). Lisi

Schoenbach, studying Stein's pragmatism, argues for a methodology of *contextualizing* innovations to illuminate the connection rather than the breach with the past.

5. See Laura Doyle, Daylanne English, and G. F. Mitrano. For a reading of racial science typologies in "Melanctha," see Paul Peppis, "Thinking Race in the *Avant Guerre*: Typological Negotiations in Ford and Stein" (*Yale Journal of Criticism* 10: 2 [1997] 371–395).

6. See Jessica Berman, Clive Bush, Janice Doane, George Moore, Allegra Stewart, Jayne Walker, Barrett Watten, and Norman Weinstein.

7. Robert Chodat, meanwhile, encourages skepticism of Stein's claims to a scientific method in her writing, in "Sense, Science, and the Interpretations of Gertrude Stein" (*Modernism/modernity* 12.4 [2005]: 581–605).

8. Stein often referred to *The Making of Americans* as "the Long book" or "my long book" (*GS/CVV* 98 and Letter to Grant Richards, 28 September. [1911]. Yale Collection of American Literature [YCAL], Beinecke Rare Book and Manuscript Library, Yale University, New Haven, Conn.). She also referred to it this way numerous times in her notes for the novel, for example 38.791.[32]).

9. Ulla Dydo defines Stein's "audience writing" as "created to please readers, for success, rather than as writing for its own sake" (*Gertrude Stein: The Language That Rises: 1923–1934* 5).

10. Among modernist writers, William Carlos Williams was a lone voice of unabashed critical appreciation, often comparing Stein to Joyce and Pound. In the early 1930s, for example, he wrote, "If you like Gertrude Stein, study her for her substance; she has it, no matter what the idle may say" (*Selected Essays* 104).

11. Leick details the role of the popular press in making Stein a household name in the 1910s, '20s, and '30s by widely disseminating Stein's work—or the idea of her work. She also shows the common pairing of Stein and Joyce as experimenters: "in the mainstream press, Gertrude Stein's name was often linked with James Joyce's, almost as if the work of the two writers was interchangeable" (91).

12. Lewis goes on to offer mild praise of Stein's work, "For any one less strong-minded than Miss Stein this might prove a dangerous occupation" (*The Art of Being Ruled* 400). In *Time and Western Man*, Lewis made Stein the target of some of his crudest criticisms of modern prose and, in a draft of his novel *The Childermass* (1928), he uses "Stein" as a verb indicating repetitious speech (as a defect) when describing a character who "stammers and *steins*" (*The Letters of Wyndham Lewis* 176).

13. Eliot refers to the title of John Rodker's 1927 book *The Future of Futurism*.

14. While David E. Chinitz, in *T. S. Eliot and the Cultural Divide*, considers reading Eliot's reference to jazz more positively, the over-all tenor of Eliot's review

seems sour, something that makes plausible Stein's bitter account in *The Autobiography of Alice B. Toklas* of meeting Eliot and not being published by him.

15. Wilson was interested in publishing Stein's work in *Vanity Fair*, where he had reviewed her 1922 volume *Geography and Plays*. See Dydo (*Language That Rises* 75 and 75n) and Stein (*GS/CVV* 66–88).

16. Eliot, too, claimed, "There is something precisely *ominous* about Miss Stein. Her books of 'about one thousand pages' may, and will, remain unread; but Miss Stein is going to make trouble for us just the same" ("Charleston, Hey! Hey!" 595). Richard Bridgman (xiii), Charles Caramello ("Gertrude Stein as Exemplary Theorist" 1), Carolyn Copeland (46), Mary Dearborn (162), Marianne DeKoven ("Gertrude Stein and the Modernist Canon" 16), Norman Weinstein (37), and Allegra Stewart (10) cite similarly disparaging remarks by Wilson.

17. E. E. Cummings compares Stein's girth to her epic 900-page novel, writing: "I did once glimpse an immense shelike It rolling along Boulevard Montparnasse on top of a microscopic automobile; & thought 'that must be Gertrude Stein.' and once, en route to France, I tried to read a hugely fat hyperopus stuffed-to-bursting with repetitions & labelled The Making of Americans; finally quitting at page thirtysomething" (*Selected Letters* 267).

18. In a 1929 letter to the American poet Louis Zukofsky, Pound mused to his young Jewish disciple, "Capital in idea that next wave of literature is jewish (obviously) Bloom casting shadow before, prophetic Jim. [Joyce] etc. / also lack of prose in German due to all idiomatic energy being drawn off into yiddish. (not concerned with the 'truth' of these suggestions but only with the dynamic)" (*Pound/Zukofsky* 26–27). See Humphrey Carpenter on Pound's description of Stein's work as "Yiddish" (400). Women writers were not immune to criticizing Stein's style as Jewish. Virginia Woolf wrote, in a letter to her sister, "We were at a party at Edith Sitwell's last night, where a good deal of misery was endured. Jews swarmed. It was in honour of Miss Gertrude Stein who was throned on a broken settee. . . . This resolute old lady inflicted great damage on all the youth. According to Dadie, she contradicts all you say; insists that she is not only the most intelligible, but also the most popular of living writers; and in particular despises all of English birth. Leonard, being a Jew himself, got on very well with her. But it was an anxious exacerbating affair. . . ." (*Letters of Virginia Woolf*, Vol. 3, 269–270).

19. Taine's philosophy influenced Zola's naturalism and American realism. See Gert Mattenklott, "'Dégénérescence' La Théorie de la Dégénération Culturelle Chez Max Nordau." Eds. Delphine Bechtel, Dominique Bourel and Jacques Le Rider. *Max Nordau (1849–1923): Critique de la Dégénérescence, Médiateur Franco-Allemand, Père Fondateur du Sionisme* (Paris: Cerf, 1996) 161–173.

20. See also Cesare Lombroso and Joseph Jacobs.

21. For Judaized estimations of Heine, see French ethnographer Anatole

Leroy-Beaulieu (236, 251–252), Italian criminologist Cesare Lombroso (135–136, et al.), German psychologist William Hirsch (41), English anthropologist Francis Galton (234), Viennese psychologist Otto Weininger (316), and German sexologist Richard von Krafft-Ebing (21).

22. I borrow the term "multiverse" from William James (*Is Life Worth Living?* 26).

23. See Brenda Wineapple 15–19. Stein's mother Milly lists her purchase of Matzos and contributions to the Hebrew Society in her Vienna diary (*Amelia Stein Diaries* 11 Mar. and 10 Apr. 1878).

24. Stein's brother Leo remembered that their mother "had some time in her youth to read a couple of novels by a gentle Jewish writer named Grace Aguilar (*Home Influence* and its sequel, *A Mother's Recompense*), and so far as I know she had never read anything else—so Gertrude and I do not come of a literary stock" (*Journey Into the Self* 187).

25. Neighboring San Francisco was the cosmopolitan center of the American West, attracting international art and theater. In 1884, for example, the family attended productions of "Daughter of the Regiment" at the Tivoli Theater and "Uncle Tom's Cabin" at the Coliseum (*Amelia Stein Diaries* 22 Mar. and 5 Apr. 1884).

26. In her lecture "Plays," Stein recalls her early experiences with German operas: "The next thing was the opera the twenty-five cent opera of San Francisco and the fight in Faust. But that I imagine was largely because my brother had told me about the fight in Faust. As a matter of fact I gradually saw more of the opera because I saw it quite frequently. . . . And then there was Lohengrin, and there all that I saw was the swan being changed into a boy, our insisting on seeing that made my father with us lose the last boat home to Oakland, but my brother and I did not mind, naturally not as it was the moment" (*LA* 113).

27. In a 1931 letter to Carl Van Vechten, Stein insisted that she was not German. She informs him of her response to Edmund Wilson's recent criticism of her in *Axel's Castle*: "I was not born in Baltimore, and I am not *german*, and I do make poetry, which can be read otherwise I was pleased [with what Wilson wrote]" (*GS/CVV* 239). As editor Edward Burns notes, Stein seems to have misread Wilson who correctly cited her birthplace as Allegheny, PA, and referred, not to Stein, but to her characters as either German or German-Jewish.

28. In *The Making of Americans*, Stein alludes to her discovery of this ideology as differentiating people who believe in an afterlife (that "dead is not dead") from those particularly Jewish folks who do not believe in one and think that "dead is dead" (498). Virgil Thompson recollected speaking to Alice Toklas about this in a conversation in which the Jewish signification of this phrase is made explicit. Toklas addresses Thompson: "You and Gertrude had it settled between you as to

why Jews don't make up their quarrels, and I went along with you. But now I've found a better reason for it. Gertrude was right, of course, to believe that 'when a Jew dies he's dead.' And that's exactly why Jews don't need to make up. When we've had enough of someone we can get rid of him. You Christians can't, because you've got to spend eternity together" (qtd. in Malcolm 220).

29. Like Leo, whose "core group of friends was German Jewish," Stein's collegiate social circle was made up largely of Jews (Wineapple 50). When Stein enrolled at Radcliffe a year after Leo began at Harvard, "her closest female friend, Mabel Earle, a housemate at Buckingham Street [boardinghouse], was not Jewish, [but] outside the boardinghouse almost all her friends were. Several she had met through Leo" (56). Dubbed the "lackadaisical, unconventional best circle in Cantabrigia," Stein's Cambridge crowd included her cousins Fred Stein and Howard Gans, and friends Leo Friedman, Francis Pollak, Inez Cohen, and Adele and Ben Oppenheimer (Leo Victor Friedman. Letter to Gertrude Stein. Aug. 10, 1895. YCAL).

30. See Eric Goldstein on Jewish race feeling in nineteenth-century America.

31. Hapgood remembers that they spoke in a rather romantic setting, "when sitting in the moonlight at the Schloss" (535). One wonders whether Stein's passionate inveighing against intermarriage was also expressing her disinterest in marriage with the gentile Hapgood—or any man.

Chapter 1. An Israel of the Imagination: The Sciences of Race, Matthew Arnold, and Stein's Modern Jew

1. Stein wrote the essay on modern Jews the same year that her first scientific publication, "Normal Motor Automatism," appeared in the *Harvard Psychological Review*, co-authored with graduate student Leon Solomons and based on their Harvard Psychology Laboratory research. Her single-authored study, "Cultivated Motor Automatism: A Study of Character in Its Relation to Attention," appeared in May 1898. These studies aimed to understand second-personality disorders in hysterics by learning how much of what was considered a second personality might be automatic body movements to which the mind had ceased paying attention.

2. The Jews' cosmopolitan ability to "adapt and thrive in all places" was considered a symptom of degeneracy because it contradicted the reigning theories that place bred race (Stepan "Biological Degeneration" 104). For example, French Orientalist Ernest Renan argued that the Semites had always been either nomads or intemperate despots (Renan 155) and Viennese psychiatrist and sexologist Richard von Krafft-Ebing observed that "the Jews, 'uprooted from the land' . . . and urbanized en masse, suffered to an extraordinary degree from nervousness" (qtd. in Hart 116). Considering Jews to be "la race bohémienne," French psychologists revived

the stock figure of the Wandering Jew—whose ceaseless locomotion was supposed to be punishment for slighting Christ—when diagnosing cases of Jewish hysteria (Théodule Ribot, *L'Hérédité psychologique,* 1871, qtd. in Laarse 24n). Neurologist Jean-Martin Charcot, in his studies of hysteria, presented a "representative" case of an "israelite" named Klein whose unsettled suffering ("névropathes voyageurs") showed him to be heir to the affliction of Wandering Jews (348).

3. French doctor Bénédicte Auguste Morel (1809–1873) theorized that degeneration—a morbid deviation from the norm ("*déviation maladive*")—reversed the progress of man's biological development. The hereditary nature of Morel's definition influenced most subsequent writing on the subject, which undertook to classify all sorts of excessive behaviors as symptoms of degeneration. Equating Judaism with capitalism, for example, Marx referred to the "*chimerical* nationality" of the Jews and "the practical Jewish spirit" ("On the Jewish Question" 51, 49). Renan credited the Jews for inventing monotheism and yet found the Jewish reluctance to embrace Christ pathologically narrow-minded. He advised that "Progress for the Indo-European people will consist in departing farther and farther from the Semitic spirit" (165). Jews as iconic degenerates were portrayed as unwilling or constitutionally unable to adhere to Christian morals. As Krafft-Ebing declared, "despite periodic relapses, public morality has made steady progress, and [. . .] Christianity is the chief factor in this advance" (6).

4. For readings of Jewishness in Disraeli's trilogy *Coningsby* (1844), *Sybil, or the Two Nations* (1845), and *Tancred, or the New Crusade* (1847), see Todd Endelman, "Benjamin Disraeli" and "'Hebrew to the end'"; Michael Ragussis 174–233; and Patrick Brantlinger's criticism of Edward Said's monolithic "East" in "Disraeli and Orientalism."

5. Stein owned at least two of Disraeli's novels, *Alroy* (1846) and *Venetia* (1853) (BGS). In one of her poems from 1919, she quotes from a third novel, *Lothair* (1870), an allusion I discuss in chapter 5.

6. Although most critics attribute Arnold's ideas on Hebraism to Heine, Michael Ragussis contends that Arnold's ideas about the "Hebraic" aspects of the British people draw heavily from Disraeli (211–233).

7. That Arnold's Hebraism vilified real Jews was not happenstance according to Lionel Trilling's account of Arnold's antisemitism: "But with Jews he was intransigent, believing that they should be barred from the universities and from citizenship. . . . England, he said, was the land of Englishmen, not of Jews, and 'lodgers' had no claims to more than an honorary citizenship which gave them no share in government" (60).

8. As Trilling writes about Heine's division of people into either Jews or Greeks, "Heine derived the antithesis from Ludwig Börne. It was a not uncommon comparison, especially among Jewish writers" (256n). He also suggests that Heine

"followed" Moses Hess, whose *Rome and Jerusalem: A Study in Jewish Nationalism*, published in German in 1862, has an epilogue on Hellenes and Hebrews (Trilling 235).

9. Some degenerationists cast Jewish genius itself as an abnormal mental state, a claim supported by Anglo-Jewish anthropologist Joseph Jacobs, a student and colleague of Galton's. In his widely cited study, "The Comparative Distribution of Jewish Ability" (1886), Jacobs concluded that Jews had both a higher-than-average number of both geniuses and insane people. Relying on Jacobs's study, Cesare Lombroso, an Italian Jewish criminologist, determined that the Jews of Europe were an "eloquent example" of the shared hereditary and racial nature of genius and insanity (*The Man of Genius* 133). Lombroso's book *Genius and Insanity*, retitled and expanded in later editions as *The Man of Genius* (in English 1891), went through at least six editions in Italian and was read and translated throughout Europe and the United States. Lombroso and others with scientific pretensions read literary texts to prove the degeneracy of certain writers, something that became common among those seeking to obviate the invisible dangers of race and mental disease. For more on Jacobs, see John M. Efron, *Defenders of the Race: Jewish Doctors and Race Science in Fin-de-Siecle Europe* (New Haven, CT: Yale University Press, 1994) and Sander Gilman, *Smart Jews: The Construction of the Image of Jewish Superior Intelligence* (Lincoln: University of Nebraska Press, 1996).

10. Frenchman Hippolyte Adolphe Taine wrote a five-volume *History of English Literature* (1863–1864, in English 1871), which classified works of English literature as either Anglo-Saxon or Semitic, praising the former as civilized and deriding the latter as uncivilized (14). Citing Ernest Renan's *Histoire des Langues Sémitiques* (1855), and in accordance with the traits that the race scientists would designate for the Jewish people, Taine characterized Semitic literature as a morbid deviation from the slow, measured, and sensible evolution of Anglo-Saxon literary production. For Taine and others, the immoderate lyricism, passion, and instinctual barbarism of Semitic literature encapsulated all the vainglorious attributes of a degenerate Jewish genius.

11. None of the major figures writing on the nature of genius ever arrived at a concrete definition of the term or drew any conclusions about what they were describing as genius. German psychologist William Hirsch saw no psychological meaning in the word *genius* (68). Similarly, in later editions of *Hereditary Genius*, Galton wrote that he regretted using the title word *genius* because of its lack of scientific value ("Preface of 1892" viii). In *A Study of British Genius* (1904), Havelock Ellis acknowledged the slippery nature of the key terms and the inadequacy of the "vague and general discussion of genius" in the major works on the subject and yet defined genius as "the happy result of a combination of many concomitant circumstances" (232, 234).

12. Nordau's 560-page tome blamed the decline of Western civilization on degenerate literature and music—arts he considered to pose equal or greater dangers than the vices of industrialization, speedy transportation, modern dress and hair styles, and the intrusive proficiency of the postal system. Nordau seized upon poetic devices to indict as degenerates D. G. Rossetti, Whitman, Wilde (before the trials), Tolstoy, Nietzsche, Ibsen, and Zola. Nordau admitted his practices were unscientific but believed they would have been corroborated by physical examination, if that had been possible: "it is not necessary to measure the cranium of an author, or to see the lobe of a painter's ear, in order to recognise the fact that he belongs to the class of degenerates" (17). Perhaps the most famous application of Nordau's practice occurred at the trials of Oscar Wilde in 1895, during which the male love affairs in *The Picture of Dorian Gray* were brought as evidence to convict Wilde for acts of "gross indecency." See Richard Ellmann's biography of Wilde (421–422, 436). For a methodological comparison of Lombroso to Nordau, see Jens Malte Fischer. Nordau's methods of cultural criticism were later embraced by the Nazis who, in Munich in 1937, held an exposition of Degenerate Art for the purposes of ridiculing such art. See Peter Adam, *Art of the Third Reich* (New York: Abrams, 1992) and Stephanie Barron, ed., *"Degenerate Art": The Fate of the Avant-Garde in Nazi Germany* (New York: Abrams, 1991).

13. James's notes for the lectures provide a detailed survey of his reading on degeneration, including not only Nordau and Lombroso, but Galton, Hirsch, Morel, and the American John Nisbet, author of *The Insanity of Genius and the General Inequality of Human Faculty Physiologically Considered* (*EMS* 132–133). Eugene Taylor's edition, *William James on Exceptional Mental States: The 1896 Lowell Lectures*, pieces together the texts of the lectures from James's notes and newspaper accounts.

14. In 1867, writing from Germany, the twenty-five-year-old James thought, "The jews, (with all that may be urged against them) are the best looking people here on the whole" (*CWJ* 4: 183). He was especially taken by one particular "young jewess," so much so that the "curve of her nose, the curl of her nostril, and the splendor of her eye" made James wish he himself were Jewish and "also one of the Nation" (183).

15. When writing to a friend about vacation plans in New Hampshire, James advised, "The Willey House circular appears this year with the precious addition: 'Applications from Hebrews cannot be considered.' I propose to return the boycott, but should like to make sure of a bed elsewhere first" (*CWJ* 8: 523). Perhaps recalling his own youthful affections for Jews in Germany, James later joked to his son, who was then (in 1903) abroad in Germany, that he should not marry a Jew because his mother was too antisemitic, as evinced by her iciness at a reception the Jameses had attended given by his Jewish colleague Münsterberg the previous

evening (10: 206). A few years later, when the Jameses were themselves in Germany visiting Jewish friends, James was able to report with relief about his wife that, "she loved them, and antisemitism was nowhere" (12: 559).

16. In 1898, when writing about an attempt to outlaw "mind-curers" and Christian Science healers as harmful, for example, James compares it to antisemitism: "The [medical] profession claims a law simply on the grounds of personal dislike. It is antisemitism again" (*CWJ* 8: 351).

17. See Harrowitz and Hyams on Joyce et al. Ford reminisced about the moment in 1906 when the English translations appeared:

> in the men's clubs of England and in the cafés of France and Germany—one began to hear singular mutterings amongst men. . . . The idea was that a new gospel had appeared. I remember sitting with a table full of overbearing intellectuals in that year, and they at once began to talk—about Weininger. It gave me a singular feeling because they all talked under their breaths. ("Women and Men, II: The Literature of the Subject," *The Little Review* 11 [March 1918]: 40–41. qtd. in Sengoopta 141)

18. See Wineapple, Wald, Will *Gertrude Stein, Modernism, and the Problem of "Genius,"* and Katz "Weininger and *The Making of Americans*."

19. I have corrected the 1908 English translator's mistake in not maintaining the parallel clauses from Weininger's original, which equates Judaism with femininity: "Zwischen Judentum und Christentum, zwischen Geschäft und Kultur, zwischen Weib und Mann, zwischen Gattung und Persönlichkeit, zwischen Unwert und Wert, zwischen irdischem und höherem Leben, zwischen dem Nichts und der Gottheit hat abermals die Menschheit die Wahl. Das sind die beiden Pole: es gibt kein drittes Reich" (*Geschlecht und Charakter* [Wien: Wilhelm Braumüller, 1904] 452).

20. Despite similarly codifying symbolic Judaisms, Weininger does not name Arnold as an influence even though he appears to have read widely, if disapprovingly, among Arnold's English contemporaries and antecedents, citing Bentham, Berkeley, Darwin, Hume, Hobbes, George Eliot, Mill, Ruskin, Spencer, and Carlyle.

21. See Wineapple 262–265 on letters to Stein from different correspondents (Emma Lootz Erving, Mabel Foote Weeks, and Marian Walker Williams) that indicate that Stein had read and enthusiastically written to her friends about Weininger in 1908. That same year Mary Costello Berenson wrote in her diary that Stein was recommending Weininger (Wineapple 464).

22. In a notebook study for *The Making of Americans*, Stein writes: "the danger with the fanatic group is the denial of their experience, this may make them moral enthusiasts, as Leon, Weininger, it may make them, aesthetic visionaries

as Raymond & (I hope not) Pablo" (37.764.[8a]). I return to Stein's interest in Weininger in chapter 3.

23. T. H. Huxley, in his 1880 lecture "Science and Culture," dubbed Arnold the "apostle of culture" (8). R. H. Super, editor of Arnold's prose works, notes that Henry Sidgwick described Arnold as "The Prophet of Culture" in *Macmillan's Magazine* XVI 274 (Aug 1867), (5:422–423).

24. Some considered Arnold's preference for thought over deed as an "indifference to direct political action," which, as he notes, inspired newspapers to call him "sometimes an elegant Jeremiah, sometimes a spurious Jeremiah" (*C&A* 88). Arnold chides the newspaper for comparing him "with just that very one of the Hebrew prophets whose style I admire the least" (88).

25. Cheyette contextualizes Arnold's notions of race in *Culture and Anarchy* in *Constructions* 13–23. For Renan's influence on Arnold see Frederic E. Faverty's *Matthew Arnold, the Ethnologist* (Evanston, IL: Northwestern University Press, 1951) and Donald D. Stone's *Communications with the Future: Matthew Arnold in Dialogue.*

26. In a letter from June of 1897, Stein's friend Francis Pollak reflects: "I used to think last year that the part of Cambridge life that wasn't Harvard life was more valuable than the part that was. . . . Certainly if the object of life is 'to live and learn' and most particularly if the aim of learning is to 'Know thyself' (and thy neighbor better than thyself) that very '95–'96 year was the best spent of them all" (YCAL).

27. Although Arnold popularized the latter phrase, he took it, appropriately enough, from Swift's 1704 *Battle of the Books*, where "Aesop" speaks on behalf of the ancients, countering modern satirists by asserting that with their words, the ancients have provided humanity with "the two noblest of things, which are sweetness and light" (21).

28. The widespread nature of this Arnoldianism may be evinced by Wyndham Lewis's use of it in his 1927 volume *Time and Western Man* (10, quoted below), Stein's allusion to it (also quoted below), and William James's borrowing of it in a letter from 1900 when he enthusiastically addresses a friend with the "hope [that] you are a power for righteousness" (*CWJ* 9: 137).

29. See Maud Ellmann.

30. "Things as they are" appears over twenty times in *Culture and Anarchy*. Stein uses it in two works from 1903, the first draft of "The Making of Americans" (167) and "Q.E.D." (133), and kept it in the final 1911 draft of *The Making of Americans* (33).

31. Leo first purchased a Cézanne in the spring of 1904, when Gertrude had returned to America for a visit. She joined him in Florence that summer, where

he spent a great deal of time studying Charles Loeser's privately held Cézannes. See Irene Gordon, "A World Beyond the World" 24–25.

32. See Stone on George Eliot ("Matthew Arnold" 183), Ira B. Nadel on Joyce (*Joyce and the Jews* 1–3), T. J. Lustig on Henry James, Anne Dewitt on Hardy, Trubowitz on Lewis (159), John Attridge on Ford and Forster, and Donald Childs on Woolf and T. S. Eliot. Sarah Orne Jewett considered Arnold's *Literature and Dogma* (1873) to have paved the way for James's *The Varieties of Religious Experience* (*CWJ* 10: 83). Wyndham Lewis relied on *Literature and Dogma* for some of his ideas about Jews: "It was that keen awareness of the Not-self, and the consequent conception of 'righteousness,' that Matthew Arnold pointed to (in his *Literature and Dogma*) as constituting the originality of the ancient Jewish people" (*Time and Western Man* 10).

33. Biographer Leon Edel suggests that from very early on James considered Arnold his "intellectual kinsman" (143). James mentions Hebraism in his novel *Roderick Hudson* and Stone argues that James fictionalizes Hebraism and Hellenism throughout his work as, respectively, "the New England conscience and the free play of the mind" (*Communications* 14–15). For more on Stein and James, see Caramello, (*Henry James* 169–200), Ira Nadel ("Gertrude Stein and Henry James" 81–97), and Copeland 10–12, 66–67.

34. These notes, formerly catalogued as "Q.E.D.—Notes and Drafts," are now listed more generally in Stein's archive, YCAL MSS 76, as a "Collection of notes and quotations," ca. 1890s, Box 139, Folder 3274.

35. Stein's concern for Jewish degeneracy continued after she left Harvard for Johns Hopkins medical school in the fall of 1897. From Baltimore, Stein wrote to Leon Solomons, still at the Harvard Psychology Laboratory, asking about the possibility of a racially specific degenerative malady among Jews. In January of 1898, Solomons replied, "I do not think there is any special tendency toward melancholia among our people, but there is a much higher percentage of all kinds of abnormality, due in all probability to the close intermarriage which necessarily prevails among a people scattered widely in small groups" (YCAL). While Stein earlier concludes that Jewish "brain-power" and good deeds should be preserved through endogamy, it is interesting that Solomons confirms the idea of a particularly Jewish degeneracy by explaining that it would be an expected result of endogamy (although Solomons's generalized diction indicates that this would be true of any diasporic people). In her letter to Solomons, Stein may have been responding to the racism and sexism of faculty at Johns Hopkins and of fellow students who were disgusted by her "Hebrew" looks and disheveled appearance (Wineapple 141). For more on Stein's reception at Johns Hopkins, see Wineapple 124–125 and Hovey 555–556. For an illuminating study of the more progressive voices at Johns Hopkins, especially concerning gender differences, see Farland.

36. James had reviewed Nordau and Lombroso for the *Psychological Review* the previous year, in 1895, and would have been preparing for his Lowell lectures to be delivered that autumn on the "Exceptional Mental States" of genius, degeneration, hypnotism, automatism, and hysteria. James's assigned textbook for Stein's graduate seminar on abnormal psychology was *Pathology of Mind* (1867) by Henry Maudsley, a Lamarckian who believed the experiences of past generations were inscribed on the body.

37. Apart from her university studies, Stein's exposure to degeneration theory may have come as early as the summer of 1895, when her brother Leo, then her constant intellectual companion, wrote to her that Nordau's *Degeneration* was "a durn fool book." Leo faulted the book as part of "a great mass of pretentious scientific literature in that it takes morality to be evidence of identity" and concluded, "Of course the book is occasionally suggestive as any book of that kind is often found to be but it is on the whole not worth reading" (Letter from Leo Stein to Bird Sternberger Gans YCAL). Stein would go on to examine the gendered aspects of degeneration in medical school at Johns Hopkins and deliver a lecture to a Baltimore women's group in early 1899 entitled "The Value of College Education for Women" (Dr. Claribel and Miss Etta Cone Papers. Archives and Manuscript Collections, Baltimore Museum of Art, Baltimore, Maryland). Stein's talk was, she admitted, largely an enthusiastic review of Charlotte Perkins Stetson's (later Charlotte Perkins Gilman) *Women and Economics: A Study of the Economic Relation Between Men and Women as a Factor in Social Evolution* from 1898. In 1901, in the *Journal of the American Medical Association*, Stein published "Degeneration in American Women," a lengthy review and response to George J. Engelmann's "The Increasing Sterility of American Women." In that paper, Stein addresses the scientific discipline of human psychology and its practical uses for raising children compared to the parenting of most women uninformed by academic psychology. See Wineapple's edition of this previously unattributed essay 411–414.

38. Ellery Sedgwick, who graduated from Harvard in 1894, a year after Stein began there, recalled his own questioning of the Arnoldian dominance at Harvard, since hitherto "the criteria of Matthew Arnold were secretly woven into all my literary enthusiasms" (qtd. in Raleigh 140). Years later, as the editor of *The Atlantic Monthly*, Sedgwick would correspond with Stein and express guarded interest in her submissions. Only when receiving portions of *The Autobiography of Alice B. Toklas* from an agent for an unnamed writer did Sedgwick finally agree to publish work he was surprised to discover was hers. Donald Gallup published their exchanges in *The Yale University Library Gazette* 28 (Jan. 1954) 109–28.

39. Gates published *Selections from the Prose Writings of Matthew Arnold* with Henry Holt in 1897.

40. One hears William James's dismal scientific opinion of Arnold in the

complaint: "His ultimate heads of classification, too, are lamentable. Think of the 'interesting' used as an absolute term!!" (*CWJ* 2: 86). James read Arnold's letters, however, and enjoyed them enough to send copies to his friends (*CWJ* 8: 113).

41. In the era of Anglo-Saxon nativism, "native" Americans (the earlier white settlers) donned the racial mantle of the American Anglo-Saxonism to differentiate themselves from the influx of European immigrants arriving over the course of the nineteenth century. See John Higham 9–11 and 132–49, and Matthew Frye Jacobson 39–78.

42. In 1901, Leo Stein read Wendell's *A Literary History of America* and recommended it to Gertrude (*Journey to the Self* 7). While Stein never took a class with Wendell, her early work, set amid the contentious American "fever to be an Anglo Saxon and a gentleman" (MA 137), echoes many of Wendell's obsessions with "Americans of 'the better sort,'" (Fredman 109). Wendell's biographer also notes that he was "fond of using the word 'gentleman,' and prepared to accept equally the privileges and the responsibilities implied in the term" (qtd. in Fredman 109). See also Higham 139.

43. The major American Jewish periodical of the era was *The American Hebrew* (1879–1902). In her 1896 essay, Stein uses both "Jew" and "Israelite" and, later, affectionately wrote to Alice B. Toklas as "my little Hebrew." On Jewish nomenclature, see Goldstein 38 and Diner 206–207.

44. Wald usefully compares Stein to Wendell and Kallen on the topic of immigration, 243–245 and 251–252.

45. Stein quotes Arnold correctly (*L&D* 200).

46. Adler founded the Ethical Culture Society in 1884. In her essay, Stein lists "the working-man's school of New York founded by Felix Adler a Jew" as one of her examples of the inclusive nature of Jewish philanthropy (426).

47. Leo refers to Arnold's Hellenic definition of criticism as "a disinterested endeavour to learn and propagate the best that is known and thought in the world" (FC 283).

Chapter 2. Brother Singulars: The "Hidden Tradition" of Jewish Culture in Stein's First Fictions

1. In the morning prayers (*Birkhot HaShahar*) recited upon waking up, the traditional Jew thanks God for not making [him] a woman (*shelo assani ishah*). See, for instance, *The Artscroll Siddur*.

2. As Catharine Stimpson has observed, "Consistently, the language of self was male and masculine" ("The Mind, the Body, and Gertrude Stein" 496). See also Ruddick 53.

3. "Brother Singulars" appears capitalized on page 153 of "The Making of

Americans" and on page 21 of *The Making of Americans*. It appears again in lowercase on page 47 of *The Making of Americans*.

4. Damon positions Stein's invocation of Brother Singulars as an "interlapping of 'queerness,' Jewishness, creativity, womanliness" or as "overlapping communities of fellow renegades" ("Women, Dogs, and Jews" 230). Anne Herrmann argues more generally that "The multiple ways in which one can be odd or at odds simultaneously recognize and serve as cover for those who are sexually queer" (6). Ruddick acknowledges that "male identification had pervaded [Stein's] earlier writings" but insists on the "near-feminist" (53) veiled lesbianism of Stein's singulars (63–65). Ulla Dydo notes that in French the term "Brother Singulars" means homosexual (*Language that Rises* 292). For Doane, Stein "assert[ed] . . . 'maleness'" to cope with the anxieties of authorship but ultimately "den[ies] culturally produced categories" of gender (*Silence and Narrative* 85).

5. For more on Eliot and Arnold and the relationship between the former's "impersonality" and the latter's "disinterestedness," see Lee Oser's *The Ethics of Modernism* (New York: Cambridge University Press, 2007).

6. Damon considers *Q.E.D.* to be equally about Stein's Jewish identity and romance, arguing that Stein "uses 'woman' as metaphoric for 'Jew'" in a story of "(self-)exploration of 'racialism' and 'national character' and a forbidden love entanglement" ("Women, Dogs, and Jews" 235, 230). For Jaime Hovey, Stein "uses race to signal sexuality" by highlighting the confluence of lesbian sexuality and racial difference in fin-de-siècle medical science (564). I agree with Hovey's thesis as a partial explanation of the use of racial metaphors in the novella. See also Will, *Gertrude Stein, Modernism, and the Problem of "Genius"* 38–41 and Doane, *Silence and Narrative* 18.

7. Stein specifically associated insistence with her own Jewish middle-class family. In her later lecture "Portraits and Repetition," Stein describes how she considers exact repetition to be a deadened, unchanging expression while insistence is alive, almost the epitome of "human expression" (*LA* 167–168). In that lecture, she recalls that she first realized the nature of insistence when she moved from her solitary orphaned adolescence in California to the warm embrace and insistent chorus of a dozen Baltimore aunts. She was living "with a lot of [her] relations and principally with a whole group of very lively little aunts who had to know anything. If they had to know anything and anybody does they naturally had to say and hear it often, anybody does, and as there were ten and eleven of them they did have to say and hear said whatever was said and any one not hearing what it was they said had to come in to hear what had been said. That inevitably made everything said often" ("Portraits and Repetition" 168–169). See DeKoven, *A Different Language* 46–62.

8. Damon argues that Adele unites the categories of Jewish and middle class,

"in the context of what Weininger terms 'faulty' Jewish language use, that is, a tendency toward free-association and illogic" ("Women, Dogs, and Jews" 231).

9. See Wineapple on Stein's "complicated" racism in *Q.E.D.* and *Three Lives* (234–238).

10. Hasia Diner writes that "Jews—associated with business and almost totally absent from agriculture—became symbols of material acquisition. In the press, theater, literature, and politics, they were linked with money" (185). See Higham on a similar reputation for mercantilism among German-Americans. The association of Jews and business was not always positive: Higham records how during the Civil War, "Jews were often singled out for exploiting the war effort" (13). After the war, he continues, "The very real economic exploits of the age underwrote its booster spirit" (16). However, "Jews . . . lost in reputation as they gained in social and economic status. Alone among European immigrant groups, the Jews during this period met a distrust that spread along with their increasing assimilation" (26). Confirming the Americanness of what Higham calls "the parvenu spirit" (27), Foote offers evidence that in the Gilded Age, "In Europe, the etiquette writers noted, all Americans were parvenus and upstarts" (47).

11. Such identification with the middle class would, in its American version, be "notoriously" Hebraic, what Cuddihy describes as "the curious, secret, adversary relationship of the secular Jewish intellectual to the Jewish bourgeoisie (that is, the ordinary, Jewish, middle-class community). The intellectual is sensitive and refined; the bourgeoisie, obviously, is vulgar" (225).

12. The vocabulary of outcast Jewish apostles was something Stein shared with her brother, Leo. In a 1913 letter to friend Mabel Weeks, he complained about disliking his sister's recent writing, "But as I said, I'm a rank outsider. I am no longer a prophet in Israel or at best only a Jeremiah" (*Journey Into the Self* 49).

13. See Hess.

14. See Doane, *Silence and Narrative* 24–31.

15. Henry James's *The Ambassadors* deploys a similarly Arnoldian phrasing: "He must approach Chad, must wait for him, deal with him, master him, but he mustn't dispossess himself of the faculty of seeing things as they were" (82).

16. On the compositional history of the novel, see Mellow 267–270, 318–320, Bridgman (59–60), and Gallup.

17. Yuri Slezkine makes the broadest claim for the Jew as mercantilist model of modernity. See also Gary Levine on Stein in this vein.

18. Jews were prohibited from vacationing at many resorts. In 1899, as I note in the previous chapter, William James proposed to "return the boycott" of a summer resort that had begun excluding Jews (*CWJ* 8: 523). See historians Dinnerstein, Selzer, and Diner.

19. Diner describes the culture of peddling as "an almost universal male Jewish

experience in nineteenth-century America" (66), and Harley Erdman discusses the peddler as a stock Jewish character in the theater. With the word "peddler" practically synonymous for "Jew," Stein omits it in the published version of the novel, where she describes "the man who comes . . . to do a little selling to the servants in the kitchen" (*MA* 14).

20. In *Staging the Jew: The Performance of an American Ethnicity, 1860–1920*, Erdman includes a poster for the play *Sam'l of Posen, as The Drummer on the Road (Spot Cash)* which, like Stein's narrator in "The Making of Americans," shows the Jew's evolution from itinerant young peddler just off the boat to more refined merchant and then gentleman of means (85).

21. In the 1936 memoir, *Everybody's Autobiography*, Stein recalled: "so there was a grandmother she was dead and her name not an easy one began with G so my mother preferred it should be an easy one so they named me Gertrude Stein" (115).

22. There is substantial critical conversation concerning the idea of a Jewish home in language. See Hana Wirth-Nesher, "Language as Homeland in Jewish-American Literature," in *Insider/Outsider: American Jews and Multiculturalism*, Eds. David Biale, Michael Galchinsky, and Susannah Heschel (Berkeley: University of California Press, 1998) 212–230. Also see Sidra DeKoven Ezrahi, *Booking Passage: Exile and Homecoming in the Modern Jewish Imagination* (Berkeley: University of California Press, 2000).

23. Higham claims that American Jews were alone among recent immigrants sending their children to college at the beginning of the twentieth century (161). Slezkine finds a similar dynamic in Central Europe: "Throughout modern Europe, education was expected to lead to money; only among Jews, apparently, was money almost universally expected to lead to education" (49). Women lacked such access to education, as Paula E. Hyman notes in *Gender and Assimilation in Modern Jewish History* (Seattle: University of Washington Press, 1995) 18–19.

24. The narrator agrees that learning about love, courtship, and marriage solely from books is not wise and warns readers of our tendency to be "slaves to a storybook tradition" (MA 148). For more on Stein's use of the marriage plot and the influence of literature, see Priscilla Wald 282–283, 293–294.

25. Stein's use of the word "interesting" to convey Julia's Arnoldian idealism was commonplace. In *Q.E.D.*, Helen conflates "interesting" with "queer" when she lovingly badgers Adele into admitting that she is admirably both "queer and interesting" (77). As quoted above, William James complained of Arnold that, "His ultimate heads of classification, too, are lamentable. Think of the 'interesting' used as an absolute term!!" (*CWJ* 2: 86).

26. The final version of the novel maintains this Arnoldianism: "now it had come to her, to see . . . clearly and freely things as they are and not as she had wished them to be for her" (*MA* 33).

27. Similarly, Laura Doyle notes that with this anecdote, "Stein signals her awareness of the narrative tension between repetition and progress, or pastness and futureness" (256). This Aristotelian allusion grows in importance, becoming the opening passage of the published version of the novel. See Bridgman 66–67, Brinnin 93, Dearborn 166, Doane 91–93, and Wald 253–257, 344.

28. Stein first used the line, "There is nothing we are more intolerant of than our own sins writ large in others," in an 1894 Radcliffe theme, and her instructor imagined it to have been taken from Montaigne or Confucius ("Radcliffe Manuscripts" 120). She may have read Wilde's *The Picture of Dorian Gray* (published 1890 or 1891), in which Lord Henry quips, "But I can't help detesting my relations. I suppose it comes from the fact that none of us can stand other people having the same faults as ourselves" (12).

29. Stein planned to use this speech yet again, writing in her notes for the novel, "Use that middle class conversation of mine in the other book that begins things as David's beginning of more intimate relations with moonlight walk with Rena Barkholdt" (37.759.13). The published novel keeps the more anonymous version of the passage in the voice of the narrator (*MA* 34).

30. In a 1933 review of *The Autobiography of Alice B. Toklas*, William Troy wrote:

> what Miss Stein has in common with James she has in common with Poe, Hawthorne, Melville, and several other important and characteristic American writers: an orientation from experience towards the abstract, an orientation that has been so continuous as to constitute a tradition, if not actually *the* American tradition. Of this tradition it is possible to see in Miss Stein's writing not only a development but the pure culmination. (275)

31. In her lecture "The Gradual Making of The Making of Americans," Stein describes this process as the result of a historical progression:

> the 18th century had concerned itself with sentences, the 19th with phrases, and the 20th with paragraphs.
>
> And so it was natural that in writing The Making of Americans I had proceeded to enlarge my paragraphs so as to include everything. What else could I do. In fact inevitably I made my sentences and my paragraphs do the same thing, made them be one and the same thing. (*LA* 159)

Damon, in contrast, reads Stein's style alongside biblical tradition to underscore the "prodigal" nature of the avant-garde and the Jewishness of American beginnings, since "European American immigrants from the 1600s onward have seen [a connection] between their journey and that of the biblical Jews" ("Women, Dogs, and Jews" 225–226).

32. While Wald sees this passage as evidence of the narrator's own confusion in

story-telling (277–278), Doyle takes it more seriously as a critique of sentimental novelistic traditions (265).

33. Slote finds commonalities between Joyce's "Eumaeus" and Proust, noting that Proust's narrator explains that the apparent "monotony" of a great writer's repetition reveals that they have just one work or that they have a singular "beauty" "refracted"—Stein might say "insistent"—across their entire oeuvre: "En repensant à la monotonie des oeuvres de Vinteuil, j'expliquais à Albertine que les grands littérateurs n'ont jamais fait qu'une seule oeuvre, ou plutôt réfracté à travers de milieux divers une même beauté qu'ils apportent au monde" (Marcel Proust, *À la recherche du temps perdu*. 1913. Vol. 3 [Paris: Gallimard, 1988] 877, qtd. in Slote, "A Eumaean Return," *Hypermedia Joyce Studies* 6.1 [2005]. n17).

34. Two years before affirming her connection to Joyce and Proust, Stein had distanced herself from Joyce. She recalled Picasso's comradely affirmation of his own difference from Braque and hers from Joyce, saying, "yes, Braque and James Joyce, they are the incomprehensibles whom anybody can understand. Les incompréhensibles que tout le monde peut comprendre" (*ABT* 212).

Chapter 3. "So much like a yid": An Associative Genealogy of "Jewish Types" in the Notebooks for *The Making of Americans*

1. For more on this chronology, see Gallup.

2. Stein indicates her changing intentions with the note—"A long book, a History of Everybody" (38.791)—which, with its capitalization may be an emendation to the 1903 subtitle "Being the History of a Family's Progress." Stein slightly modified the original subtitle when she published the book in 1925, replacing the definite article with an indefinite article, *"Being a History of a Family's Progress."* This change previews the movement within the novel itself from definite to indefinite claims, which I discuss in chapter 4.

3. Ulla Dydo and Leon Katz organized and catalogued the notebooks at the Beinecke according to corresponding passages in the novel. Early and important studies that examine or refer to Stein's notebooks include Leon Katz's widely circulated but unpublished 1963 dissertation, "The First Making of *The Making of Americans*: A Study Based on Gertrude Stein's Notebooks and Early Versions of Her Novel (1902–1908)" and Marianne DeKoven's *A Different Language*. See also Jayne Walker, Lisa Ruddick, and Wendy Steiner.

4. Stein later wrote of her first experiment in the Harvard Psychology Laboratory, a study of fatigue and automatic writing in almost 100 Harvard and Radcliffe students, where she became very interested in the student-subjects as types of people: "I was very much interested in the way they had their nature in them and sitting there while their arm was in the [automatic writing] planchette and hardly vaguely talking, it was interesting to me to see how I came to feel that I

could come sometime to describe every kind there is of men and women and the bottom nature of them and the way it was mixed up with the other natures in them" (*EA* 266).

5. In one notebook entry Stein characterizes her influence over Annette and Harriet as a "male influence" not unlike the "hypnotic influence" sometimes observed in friendships between similar kinds of people (38.790). Katz claims that Stein records her process of learning Annette Rosenshine on pages 308–311, 317, and 318 of *The Making of Americans* ("First Making" 236). Leo, too, continued to have a lively characterological practice. In recounting her early courtship with Leo, Nina Auzias claimed that in lieu of inviting her to pose for him as an artist's model, he invited her to "come to visit [him] as a psychological model" (qtd. in Leo Stein, *Journey Into the Self* 28).

6. Stein was intent on describing as many variations between major types as possible: "In big book after doing most xquisite flavor to the pure genius, Chalfin to Pablo, Janet to B.B. and Alice show the basis of all Simon to Chalfin to Pablo. Bertha to Alice to Janet and the infinite variations that spring from these" (38.788).

7. Stein may have also found models for her character study in *The Ambassadors* where James presents both his central protagonist, Strether, and his mentor, Miss Gostrey, as concerned with types. Gostrey identifies people in a restaurant with the remark, "Oh yes, they're types!" and Strether continues thinking about this as they attend a play: "It was an evening, it was a world of types, and this was a connexion above all in which the figures and faces in the stalls were interchangeable with those on the stage. . . . However he viewed his job it was 'types' he should have to tackle" (36).

8. For beauty's opposition to the earth type, see 37.761.[32]. Stein also explains: "May call Jewish type ethical & earthy opposed to Man of the world the most idealist and finest form of the conventional success" (37.761.[28–29]). "Idealist" and "Beauty" types appear together on a list of Anglo-Saxon types, and one diagram shows the "Beauty group" counterposed with "earthy success man justice" (37.761.[27]). In another diagram, Stein considers the writer Neith Boyce, wife of her old friend Hutchins Hapgood, to have a top nature in the Anglo-Saxon beauty group ("upper flavor beauty") and a bottom nature in the Jewish earth group's female iteration, the servant girl ("lower layer servant girl") (37.761.back cover). For "faith" as a characteristic lacking in the "jewish side," see 37.764.[2a-verso], quoted below note 26.

9. Katz mistakenly identifies male and female types as the primary division of character in the notebooks and maps that division onto the later references to "attacking" and "resisting" kinds in the novel ("First Making" 289). Stein's types were more racial than gendered. In the Harvard Psychology Laboratory, she had

grouped noteworthy subjects as "Types I and II" and observed great variation within the two types and among several intermediary types. Like the Jewish and Anglo-Saxon types to follow, Stein considered Types I and II in a racial-national manner, noting with exasperation the characteristic "self-repression . . . so prominent an element in the New England character" that it was an impediment to her experiments ("Cultivated Motor Automatism" 299). Her classification of "New England character" was the regional expression of Anglo-Saxonism in America, a type she later recalled observing in her college rooming-house in Cambridge, where "Everybody was New England" (*EA* 155).

10. Stein, in Toklas's voice, roots her use of the attacking and resisting kinds in a conversation with Matisse:

> Matisse intimated that Gertrude Stein had lost interest in his work. She answered him, there is nothing within you that fights itself and hitherto you have had the instinct to produce antagonism in others which stimulated you to attack. But now they follow.
>
> That was the end of the conversation but a beginning of an important part of The Making of Americans. Upon this idea Gertrude Stein based some of her most permanent distinctions in types of people. (*ABT* 65)

11. Stein's note instructs: "Make the independent depence [*sic*] and dependent independence attacking and resisting attacking like Martha Hersland for one and Bruner for another" (38.792.[43]) Stein likely derived this bipartite nomenclature from Herbert Spencer's widely taught *First Principles* (1864). Spencer differentiates between "two orders of manifestations" modified dialectically as "passive but independent . . . [and] active but dependent" (130, 171).

12. Like *Q.E.D.*'s Adele, who demands her community live up to the "middle-class ideal" to "avoid excitements and cultivate serenity," Jefferson Campbell is an outcast apostle, who wants his community "to be regular in all your life, and not to be always wanting new things and excitements" (*Q.E.D.* 59; *TL* 116, 117).

13. The "moral Caliban" was a popular turn-of-the-century character type appearing in poems, fiction, and nonfiction from England, New Zealand, Texas, and San Francisco. A Google search turns up several appearances of the phrase in books and periodicals from the 1850s through 1910, including critical writing about Shakespeare's *The Merchant of Venice* and Jack London's *The Sea-Wolf*.

14. For more on the physiological stereotypes that empirical scientists had about Jews, see Sander Gilman, *The Jew's Body*. New York: Routledge, 1991.

15. Stein describes Jewish or "resisting" types with the dark eyes—"dependent independent / dark-eyed" (38.785)—, and dark or red hair common to the costume of the stage Jew, such as the note that states, "I think she is quite clear now, red headed brown eyed resistants" (38.798).

16. Stein diagnoses her nephew Allan, for example, as likely suffering from neurosis and determines his Jewish nature from his lower lip, which either suggests his melancholy (from pouting) or his physiognomy (a notably fleshy lip):

> Interesting that all the earthy ones are afraid of heart trouble and poisoning etc and acknowledge it Marie Lorenzin, Harriet, Pablo, Mike and me. All the independent dependents not, Alice, Leo, Sally, Fernande. This is what makes me quite sure that Allan will turn out an earthy one. His lower lip says so too. (38.790)

17. Stein draws explicit correspondences in a gendered chart in the "Diagram book," which lists:

Men	Women
Idealist	free soul.
Fanatic	—
Beauty	lady-flavor
Intellectual	Mabel–Miss Franke.
Earthy	servant girl.
lurid	lurid.
Bazarofs	ethical. (37.761.[50])

18. Stein's use of a Jewish-tinged dirty water in Adele's reflection echoes and reappropriates antisemitism of the era. Trubowitz quotes from a 1901 issue of London's *Pall Mall Gazette* where an anonymous writer compares Jewish immigration to diseased and dirty water: "[T]he small-pox now creeping through London, this agony now throbbing and scorching in my arm is caused (make no mistake about it) by the scum washed to our shores in the dirty waters flowing from foreign drainpipes" (40–41).

19. Linda Wagner-Martin includes a rendering of Stein's diagram of the "Jewish group" as an example of Stein's development of a "teleology of personalities" but does not explain the role it plays (84). Katz makes no mention of "Jewish" or "earthy" types in his account of Stein's diagram of male types, even though Stein titled the diagram as the "Jewish group" ("First Making" 277–278). Jayne Walker affirms the fundamental nature of Stein's attacking and resisting or "independent dependent" and "dependent independent" types to her early fiction and as the major divisions "that inform all human behavior," but misses their roots in Anglo-Saxon and Jewish types (48–49). Wineapple inconclusively links Stein's Jewish type to the behavior of running oneself by the mind, "whatever that ultimately meant" (319).

20. Katz is correct that Stein briefly used "german" in early drafts of the novel, but there is absolutely no evidence for his claim that Stein first (or ever) openly

described the families in her novel as "Jewish." The notesheets he cites as the "original" or "first" draft cannot be what he claims since, by his own description, those notes themselves make reference to earlier drafts of the novel: Katz cites two notes (37.752 and 37.753) that do not show Stein "deleting" the word "Jewish," but instead, as he states, they are "very clearly plans for revising old material" ("First Making" 206–207, 36).

21. From November 1952 to February 1953, Katz relied on Toklas's "kindness . . . [in] adumbrat[ing] and orally annotat[ing] the Notebooks out of her store of memories" ("First Making" vi). Toklas's memories, as recorded by Katz, included the recollection of Stein wryly noting "they have never accused me of being a Jew. At least I'm not typical" (208). Toklas led Katz to conclude that "Stein was hard put to it all her life to reconcile herself to her own Jewishness" (204).

22. Damon, "Gertrude Stein's Doggerel 'Yiddish': Women, Dogs, and Jews" 232; Burke 131; Bridgman 161; Moore 18.

23. Katz thought Stein's character studies in *The Making of Americans* were a big mistake. He imagined that if Stein had held onto plot and maintained the repetitious style of *Three Lives,* the novel "would unquestionably have been accepted by general readers as one of the greatest of the twentieth century" ("First Making" 223).

24. The script of the play renders the line: "I guess it's all a dream. It was too good to be true.—No, by Golly, I seen him—I saw him with my eyes—I was speaking with him" (Klein with Arthur, *The Auctioneer*, Act III, page 19). For more on *The Auctioneer* and other plays of this kind, see Erdman.

25. The typological categories in Stein's notebooks exhibit a remarkable fluidity. For example, Stein notes of the Jewish "earth group": "this is essentially the servant group although it may transform itself into *mistress* by a practical intelligence . . . [or] to real *intellect* like mine [. . .] or to pure *lady*, as it does in Mrs. Rosenshine carried farther than it goes into pure *servant girl* group into *ethical*" (37.761.[145–146], emphasis added to identify names of Stein's types).

26. Her diagram of the "Jewish group" positions brother Leo under the "intellectual group" (37.764.[3a-verso]; see figure 2), and, as noted above, she lists "practical intelligence" and "real intellect" as two varieties of the "earth group" (37.761.[145, 146, 145]). In another note, Stein describes varieties of intellectual character of the "jewish side" of a character type exemplified by the writer Henri-Pièrre Roché:

> The jewish side of them lacks this sensibility this real faith and it is replaced by a lyrical pretty quality and a passion for rather confused emotional and transcendental thinking and an intelligent facile practical intellect in their real business whatever it is. It goes over with them into the purely intellectual group, the untemperamental intellectual as the other group the

Christian side goes over into the idealistic group. (37.764.[2a-verso continuing onto 3a])

27. Stein's note conforms to Weininger's consideration of Goethe as one of "the most introspective of men" (316). Stein owned *The Autobiography of Goethe* (1903) and *Conversations of Goethe with Eckermann and Soret* (1906) (BGS). Stein prided herself on having read Carlyle's epic biography of Frederick the Great and noted her plans to use this autobiographical detail for one of her fictional stand-ins: "Jane reading Frederick the great" (37.760.[39]). Later, she has Toklas describe the adolescent Stein's "bookish life":

> She read a tremendous amount of history, she often laughs and says she is one of the few people of her generation that has read every line of Carlyle's Frederick the Great and Lecky's Constitutional History of England besides Charles Grandison and Wordsworth's longer poems. (*ABT* 74)

28. Stein owned a two-volume edition of *The Life and Letters of Charles Darwin, 1888–1889* (BGS).

29. In *Howards End* (composed 1908–1910), Forster's protagonist imagines a "rainbow bridge" of love that will "connect the prose and the passion.... the beast and the monk" (158, 159).

30. In the Diagram book, Stein analyzes two "moral Calibans" who were Jewish by birth: doctor Claribel Cone, a Baltimore friend of Stein's, and Harriet Levy, a fellow Californian who had accompanied Toklas to Paris in 1907. Stein copied the "moral Caliban" study out of the Diagram book onto folio sheets, striking out Claribel's name to focus solely on Harriet as a representative of this problematic type. A few years later, Stein drew on her study for two literary creations: "Harriet Fear" (*Two* 343–346), which echoes the notebook entry, "Harriet is quite right to fear me, for her" (38.797), and the portrait "Harriet" (*Portraits and Prayers* 105–107).

31. In Kipling's 1891 poem "Tomlinson," Saint Peter complains to the eponymous protagonist, "'Ye have read, ye have heard, ye have thought,' he said, 'and the tale is yet to run: / 'By the worth of the body that once ye had, give answer— what ha' ye done?'" (131). Stein owned numerous volumes by Kipling including a collection of ballads with this poem (BGS).

32. Stein heard about the American intolerance for daring works of art when Mike and Sally brought Matisse paintings home to San Francisco from Paris after the 1906 earthquake. See Golson 43.

33. See Leo Stein, *The A-B-C of Aesthetics* (1927) and *Appreciation: Painting, Poetry, and Prose* (1947).

34. In addition to notebook references to "Tomlinson" and Kipling's writing, Stein discusses his influence in her lecture "What Is English Literature" (*LA* 46).

She also addresses Kipling's notion of Anglo-Saxonism, the "white man's burden," in the 1906 draft of *The Making of Americans* (40.835) and in *Wars I Have Seen* (36–37, 48).

35. Here Stein alludes to her typology of attacking and resisting kinds, of which Cézanne was the resisting Jewish kind. Elsewhere in the notebooks she determined, "Cezanne-earthy resis" (38.798) and concluded, "Cezanne resistance great but dragged along" (39.813.[29]). She also uses Cézanne's Jewish nature as a point of reference: "earthy bottom like Cezanne or Pablo or mine" (38.791).

36. Jayne Walker, in her discussion of this notebook passage, provides a very plausible reading of Stein's reference to Cézanne by quoting the painter on the subject of reality: "To paint after nature is not to copy the objectively given, it is to realize one's sensations" (qtd. in Walker 3). See also Dydo, "To Have the Winning Language" 60; Katz, "Matisse, Picasso and Gertrude Stein" 59–62; and Ruddick 95–100.

37. Stein's thoughts on objects and the self have their roots in her philosophy studies at Harvard. In addition to courses, seminars, and labs each year with the psychology branch of the Philosophy Department, Stein took George Santayana's "Introduction to Philosophy. History of Philosophy" in 1893–1894, followed by "Metaphysics" with Josiah Royce in 1894–1895 ("Typed list of Gertrude Stein's courses and instructors").

38. In chapter 2, I discuss the racial (and racist) stereotypes in Stein's college writings and first fictions, where she characterizes locales like Baltimore as a place "where no one is in a hurry and [one hears] the voices of the negroes singing as their carts go lazily by" ("Radcliffe Manuscripts" 139). In the notebooks, Stein characterizes half of her nature as "the Rabelasian, nigger abandonment, Vollard, daddy side" (37.761.[64]).

39. The complete note recalls a conversation with Harriet Levy as the catalyst for Stein's realization that character study was paramount: "Must make my hero grow into realisation of B. as I did of Sally, through experience, quarrels in the summer, that epoch making for me conversation with Harriet about her when I explained her after Harriet had given me her version which was alright except the bottom and then one with Leo about her originality" (38.792).

40. Other than these notes, Stein rarely writes explicitly about her conception of pragmatism. Whatever similarities her pragmatism bore to that of her Harvard professors Charles Peirce or William James, Stein thought she was breaking with the old and making semiotics new. See Lisi Schoenbach on Stein and pragmatism.

Chapter 4. Pariah Modernism: Estranging Narration in *The Making of Americans*

1. In chapter 6 I discuss Stein's later use of the word "stimulating" to refer specifically to Jews and immigrants and their positive effect on modern society.

2. Stein eventually makes explicit what she sees as the Jewish quality of a parvenu posture and its irredeemable nature. See my "Gertrude Stein, Alice Toklas, and Albert Barnes: Looking Like a Jew in *The Autobiography of Alice B. Toklas*."

3. Begun in 1903, Stein completed the manuscript of *The Making of Americans* in 1911, though she made several changes between the portions serialized in the *Transatlantic Review* in 1924 and the first printing of the book, Robert McAlmon's Contact Edition, in 1925. See Mellow 266–270, 316–320.

4. Stein changes the name of Julia's betrothed from "Henry" in the 1903 draft to "Alfred" in the 1911 draft. She also changes the names of several characters from the typically Biblical names of Jewish tradition in the 1903 draft to German names in the 1906–1908 draft and then to more Anglicized names by 1911. The patriarch Abe Dehning becomes "Henry" (and "Herman") Dehning (*MA* 7 and 18), his brother Sam becomes "Adolphe" (*MA* 10), and the Hersland matriarch née Fanny Heizman becomes the more Anglicized "Fanny Hissen" (*MA* 43). The Hersland patriarch, meanwhile, who had been Gustav Hersland in the 1903 draft, becomes "David" in the final draft, a name he shares with his father and his son (*MA* 21, 38, 47).

5. See Dearborn, Doyle, Wald, and Wilson. Stein herself encouraged this biographical reading, reflecting, "We had a mother and a father and I tell all about that in The Making of Americans which is a history of our family" (*EA* 135).

6. In the first notes and notebooks, Stein recorded biographical sources for her plots and characters (37.755–760). From these, Katz reconstructs "the buried narrative" of the novel's first schema ("First Making" 159–194). Beginning with the Diagram book, however, Stein made studies of character type with minimal reference to the book's characters (37.761).

7. The manuscript drafts of the novel in the *cahiers* from 1906–1908, demonstrate Stein's purposeful diction regarding the metaphorically Jewish origins of the Hersland and Dehning families depicted in the novel. In the 1906 draft, Stein writes openly of the "german" family's struggle with "Anglo-Saxon" ways of American living (40.835). The family is explicitly *not* Anglo-Saxon and is thus free from Kiplingesque duty: they have "no primal upheaving Anglo-saxon, white man's burden to uplift" their way of living (40.835). The family maintain from the 1903 draft the metaphorically Jewish descriptors celebrated as "sordid unaspiring, ordinary, middle class decent enough" (40.835). After 1908, Stein replaces the *german* origins of the older generation of the Hersland family with the adjectives "ordinary" and "foreign," and replaces *Anglo-Saxon* with "american" (*MA* 6, 17, 15). As the novel proceeds, however, Stein selectively omits even the "foreign" and "american" designation for the Herslands, leaving only their "middle class living"

to characterize them (*MA* 53). This change occurs in the 1925 book publication, whereas in the 1924 serialization of the novel in the *Transatlantic Review*, the Herslands are people with "middle class foreign american living" ("The Making of Americans," *Transatlantic Review*, 188–202).

8. See Ruddick 63, Walker 51, and Dearborn 164. Dearborn identifies the narrator as Stein but adds that "Stein is autobiographically invested in each character in *The Making of Americans*, including the servants" (258n32). Doyle, meanwhile, reads the narrator's melancholic exclamations as the feminine sentimentality "of a weeping heroine-narrator, betrayed and undone by her own belief in the 'bottom natures' of her characters" (256).

9. Except for Maria Damon, most of Stein's critics have avoided connecting narrative style and characterology to Jewish nature in *The Making of Americans*. Jessica Berman, for example, situates Proust in the context of Jewish thinker Bernard Lazare's notion of the "conscious pariah" and yet her chapter on Stein's "wandering" and "singular" heroes never mentions Jewish identity (157–158, 169).

10. In the quotation from *Everybody's Autobiography* it is difficult to determine where James's words end and Stein's begin. However, Stein had earlier used the phrase "abject truth" in an anecdote about James in *The Autobiography of Alice B. Toklas*: "William James delighted her. His personality and his teaching and his way of amusing himself with himself and his students all pleased her. Keep your mind open, he used to say, and when some one objected, but Professor James, this that I say, is true. Yes, said James, it is abjectly true" (78–79).

11. See Arendt's "Creating a Cultural Atmosphere," "We Refugees," and "The Jew as Pariah: A Hidden Tradition" in *The Jew as Pariah: Jewish Identity and Politics in the Modern Age*.

12. Lazare (1865–1903) was a French-Jewish writer, Dreyfusard, and Zionist, who sought to provoke Jews to political action by unpopular means. According to Arendt, Lazare's "conscious pariah" is a Jeremiah who "must awake to an awareness of his position and, conscious of it, become a rebel against it—the champion of an oppressed people" (76). See Lazare's *Job's Dungheap* (New York: Schocken Books, 1948).

13. Stein included John Stuart Mill in her notebooks characterology (38.785), and her thinking on singularity may draw from his "Of Individuality, as One of the Elements of Well-being" from *On Liberty* (1859). In that essay, Mill argues that protections of eccentricity are a good measure of a society's protection of freedom and "moral courage" (121).

14. In the novel, Stein quietly alludes to the experimental sentences by naming the Herslands's hometown Gossols, a reference to the small Catalonian village of Gósol. Picasso visited Gósol in the summer of 1906 and began experimenting with portraiture there by abstracting identities into iconic types. Art historian

Vincent Giroud describes Picasso's stay there as "a very productive period for him" influenced by "the twelfth-century Romanesque sculpture known as the Gósol Madonna" (29). Stein was privy to what would become a revolution in Picasso's style since it occurred as he was trying to finish his *Portrait of Gertrude Stein*, which became a "cornerstone" of the new abstract style (qtd. in Giroud 30). He completed Stein's portrait after his return from Gósol by rendering her face as a mask that echoes the wide-eyed expression of Gósol's Romanesque statuary, the protruding eyes of "archaic Andalusian sculptures he saw displayed at the Louvre that spring," and the portraits and "face mask" sketches he made of his 90-year-old innkeeper in Gósol (Giroud 26, 28–30). As Stein has Toklas recall in *The Autobiography of Alice B. Toklas*, "The day he returned from Spain Picasso sat down and out of his head painted the head in without having seen Gertrude Stein again" (57). The autobiography revisits the synchronicity of their stylistic changes and, obliquely, the novel's allusion to Gósol, when Toklas points to the coincidence of Stein's "working tremendously over the beginning of The Making of Americans" precisely when Picasso was engaged in the "intensive struggle which was to end in cubism" (*ABT* 57, 54).

15. See Mitrano (31), Moore (12), Ruddick, and Watten on the usefulness of psychoanalytic discourse for interpreting the narrator's annunciation of his endeavor despite, as Ruddick notes, Stein's lack of interest in Freud.

16. Of course, the narrator's reticence is something commonly felt by writers. Stein may have borrowed a page from Henry James's *The Ambassadors*, whose protagonist recalls a childhood embarrassment: "He could perform before strangers, but relatives were fatal" (122). Similarly, Herbert Spencer wrote of his autobiography's "constitutional . . . frankness," which sounded like he was "addressing the public as though it consisted of personal friends" (Spencer ix–x). Finding such frankness impolite, he asked that it be published posthumously, which it was. In a letter to publisher Grant Richards from 1906, Joyce famously claims to have anticipated the "objections" readers might have to the "scrupulous meanness" of his *Dubliners*: "All these objections of which the printer is now the mouthpiece arose in my mind when I was writing the book, both as to the themes of the stories and their manner of treatment. Had I listened to them I would not have written the book. I have come to the conclusion that I cannot write without offending people" (*Letters of James Joyce* Vol. 2, 134). It is not surprising then to learn that, in 1911, Richards rejected Stein's *Three Lives*, concerned that the form, a collection of stories, would be "a great barrier to its popularity," and that the "scene and atmosphere" were "so very American that the ordinary English reader would be a little at a loss" (Letter from Grant Richards to Gertrude Stein, September 27, 1911. YCAL). He nonetheless invited Stein to send her "long book" and, while avowedly eager "to have a book of yours on our list," he rejected *The Making of*

Americans fearing "it would not be successful" (October 17, 1911. YCAL). For more on the conscious positioning of the writer as necessarily at a remove from criticism, see Barbara Herrnstein Smith, *Contingencies of Value: Alternative Perspectives for Critical Theory* (Cambridge, MA: Harvard University Press, 1988).

17. For more on Stein and dialects, see Juliana Spahr.

18. Later in the novel, the Herslands do not live among other wealthy families in Gossols, but, instead near, "for them, poor queer kind of people" (89). As with hygiene, "queer" and "natural way[s] of being" vary according to perspective, something the narrator indicates by always clarifying who considers others queer (89). For example, the poor folks *themselves* perceive Mr. Hersland to be queer: "he was, in the beginning of their knowing him, to them, a queer man, with his big ways in buying and his way of owning everything around him to his feeling" (140).

19. This association between Brother Singulars and Jewish identity has not gone unnoticed. Doyle's nagging feelings about "perhaps Jewish immigrant figures" in Stein's first fictions and "the untouched question of whether these Germans are Jews or Christians" in *The Making of Americans* leads her to wonder, "Is this a Jewish narrator?" (255, 258, 259).

20. Unlike the vitality of Brother Singulars, servant girls are singulars who do not thrive on isolation: "Many servants get to have in them something that is almost a craziness in them, many have a very lonesome feeling in them not a lonesome feeling of themselves inside them just a lonesome feeling that makes queer, sometimes a little crazy women of them" (168–169). This sounds like the picture historian Faye Dudden paints of women in service in late nineteenth-century America: "Most domestics toiled alone, and isolation was greatest for the maid-of-all-work who shouldered the heaviest workload at the lowest pay. . . . [and] especially hard on immigrants" (198).

21. On a chart listing male and female correspondences, Stein positions the "servant girl" as the female equivalent of the "earthy" type (37.761.[50]) and elsewhere notes, "Servant class particularly earthy" (37.774).

22. For a contemporary account, see Harriet Elizabeth Prescott Spofford, *The Servant Girl Question* (Boston: Houghton Mifflin, 1881). Stein was not the only novelist to discuss this question in her immediate circle of acquaintance. Alfred Hodder was an author and academic whose romantic affairs became the subject of Stein's 1904 story "Fernhurst," later incorporated into *The Making of Americans* (427–476). Hodder's 1901 novel *The New Americans*, read by Stein, has a character who insists that "The 'servant-girl' question is not to be compared with" the woman question (418).

23. The narrator finds that differences in race and nation explain the propensity for queerness in servant girl character. He concludes that German servants were

"very steady women" who did not develop queerness, while Irish, Italian, and Mexican women might (171).

24. In *The Spoils of Poynton* (1896), James's middle-class protagonist, whose family has fallen on hard times, denigrates the showy decor of her rival's family. Later, the protagonist self-consciously mocks her own appreciation for a painting in a shop window because it makes her feel like "a servant-girl taking her 'afternoon'" (177).

25. The word "queer" was used similarly by members of Stein's circle to describe her. Bernard Berenson, for example, complained to Isabella Stuart Gardner that Leo and Gertrude were "a tribe of queer, conceited, unworldly, bookish, rude, touchy, brutal, hypersensitive people" (qtd. in Tinterow 83). In the same letter Berenson refers to Stein as "a sort of Semitic primeval female straight from the desert," confirming the antisemitism in his distaste for her "queer" tribe.

26. The narrator's linking of these several or singular "yous" underscores the uncertainty as to which "you" is being addressed. Ashton connects this Steinian ambiguity of the second-person address to Derrida's determination that "uncertainty is essential to all linguistic signs" (594). Even when someone addresses another person in the most personal manner possible, with "his or her most proper name, possibly the most secret," Derrida asserts that a fundamental ambiguity still remains: "I can never be sure when someone says to me—or to you—says to me 'you, you,' that it might not just be any old 'you'" (qtd. in Ashton 594).

27. Ruddick reads the passage as the declaration of the lesbian writer and, using evidence from the notebooks, identifies Alice Toklas as the one who first accepts this outlaw (108). See Doane for a feminist reading of this passage.

28. Although Stein uses the term *equilibration* to connote an unconscious process of mental and psychological *equivocation*, she may have drawn on William James's use of the term "*déséquilibration*," which indicated the unbalanced mental state that most race scientists identified with degeneracy ("Degeneration and Genius" 287). Stein's use may also derive from Spencer's *First Principles*.

29. According to Meyer, Stein "created [in David Hersland] a late-nineteenth-century American rationalist for whom the experience of life's fortuitousness was definitive, and devastating" ("Introduction" xxxiv). Hersland thinks a lot about death and dies young, possibly a suicide, which, for Meyer, suggests that Stein modeled him on Leon Solomons, her partner in the Harvard Psychology Laboratory, who died young from illness (xxxiv). Further, according to family lore, Stein and her brother Leo had only been born because two others had died, which is also David's situation.

30. Neil Schmitz reads this shift as a powerful tool: "The concept of *A Man* or *A Woman* standing behind *he* and *she* (as Platonic mannikins) slowly erodes, and then finally *he/she* also disappears. In this cleared space the massive coda of

The Making of Americans lovingly relishes the indefinite pronoun. . . . Gertrude Stein had thoroughly neutered discourse, and in much of her later experimental portraiture she would use this ambiguous reference (this one, some one, very many) as if indeed it were (for anyone) superbly illustrative" ("Portrait, Patriarchy, Mythos" 76).

31. The few critics who have discussed the epilogue in detail read it as distinct from the rest of the novel, despite numerous textual echoes. Wald dismisses Stein's syntax in the majority of the novel as "unremitting wordplay" and struggles to read the last line of the epilogue, claiming that "Context is generally unhelpful in reading this passage" (286, 297).

Chapter 5. "Can a Jew be wild": A Radical Jewish Grammar in the Voices Poems

1. Marjorie Perloff contrasts the "structure of accumulation" in the prose of *The Making of Americans* with the "reduction" that would follow it in *Tender Buttons* (99). In the revolutionary *Tender Buttons*, composed from 1910 to 1912 and published in 1914, Stein conjoined syllables, words, and phrases by "non-sequitur and logical fallacy," in what Cyrena Pondrom describes as "the brilliantly irrational style" (xv). Stein described it as one in which "words have the liveliness of being constantly chosen," from which Marianne DeKoven dubs it the "lively words" style (*LA* 25; *A Different Language* 67).

2. DeKoven dubbed these poems the "voices" style (*A Different Language* 88). Rosalind Moad elaborates that they are "voice-montages" in which Stein attempts to "c[atch] ephemeral voices in literary forms" (1). Dana Cairns Watson looks more broadly at Stein's conversational voices.

3. Stein's 1913 composition "Yet Dish," from the "lively words" style that directly preceded the voices style, is often read as a transyllabification of the word "Yiddish." Although this may be the first time Stein *pronounces* a Jewish topic in her work, it is still visually veiled by the punning homophones.

4. Beyond the critical writings on Joyce's *Ulysses*, see Cheyette's *Constructions*, Linett, Loewenstein, and Trubowitz.

5. In addition to Quartermain, see Benstock (*Women of the Left Bank*), DeKoven (*A Different Language*), Ruddick, and Schmitz (*Of Huck and Alice*). See also Elizabeth Fifer, *Rescued Readings: A Reconstruction of Gertrude Stein's Difficult Texts* (Detroit: Wayne State University Press, 1992). Notably, Lorna Smedman calls this liberatory reading into question by looking at Stein's use of black racial epithets, and Wanda Van Dusen argues for Stein's fascism.

6. See Mellow 149–150. Moad gives the Stein-Toklas dates as 1909 and 1914 (238).

7. Many of these notes appear in her drafting notebooks where, as Dydo argues, they were used to communicate Stein's affection, sometimes as dedications at the beginning of a composition. Kay Turner published a selection of Stein's loose love notes (not taken from drafting notebooks), and one finds several "jews" there: often Alice, "my baby jew bless / you" (148), sometimes Gertrude, "baby precious her / little jew is all to you" (143), and others, "she's got me like the jewish gentleman / said bless my baby precious bless / she" (100).

8. See Damon's "Gertrude Stein's Doggerel 'Yiddish': Women, Dogs, and Jews."

9. Stein's familial Jewish vocabulary extended to her close relations outside the home as well; in correspondence, for example, Stein notes that she is "rather pleased" that Picasso considers her to be "a real Jewish mother" to his children (Letter to Robert and Diana Abdy, c. 1938. YCAL).

10. Blanche Cook, Penelope Engelbrecht, and Gilbert and Gubar dislike what they see as Stein's embrace of stereotypical gender roles while Turner, Benstock (*Women of the Left Bank*), Norris, DeKoven (*A Different Language*), and Ruddick approve of it. Stimpson, meanwhile, outlines Stein's simultaneous repudiation and reconstitution of heterosexual and patriarchal norms ("Stein and the Transposition of Gender").

11. See Jonathan D. Sarna. "The Pork on the Fork: A Nineteenth Century Anti-Jewish Ditty," *Jewish Social Studies* 44.2 (Spring 1982): 169–172.

12. Stein also has voices that discuss fattening "the Jew" with butter in the poem "As Fine as Melanctha," where, as quoted above, a speaker is determined to "choose a robust jew": "Fill the jew. With what. With butter. Thank you so much for all that good butter" (267, 263). Such concern over the Jew's diet accords with Turner's claim that Stein, in her love notes, often expressed concern for Toklas's digestive health (27).

13. In her appendices, Moad assiduously dates and documents Stein's and Toklas's lives and locations from 1913 to 1922, including their stays in Mallorca (393–455). Stein and Toklas were on the island of Mallorca from April 1915 to June 1916 to avoid being in Paris during the war (Dydo *Gertrude Stein* 44). The exuberant tone of the speaker conveys the proud public parading of this happy couple as they go walking about Mallorca, "Visiting the sea," and greeting passersby ("Look At Us" 264). Moad classifies this poem under her category of those voice-montages with "*repeating title phrase*," a category that also includes "Lifting Belly" (235).

14. In the *carnets* for "An Elucidation" (1923) Stein refers to herself and Alice as "baby and its Jew" near a mention of a birthday: "Please remember me on my birthday / I do / conversation between / baby and its Jew" (qtd. in Dydo *Gertrude Stein* 56n).

15. The manuscript of this line from "Look At Us" reads "That is like the Jewish new year," suggesting that anything—maybe even "to-day"—has a resemblance to "the Jewish new year" (YCAL). Both typescripts of the poem and the posthumously published edition of "Look At Us" in *Painted Lace* omit the word "like" (YCAL). The poem "Coal and Wood," contains a possible allusion to the Jewish New Year and its tradition of sounding the *shofar*—"Remember the ram's horn"— a stanza after an instruction to "Think of Moses" (9). Mention of the Jewish New Year in "Look At Us" is therefore remarkable, especially compared to the solely syllabic mention of *Passover* in the poem "Dates," which reads: "Pass over. / Pass over. / Pass. / Pass. / Pass. / Pass. / Pass pass" (170).

16. See *Gertrude Stein: A Bibliography* by Robert A. Wilson with Arthur Uphill (Rockville, MD: Quill & Brush, 1994).

17. Crowninshield may have considered omitting the Jewish reference, but perhaps the power of the word, even in this uncertain and experimental voices context, convinced him to include it. In the version later published in *Selected Writings*, the "J" in "jew" is capitalized although it was not capitalized in Stein's manuscript notebook or in *Vanity Fair*.

18. The overarching concern with marriage in Stein's poem cannot have been missed by Crowninshield, reinforced as it was by the surrounding pages of the June bridal issue. Stein's poem appears alongside ads for "June Bridal Gifts" from Bailey, Banks, and Biddle of Philadelphia (8) and for *Vanity Fair* itself. Subscribing to the magazine, an ad suggests, would ease the laboriousness of being married by helping husbands and wives "be amusing, though married" (4).

19. On 16 October 1919, Stein sent the poems "The Revery of the Zionist," "IRELAND," and "Land of Nations" to Ellery Sedgwick, the editor of the *Atlantic Monthly*, describing them as part of her "World Series" (Letter to Ellery Sedgwick. YCAL). Dydo notes that the poem "More League" also appeared as one of "Two Cubist Poems. The Peace Conference" in the *Oxford Magazine* (*Gertrude Stein* 94n).

20. The poem was composed between January and October of 1919. I am quoting from the corrected typescript of the poem from Stein's Bound Volume 15 (YCAL), rather than the version published in the posthumous volume *Painted Lace*, which spells "Reverie" with an "ie" and has a "singing dell" rather than a "singing doll."

21. In *The Autobiography of Alice B. Toklas*, Stein also mentions antagonism toward an "expert" in Toklas's account of the sale of one of Braque's paintings (109).

22. Stein and Toklas owned several novels by Disraeli: *Alroy, Coningsby, Lothair, Venetia,* and *Vivian Grey* (BGS).

23. For Damon, "The piece appears to be shot through with contradictions. . . . [that] enact the internal heterogeneity, the contentious pluralism that comprises

the Jewish interpretive community ("Gertrude Stein's Jewishness" 503). Will points to the way that the voices style "emphasizes heterogeneity rather than agreement, pluralism rather than univocality" ("Gertrude Stein and Zionism" 440).

24. See Genesis 10 and Stephen R. Haynes, *Noah's Curse: The Biblical Justification of American Slavery* (New York: Oxford University Press, 2002).

25. Stein's inspiration for the poem's voices may also have come from George Eliot's *Daniel Deronda*, where the Philosopher's Club roundtable of heterogeneous voices debates a proto-Zionist answer to the Jewish question. An admirer of Eliot from her youth, Stein owned the novel and six other volumes by Eliot (BGS).

26. Will notes that this voice's claim "'[r]ace is disgusting if you don't love your country' . . . open[s] the door for the argument that racialist or racist thinking is acceptable if you *do* love your country" ("Gertrude Stein and Zionism" 451). Will warns that despite its ambiguity, such thinking—which she attributes to Stein—hints at a linguistic congruity between Stein's diction and the nationalistic creeds of fascism. Her choice to hear this particular voice as Stein's previews her argument in *Unlikely Collaboration* that Stein collaborated and supported French collaborators with Nazism.

27. Other references to Palestine appear in "Nest of Dishes" from 1921 (100) and "Natural Phenomena" from 1925 (202).

28. In the treaty signed in the Paris suburb of Sèvres in August 1920, the British acquired mandates in Iraq and Palestine. Historian Stephen Stillwell claims that Britain "used the League of Nations apparatus . . . to forward the aims of their imperial policy" (67). See Trubowitz 156–160 for Wyndham Lewis's criticism of the League of Nations as a Jewish and internationalist institution.

29. According to Bülent Gökay, in late 1918 British forces followed the Ottoman army to occupy the Baku oil fields (39). And, as Marian Kent argues, "By 1920 Mesopotamian oil . . . had come to occupy a major place in British diplomatic and military concerns in the Middle East" (157).

30. "Coal and Wood," written in 1920, refers directly to Jessie (Whitehead), about whom Stein would later write, "Jessie always made friends with foreigners from strange places, she had a passion for geography and a passion for the glory of the British Empire" (*ABT* 146). In "Coal and Wood," Jessie and perhaps "James" or another voice, discuss the global reach of the British Empire (8).

31. According to Alice's account in *The Autobiography of Alice B. Toklas*, Stein was reading newspapers such as the *Herald* and "the Daily Mail, although, as she said, she was not interested in Ireland" (144).

32. See a short survey of Stein's writing on Napoleon in my conclusion.

Chapter 6. "Everybody can persecute anybody": What's Funny about Jewish Identity in *Wars I Have Seen*

1. Of the anti-Jewish directives historian Michael Curtis notes that "In the four years of Vichy, 168 discriminatory texts on Jews were issued and Jews were thus injected into every branch of the legal system, and in all subjects, especially those of individual rights and property" (106–107). Historian Renée Poznanski weighs in on the application of the statutes: "While the Vichy government decided on matters of policy and promulgated its law accordingly, it was French society—in other words both administrative offices and public opinion—that determined the application of these measures" (476). Application differed, Poznanski claims, "from one département to another. . . . [and] varied greatly from one region to another" (478). She concludes that any "flexibility" in enforcing the antisemitic and other laws of persecution "was always of local origin: it was never encouraged by ministerial memoranda, which always pleaded for a more rigorous application of rules and regulations. This rigor of application changed over time: there was the period of 'chaos' in the aftermath of the defeat as well as the deterioration that in some places marked the final phase of the Occupation beginning in autumn 1943" (478).

2. Reporter Eric Sevareid shared Stein's account that "The mayor had always protected her secret from the Germans and so had all the people of the village, who knew perfectly well who and what she was. When the Germans began rounding up enemy aliens, the mayor simply forgot to tell them about the Stein household" (458–459). Burns and Dydo add that Stein's neighbor Romain Godet, a member of the Resistance, claimed to have been keeping a protective an eye on her (416). They also mention that because of her connection to René Tavernier, editor of the left-wing journal *Confluences*, which published her work throughout the war, Stein was issued a German-recognized *passeport de protection* in February of 1944, guaranteeing her safe and *legal* passage to Switzerland, though she did not use it (421). Stein herself alludes to many instances of protection in the memoir, such as the "comforting" Swiss who provide her *passeport de protection* (*WIHS* 153), the surprising financial assistance of a Lyon industrialist who had hitherto not been of their acquaintance (112), and the offer by her lawyer to hide in his house in the mountains or to help them cross illegally into nearby Switzerland (50). She writes affectionately, too, of "our friend the captain of gendarmes who has always been so nice to us" and who "helps us get around and helps us get a goat, and helped us every way they help anybody every day often to get away, they do do that" (170, 117).

3. In the 1930s, when "everybody was once again talking revolution," Stein chronicled her acquaintance with Bonapartists, fascists, ultranationalist *croix de feu*, and communists (*EA* 305). Birgit Van Puymbroeck illuminates the importance

of Stein's friendship with the "communist duchess Elisabeth de Gramont, Madame de Clermont-Tonnerre" (85).

4. Historians Marrus and Paxton assert that Faÿ was on the German embassy's list of possible candidates to run their Jewish operations in France before deciding to let Vichy organize such an administration themselves (82).

5. Stein, in a postwar letter, acknowledges Faÿ's "monarchist" politics but assures her correspondent that Faÿ did not denounce anyone during the Occupation (qtd. in Will, "Gertrude Stein, Bernard Faÿ" 660). Will corrects Stein to affirm that Faÿ denounced several employees of the Bibliothèque Nationale as Freemasons and was convicted of collaboration in 1946. Was Stein ignorant of Faÿ's crimes, or did she knowingly deny them? For an extraordinary study of the decades-long social, intellectual, and political dance between Stein and Faÿ, see Will's *Unlikely Collaboration: Gertrude Stein, Bernard Faÿ, and the Vichy Dilemma*.

6. In his postwar memoir, *Les Précieux* (1966), Faÿ claims to have assured Stein that it was his duty ("mon devoir") to keep her safe ("de la garder à l'abri") and describes how he intervened on her behalf over a long lunch with Pétain (162). Faÿ even recalls Stein's indisputable belief that he was Jewish, which rings true, given her past interest in Jewish types. Faÿ claims that Stein insisted, despite his protestations, "Bernard, admit it, you are much too intelligent not to be Jewish" (143, my translation of "Bernard, avouez-le, vous êtes bien trop intelligent pour n'être pas juif").

7. Burns and Dydo published Stein's "Introduction" two years earlier in *The Letters of Gertrude Stein & Thornton Wilder* (406–408), but Van Dusen's outraged (and posthumously published) essay accompanying her edition provocatively threw down the gauntlet by casting Stein's portrait of Pétain in the "Introduction" as a "Portrait of a National Fetish."

8. See Will ("Lost in Translation: Stein's Vichy Collaborations"), Rachel Galvin ("Gertrude Stein, Pétain, and the Politics of Translation"), and Václav Paris. I discuss this debate in greater detail in my conclusion.

9. Will condemns, for example, Stein's 1940 *Atlantic Monthly* essay, "The Winner Loses," as "the most notorious instance" of "Stein's ignorance about the darkening world around her" and argues that its titular language of winning and losing—as borrowings from Faÿ—show Stein's propagandistic aims (*Unlikely* 103). In contrast, Lesinska hears in the *Atlantic* piece Stein's lukewarm affection for Pétain and finds that Stein "conveys a more complex picture of the French response to the war" (38).

10. Neither Stein's "Introduction" nor *Wars I Have Seen* include accents in French names and places, and I have reflected that absence in my quotations.

11. In *Wars I Have Seen*, Stein gets more specific about the "man at the bank" who "explained. . . . there are a great many different points of view and one single man can have quite a great number of them" (81).

12. The anecdote may also celebrate what she saw as Pétain's restraining impulse, something Galvin suggests that Stein admired in the French. Galvin observes that a "rhetoric of understatement [was] a familiar tactic among noncombatant writers," and reminds us that Stein's "use of understatement [in the memoir] is inflected by her idiosyncratic understanding of cultural restraint among the French (*retenue*), which she aimed to emulate in life and in her writing" (*News of War* 280).

13. See *Mrs. Reynolds* 170–172 and *Wars I Have Seen* 87.

14. "Funny" appears numerous times in *The Making of Americans*, such as the narrator's admission, "It makes me a little unhappy that many things are funny and peculiar and strange to me" (482). In 1936, Stein would pen a series of articles in *The Saturday Evening Post* on the topic of money, quipping at the beginning of "All About Money" that "It is very funny about money" (110).

15. The protagonist in *Mrs. Reynolds* notices that amidst a general gauntness, "it was funny that some people did continue to be stout" (224). Reynolds's comment shows how wartime scarcities lead to suspicion, something Stein returns to repeatedly in the memoir. And the wartime protagonist of *Yes Is for a Very Young Man* worries over her young lover's departure, "Oh dear, that does make me feel funny" (24).

16. For Will, "there is no question that Stein sees herself on the side of 'the chosen people'" in the memoir (*Unlikely* 73). Most other critics disagree, however, and, like Malcolm, give cursory readings of what they see as Stein's cursory mention of her Jewish identity or the plight of Jews in France. Malcolm writes: "In *Wars I Have Seen* Stein continues to leave out the essential. She just can't seem to bring herself to say that she and Toklas are Jewish. But the Nazis' persecution of the Jews is clearly on her mind, and the book is full of indirect allusions to it" (79).

17. Davis notes that the publisher had presented *Wars I Had Seen* as "a journalistic firsthand account of the war, smuggled to them across enemy lines" (572). Lesinska points out the documentary significance of these conversations as a "representation of ideologies circulating in France between 1939 and 1945," since Stein so "often repeats somebody else's observations" (33). Galvin, meanwhile, argues that the "journal-like, genre-mixing book is also an anti-newspaper. . . . [that] signals, encodes, and dwells on moments of fear and danger as an alternative to the norms of war reportage" (*News of War* 280).

18. Whittier-Ferguson finds that Stein's late writing "capture[s] something essential about war itself," which he deems typical: "The attempts of every writer to narrate experience during war founder as he or she confronts events that cannot be told, occurrences that refuse grammatical parsing and the shapes of narration" (*Mortality and Form* 93). Galvin argues that Stein transforms such foundering experiences into moments of authorial agency, "enact[ing] the difficulty of

expression through lyric outbursts instead of direct declarations by a first-person speaker" (*News of War* 280).

19. As Davis notes, many readers complain of Stein's "almost unbelievable . . . naïveté" or solipsism, given the quotidian and local scope of the narrative (572). They criticize Stein's seemingly abortive approach to "the question of the holocaust" (Diedrich 102), her "apparent refusal to face [the war's] horrors, her inability to commit to one side or the other" (Mills 17), and claim that she "avoids confronting the mass destruction and death intensifying around her" (Olson 343). Benstock criticizes what she sees as an appalling ignorance, since "it remains unclear whether she ever understood what was at stake in this war, what had led to it, or what her own position was in it" ("Paris Lesbianism" 342). Benstock condemns Stein's apparent "anti-Semitism [as] a mark of her own self-hatred as a Jew" that "allowed her to turn a blind eye to the fate of other Jews, and . . . blinded her to the gravity of her own situation" (338). Lesinska summarizes these readings under the heading "Stein's Postwar Critics: Reproaches and Excuses," and she, too, finds Stein's "perceptible evasions" (43) problematic, complaining that "the fate of the Jews" is "a topic that [Stein] frequently invokes but abandons after a few hints" (47). Patrick Shaw complains that Stein presents her Jewish identity "only through inference" and "tacit admission" (21).

20. In contrast, Galvin finds an active, engaged, and partisan voice in Stein's masterful mixing of genres in the memoir. She asserts that Stein punctuates the stories of everyday struggles with "lyric outbursts" of "rhyming, rhythmic language" (*News of War* 280, 292). For Galvin, these poetic passages actively "work to contain disturbing incidents and to rein in the perception of threat" and show Stein's writerly means of "encoding . . . sensitive material, such as the expression of fear or dissent" (280, 295–296).

21. I visited Culoz in the summer of 2013 and saw why Stein's house was so coveted for billeting by occupying authorities: a small stately mansion on the grounds of the local chateau, the house is centrally located and yet protectively isolated from the town by its perch on a hill at the top of a gated park overlooking the cathedral. In *Yes Is for a Very Young Man*, one of the protagonist's servants reports on the strategic benefits of the park requested by the German captain: "he only wished to have the key of the park gate, so that the soldiers could camp there in case of bombardment by the English and Americans while they were passing through the village" (20).

22. See Wieviorka for a detailed account of *what* the French knew *when* concerning the fate of deportees before the opening of the camps (47–66). As Marrus and Paxton warn, "it is naïve to select retroactively—out of the myriad conflicting signals of wartime news, rumor, and propaganda—those reports that conform to the truth finally established upon the opening of the camps in May 1945, and to

declare that, once these reports had arrived in the West, everyone of good faith 'knew'" (350). In January of 1944, Stein complains, "we have the terror of the Germans all about us, we have no telephone, we hear stories and do not know whether they are true, we do not know what is happening to our friends in Belley, except for the life of this village of Culoz we seem separated from everything, we have our dog, we have the radio, we have electricity, we have plenty to eat, and we are comfortable but we are completely isolated and rumor follows rumor" (*WIHS* 145). The journal of Hélène Berr, a young Jew who remained in Paris until she was detained and deported in March of 1944, shows that even a well-connected Parisian relied on rumors concerning the fate of those deported East: "We never heard anything more about the convoy of March 27, 1942 (the one that took Mme Schwartz's husband away). There was talk of the eastern front, with deportees being made to walk ahead of the front lines to detonate the Russian mines. There was also talk of asphyxiating gas being administered to the convoys at the Polish border. There must be some truth behind these rumors" (194; Nov 1, 1943). A few days later Berr hears that "British radio has apparently rebroadcast frightful details about the life in the camps in Poland" (200; November 6, 1943). To explain the deportations of whole families, Berr imagines that the Germans must be planning to create a "Jewish slave state," though she can't imagine how they would keep people there after the war (214; Nov 14, 1943). Another contemporary account that shows the French ignorance of extermination camps concerns writer Irene Némirovsky, who, in July 1942, was interned briefly at Drancy and then deported to Auschwitz where she died. Her husband Michel Epstein wrote to the German ambassador Otto Abetz to beg for his wife's release, because due to her chronic asthma, "internment in a concentration camp would be fatal for her" (Némirovsky, Appendix II, 404). Postwar estimates put the return rate of Jews expelled from France to Nazi death camps at 3 to 4 percent (Marrus and Paxton 343).

23. See Marrus and Paxton 249–252 and Zuccotti 81–117.

24. Wieviorka's original reads, "la déportation ne concerna pas les seuls Juifs" (20). Wieviorka notes that among the non-Jewish deportees were resistance fighters, hostages, and people picked up in raids, as well as political prisoners, mostly communists, but also "mayors of all allegiances arrested because their attitude displeased the [German] occupier or the Vichy government" (26, my translation). She adds that common criminals also were deported after the Germans emptied France's prisons (47).

25. On the STO's impact on French society, see Marrus and Paxton 321–322, Curtis 260–261, and Zuccotti 177–178.

26. Marrus and Paxton "found an important root of Vichy's anti-Jewish program in the increasingly severe restrictions imposed upon refugees by the [Third]

Republic, and a hitherto unnoticed continuity between the anxiety and hostility aroused by refugees in the late 1930s and Vichy's xenophobia" (xii). The very first statutes passed by Vichy restricted the rights of foreign-born Jews, a move that played to the xenophobia of the general population and the snobbism and insecurities of the French-Jewish establishment.

27. The abdication of Edward the Eighth in 1936 coincided with the rise of the British Union of Fascists headed by Oswald Mosley, whose blackshirts raided London's East End Jewish quarter, especially in the years 1935–1937. See Endelmann, *The Jews of Britain*, 202–209.

28. Will does not read the comment as ironic and struggles to reconcile what she sees as a "disparity between . . . two contemporaneous perspectives" on the idea of "peace" in Stein's 1930s writings (*Unlikely* 74–75). Such a disparity is only present, however, if one reads the Nobel Peace Prize comment unironically. As Will admits, all the evidence she finds to contextualize her unironic reading is "utterly at odds with Stein's Hitler comments" (74). In my conclusion, I return to the irony in Stein's Hitler comment.

29. According to Marrus and Paxton, an accurate sense of the number of foreigners in France in the 1930s and during the war was difficult to attain because refugee populations were not well documented, but they estimate that in 1940 about half the French-Jewish population of 300,000–350,000 were foreign born (xiv). Further, they consider that France had approximately "515 immigrants for every 100,000 inhabitants, against 492 per 100,000 in the next largest country of immigration, the United States" (35).

30. Marrus and Paxton note that in February 1943, "French police in the southern zone" resumed "mass arrests of foreign Jews"; by March, 49,000 Jews had been sent east (306, 307). See also Poznanski 371.

31. One of these "difficult moments" is the internment of her friends, the American consuls in Lyon, in January or February of 1943. Their experience gave Stein a rosy if unrepresentative picture of internment: "although in prison . . . [our friends] are very free and amusing themselves and have flowers in their rooms and play tennis and send messages and make excursions" (*WIHS* 47).

32. Marrus and Paxton describe the closing of the Swiss border and the opening of a market in illegal crossings (308–309).

33. When France had first fallen to the Germans, Stein and Toklas grappled with the decision of whether to stay in France, eventually heeding the advice of their friend Doctor Chaboux: "I can't guarantee you anything, but my advice is to stay. . . . I think unless your house is actually destroyed by a bombardment, I always think the best thing to do is to stay. . . . Everybody knows you here; everybody likes you; we all would help you in every way. Why risk yourself among strangers?" ("The Winner Loses" 624). Stein likely drew on this summer

1940 conversation when writing *Mrs. Reynolds*, where Mr. Reynolds worries about the Hitler character and announces "we are going away for a while," and then promptly changes his mind, leaving his wife feeling "a little uneasy but she said very well very well she said and they decided to stay at home they decided not to go away" (126–127).

34. Lesinska complains, "It is quite easy to overlook a short paragraph" that mentions the threatened internment, adding that "this incident is quickly overshadowed in the text by the description of her new house, new park and new domestics." She concludes, "Undoubtedly, this episode must have haunted Stein for a long time, and yet she does not discuss it at length" (44).

35. In *Mrs. Reynolds*, Stein uses the phrase "go away" to refer to the plight of the refugee: "Not to be afraid to be home again is something said Caesar Rivers and he always said things like that. . . . Caesar Rivers was a refugee. Anybody was a refugee who had to go away" (169).

36. The thinly veiled account of the February threatened internment (26–27) appears in the memoir after the January 1943 events in Marseilles (11) and the February 1943 announcement of the STO: "the young men . . . are now all being taken away" (13). The episode appears prior to passages dated from "April," when Stein and Toklas "are just in this house [in Culoz]. . . . which we have taken and where we are very comfortable," and "June 1943," when two young men they know depart for Germany as part of the STO (31–32, 35). Although the April passage is dated in the published memoir with the comment, "Now in 1942 in April 1942," it is sandwiched between paragraphs dated "now in 1943" (31). Stein's manuscript draft of the passage reads, "Now in 1943 in May 1943," and, above it, a note penciled in Toklas's handwriting suggests, "Perhaps you'd like to make it April" (YCAL 80.1470). I have no explanation for the change of month or year in the published text.

37. France and other European nations proposed the use of concentration camps and other territorial solutions to the Jewish refugee crisis that followed the 1938 *Anschluss*. But, as Marrus and Paxton report, concern was already heightened about refugees in France as Jews fled German lands earlier in the 1930s. (These refugees were on Stein's radar, as attested to by her mention of Jewish expulsions from Germany in the 1934 *New York Times* interview.) The French first set up *camps de concentration* in March 1939, when 400,000 refugees entered France at the end of the Spanish Civil War. In September 1939, with the beginning of war with Germany, many Spaniards had returned to Spain and the French refilled the camps with 15,000 German and Austrian males (many of whom were Jews), releasing about half by December 1939. In May 1940, with the German Army entering France, the French again rounded up foreigners. By the end of 1940, 70 percent of the 40,000 civilians interned in now-Vichy and occupied France

were Jewish. As Marrus and Paxton argue, the xenophobic and antisemitic Vichy internment policies were very much a continuation of those of the Third Republic. See Marrus and Paxton "The Refugee Crisis 1938–41" in *Vichy France and the Jews* 58–71.

38. References like this to the Marseilles roundup, upon which Stein ruminates for pages and pages, make it hard to believe Olson's claim that "Rather than focus on the facts or chronology of war, Stein and Toklas protect themselves from the shock of war's events. . . . [preferring] to live calmly through occupation, with a sense of control—however self-deceiving—over their lives" (341). By mentioning the massive roundups in Marseilles, Stein may even be hinting at the specifically Jewish reverberations associated with the event, though she does not mention Jews. Poznanski suggests that despite attempts by the authorities to suggest otherwise, people would likely have understood the clearing of the Old Port and the roundups of Jews as related events (372).

39. Historian Donna Ryan identifies the roundups (internally labeled Operation Tiger) as a landmark event: "For the first time French Jews who had committed no infraction at all were subject to the roundups, marking a new phase in the persecution of Jews in France" (184). Marrus and Paxton report that the stated plan was as follows: "On 22–27 January 1943, 10,000 French Police and several thousand German police were concentrated in Marseilles to move 22,000 inhabitants to other areas and to raze the Old Port" (307). Poznanski asserts that "Nearly 30,000 people were thus evacuated, and 5,956 others arrested (3,977 of whom were released)," adding that 1642 people were deported, 782 of whom were Jews (372).

40. Stein and her brother Leo spent many months in Europe during the Boer War. It officially ended on May 31, 1902, and the Steins spent that September outside London with Bernard and Mary Berenson before moving to Bloomsbury Square for the fall (Mellow 46–49, Wagner-Martin 56–57, Wineapple 169–178). That puts Stein in England for the aftermath of the war when the Parliament and newspapers were consumed by the concentration camp issue. She likely heard about or read Hobhouse's "Report of a Visit to the Camps of Women and Children in the Cape and Orange River Colonies" (London: Friars Printing Association, 1901), delivered to the British government in June 1901. Because of this report, a formal commission was set up and a team of official investigators headed by Millicent Fawcett was sent to inspect the camps. For more on the public discourse surrounding the camps see Paula M. Krebs, *Gender, Race, and the Writing of Empire: Public Discourse and the Boer War* (New York: Cambridge University Press, 1999).

41. See Spies on the retaliatory policy of burning farms and "clearing the country" (20). In the 1930s, writing about World War I, Stein mentions Kitchener as a still-influential friend of the Whiteheads, her English hosts (*ABT* 148).

42. Stein recalls the Dreyfus Affair as one of three formative examples of a national government being the corrupt agent of injustice. It is the only one of the three that she explores at length in the memoir. The other awakenings to "officialdom and what one did by bribing" were her eldest brother's military service and the Oscar Wilde trial (51). The latter, of course, another celebrated imprisonment of the fin-de-siècle, was for Stein "the first thing that made me realise that it could happen, being in prison" (55).

43. Malcolm notes this textual echo (82).

44. I have corrected this passage, which appears in the published memoir as "they to cling to a century," restoring the word "like" that had been accidentally omitted (56). Another omission from the manuscript, perhaps intentional, was the following italicized sentence at the end of the passage: "Anyway financially there is no sense in anti-semitism. *For other reasons yes but financially now to-day they are insignificant.* That is what I say" (YCAL 80.1470. Notebook 2 of 6).

45. In her 1896 Radcliffe essay, Stein rehearses the commonly held belief that Jews, by maintaining their distinctiveness, invite persecution. Playing the devil's advocate there, she asserts, "A wealthy race holding itself apart from the rest of the nation they belong to, is too convenient a political scapegoat to ever hope to be left alone" (TMJ 426). Stein goes on to dismiss this notion in the essay by arguing that "practical benefits" gained by Jews in segregating themselves override the potential for persecution (426).

46. In the memoir, Stein is fascinated by "the Germans talking English on the radio," though their propaganda makes her ruefully conclude "the world to-day is not adult it has the mental development of a seven year old boy just about that. Dear me" (121). She goes on to blithely comment on the hatefulness and ubiquity of propaganda: "any evening one can go on listening to any one propagandizing over the radio and one thing is very certain nobody seems to be loving any one" (125). In a love note to Toklas, likely from this period, Stein relishes a reprieve from propagandizing. She croons, "Sweetness sweetness my own jelly / belly sweetness is getting better and / better, not a german voice on the radio anywhere / to-night, god bless my sweetness my joy" (Turner 111).

47. According to Curtis, Les Chantiers de la Jeunesse, begun in July 1940, was "originally intended as an emergency measure to find work for six months for men who had been demobilised or were of draft age. Over 92,000 had been called up for military service in June 1940, but the war ended before they were part of a military unit. In a sense the *Chantiers* replaced conscription. The *Chantiers* became a mandatory body . . . and a substitute for military service" (99).

48. Kedward, historian of the *maquis*, discusses the significance of their youthfulness, something Stein constantly remarks upon (153). He also notes that Belley, the town closest to Stein's first residence and not far from Culoz, was a majority

right-wing *département* and yet conducive to "*maquis* growth and development" (153–154).

49. Némirovsky depicts this degradation of communal trust in the second movement of *Suite Française*, where a character's insistence that "Frenchmen don't denounce one another," is contradicted by the German officer's account of occupying their town. He confides to the protagonist:

> The very first day we arrived . . . there was a package of anonymous letters waiting for us at Headquarters. People were accusing one another of spreading English and Gaullist propaganda, of hoarding supplies, of being spies. If we'd taken them all seriously, everyone in the region would be in prison. I had the whole lot thrown on to the fire. People's lives aren't worth much and defeat arouses the worst in men. In Germany it was exactly the same. (338–339)

50. Following Hitler's annexation of Austria in March 1938, 544,000 Jews were rendered stateless and, due to xenophobic measures to block immigration across Europe and the United States, "France received proportionally more refugees than any other country" (Marrus and Paxton 63). In March 1939, the end of the Spanish Civil War brought 400,000 Spanish refugees across the southern border, though many of them would return within the year. Historians calculate that within France, "the great exodus of June 1940, ahead of the German Army's advance" consisted of "eight million persons . . . uprooted," including "about a million Belgians and roughly two hundred thousand Luxemburgers, Dutch, Poles, and Jewish refugees from the Reich" (Marrus and Paxton 65).

51. Stein's mention of refugeed "Alsatians and Lorrainers" is a good example of how Nazi expulsions of Jews could be paired with expulsions of gentiles, in this case, people the Nazis did not consider to be ethnic Germans. Raul Hilburg notes the heterogenous origins of those trucked out of Alsace-Lorraine by the Germans in the fall of 1940, "Most of the Alsace Jews lived in Strasbourg and Mulhouse. Few Jews lived in Lorraine. The Alsace expulsions of 1940 affected 105,000 people, including Jews, Gypsies, criminals, 'asocials,' mental patients, Frenchmen, and Francophiles" (*The Destruction of the European Jews, Volume 2*. Third Ed. [New Haven, CT: Yale University Press, 2003] 651n13).

52. See Toklas's Cookbook chapter "Food in the Bugey During the Occupation" on the "blessed black market" (205).

53. Because the French, in Stein's experience, are "awfully careful" with money, she thinks that they are unlikely to provide financial assistance to others (*WIHS* 112). At war's end, however, Sevareid reports Stein's reflection that "The village people had learned to share, not only their sorrows, but their little pleasures and their material goods in a way one would not have believed of the parsimonious French" (Sevareid 459).

54. According to Marrus and Paxton, American and British nationals were exempted from 10 December 1942 orders to concentrate all foreign Jews pending deportation East (305).

55. The new friend, Paul Genin, was also a writer. For more about Genin and his family, see Burns and Dydo with Rice.

56. Toklas renews this phrase in her cookbook, reflecting on their luck with obtaining food and other provisions on the black market. Her friend Madame Pierlot underscores the importance of being in favor, "for it is not with money that one buys on the black market but with one's personality," and Toklas agrees, noting, "Gertrude Stein when no one else did would return from a walk with an egg, a pound of white flour, a bit of butter" (207). The move from Bilignin to Culoz was worrisome, Toklas admits, since "At Culoz we should be less favoured" (210). In *Mrs. Reynolds*, Stein includes Madame Pierlot's assessment about currency on the black market as the protagonist's "prophesy" as the war gets underway. Mrs. Reynolds says, "purchase bye and bye will be not a matter of money but a matter of personality. If you are popular you can buy if you are not popular you can die" (34). Stein repeats Pierlot's saying in *Wars I Have Seen* (45), before expressing sadness about those without friends, "they poor dears have nothing to eat, neither do the indiscreet" (46). Uncertain access to food means that many go without, and Stein opines that middle-aged women's bodies seem to hold out better than middle-aged men's. The published memoir omits from this passage a possibly indiscreet sentence that appears in the manuscript about her friend Faÿ and his access to food: "They have just told me that Bernard Faÿ has gotten very fat, that must be potatoes, as he has a place in the country" (YCAL 40.1470).

57. Stein's statement of "favored" status refers most directly to special travel privileges that flouted restrictions on Jewish movements. Marrus and Paxton note that "Several ordinances in early 1943 forbade Jews to reside in fourteen departments. . . . A 16 March decree further tightened the vise on foreign Jews: they had to report to the police whenever they moved, even within a single commune" (305).

58. As Poznanski asserts, there was serious risk for Jews who submitted to have their cards stamped: "Even as late as January 1943, Jews in Paris who had gone to have their food ration cards stamped in order to comply with the new French law wound up at Drancy" (478).

59. See Patrick Shaw 20, Malcolm 79, and Anne-Marie Levine's "Gertrude Stein's War" (*Contemporary French Civilization* 23.2 [Summer/Fall 1999]: 223–243, esp. 227).

60. In *Mrs. Reynolds*, Stein creates a character, Mrs. Coates, who likewise stops suffering "imbeciles"—like those who admire the novel's Hitler figure—gladly: "Mrs. Coates had greatly respected Mr. and Mrs. Madden-Henry, but when she

heard them say that they admired Angel Harper because he never coughed, she began to think badly of them, and gradually she came to despise them" (96). Mrs. Coates reckons that emotion and reason (or lack thereof) wholly determine politics: "eighty percent of the people are afraid and of the remaining twenty percent half are imbeciles and the other half fanatics" (97).

61. As Galvin notes, Raymond Queneau's *Exercises de Style*, written from 1943 to 1945 (the same years Stein was writing her memoir), also satirizes this stated desire for order by Pétainists and other right-wingers. In the voice of a "Réactionnaire," we hear, "Et puis les Français manquent d'organisation et de sens civique; sinon, il ne serait pas nécessaire de leur distribuer des numéros d'ordre pour prendre l'autobus—ordre est bien le mot" (Galvin's translation: "And also the French lack organization and a civic sense; otherwise, it would not be necessary to hand out numbers to take the bus—order is really the word") (qtd. in *News of War* 223). I quote the original French to emphasize that Queneau has his "Reactionary" say the word "order" (and the sibling term "organization") and then reflect and insist on the word's importance by repeating it, "order est bien le mot" ("order is really the word").

62. The phrase also appears in the Book of Revelation (13:10): "He that leadeth into captivity shall go into captivity: he that killeth with the sword must be killed with the sword. Here is the patience and the faith of the saints." Stein returned to this epigram in the opening lines of *The Mother of Us All*, her opera about Susan B. Anthony, composed in 1945–1946.

63. Stein's last mention of Pétain in the memoir confirms this note of anti-Pétainism, even if it is in the voice of a man who surpasses other French people by being "anti-Pétain . . . anti-De Gaulle . . . anti-everything" (213). Stein's penultimate anecdote about Pétain also ends with a sense of inevitable disappointment, though it includes some elated praise of his actions, "it is like Verdun again," which some critics have quoted out of context (175). A fuller reading shows Stein recounting reports of Pétain trying to resurrect himself in the spring of 1944 by raising the French flag atop Paris city hall in front of cheering crowds, dispelling the sense, ever "since the young men had been taken away" to forced labor, that he was "forgotten . . . frightfully helpless and not interested in doing anything" (174). Stein momentarily applauds this heroically staged return—"it is like Verdun again it is complete and incomparable"—before complaining of his inevitable betrayal: "And then the next day we were all disappointed because Petain had to go on talking about the partisans and all the rest of it" (175). For other contemporary accounts of Pétain's visit to Paris, see David Drake's *Paris at War, 1939–1944* (Cambridge, MA: Harvard University Press, 2015) 363–366.

64. Stein had long considered her literary creations to have had epoch-changing effects. In *The Autobiography of Alice B. Toklas*, for example, Toklas states that

"Gertrude Stein had written the story of Melanctha . . . of *Three Lives* which was the first definite step away from the nineteenth century and into the twentieth century in literature" (54).

65. Although Stein is critical of those who denigrate the *maquis*, she does not think their point of view should be a death sentence. As the Resistance strengthens, she worries about the safety of some "charming neighbors," "some firm reactionaries who are convinced that all maquis are terrorists" (*WIHS* 206). After the liberation, Stein nonetheless affirms her condemnation of those who call the *maquis* terrorists in *Yes Is for a Very Young Man*, where Henry, the husband of a "mixed up" Pétainist neighbor, takes umbrage at his wife's use of the term "terrorists." In Steinian repetitions, he angrily retorts, "Hell what are terrorists, who are terrorists, which are terrorists, where in hell, you make me sick, which is hell, where is hell" (27).

66. As a dramatist, too, Stein cast herself as a war hero. Constance, the Steinian character in *Yes Is for a Very Young Man*, is an American who is "in with the terrorists," as part of the resistance movement, serving as a messenger for the *maquis* and helping to arrange for the storage of explosives (27). For a fuller estimation of the play in the context of Stein's other wartime and postwar plays, see Sarah Bay-Cheng's *Mama Dada: Gertrude Stein's Avant-Garde Theater* 93–113. As Whittier-Ferguson notes, the title of the play's first edition is "*In Savoy or Yes is for a Very Young Man (A Play of the Resistance in France)*" (*Mortality and Form* 129).

67. Annalisa Zox-Weaver notes that "Stein repeatedly turned to the divination in Leonardo Blake's *Hitler's Last Year of Power* (1939) and the *Last Year of the War* (1940)," the latter of which contains Blake's summaries of the prophecies of Saint Odile (81).

68. See *Mrs. Reynolds* 47–48, 160–162, 203–204, 212, and 312–313.

69. Stein had earlier reconstructed this memory in *Mrs. Reynolds*, where the protagonist, who "never gave a dinner party," announces to the assembled company that Harper, the novel's Hitler-figure, "is a stranger and a stranger can do things nobody born in a country can do" (120–121).

Conclusion: Making Sense of a Sensationally Jewish Stein

1. The previous year, exhibits on Stein in San Francisco and Washington, D.C., had provoked inquiries and accusations, such as "Exhibit Leaves Out How Gertrude Stein Survived Holocaust" (Sonia Melnikova-Raich, *JWeekly.Com*, June 10, 2011) and "Did You Know Gertrude Stein Allegedly Advocated Adolf Hitler for a Nobel Peace Prize? It Gets Worse" (Bill Berkowitz, *The Buzzflash Blog*, Sept. 12, 2011). With the New York City opening of "The Steins Collect" exhibition at the Met on February 28, 2012, Will, promoting her book released six months prior,

alerted "those filling the rooms of several recent major museum exhibits on Stein" to her revelations about "Stein's Vichy past" ("The Strange Politics of Gertrude Stein" March/April 2012). Soon, city officials demanded that the museum post signage about Stein's wartime life. The news media exploded: from bookish periodicals (*New York Review of Books*, *The New Yorker*, and *The New Republic*) and the popular press (the *Huffington Post*, *New York Daily News*, and *The New York Observer*), to Jewish newspapers, magazines, and websites (*Haaretz*, *Tablet*, *The Algemeiner*, and *Tikkun*).

2. In response to Dershowitz, poet and Stein scholar Charles Bernstein convened and edited a "dossier" in the online journal *Jacket2* called "Gertrude Stein's War Years: Setting the Record Straight." Dershowitz demanded that the Met sell Will's book, *Unlikely Collaboration: Gertrude Stein, Bernard Faÿ, and the Vichy Dilemma*, in their giftshop, which they did. Now, however, the museum website links the gallery inventories for "The Steins Collect" to the *Jacket2* dossier.

3. Bernstein notes the absence of demands for accountability regarding MoMA's 2016–2017 retrospective of the non-Jewish painter Francis Picabia, who, like Stein, lived and worked in Vichy France: "Perhaps European Jews are held to a different standard, perhaps they are expected to be heroic resistance fighters" ("Gertrude and Alice in Vichyland").

4. Greenhouse, writing from *The New Yorker*'s culture desk, breezily ascertained Stein's "pro-Fascist ideology" and suggested that her translations of Pétain were merely the latest example of "Stein's pro-Nazi expression" ("Gertrude Stein," "Why Won't").

5. Dershowitz understands that modernist writers Pound and Eliot admired Fascism, "but Stein's support for Fascism was more bizarre because she was Jewish" ("Suppressing Ugly"). For Greenhouse, too, the monstrosity of Stein's Jewish antisemitism is "ugly" and yoked to her lesbianism and masculine appearance ("Why Won't"). In order to describe Stein as a "transgressive, lesbian Jewish writer," Greenhouse cites Malcolm's details regarding the "perverse undercurrents of [Stein and Toklas's] romantic union" ("Gertrude Stein").

6. As I discuss in chapter 6, critics still mistake Stein's familiarity with French concentration camps for knowledge about Nazi Final Solution extermination camps.

7. Marrus and Paxton refer to May 1945 as the time when the "truth [was] finally established" that the Nazi camps were extermination facilities (350). As French cultural historian Tal Bruttmann reminds us, "before the end of 1944 . . . in France there was almost no knowledge of the death camps. At this time, only one camp, Majdanek, on the outer edges of Poland, had been discovered (empty). In the west, not a single concentration camp had been liberated: the first, KZ Natzweiler, in Alsace, albeit empty of all prisoners, saw the arrival of Allied troops on November 23, 1944. Thus, neither the *univers concentrationnaire*, nor

the systematic extermination of the Jews of Europe had been revealed to contemporaries" (181). Bruttman's timeline depends on Annette Wieviorka's *Déportation et Génocide*, which I discuss in chapter 6.

8. See "The Strange Politics of Gertrude Stein," her Oct. 23, 2011 interview on Rorotoko.com (rorotoko.com/interview/20111024_will_barbara_on_unlikely_collaboration_gertrude_stein_bernard_fay/?page=3), and an interview at the Museum of Jewish Heritage: A Living Memorial to the Holocaust in New York City with *The New Republic*'s Ruth Franklin on March 2, 2012, viewed on YouTube (www.youtube.com/watch?v=e9PAL3K0iWM).

9. In the 1990s, in order to cast anti-Zionism as Nazism, Zionists circulated the idea that Stein had submitted a nomination of Hitler to the Nobel Committee. This claim was later proven false. However, there had been an actual nomination of Hitler for the Nobel Peace Prize in 1938 by a Swedish member of parliament who was protesting the Nobel Peace Prize nomination of Britain's Neville Chamberlain for his signing the nonaggression pact ceding the Sudetenland to Hitler. Stein's comment was ironic, as were the actions of the Swedish member of Parliament who nominated Hitler for a Nobel Prize. See Charles Bernstein's scrutiny of this "fake news" in "Gertrude Stein Taunts Hitler in 1934 and 1945."

10. Watson reminds us that Stein continues to complain about German obedience, both in the 1944 play *Yes Is for a Very Young Man* (15–16) and in her 1945 *Life* magazine article, "Off We All Went To See Germany," subtitled "Germans Should Learn To Be Disobedient And GIs Should Not Like Them No They Shouldn't" (Watson 178).

11. Van Puymbroeck notes this reference to Hitler (95).

12. For example, Laughlin misremembered meetings with Louis Zukofsky in Italy with Ezra Pound. See Ian S. MacNiven's *'Literchoor Is My Beat': A Life of James Laughlin, Publisher of New Directions* (New York: Farrar, Straus and Giroux, 2014) 48.

13. Stein's notes on the Napoleonic character type appear in the Diagram book in a study of Alice Toklas. Stein expresses relief that Toklas is a "failure," unlike the successful "Napoleonic types," who "do not conceive themselves as low" and are thus "a misfit between the evil, overpowering nature and the ideals" (37.761. [104–105]). Elsewhere in the Diagram book she disapprovingly notes that Napoleonic types lack a vaunted quality of the Arnoldian Hellene: "Napoleonic type not disinterested" (34).

14. At the end of the war, horrified by Hitler's refusal to give up and end the killing, Stein compares Hitler to Napoleon as a foreign leader butchering his adopted nation: "it is like Napoleon who was an Italian and naturally was indifferent as to how many Frenchmen were killed" (*WIHS* 231). Other hearsay accounts of Stein from the early 1930s, meanwhile, portray Stein as both calmly skeptical

and vehemently critical of Hitler and of Germany. See Sevareid 90 and 460–461, Steward 36–37 and 53, and Paul Bowles, *Without Stopping: An Autobiography* (New York: Ecco Press, 1991) 118.

15. Hell recalls Stein's explanation that the Maréchal was "un héros presque légendaire, dont on a fait l'incarnation des vertus militaires d'un peuple, et qui ne veut plus faire la guerre; voilà qui est intéressant" (428–429). Stein gives Hell a small cameo in *Mrs. Reynolds* on page 316.

16. Stein's letter is concerned with truth and the difficulty of knowing it. She tells Cerf that she is sending a friend to convey what she cannot adequately explain in writing about the current French situation: "he will make you understand things as they are which I think you over there do not quite see" (qtd. in Burns and Dydo 413). The Arnoldian phrasing of *things as they are* might indicate her sense of once again being a prophet crying in the wilderness. She does not specify what about the current situation is so difficult to communicate but, given the alternating tedium and tumultuousness of France's defeat and subsequent occupation, one imagines it was complicated. Her introduction to the planned volume of translated speeches proposes to explain her own "strong ups and downs" about the Maréchal (413). She ominously suggests, furthermore, that her circumstances—and perhaps that of all of France—are compromised in a manner that she is just starting to comprehend: "we all now over here can begin to understand that life with its reverses, are not what they were when all went alright" (413).

17. In 1941 there were exhibitions of Stein's writing at Yale and Columbia Universities, a concert performance of her opera *Four Saints in Three Acts* at the Museum of Modern Art and NYC's Town Hall, and interest on the part of young academics and writers, some of whom were intent on publishing her in small presses (*GS/CVV* 707–719). And although Scribner's published the "straightforward" *Paris France* in 1940, Scribner's, Random House's Bennett Cerf, Alfred Harcourt, and others were still loath to publish her more experimental writing (*GS/CVV* 700n).

18. Stein knew of the "OTTO" lists, joint ventures of French publishers and German propaganda arms in France, which banned the publication and sale of books by Jews and Communists or books that criticized Germany or Nazism. Her name appeared on the third OTTO list of May 1943 for her book *Picasso* (1938).

19. See Gisèle Sapiro, *The French Writers' War, 1940–1953* (Durham, NC: Duke University Press, 2014); Alan Riding, *And the Show Went On: Cultural Life in Nazi-Occupied Paris* (New York: Knopf, 2010); and Frederic Spotts, *The Shameful Peace: How French Artists and Intellectuals Survived the Nazi Occupation* (New Haven, CT: Yale University Press, 2008).

20. Edmond Charlot was the "resistant" in Algiers who published two of Stein's books during the war on behalf of the journal *Fontaine*. Stein's *Paris France* (1940) and her *First Reader* appeared in French translations—*Paris-France* (1941)

and *Petits poems pour un livre de lecture* (1944)—thanks to his *Éditions Charlot*. I consider Charlot's "resistant" moniker to be self-attributed, even though in an uncorroborated account he alleges that Stein boasted about him on the radio in February 1942, happy to have him as "un éditeur dynamique et resistant" [a dynamic and resistant publisher]. He claims this broadcast led to his imprisonment (*Le Monde*, Friday, 28 February, 1997, p. v). Elsewhere, however, Charlot recalls that his imprisonment was part of the "ventilation des intellectuels" in the first few months of 1942, when the Algiers police began rounding up intellectuals, including those in the *Fontaine* circle (qtd. in Vignale 127).

21. See the letter from Paul Marion, the General Secretary for Information at Vichy (Corpet and Paulhan 250).

22. A great deal of literary history remains to be written about the "French" Gertrude Stein. A fuller understanding of the publication of her work in French translation and her role in French literary life would provide important context for her Vichy-era writings.

23. Burns and Dydo enumerate most of Stein's publications in wartime leftist literary reviews (418–421) and mention Stein's essay in *Patrie* (299 n8, 403). Burns gives a more expansive account in "Gertrude Stein: A Complex Itinerary, 1940–1944." Vignale tells the story of *Fontaine*'s 1941 publication of *Paris France* under its own imprint and Stein's inclusion in *Fontaine*'s celebrated 1943 double issue on writers of the United States. Feinstein mentions the *Confluences* publications (Introduction 419). See also Lottman 209 and Wagner-Martin 247.

24. Some of the context for Stein's *Patrie* essay can be gleaned from recent work on the major figures of the Mediterranean literary milieu that became so prominent in the Vichy era. See, for example, Vignale on Max-Pol Fouchet and his circle, and two collections edited by Guy Dugas, *La Méditerranée de Audisio à Roy* (Paris: Éditions Manucius, 2008), and *Edmond Charlot, passeur de culture* (Pézenas: Domens, 2016).

25. See the 1945 "Portrait of Gertrude Stein" photograph by André Ostier in Burns and Dydo 320 and Corpet and Paulhan 336. Also YCAL MSS 76 Photo Negative Collection.

26. Michael Lerner castigates Stein for committing "the sin of silence" by not taking one of the "many opportunities for creative writers and thinkers to combat fascism" ("Editor's Note on 'Why the Witch-Hunt Against Gertrude Stein?' By Renate Stendhal" *Tikkun*, June 4, 2012). Maayan P. Dauber condemns Stein for not speaking out as a Jew or at all in "Gertrude Stein's Passivity: War and the Limits of Modern Subjectivity" (*Texas Studies in Literature and Language* 58:2 [Summer 2016] 129–143).

27. In chapter 3, I refute Leon Katz's story of Jewish erasure in the composition of *The Making of Americans*. His story was undisputed for decades and thus may

reasonably have shaped Benfey's and several generations of scholars' understandings of Stein.

28. Richard Bridgman, in his early and encyclopedic *Gertrude Stein in Pieces* (1970), reads this line as one that "underlined her views" (315). For him, it shows that Stein had adopted the wartime politics of her extreme-right-wing friends and neighbors and their fierce anticommunism and antipathy for constitutional governments. Will quotes the line to punctuate a paragraph about Stein's political conservatism (*Unlikely* 118). Greenhouse quotes this line to link Stein's conservatism with her Pétain-loving politics ("Gertrude Stein"). Even Renate Stendhal, in her defense of Stein, quotes the line as an acknowledgment of Stein's conservative politics ("Why the Witch-Hunt Against Gertrude Stein?" *Tikkun,* June 4, 2012).

29. This odd sentence sounds to me like Stein may have meant to introduce the notion of needing to be conservative or traditional to be free, a phrase she then repeats on the next page. If this was indeed an omission, it was never caught by Stein or other readers before publication, for that is the way it appears in her manuscript notebook for *Paris France.*

WORKS CITED

Abraham, Julie. *Are Girls Necessary? Lesbian Writing and Modern Histories.* London: Routledge, 1996.
Adler, Felix. *Creed and Deed.* 1877. New York: Arno Press, 1972.
Aguilar, Grace. *Home Influence: A Tale for Mothers and Daughters.* 1847. New York: D. Appleton, 1871.
———. *The Mother's Recompense: A Sequel to* Home Influence. London: Groombridge and Sons, 1851.
Arendt, Hannah. *The Jew as Pariah: Jewish Identity and Politics in the Modern Age.* Ed. and Intro. Ron H. Feldman. New York: Grove, 1978.
Aristotle, *Nicomachean Ethics.* Trans. Sarah Broadie and Christopher Rowe. Oxford: Oxford University Press, 2002.
Arnold, Matthew. *The Complete Prose Works of Matthew Arnold.* Ed. R. H. Super. 11 Vols. Ann Arbor: University of Michigan Press, 1960–1977.
———. *Culture and Anarchy.* In *The Complete Prose Works*, Vol. 5, 85–256.
———. "The Function of Criticism at the Present Time." In *The Complete Prose Works*, Vol. 3, 258–285.
———. *Literature and Dogma.* In *The Complete Prose Works*, Vol. 6, 139–411.
———. "My Countrymen." In *The Complete Prose Works*, Vol. 5, 3–31.
The Artscroll Siddur. New York: Mesorah Publications, 1984.
Ashton, Jennifer. "'Rose is a Rose': Gertrude Stein and the Critique of Indeterminacy." *Modernism/modernity* 9: 4 (Nov. 2002): 581–604.
Attridge, John. "Steadily and Whole: Ford Madox Ford and Modernist Sociology." *Modernism/modernity* 15: 2 (2008): 297–315.
Axelrod, Steven Gould. "*Mrs. Reynolds*: Stein's Anti-Nazi Novel." *Primary Stein: Returning to the Writing of Gertrude Stein.* Eds. Janet Boyd and Sharon J. Kirsch. New York: Lexington Books, 2014, 259–276.
Bauman, Zygmunt. "Allosemitism: Premodern, Modern, Postmodern." In *Mo-

dernity, Culture, and "the Jew." Eds. Bryan Cheyette and Laura Marcus. Stanford, CA: Stanford University Press, 1998, 143–156.

Bay-Cheng, Sarah. *Mama Dada: Gertrude Stein's Avant-Garde Theater.* New York: Routledge, 2005.

Benfey, Christopher. "The Alibi of Ambiguity." *The New Republic.* June 7, 2012. Online. https://newrepublic.com/article/103918/barbara-will-gertrude-stein-christopher-benfey

"Bequest of Gertrude Stein, Books." 8 May 1947, document copy provided by Yale Collection of American Literature Curator, Patricia Willis in 2006. Online: www.library.yale.edu/~nkuhl/Gertrude%20Stein%20Bequest%20complete.pdf

Benstock, Shari. "Paris Lesbianism and the Politics of Reaction, 1900–1940." *Hidden from History: Reclaiming the Gay & Lesbian Past.* Eds. Martin Duberman, Martha Vicinus, and George Chauncey, Jr. New York: Meridian, 1990, 332–346.

———. *Women of the Left Bank: Paris, 1900–1940.* Austin: University of Texas Press, 1986.

Bercovitch, Sacvan. *The American Jeremiad.* Madison: University of Wisconsin Press, 1978.

Berman, Jessica. *Modernist Fiction, Cosmopolitanism, and the Politics of Community.* Cambridge: Cambridge University Press, 2007.

Bernstein, Charles, ed. *Gertrude Stein's War Years: Setting the Record Straight.* In *Jacket2.* May 9, 2012–present. Online: https://jacket2.org/feature/gertrude-steins-war-years-setting-record-straight.

———. "Gertrude and Alice in Vichyland." *Gertrude Stein's War Years.* Ed. Charles Bernstein. *Jacket2.* May 30, 2017. Online: jacket2.org/commentary/gertrude-and-alice-vichyland

———. "Gertrude Stein Taunts Hitler in 1934 and 1945." *Gertrude Stein's War Years.* Ed. Charles Bernstein. *Jacket2.* May 9, 2012. Online: jacket2.org/article/gertrude-stein-taunts-hitler-1934-and-1945

———. "Stein's Identity." *Modern Fiction Studies* 42: 3 (Fall 1996): 485–488.

Berr, Hélène. *The Journal of Hélène Berr.* Trans. and Intro. David Bellos. New York: Weinstein Books, 2008.

Blair, Sara. "Home Truths: Gertrude Stein, 27 Rue de Fleurus, and the Place of the Avant-Garde." *American Literary History* 12: 3 (2000): 417–437.

The Book of the Prophet Jeremiah, Together with the Lamentations, with Map Notes and Introduction. Intro. and notes A. W. Streane. *The Cambridge Bible for Schools and Colleges.* Gen. Ed. J.J.S. Perowne. Cambridge: Cambridge University Press, 1899.

Brantlinger, Patrick. "Disraeli and Orientalism." In *The Self-Fashioning of Disraeli,*

1818–1851. Eds. Charles Richmond and Paul Smith. Cambridge: Cambridge University Press, 1999, 90–105.

Bridgman, Richard. *Gertrude Stein in Pieces*. New York: Oxford University Press, 1970.

Bruttman, Tal. "The Holocaust through Comic Books." *Re-Examining the Holocaust Through Literature*. Eds. Aukje Kluge and Benn E. Williams. Newcastle upon Tyne: Cambridge Scholars Publishing, 2009, 173–200.

Burke, Carolyn. *Becoming Modern: The Life of Mina Loy*. New York: Farrar, Straus & Giroux, 1996.

Burns, Edward M. "Gertrude Stein: A Complex Itinerary, 1940–1944." *Gertrude Stein's War Years*. Ed. Charles Bernstein. *Jacket2*. May 9, 2012. Online: jacket2.org/article/gertrude-stein-complex-itinerary-1940–1944

Burns, Edward M., and Ulla E. Dydo, eds., with William Rice. *The Letters of Gertrude Stein and Thornton Wilder*. New Haven, CT: Yale University Press, 1996.

Bush, Clive. *Halfway to Revolution: Investigation and Crisis in the Work of Henry Adams, William James, and Gertrude Stein*. New Haven, CT: Yale University Press, 1991.

Caramello, Charles. "Gertrude Stein as Exemplary Theorist." In Neuman and Nadel, 1–7.

———. *Henry James, Gertrude Stein, and the Biographical Act*. Chapel Hill: University of North Carolina Press, 1996.

Carpenter, Humphrey. *A Serious Character: The Life of Ezra Pound*. Boston: Houghton Mifflin, 1988.

Charcot, Jean-Martin. *Leçons du Mardi à la Salpêtrière. Policlinique 1887–1888. Notes de cours de MM. Blin, Charcot, Henri Colin, élèves du service*. Paris: Bureaux du Progrès Médical, 1888–1889.

Chesnoff, Richard. "A Nazi Collaborator at the Met," *New York Daily News*, April 29, 2012.

Cheyette, Bryan. *Constructions of "the Jew" in English Literature and Society: Racial Representations, 1875–1945*. Cambridge: Cambridge University Press, 1993.

Cheyette, Bryan, ed. *Between "Race" and Culture: Representations of "the Jew" in English and American Literature*. Stanford, CA: Stanford University Press, 1996.

Childs, Donald. "Mrs. Dalloway's Unexpected Guests: Virginia Woolf, T. S. Eliot, and Matthew Arnold." *Modern Language Quarterly* 58.1 (March 1997): 63–82.

Chinitz, David E. *T. S. Eliot and the Cultural Divide*. Chicago: University of Chicago Press, 2003.

Cook, Blanche. "'Women Alone Stir My Imagination': Lesbianism and the Cultural Tradition." *Signs* 4.4 (Summer 1979): 718–739.

Copeland, Carolyn Faunce. *Language and Time and Gertrude Stein*. Iowa City: University of Iowa Press, 1975.

Corpet, Olivier, and Claire Paulhan. Trans. Jeffrey Mehlmen et al. *Collaboration and Resistance: French Literary Life under the Nazi Occupation*. New York: Five Ties, 2009.

Cuddihy, John. *The Ordeal of Civility: Freud, Marx, Lévi-Strauss, and the Jewish Struggle with Modernity*. New York: Basic Books, 1974.

Cummings, E. E. *Selected Letters*. Eds. F. W. Dupee and George Stade. New York: Harcourt, Brace, 1969.

Curtis, Michael. *Verdict on Vichy: Power and Prejudice in the Vichy France Regime*. New York: Arcade, 2002.

Damon, Maria. "Gertrude Stein's Jewishness, Jewish Social Scientists and the 'Jewish Question.'" *Modern Fiction Studies* 42.3 (Fall 1996): 489–506.

———. "Gertrude Stein's Doggerel 'Yiddish': Women, Dogs, and Jews." *The Dark End of the Street: Margins in American Vanguard Poetry*. Minneapolis: University of Minnesota Press, 1993, 202–235.

Davis, Phoebe Stein. "'Even Cake Gets to Have Another Meaning': History, Narrative, and 'Daily Living' in Gertrude Stein's World War II Writings." *Modern Fiction Studies* 44.3 (1998): 568–607.

Dearborn, Mary V. *Pocahontas's Daughters: Gender and Ethnicity in American Culture*. New York: Oxford University Press, 1986.

DeKoven, Marianne. *A Different Language: Gertrude Stein's Experimental Writing*. Madison: University of Wisconsin Press, 1983.

———. "Gertrude Stein and the Modernist Canon." In Neuman and Nadel, 8–20.

———. "'Why James Joyce Was Accepted and I Was Not': Modernist Fiction and Gertrude Stein's Narrative." *Studies in the Literary Imagination* 25.2 (1992): 23–30.

Dershowitz, Alan. "Suppressing Ugly Truth for Beautiful Art," *Huffington Post*, May 1, 2012. Online: huffpost.com/entry/met-gertrude-stein-collaborator_b_1467174

Detloff, Madelyn. *The Persistence of Modernism: Loss and Mourning in the Twentieth Century*. New York: Cambridge University Press, 2009.

Dewitt, Anne. "'The Actual Sky Is a Horror': Thomas Hardy and the Arnoldian Conception of Science." *Nineteenth-Century Literature* 61.4 (2007): 479–506.

Diedrich, Maria. "'A Book in Translation about Eggs and Butter': Gertrude Stein's World War II." *Women and War: The Changing Status of American Women from the 1930s to the 1950s*. Eds. Maria Diedrich and Dorothea Fischer-Hornung. New York: Berg, 1990, 87–106.

Diner, Hasia R. *A Time for Gathering: The Second Migration, 1820–1880. The Jewish People in America*. Vol. 2. Baltimore: Johns Hopkins University Press, 1992.

Dinnerstein, Leonard. *Antisemitism in America*. New York: Oxford University Press, 1994.

Disraeli, Benjamin. *Lothair*. 1870. London: Longmans and Co., 1882.
Doane, Janice. *Silence and Narrative: The Early Novels of Gertrude Stein*. Westport, CT: Greenwood Press, 1986.
Douglas, Alfred. "Two Loves." 1894. *"Two Loves" & Other Poems: A Selection*. East Lansing, MI: Bennett & Kitchel, 1990.
Doyle, Laura. "The Flat, the Round, and Gertrude Stein: Race and the Shape of Modern(ist) History." *Modernism/modernity* 7.2 (2000): 249–271.
Dudden, Faye E. *Serving Women: Household Service in Nineteenth-Century America*. Middletown, CT: Wesleyan University Press, 1983.
Dydo, Ulla. "*Stanzas in Meditation*: The Other Autobiography." *Gertrude Stein Advanced: An Anthology of Criticism*. Ed. Richard Kostelanetz. Jefferson, NC: McFarland, 1990, 112–127.
———, ed. *A Stein Reader*. Evanston, IL: Northwestern University Press, 1993.
———. "To Have the Winning Language: Texts and Contexts of Gertrude Stein." *Coming to Light: American Women Poets in the Twentieth Century*. Eds. Diane Middlebrook and Marilyn Yalom. Ann Arbor: University of Michigan Press, 1985, 58–73.
Dydo, Ulla, with William Rice. *Gertrude Stein: The Language That Rises (1923–1934)*. Evanston, IL: Northwestern University Press, 2003.
Edel, Leon. *Henry James: A Life*. New York: HarperCollins, 1987.
Eliot, George. *Daniel Deronda*. 1876. New York: Penguin, 2003.
Eliot, T. S. "Charleston, Hey! Hey!" *The Nation & Athenaeum* 40. 17 (29 January 1927): 595.
———. *The Complete Poems and Plays (1909–1950)*. New York: Harcourt, Brace, 1971.
———. *Poems*. New York: Knopf, 1920.
———. *Poems*. Richmond, England: Hogarth Press, 1919.
———. *Selected Essays 1917–1932*. New York: Harcourt, Brace, 1932.
Ellis, Havelock. *A Study of British Genius*. London: Hurst and Blackett, 1904.
Ellmann, Maud. "The Imaginary Jew: T. S. Eliot and Ezra Pound." In Cheyette, *Between 'Race' and Culture*, 84–101.
Ellmann, Richard. *Oscar Wilde*. New York: Vintage, 1988.
Endelman, Todd. "Benjamin Disraeli and the Myth of Sephardi Superiority." *Jewish History* 10.2 (1996): 21–35.
———. "'Hebrew to the end': The Emergence of Disraeli's Jewishness." *The Self-Fashioning of Disraeli, 1818–1851*. Eds. Charles Richmond and Paul Smith. Cambridge: Cambridge University Press, 1999, 106–130.
———. *The Jews of Britain, 1656 to 2000*. Berkeley: University of California Press, 2002.
Engelbrecht, Penelope. "'Lifting Belly is a Language': The Postmodern Lesbian Subject." *Feminist Studies* 16.1 (1990): 85–114.

English, Daylanne. "Gertrude Stein and the Politics of Literary-Medical Experimentation." *Literature and Medicine* 16 (Fall 1997): 188–209.

———. *Unnatural Selections: Eugenics in American Modernism and the Harlem Renaissance*. Durham: University of North Carolina Press, 2004.

Erdman, Harley. *Staging the Jew: The Performance of an American Ethnicity, 1860–1920*. New Brunswick, NJ: Rutgers University Press, 1997.

Eshel, Amir, and Todd Presner. "Introduction: Between Spontaneity and Reflection: Reconsidering Jewish Modernism." *Modernism/modernity* 13.4 (2006): 607–614.

Farland, Maria. "Gertrude Stein's Brain Work." *American Literature* 76.1 (March 2004): 117–148.

Faÿ, Bernard. *Les Précieux*. Paris: Librairie Académique Perrin, 1966.

———. *George Washington, Republican Aristocrat*. New York: Houghton Mifflin, 1931.

Feinstein, Amy. "Gertrude Stein, Alice Toklas, and Albert Barnes: Looking Like a Jew in *The Autobiography of Alice B. Toklas*." *Shofar: An Interdisciplinary Journal of Jewish Studies* 25.3 (Spring 2007): 47–60.

———. Introduction. "The Modern Jew Who Has Given Up the Faith of His Fathers Can Reasonably and Consistently Believe in Isolation." By Gertrude Stein. *PMLA* 116 (2001): 416–421.

Fischer, Jens Malte. "Max Nordau: Dégénérescence." Eds. Delphine Bechtel, Dominique Bourel, and Jacques Le Rider. *Max Nordau 1849–1923. Critique de la Dégénérescence, Médiateur Franco-Allemand, Père Fondateur du Sionisme*. Paris: CERF, 1996, 107–119.

Foote, Stephanie. "Henry James and the Parvenus: Reading Taste in *The Spoils of Poynton*." *The Henry James Review* 27.1 (2006): 42–60.

Forster, E. M. *Howards End*. 1910. New York: Penguin, 2000.

Fredman, Stephen. *A Menorah for Athena: Charles Reznikoff and the Jewish Dilemmas of Objectivist Poetry*. Chicago: University of Chicago Press, 2001.

Friedman, Leo Victor. Letter to Gertrude Stein. 10 Aug. 1895. Yale Collection of American Literature (YCAL), Beinecke Rare Book and Manuscript Library, New Haven, CT.

Galchinsky, Michael. "Africans, Indians, Arabs, and Scots: Jewish and Other Questions in the Age of Empire." *Jewish Culture and History* 6.1 (Fall, 2003): 46–60.

Gallagher, Jean. "Occupation and Observer: Gertrude Stein in Vichy France." *The World Wars through the Female Gaze*. Carbondale: Southern Illinois University Press, 1998, 116–149.

Gallup, Donald. "The Making of *The Making of Americans*." *Fernhurst, Q.E.D., and Other Early Writings*. By Gertrude Stein. Ed. Donald Gallup. New York: Liveright, 1971.

Galton, Francis. *Hereditary Genius: An Inquiry into Its Laws and Consequences*. 1869. Preface 1892. New York: St Martin's Press, 1978.

Galvin, Rachel. "Gertrude Stein, Pétain, and the Politics of Translation." *English Literary History* 83 (2016): 259–292.

———. *News of War: Civilian Poetry 1936–1945*. New York: Oxford University Press, 2018.

Gates, Louis E., ed. *Selections from the Prose Writings of Matthew Arnold*. By Matthew Arnold. New York: Henry Holt, 1897.

Gilbert, Sandra M., and Susan Gubar. *No Man's Land: The Place of the Woman Writer in the Twentieth Century, II: Sexchanges*. New Haven, CT: Yale University Press, 1988.

Giroud, Vincent. *Picasso and Gertrude Stein*. New York: Metropolitan Museum of Art, 2006.

Gökay, Bülent. *A Clash of Empires: Turkey between Russian Bolshevism and British Imperialism, 1918–1923*. New York: Taurus Academic Studies, 1997.

Goldsmith, Meredith. "White Skin, White Mask: Passing, Posing, and Performing in *The Great Gatsby*." *Modern Fiction Studies* 49.3 (Fall 2003): 443–468.

Goldstein, Eric L. "'Different Blood Flows in Our Veins': Race and Jewish Self-Definition in Late Nineteenth Century America." *American Jewish History* 85.1 (1997): 29–55.

Golson, Lucile M. "The Michael Steins of San Francisco: Art Patrons and Collectors." Gordon, 35–49.

Gordon, Irene, ed. *Four Americans in Paris: The Collections of Gertrude Stein and Her Family*. New York: Museum of Modern Art, 1970.

Gordon, Irene. "A World Beyond the World: The Discovery of Leo Stein." Gordon, 13–33.

Greenhouse, Emily. "Gertrude Stein and Vichy: The Overlooked History." *The New Yorker*, May 4, 2012.

———. "Why Won't the Met Tell the Whole Truth about Gertrude Stein?" *The New Yorker*, June 8, 2012.

Hapgood, Hutchins. *A Victorian in the Modern World*. New York: Harcourt, Brace, 1939.

Harrowitz, Nancy A., and Barbara Hyams. *Jews and Gender: Responses to Otto Weininger*. Philadelphia: Temple University Press, 1995.

Hart, Mitchell B. *Social Science and the Politics of Modern Jewish Identity*. Stanford, CA: Stanford University Press, 2000.

Hawkins, Stephanie L. "The Science of Superstition: Gertrude Stein, William James, and the Formation of Belief." *Modern Fiction Studies* 51.1 (2005): 60–87.

Heine, Heinrich. *Jewish Stories and Hebrew Melodies*. New York: M. Wiener, 1987.

Hell, Victor. "Gertrude Stein et l'Esthétique du XXe Siècle," *Proceedings of the 7th Congress of the International Comparative Literature Association*. Stuttgart: Erich Bieber, 1979, 427–431.

Herrmann, Anne. *Queering the Moderns: Poses/Portraits/Performances*. New York: Palgrave, 2000.

Hess, Moses. *Rome and Jerusalem: A Study in Jewish Nationalism*. 1862. Trans. Meyer Waxman. New York: Bloch Publishing, 1918.

Higham, John. *Strangers in the Land: Patterns of American Nativism, 1860–1925*. New Brunswick, NJ: Rutgers University Press, 2002.

Hirsch, William. *Genius and Degeneration: A Psychological Study*. New York: D. Appleton, 1896.

Hodder, Alfred. *The New Americans*. New York: Macmillan, 1901.

Hovey, Jaime. "Sapphic Primitivism in Gertrude Stein's *Q.E.D.*" *Modern Fiction Studies* 42.3 (Fall 1996): 547–568.

Huxley, T. H. *Science and Culture, and other Essays*. New York: D. Appleton, 1882.

Jacobs, Joseph. "The Comparative Distribution of Jewish Ability." *Journal of the Anthropological Institute of Great Britain and Ireland* 15 (1886): 351–379.

———. "On the Racial Characteristics of Modern Jews." *Journal of the Anthropological Institute of Great Britain and Ireland* 15 (1886): 23–62.

Jacobson, Matthew Frye. *Whiteness of a Different Color: European Immigrants and the Alchemy of Race*. Cambridge, MA: Harvard University Press, 1998.

James, Henry. *The Ambassadors*. 1903. New York: Oxford University Press, 1998.

———. *The Spoils of Poynton*. 1896. *The Spoils of Poynton; A London Life; The Chaperon. The Novels and Plays of Henry James, New York Ed.* Vol 10. New York: Scribner's, 1922.

James, William. *The Correspondence of William James*. Eds. Ignas K. Skrupskelis and Elizabeth M. Berkeley. 12 Vols. Charlottesville: University Press of Virginia, 1992–2002.

———. "Degeneration and Genius." *Psychological Review* 2 (1895): 287–294.

———. *Is Life Worth Living?* Philadelphia: S. Burns Weston, 1896.

———. *Pragmatism: A New Name for Some Old Ways of Thinking*. New York: Longman Green, 1907.

———. *William James on Exceptional Mental States: The 1896 Lowell Lectures*. Ed. Eugene Taylor. New York: Charles Scribner's Sons, 1982.

Joyce, James. *Dubliners*. 1914. Mineola, NY: Dover, 1991.

———. *Letters of James Joyce*. Ed. Richard Ellmann. Vols. 2 and 3. New York: Viking, 1966.

———. *Ulysses*. 1922. New York: Random House, 1986.

Kafka, Franz. *The Castle*. 1926. New York: Vintage, 1974.

Katz, Leon. "The First Making of *The Making of Americans:* A Study Based on Gertrude Stein's Notebooks and Early Versions of her Novel (1902–1908)." 1963. Columbia University, PhD dissertation.

———. Introduction. *Fernhurst, Q.E.D., and Other Early Writings.* By Gertrude Stein. New York: Liveright, 1971, ix–xlii.

———. "Matisse, Picasso and Gertrude Stein." Gordon, 51–63.

———. "Weininger and *The Making of Americans.*" *Twentieth Century Literature* 24.1 (Spring 1978): 8–26.

Kedward, H. R. *In Search of the Maquis: Rural Resistance in Southern France, 1942–1944.* New York: Oxford University Press, 1994.

Kent, Marian. *Oil and Empire: British Policy and Mesopotamian Oil, 1900–1920.* London: MacMillan, 1976.

Kessner, Carole Schwartz, ed. *The "Other" New York Jewish Intellectuals.* New York: New York University Press, 1994.

Kipling, Rudyard. *Ballads and Barrack-room Ballads.* New York: Macmillan and Co., 1893.

Klein, Charles, with Lee Arthur. *The Auctioneer: A Character Comedy in Three Acts.* 1901. Ts. Property of David Belasco. Set No. 2. Harry Ransom Center, University of Texas at Austin.

Knowlson, James. *Damned to Fame: The Life of Samuel Beckett.* New York: Simon and Schuster, 1996.

Krafft-Ebing, Richard von. *Psychopathia Sexualis with Especial Reference to the Antipathic Sexual Instinct: A Medico-Forensic Study.* Trans. F. J. Rebman from 12th German ed. 1906. Rev. ed. Brooklyn: Physicians and Surgeons Book Co., 1926.

Laarse, Robert van der. "Masking the Other: Max Nordau's Representation of Hidden Jewishness." *Historical Reflections* 25 (1999): 1–31.

Laughlin, James. "About Gertrude Stein." *Yale Review* 77:4 (Summer 1988): 535.

Lawrence, Karen. "Who Could Have Read the Signs? Politics and Prediction in Gertrude Stein's *Mrs. Reynolds* and Christine Brooke-Rose's *Amalgamemnon.*" *Western Humanities Review* 59:2 (Fall 2005): 18–38.

Leick, Karen. *Gertrude Stein and the Making of an American Celebrity.* New York: Routledge, 2009.

Leroy-Beaulieu, Anatole. *Israel among the Nations: A Study of the Jews and Antisemitism.* Trans. Frances Hellman. New York: Putnam, 1895.

Lesinska, Zofia P. *Perspectives of Four Women Writers on the Second World War: Gertrude Stein, Janet Flanner, Kay Boyle, and Rebecca West.* New York: Peter Lang, 2002.

Levine, Gary. *The Merchant of Modernism: The Economic Jew in Anglo-American Literature, 1864–1939.* New York: Routledge, 2003.

Lewis, Wyndham. *The Art of Being Ruled.* London: Chatto and Windus, 1926.

———. *Blasting and Bombardiering.* 1937. London: John Calder, 1982.

———. *The Letters of Wyndham Lewis*. Ed. W. K. Rose. New York: New Directions, 1963.

———. *Time and Western Man*. New York: Harcourt Brace, 1928.

Linett, Maren. *Modernism, Feminism, and Jewishness*. New York: Cambridge University Press, 2007.

Loewenstein, Andrea Freud. *Loathsome Jews and Engulfing Women: Metaphors of Projection in the Works of Wyndham Lewis, Charles Williams, and Graham Greene*. New York: New York University Press, 1993.

Lombroso, Cesare. *The Man of Genius*. New York: Charles Scribner's Sons, 1891.

Lottman, Herbert. *The Left Bank: Writers, Artists, and Politics from the Popular Front to the Cold War*. Chicago: University of Chicago Press, 1982.

Lustig, T. J. "James, Arnold, 'Culture,' and 'Modernity'; or, A Tale of Two Dachshunds." *The Cambridge Quarterly* 37.1 (2008): 164–193.

Malcolm, Janet. *Two Lives*. New Haven, CT: Yale University Press, 2007.

Marrus, Michael R., and Robert O. Paxton. *Vichy France and the Jews*. Stanford, CA: Stanford University Press, 1981.

Marx, Karl. "On the Jewish Question." 1843. *The Marx–Engels Reader*. Ed. Robert C. Tucker. 2nd ed. New York: Norton, 1978, 26–52.

McAlmon, Robert. *McAlmon and the Lost Generation: A Self-Portrait*. Ed. Robert E. Knoll. Lincoln: University of Nebraska Press, 1962.

Mellow, James R. *Charmed Circle: Gertrude Stein & Company*. New York: Avon, 1974.

Meyer, Steven. Introduction. *The Making of Americans*. By Gertrude Stein. xiii–xxxvi.

———. *Irresistible Dictation: Gertrude Stein and the Correlations of Writing and Science*. Stanford, CA: Stanford University Press, 2001.

Mill. J. S. *On Liberty*. 1859. 3rd ed. London: Longman, 1864.

Miller, Matt. "Makings of Americans: Whitman and Stein's Poetics of Inclusion." *Arizona Quarterly* 65.3 (Autumn 2009): 39–59.

Mills, Jean E. "Gertrude Stein Took the War Like a Man." *The Gay and Lesbian Review* 10.2 (March–April 2003): 16–17.

Mitrano, G. F. *Gertrude Stein: Woman without Qualities*. Aldershot, England: Ashgate, 2006.

Moad, Rosalind. *1914–16: Years of Innovation in Gertrude Stein's Writing*. 1993. University of York, PhD dissertation.

Moore, George. *Gertrude Stein's "The Making of Americans": Repetition and the Emergence of Modernism*. New York: Peter Lang, 1998.

Morel, Bénédicte Auguste. *Traité des Dégénérescences Physiques, Intellectuelles et Morales de L'Espèce Humaine et des Causes Qui Produisent ces Variétés Maladives*. New York: H. Baillière, 1857.

Nadel, Ira B. "Gertrude Stein and Henry James." In Neuman and Nadel, 81–97.
———. *Joyce and the Jews: Culture and Texts*. Gainesville: University Press of Florida, 1989.
Nazaryan, Alexander. "Gertrude Stein Exhibit at the Met Will Now Allude to Her Hitler-loving Past and Collaboration with Vichy Regime." *New York Daily News*, May 7, 2012.
Némirovsky, Irène. *Suite Française*. [1941–1942.] Trans. Sandra Smith. New York: Vintage, 2007.
Neuman, Shirley, and Ira B. Nadel, eds. *Gertrude Stein and the Making of Literature*. Boston: Northeastern University Press, 1988.
Nielsen, Aldon Lynn. *Reading Race: White American Poets and Racial Discourse in the Twentieth Century*. Athens: University of Georgia Press, 1988.
Nordau, Max. *Degeneration*. 1895. Intro. George Mosse. Lincoln: University of Nebraska Press, 1993.
Norris, Margot. "The 'Wife' and the 'Genius': Domesticating Modern Art in Stein's *Autobiography of Alice B. Toklas*." *Modernism, Gender, and Culture: A Cultural Studies Approach*. Ed. Lisa Rado. New York: Garland, 1997, 79–99.
Olson, Liesl M. "Gertrude Stein, William James, and Habit in the Shadow of War." *Twentieth-Century Literature* 49.3 (Fall 2003): 328–359.
Paris, Václav. "'Gertrude Stein's Translations of Speeches' by Philippe Petain." *Gertrude Stein's War Years*. Ed. Charles Bernstein. *Jacket2*. May 6, 2013. Online: jacket2.org/article/gertrude-steins-translations-speeches-philippe-petain
Paxton, Robert O. "Preface: From the Bottom of the Abyss." In Corpet and Paulhan, 7–16.
Perloff, Marjorie. *The Poetics of Indeterminacy: Rimbaud to Cage*. Princeton, NJ: Princeton University Press, 1981.
Pollak, Francis. Letter to Gertrude Stein. June 1897. YCAL.
Pondrom, Cyrena. Introduction. *Geography and Plays*. By Gertrude Stein. Madison: University of Wisconsin Press, 1993.
Pound, Ezra. *Pound/Zukofsky: Selected Letters of Ezra Pound and Louis Zukofsky*. Ed. Barry Ahern. New York: New Directions, 1987.
———. *Pound/Joyce: The Letters of Ezra Pound to James Joyce*. Ed. Forrest Read. New York: New Directions, 1970.
———. "Salutation the Third." *BLAST* 1. Ed. Wyndham Lewis. Santa Rosa: Black Sparrow Press, 1992, 45.
Poznanski, Renée. *Jews in France During World War II*. Trans. Nathan Bracher. Waltham: Brandeis University Press, 2002.
Prickett, Stephen. "'Hebrew' versus 'Hellene' as a Principal of Literary Criticism." *Rediscovering Hellenism: The Hellenic Inheritance and the English Imagination*.

Ed. G. W. Clarke with J. C. Eade. New York: Cambridge University Press, 1989, 137–160.

Quartermain, Peter. *Disjunctive Poetics: From Gertrude Stein and Louis Zukofsky to Susan Howe.* Cambridge: Cambridge University Press, 1992.

Raleigh, John Henry. *Matthew Arnold and American Culture.* Berkeley: University of California Press, 1961.

Ragussis, Michael. *Figures of Conversion: "The Jewish Question" and English National Identity.* Durham, NC: Duke University Press, 1995.

Renan, Ernest. "The Share of the Semitic People in the History of Civilization." *Studies* of *Religious History and Criticism.* Trans. O. B. Frothingham. New York: Carleton, 1864, 149–167.

Richards, Grant. Letters to Gertrude Stein. Circa 1911. YCAL.

Rodker, John. *The Future of Futurism.* New York: E. P. Dutton, 1927.

Ruddick, Lisa. *Reading Gertrude Stein: Body, Text, Gnosis.* Ithaca, NY: Cornell University Press, 1990.

Ryan, Donna. *The Holocaust and the Jews of Marseille: The Enforcement of Anti-Semitic Policies in Vichy France.* Chicago: University of Illinois Press, 1996.

Schmitz, Neil. *Of Huck and Alice: Humorous Writing in American Literature.* Minneapolis: University of Minnesota Press, 1983.

———. "Portrait, Patriarchy, Mythos: The Revenge of Gertrude Stein." *Salmagundi* 40 (1978): 69–91.

Schoenbach, Lisi. "'Peaceful and Exciting': Habit, Shock, and Gertrude Stein's Pragmatic Modernism." *Modernism/modernity* 11.2 (2004): 239–259.

Selzer, Michael, ed. *"Kike!": A Documentary History of Anti-Semitism in America.* New York: World Publishers, 1972.

Sengoopta, Chandak. *Otto Weininger: Sex, Science, and Self in Imperial Vienna.* Chicago: University of Chicago Press, 2000.

Sevareid, Eric. *Not So Wild A Dream.* New York: Knopf, 1946.

Shaw, Bernard. "The Sanity of Art: An Exposure of the Current Nonsense about Artists Being Degenerate." 1895. *Major Critical Essays.* London: Constable, 1932, 281–332.

Shaw, Patrick. "The Surrender to Ethos: Gertrude Stein's 'Introduction to the Speeches of Maréchal Pétain.'" *Chasing Esther: Jewish Expressions of Cultural Difference.* Eds. David Metzger and Peter Schulman. Santa Monica, CA: Institute for Jewish Studies and Interfaith Understanding, University of Haifa, 2005, 9–31.

Skelton, John. *The Table-Talk of Shirley: Reminiscences of and Letters from Froude Thackeray Disraeli Browning Rossetti Kingsley Baynes Huxley Tyndall and Others.* 5th Ed. Edinburgh: Blackwood, 1895.

Slezkine, Yuri. *The Jewish Century*. Princeton, NJ: Princeton University Press, 2004.

Slote, Sam. "Preliminary Comments on Two Newly Discovered *Ulysses* Manuscripts." *James Joyce Quarterly* 39.1 (Fall 2001): 17–28.

Smedman, Lorna. "'Cousin to Cooning': Relation, Difference, and Racialized Language in Stein's Nonrepresentational Texts." *Modern Fiction Studies* 42:3 (1996): 569–588.

Solomons, Leon. Letter to Gertrude Stein. 4 Jan. 1898. YCAL.

The Sorrow and the Pity [Le chagrin et la pitié]. 1969. Dir. Marcel Ophüls. Oscilloscope Pictures, 2011.

Spahr, Juliana. "'There is No Way of Speaking English': The Polylingual Grammars of Gertrude Stein." *Everybody's Autonomy: Connective Reading and Collective Identity*. Tuscaloosa: University of Alabama Press, 2001, 17–50.

Spencer, Herbert. *An Autobiography*. New York: D. Appleton, 1904.

———. *First Principles*. 1864. New York: D. Appleton, 1898.

Spies, S. B. *Methods of Barbarism? Roberts and Kitchener and Civilians in the Boer Republics, January 1900–May 1902*. Cape Town: Human & Rousseau, 1977.

Stein, Amelia. Unpublished diaries. 1878–1886. 6 Vols. Bancroft Library of Western Americana. University of California, Berkeley, CA.

Stein, Gertrude. "All About Money." *How Writing Is Written: Volume II of the Previously Uncollected Writings of Gertrude Stein*. Ed. Robert Bartlett Haas. Los Angeles: Black Sparrow Press, 1974, 110.

———. "As Fine as Melanctha." *As Fine as Melanctha (1914–1930). The Yale Edition of the Unpublished Writings of Gertrude Stein*. Vol. 4. New Haven, CT: Yale University Press, 1954, 255–269.

———. *The Autobiography of Alice B. Toklas*. 1933. New York: Vintage, 1990.

———. *Bee Time Vine and Other Pieces (1913–1927). The Yale Edition of the Unpublished Writings of Gertrude Stein*. Vol. 3. New Haven, CT: Yale University Press, 1953.

———. "Coal and Wood." *Painted Lace and Other Pieces (1914–1937)*, 3–11.

———. Collection of notes and quotations, in Gertrude Stein's hand ca. 1890s [Formerly catalogued as *Q.E.D.* Notes] YCAL.

———. "Composition as Explanation." In Dydo, *A Stein Reader*, 493–503.

———. "Cultivated Motor Automatism: A Study of Character in Its Relation to Attention." *Harvard Psychological Review* 5.3 (May 1898): 295–306.

———. "Dates." 1914. *Bee Time Vine and Other Pieces (1913–1927)*, 168–170.

———. "Degeneration in American Women." Circa 1901–2. In Wineapple, 411–414.

———. *Everybody's Autobiography*. 1937. New York: Vintage, 1973.

———. "Geography." 1923. *Painted Lace and Other Pieces (1914–1937)*, 239–243.

———. "Gertrude Stein Views Life and Politics." Interview with Lansing Warren. *New York Times Magazine* (6 May 1934): SM9 and SM23.

———. "Harriet and the person I knew once somewhat like her." Ms. n.d. YCAL.

———. "Harriet Fear." *Two: Gertrude Stein and Her Brother and Other Early Portraits (1908–1912)*, 343–346.

———. "Have They Attacked Mary. He Giggled." *Vanity Fair* 8.4 (June 1917): 55.

———. "Have They Attacked Mary. He Giggled. (A Political Caricature)." *Selected Writings*, 531–539.

———. "Introduction to the Speeches of Maréchal Pétain." 1942. Ed. Wanda Van Dusen. *Modernism/modernity* 3.3 (1996): 93–96.

———. "Land of Nations." *Geography and Plays*. 1922. Madison: University of Wisconsin Press, 1993, 408.

———. *Last Operas and Plays*. Baltimore: Johns Hopkins University Press, 1995.

———. *Lectures in America*. 1935. Boston: Beacon Press, 1985.

———. Letter to Robert and Diana Abdy. c. 1938. YCAL.

———. Letter to Grant Richards. 28 Sept. 1911. YCAL.

———. Letter to Ellery Sedgwick. 16 Oct. 1919. YCAL.

———. *The Letters of Gertrude Stein and Carl Van Vechten*. 2 Vols. Ed. Edward Burns. New York: Columbia University Press, 1986.

———. "Lifting Belly." *Bee Time Vine and Other Pieces (1913–1927)*, 63–115.

———. "Look at Us." *Painted Lace and Other Pieces (1914–1937)*, 259–268.

———. "The Making of Americans: Being the History of a Family's Progress." Ed. Donald Gallup. *Fernhurst, Q.E.D., and Other Early Writings*. New York: Liveright, 1971, 135–172.

———. *The Making of Americans: Being a History of a Family's Progress*. 1925. Normal, IL: Dalkey Archive Press, 1995.

———. "The Making of Americans." *Transatlantic Review*. (April–December 1924).

———. "Mildred's Thoughts." 1922. In Dydo, *A Stein Reader*, 356–375.

———. "The Modern Jew Who Has Given Up the Faith of His Fathers Can Reasonably and Consistently Believe in Isolation." 1896. Ed. and Intro. Amy Feinstein. *PMLA* 116 (2001): 416–428.

———. *The Mother of Us All*. 1946. *Last Operas and Plays*, 52–88.

———. *Mrs. Reynolds*. Los Angeles: Sun & Moon Press, 1980.

———. "Natural Phenomena." *Painted Lace and Other Pieces (1914–1937)*, 167–233.

———. "Nest of Dishes." *Painted Lace and Other Pieces (1914–1937)*, 97–107.

———. *Painted Lace and Other Pieces (1914–1937)*. The Yale Edition of the Unpublished Writings of Gertrude Stein. Vol. 5. New Haven, CT: Yale University Press, 1955.

———. "Painted Lace." *Painted Lace and Other Pieces (1914–1937)*, 1–3.
———. *Paris France*. 1940. New York: Liveright, 1970.
———. "A Political Series." *Painted Lace and Other Pieces (1914–1937)*, 76.
———. *Portraits and Prayers*. New York: Random House, 1934.
———. Postscript. Leo Stein Letter to Fred Stein, 20 July 1896. YCAL.
———. *Q.E.D.* Ed. Donald Gallup. *Fernhurst, Q.E.D., and Other Early Writings*. New York: Liveright, 1971, 51–133.
———. "The Radcliffe Manuscripts." Ed. Rosalind S. Miller. *Gertrude Stein: Form and Intelligibility*. New York: The Exposition Press, 1949, 108–156.
———. "A Radical Expert." *Bee Time Vine and Other Pieces (1913–1927)*, 198.
———. "Reread Another. A Play. To Be Played Indoors Or Out. I Wish to Be A School." In Dydo, *A Stein Reader*, 347–355.
———. "The Reverie of the Zionist." *Painted Lace and Other Pieces (1914–1937)*, 94.
———. "The Revery of the Zionist." YCAL, MSS 76, Box 90, Folder 1701, Bound Volume 15, 300.
———. "Saints and Singing: A Play." In Dydo, *A Stein Reader*, 381–399.
———. *Selected Writings of Gertrude Stein*. Ed. Carl Van Vechten. New York: Vintage, 1990.
———. "A Sonatina Followed By Another." *Bee Time Vine and Other Pieces (1913–1927)*, 4–32.
———. *Three Lives*. 1909. New York: Vintage, 1936.
———. "A Transatlantic Interview." 1946. *A Primer for the Gradual Understanding of Gertrude Stein*. Ed. Robert Bartlett Haas. Los Angeles: Black Sparrow Press, 1973, 11–35.
———. "Two." *Two: Gertrude Stein and Her Brother and Other Early Portraits (1908–1912)*, 1–142.
———. *Two: Gertrude Stein and Her Brother and Other Early Portraits (1908–1912)*. The Yale Edition of the Unpublished Writings of Gertrude Stein. Vol. 1. New Haven, CT: Yale University Press, 1951.
———. Unpublished ms. notebooks and ms. drafts for *The Making of Americans*. YCAL.
———. "The Value of College Education for Women." Unpublished lecture ts. (March or May 1899.) Dr. Claribel and Miss Etta Cone Papers. Correspondence, Box 5, Folder 20. Archives and Manuscript Collections. Baltimore Museum of Art, Baltimore, Maryland.
———. *Wars I Have Seen*. 1945. London: Brilliance, 1984.
———. *Wars I Have Seen*. YCAL, MSS 76, Box 80, Folder 1470, Notebook 2.
———. "The Winner Loses: A Picture of Occupied France." 1939–1940. *Selected Writings*. 613–637.

———. *Yes Is for a Very Young Man.* 1944–1945. *Last Operas and Plays*, 3–51.
———. "Yes You Do." 1922. *Painted Lace and Other Pieces (1914–1937)*, 118–123.
———. "Yet Dish." 1913. *Bee Time Vine and Other Pieces (1913–1927)*, 53–60.
Stein, Gertrude, and Leon Solomons. "Normal Motor Automatism." *Psychological Review* 3.5 (Sept. 1896): 492–512.
Stein, Leo. "The Jew in Fiction." *Jewish Comment* 11.5 (18 May 1900): 6, 8.
———. *Journey Into the Self: Being the Letters, Papers & Journals of Leo Stein.* Ed. Edmund Fuller. New York: Crown, 1950.
———. Letter to Bird Sternberger Gans. 30 Aug. 1895. YCAL.
———. "Society and Art." *Jewish Comment* 11.7 (1 June 1900): 3–4.
Steiner, Wendy. *Exact Resemblance to Exact Resemblance: The Literary Portraiture of Gertrude Stein.* New Haven, CT: Yale University Press, 1978.
Stepan, Nancy. "Biological Degeneration: Races and Proper Places." In *Degeneration: The Dark Side of Progress.* Eds. J. Edward Chamberlin and Sander L. Gilman. New York: Columbia University Press, 1985, 97–120.
Stetson, Charlotte Perkins. *Women and Economics.* 1898. New York: Dover, 1998.
Steward, Samuel, ed. and memoir. *Dear Sammy: Letters from Gertrude Stein and Alice B. Toklas.* Boston: Houghton Mifflin, 1977.
Stewart, Allegra. *Gertrude Stein and the Present.* Cambridge, MA: Harvard University Press, 1967.
Stillwell, Stephen. *Anglo-Turkish Relations in the Interwar Era.* Lewiston, NY: Edwin Mellon Press, 2003.
Stimpson, Catharine. "Stein and the Transposition of Gender." *The Poetics of Gender.* Ed. Nancy K. Miller. New York: Columbia University Press, 1986, 1–18.
———. "The Mind, the Body, and Gertrude Stein." *Critical Inquiry* 3 (1977): 489–506.
Stocking, Jr., George W. "Matthew Arnold, E. B. Tylor, and the Uses of Invention." *Race, Culture, and Evolution: Essays in the History of Anthropology.* New York: Free Press, 1968, 69–90.
Stone, Donald D. *Communications with the Future: Matthew Arnold in Dialogue.* Ann Arbor: University of Michigan Press, 1997.
———. "Matthew Arnold and the Pragmatics of Hebraism and Hellenism." *Poetics Today* 19.2 (Summer 1998): 179–198.
Suleiman, Susan Rubin. *The Némirovsky Question: The Life, Death, and Legacy of a Jewish Writer in 20th-Century France.* New Haven, CT: Yale University Press, 2016.
Super, R. H., ed. *The Complete Prose Works of Matthew Arnold.* Vol. 5. Ann Arbor: University of Michigan Press, 1965.
Swartz, Shirley. "The Autobiography as Generic 'Continuous Present': *Paris France* and *Wars I Have Seen.*" *English Studies in Canada* 4.2 (1978): 224–237.

Swift, Jonathan. *The Battle of the Books.* 1704. London: Chatto and Windus, 1908.

Taine, Hippolyte Adolphe. *A History of English Literature.* Trans. H. Van Laun. Vol. 1. 1871. New York: Frederick Ungar, 1965.

Taylor, Melanie. "A Poetics of Difference: *The Making of Americans* and Unreadable Subjects." *NWSA Journal* 15.3 (2003): 26–42.

Tinterow, Gary, assisted by Marci Kwon. "Leo Stein before 1914." *The Steins Collect: Matisse, Picasso, and the Parisian Avant-Garde.* Eds. Janet Bishop, Cécile Debray, and Rebecca Rabinow. San Francisco: San Francisco Museum of Modern Art, 2011.

Toklas, Alice B. *The Alice B. Toklas Cookbook.* Guilford, CT: The Lyons Press, 1954.

Transcript of Gertrude Stein. Radcliffe College. Office of the Registrar Records, 1874–1966. RG XII, Series 1, Vol. D./ MM-6 Radcliffe College Archives, Schlesinger Library, Radcliffe Institute, Harvard University, Cambridge, Mass.

Trilling, Lionel. *Matthew Arnold.* New York: Norton, 1939.

Troy, William. "A Note on Gertrude Stein." Rev. of *The Autobiography of Alice B. Toklas* by Gertrude Stein. *The Nation.* 6 Sept. 1933, 274–275.

Trubowitz, Lara. *Civil Antisemitism, Modernism, and British Culture, 1902–1939.* New York: Palgrave Macmillan, 2012.

Turner, Kay, ed. *Baby Precious Always Shines: Selected Love Notes Between Gertrude Stein and Alice B. Toklas.* New York: St. Martin's Press, 1999.

Typed list of Gertrude Stein's courses and instructors. Radcliffe College Alumnae Association Records, ca. 1894–2004. RG IX, Series 2, Box #298, Stein, Gertrude '98, Folder 1. Schlesinger Library, Radcliffe Institute, Harvard University, Cambridge, Mass.

Van Dusen, Wanda. "Portrait of a National Fetish: Gertrude Stein's 'Introduction to the Speeches of Maréchal Pétain' (1942)." *Modernism/modernity* 3.3 (1996): 69–92.

Van Puymbroeck, Birgit. "Triangular Politics: Stein, Bernard Faÿ, and Elisabeth de Gramont." *Gertrude Stein in Europe: Reconfigurations Across Media, Disciplines, and Traditions.* Eds. Sarah Posman and Laura Luise Schultz. New York: Bloomsbury, 2015, 85–103.

This Land is Mine. Dir. Jean Renoir. RKO Radio Pictures, 1943.

Veblen, Thorstein. *Theory of the Leisure Class: An Economic Study in the Evolution of Institutions.* 1899. New York: New American Library, 1953.

Vignale, François. *La revue "Fontaine": poésie, résistance, engagement: Alger 1938– Paris 1947.* Rennes: Presses universitaires de Rennes, 2012.

Wagner-Martin, Linda. *"Favored Strangers": Gertrude Stein and Her Family.* New Brunswick, NJ: Rutgers University Press, 1995.

Wald, Priscilla. *Constituting Americans: Cultural Anxiety and Narrative Form.* Durham, NC: Duke University Press, 1995.

Walker, Jayne. *The Making of a Modernist: Gertrude Stein from* Three Lives *to* Tender Buttons. Amherst: University of Massachusetts Press, 1984.

Walkowitz, Rebecca. *Cosmopolitan Style: Modernism Beyond the Nation.* New York: Columbia University Press, 2006.

Watson, Dana Cairns. *Gertrude Stein and the Essence of What Happens.* Nashville, TN: Vanderbilt University Press, 2005.

Watten, Barrett. "An Epic of Subjectivation: *The Making of Americans.*" *Modernism/modernity* 5.2 (1998): 95–121.

Webb, Beatrice Potter. "The Jewish Community" *Life and Labour of the People in London.* Ed. Charles Booth. Vol. 1. 3rd Ed. London: Williams and Norgate, 1891, 564–590.

Weininger, Otto. *Sex and Character.* London: Heinemann, 1906.

Weinstein, Norman. *Gertrude Stein and the Literature of Modern Consciousness.* New York: Frederick Ungar, 1970.

Whittier-Ferguson, John. *Mortality and Form in Late Modernism.* New York: Cambridge University Press, 2014.

———. "Stein in Time: History, Manuscripts, and Memory." *Modernism/modernity* 6.1 (1999): 115–51.

Wieviorka, Annette. *Déportation et Génocide: Entre la mémoire et l'oubli.* Paris: Plon, 1992.

Wilde, Oscar. *The Picture of Dorian Gray.* 1891. New York: Penguin, 2000.

Will, Barbara. "Gertrude Stein and Zionism." *Modern Fiction Studies* 51.2 (Summer 2005): 437–455.

———. "Gertrude Stein, Bernard Faÿ, and the Ruthless Flowers of Friendship." *Modernism/modernity* 15.4 (2008): 647–663.

———. *Gertrude Stein, Modernism, and the Problem of "Genius."* Edinburgh: Edinburgh University Press, 2000.

———. "Lost in Translation: Stein's Vichy Collaborations." *Modernism/modernity* 11.4 (2004): 651–668.

———. "The Strange Politics of Gertrude Stein." *Humanities* 33.2 (March/April 2012).

———. *Unlikely Collaboration: Gertrude Stein, Bernard Faÿ, and the Vichy Dilemma.* New York: Columbia University Press, 2011.

Williams, Raymond. *Culture and Society, 1780–1950.* New York: Columbia University Press, 1983.

Williams, William Carlos. *Selected Essays.* New York: Random House, 1954.

Wilson, Edmund. *Axel's Castle: A Study in the Imaginative Literature of 1870–1930.* New York: Scribner, 1931.

Wineapple, Brenda. *Sister Brother: Gertrude and Leo Stein*. New York: Putnam, 1996.
Wisse, Ruth. *Modern Jewish Canon: A Journey through Language and Culture*. New York: The Free Press, 2000.
Woolf, Virginia. *Letters of Virginia Woolf*. Vol 3. 1923–1928. Eds. Nigel Nicolson and Joanne Trautmann. New York: Harcourt Brace Jovanovich, 1980.
———. *A Room of One's Own*. 1929. New York: Harvest, 1989.
Zox-Weaver, Annalisa. *Women Modernists and Fascism*. New York: Cambridge University Press, 2011.
Zuccotti, Susan. *The Holocaust, the French, and the Jews*. Lincoln: University of Nebraska Press, 1999.

INDEX

Abraham, Julie, 127
Abstraction: Arendt on, 93; Jewish nature of, 11, 23–28; in *The Making of Americans*, 59–60, 95, 105, 112; in Stein works, 41
Adler, Felix, 35
Aesthetic Calibans, 85
Afterlife, 200–201n28
d'Aiguy, Madame Dianne (May), 157
Allosemitism, 21
Ambassadors, The (James), 62, 211n15, 215n7
Anglo-Saxon nativism, 209n41
Anglo-Saxon type, 65–68, 71, 72–73, 90, 107, 109, 113–14, 215–16nn8–9
Antisemitism: as archaic, 154; of Arnold, 9–10, 202n7; banning of Jews from vacation resorts, 211n18; of Germany under Hitler, 176, 184; in 1901 London, 217n18; of Pétain, 174–75; Stein accused of, 74, 233n19, 238n45, 243n5; under Vichy regime and German Occupation, 147, 152–54, 155, 230nn1–2, 234–35n26, 236–37n37–39, 240n57; in *Wars I Have Seen*, 161–69
Aragon, Louis, 190
Arendt, Hannah, 88, 92–93, 122, 222n12
Aristotle, 56
Arnold, Matthew: antisemitism of, 9–10, 202n7; on culture, 26–28; *Culture and Anarchy*, 21–22; influences on, 202n6; as influence on Stein, 2, 3–4, 21, 22, 28–32, 40–41, 194; as influence on Weininger, 205n20; as influence on Wyndham Lewis, 206n28, 207n32; Leo Stein on, 37; *Literature and Dogma*, 27–28, 33, 34; and Stein's genealogy of Jewish types, 64, 67, 69–70, 73, 75, 77, 79, 82; and Stein's "Oriental" Jews, 154; Swift's influence on, 206n27; and William James, 30–31, 206n28, 207n33, 208–9n40, 212n25
Ashton, Jennifer, 111, 225n26
Auctioneer, The (play), 75
Auschwitz, 151, 159, 182, 234n22
Auzias, Nina, 215n5
Axelrod, Steven Gould, 148

Barnes, Djuna, 5
Bauman, Zygmunt, 11, 21
Beckett, Samuel, 169
Benfey, Christopher, 192
Benstock, Shari, 233n19
Bercovitch, Sacvan, 58, 59
Berenson, Bernard, 68, 78, 225n25, 237n40
Berenson, Mary, 65, 237n40
Berman, Jessica, 89, 103, 118, 222n9
Bernstein, Charles, 183, 197n2, 243nn2–3

Berr, Hélène, 234n22
Biblical allusions, 43, 51, 56, 57–59, 99, 108–9, 135, 136, 141, 163, 213n31, 224n4; the chosen people, 21, 33–34, 96, 124, 163, 232n16; Jeremiah, 26, 46–47, 58–59, 74, 118, 178–79, 206n24, 211n12, 222n12
Bildung, 27, 49–50
Black racial stereotypes, 43–44, 220n38
Blair, Sara, 131
Boer War, 159, 160, 237n40
Bonaparte, Napoleon, 82, 142, 155, 185–86, 244–45nn13–14
Book of Lamentations, The, 46–47
Boston, 72
Bottom nature, 75–76
Boyce, Neith, 215n8
Bridgman, Richard, 247n28
Brother Singular(s): avant-garde writing and, 102–4; biblical tradition and, 57–59, 99; conception of, 4, 36–37; David Hersland as, 114; Flaubert as, 82; hidden *maquis* and, 173; as Jewish pariahs, 92–95, 98–99, 194; in "The Making of Americans," 49, 57–59; in *The Making of Americans* epilogue, 117–22, 194; modern Jews and, 35; narrator's address to, in *The Making of Americans*, 99, 112–13; *Q.E.D.*'s Adele as, 41–55; as queer, 39–40, 57–58, 210n4; servant girls as, 99–103; similarities to notions by Woolf and T. S. Eliot, 40
Bruttmann, Tal, 243–44n7
Burns, Edward, 153, 200n27, 230n2, 246n23

Cahan, Abraham, 37
Caliban(s), 64, 70, 79–81, 83–84, 85, 113–17, 216n13, 219n30
Cerf, Bennett, 189, 245n16
Cézanne, Paul, 28–29, 70, 71, 73, 83–84, 109, 206–7n31, 220n35, 220n36
Chaboux, Doctor, 235n33
Chalfin, Paul, 78
Chantiers de la Jeunesse, 165, 238n47

Chaplin, Charlie, 93
Characterology. *See* Anglo-Saxon type; Jewish types
Charcot, Jean-Martin, 202n2
Charlot, Edmond, 245–46n20
Chodat, Robert, 198n7
Civil War, 211n10
Cohen, Inez, 201n29
Concentration camps, 151, 155–61, 182, 234n22, 235n31, 236–37n37, 237n40, 243–44nn6–7
Cone, Claribel, 70, 219n30
Confluences, 190, 191, 246n23
Conscious pariahs, 95–100, 222n12
Cooper, James Fenimore, 166
Crowninshield, Frank, 131–32, 228nn17–18
Cuddihy, John, 32, 211n11
Culture: Arnold on, 9–10, 26–28; and tensions between Hebraism and Hellenism in "The Making of Americans," 53–55
Culture and Anarchy (Arnold), 21–22
Cummings, E. E., 87, 199n17
Curiosity, 27, 69, 70, 82
Curtis, Michael, 230n1, 238n47

Damon, Maria, 4, 39, 43, 58, 125, 136, 210n4, 210n6, 210–11n8, 213n31, 228–29n23
Darwin, Charles, 79
Dauber, Maayan P., 246n26
Davis, Phoebe Stein, 149–50, 232n17, 233n19
Dearborn, Mary, 4, 222n8
Death, 225n29
Degeneration / Degeneracy, 21, 22, 23–25, 30, 201–2nn2–3, 203n9, 207n35, 208n37
DeKoven, Marianne, 124, 226nn1–2
Derain, André, 71
Derrida, Jacques, 225n26
Dershowitz, Alan, 181, 243n2, 243n5
Detloff, Madelyn, 150

Deviance, social repercussions of, in *The Making of Americans*, 101–4
"Diagram book," 63–64, 65, 217n17, 219n30, 221n6, 244n13
Diner, Hasia, 92, 211n10, 211–12n19
Disinterestedness, 27, 70, 77, 82, 209n47, 210n5
Displacement, 125–26
Disraeli, Benjamin, 21, 135–36, 202nn5–6, 228n22
Doane, Janice, 210n4
Dougherty, Paul, 78
Douglas, Lord Alfred, 140
Doyle, Laura, 213n27, 222n8
Dreyfus Affair, 33, 161–69, 238n42
Drieu la Rochelle, Pierre, 190
Dudden, Faye, 224n20
Duncan, Raymond, 68, 81
Dydo, Ulla, 127, 153, 163, 198n9, 210n4, 228n19, 230n2, 246n23

Earle, Mabel, 201n29
Earthy Jewish type, 64, 65, 69–74, 90, 99, 100, 109, 215n8
Edel, Leon, 207n33
Edstrom, David, 78
Eliot, George, 229n25
Eliot, T. S., 8, 9, 28, 40, 87, 125, 198–99n14, 199n16, 243n5
Ellis, Havelock, 203n11
Enemies, 166–68
Epstein, Michel, 234n22
Equilibration, 107, 109, 110, 225n28
Erdman, Harley, 212nn19–20

Farland, Maria, 4, 70
Faÿ, Bernard, 143–44, 185–86, 191, 192, 231nn4–6, 240n56
Fénéon, Félix, 71
Fitzgerald, F. Scott, 88
Flaubert, Gustave, 82
Fontaine, 190, 191, 246n23
Foote, Stephanie, 211n10
Ford, Maddox Ford, 205n17

Forster, E. M., 47, 79, 219n29
Frederick the Great, 77, 219n27
Fredman, Stephen, 32
Freemasons, 175, 231n5
French cuisine, 193
Friedman, Leo, 63, 71, 201n29
"Funny," 146–47, 156–58, 187, 232n14
Futurism, 8. *See also* Modernism

Galchinsky, Michael, 11
Gallagher, Jean, 149
Galton, Francis, 23, 203n11
Galvin, Rachel, 182, 186, 189, 232n12, 232–33nn17–18, 233n20, 241n61
Gans, Howard, 201n29
Gates, Lewis E., 30
Generational change and conflict, 52–53
Genius, 10–11, 16, 24, 25, 76, 77–79, 203n9, 203n11. *See also* Degeneration / Degeneracy; Intelligence
German Jews, 9, 12, 13, 31, 44, 89, 201n29, 211n10
German Occupation, 143–44, 147, 181, 190, 230nn1–2, 233–34n22, 234n24, 235–36n33, 240n56. *See also* Vichy regime; *Wars I Have Seen* (Stein)
German opera, 200n26
Giroud, Vincent, 222–23n14
Godet, Romain, 230n2
Goering, Hermann, 166–67
Goethe, Johann Wolfgang von, 200n26, 219n27
Gökay, Bülent, 138–39, 229n29
Goldsmith, Meredith, 88
Goldstein, Eric, 45
Gósol, 222–23n14
Great Britain, 138–41
Greenhouse, Emily, 182, 243nn4–5, 247n28

Hapgood, Hutchins, 15, 65, 68, 201n31
Harvard University, 14–15, 16, 30–33, 214–15n4, 220n37
Hawkins, Stefanie, 91
Haynes, Mabel, 82

Hebraism: and Arnold's "culture," 26–27; defined, 27; as foil for Hellenism, 21; and Hellenizing of Jewish singular in *Q.E.D.*, 41–55; influence of ideology of, 32; and middle-class origins in "The Making of Americans," 55–61; and Stein's first Jewish protagonists, 40–41; and Stein's genealogy of Jewish types, 64, 67, 69–70, 73, 75, 77, 79, 82; and Stein's "Oriental" Jews, 154; Stein's reappropriation of, 3–4; tensions between Hellenism and, in "The Making of Americans," 50, 53–55
Heine, Heinrich, 10–11, 202n6, 202–3n8
Hell, Victor, 187, 188, 245n15
Hellenism: and Arnold's "culture," 26–27; and authorial type, 81–85; defined, 27; as foil for Hebraism, 21; Hellenizing of Jewish singular in *Q.E.D.*, 41–55; and Stein's first Jewish protagonists, 40–41; and Stein's genealogy of Jewish types, 64, 67, 69–70, 73, 75, 77, 79, 82; and Stein's "Oriental" Jews, 154; Stein's reappropriation of, 4; tensions between Hebraism and, in "The Making of Americans," 50, 53–55
Hemingway, Ernest, 166
Heredity, and middle-class origins in "The Making of Americans," 55–61
Herrmann, Anne, 58, 104, 210n4
Higham, John, 92, 211n10, 212n23
Higher Criticism, 33, 34
Hilburg, Raul, 239n51
Hirsch, William, 24, 203n11
Hitler, Adolf, 153, 155, 176, 178–79, 182–86, 235n28, 244n9, 244–45n14
Hodder, Alfred, 224n22
Homosexuality: compared to avant-garde writing in *The Making of Americans*, 104; and Stein's romantic Jewish lexicon, 127–31; and Stein's views on intermarriage, 201n31. *See also* Queerness
Hovey, Jaime, 4, 43, 210n6
Hyman, Paula E., 212n23

Immigration, 153–54
Imprisonment / Internment: Stein and Toklas evade, 156–59, 235–36nn33–36; in *Wars I Have Seen*, 161–69. *See also* Concentration camps
Insistence, 43, 210n7
Intelligence, 77–79, 218–19n26. *See also* Genius
"Interesting," conflated with "queer," 54, 57, 209n40, 212n25
Intermarriage, 15, 32–34, 96, 201n31
International affairs, 133–34, 138–41
Internment. *See* Concentration camps; Imprisonment / Internment

Jacob, Max, 190
Jacobs, Joseph, 203n9
Jacobson, Matthew Frye, 44
James, Henry, 28, 29–30, 62, 101, 211n15, 215n7, 223n16
James, William: Arnold and, 30–31, 206n28, 207n33, 208–9n40, 212n25; on bans against Jews, 211n18; on Christian Science healers, 205n16; on degenerationism, 6–7, 14–15, 20, 24, 208n36; and equilibration, 225n28; as influence on Stein, 222n10; on Jews, 204–5nn12–13; on scientific endeavor, 91; Stein's classification of, 78; Weininger on, 25
Jerusalem, 47
"Jew complex," 14
Jewish communal ties, 35
Jewish identity: of Adele in *Q.E.D.*, 41–43; associated with modernity, 190–91; of Stein, 4, 150–51, 218n21, 232n16, 233n19; Stein on, 33–36, 142; Stein's claiming of, 150–51, 218n21; Stein's masculine identification and, 39, 71
Jewish nationalism, 133–42
Jewish nature: of Adele in *Q.E.D.*, 43; of Cézanne, 220n35; and characterology in *The Making of Americans*, 90; determined from physiognomy, 217n16; intelligence as characteristic of, 77–79,

218–19n26; of marital bond between Stein and Toklas, 128; nineteenth-century scientific views on, 10–11; versus non-Jewish nature, 36; of Stein, 11–12, 31, 220n38; Stein's qualitative questions about, 126
Jewish New Year, 130, 228n15
Jewish nomenclature, 124, 209n43
Jewish problem / question, the, 20–21, 22, 25, 32–37, 100
Jewish tradition: American Jews' connection to, 31; hidden, 41, 49–55; households and holidays, 128–30; modernism and, 192–95; rebellion as maintenance of, 56; Stein on, 38–39; Stein's discovery of, as distinct from "Christian thinking," 14
Jewish types: and abstraction, 110–12; authorial type, 81–85; avant-garde writers in *The Making of Americans*, 101–4; and beginning again in *The Making of Americans*, 106–7; and biblical tradition, 57–59, 99, 108–9; Calibans, 64, 70, 79–81, 83–84, 85, 113–17, 216n13, 219n30; earthy, 64, 65, 69–74, 90, 99, 100, 109, 215n8; fluidity of, 64, 218n25; gendered correspondences to, 217n17; genealogy of, in notebooks for *The Making of Americans*, 62–64, 85–86, 88–90, 215–16nn5–11, 216n15; intellectual character of, 77–79, 218–19n26; in *The Making of Americans*, 88–90, 95–100; pariah types in *The Making of Americans* epilogue, 117–22; peddlers, 50–51, 61, 194–95, 212n19; resisting, 66–67, 71, 83, 90, 106, 108–9, 216n15, 220n35; tendency toward melancholia in, 105–6; truth tellers, 74–79. *See also* Anglo-Saxon type; Brother Singular(s); Cézanne, Paul; Levy, Harriet; Pariah(s); Picasso, Pablo; Servant girls
Jews: assimilation of American, 31–32; associated with middle class, 45–47, 211n11; as biblical people, 10, 23, 26, 28, 33, 43, 51, 136, 213n31; as contradictory symbol of European culture, 9–10; contributions to world culture, 35–36; degenerationist theories about, 21, 22, 23–25, 30, 201–2nn2–3, 203n9, 207n35, 208n37; depicted as pariahs, 96; deportation and genocide of French, 151–52, 156–60, 182, 233–34n22, 234n24, 236–37nn36–39, 239n51; education of, 212n23; German, 9, 12, 13, 31, 44, 89, 201n29, 211n10; nineteenth-century stereotypes concerning, 92, 211n10; nomenclature for, 124, 209n43; scholarship on images of, in modernist literature, 4–5; and "scientific" theories of racial difference, 20–21, 23–28; social analyses of, 9–11; Stein's choice on how and when to write about, 37; Stein's racialization of, 15, 43–44, 137; as symbols of refugeeism, 169–72; as wanderers, 201–2nn2–3. *See also* Antisemitism; Jewish tradition; Jewish types; Judaism; Voices poems, Jewish lexicon in
Joyce, James: anticipates opposition to *Dubliners*, 223n16; Arnold's influence on, 29; commonalities between Proust and, 61, 214n33; "The Dead," 165; Jewish presence in works of, 125; Pound's criticism of, 7; as Stein critic, 9; Stein distances herself from, 214n34; Stein linked to, 198n11; *Ulysses*, 7, 29, 60–61, 84, 101, 104; Weininger's influence on, 25
Joyce, Stanislaus, 7
Judaism: Arnold's influence on Stein's understanding of, 27–28; Stein on orthodox practice of, 38; Stein's understanding of, 22, 32–36; Weininger on, 25–26. *See also* Jewish tradition; Jews

Kafka, Franz, 93–94, 122
Kallen, Horace Meyer, 31–32
Katz, Leon, 74, 215–16n9, 217–18nn19–21, 218n23, 221n6, 246–47n27
Kedward, H. R., 170, 238–39n48

Kenner, Hugh, 5
Kent, Marian, 229n29
Kipling, Rudyard, 81–82, 219n31, 219–20n34, 221n7
Knowlson, James, 169
"Know thyself," 27, 49–50, 206n26
Krafft-Ebing, Richard von, 201n2, 202n3

Laughlin, James, 185–86
Lawrence, Karen, 150
Lazare, Bernard, 93, 222n12
League of Nations, 133, 138, 229n28
Leick, Karen, 7, 131, 198n11
Lerner, Michael, 246n26
Lesinska, Zofia, 151–52, 168, 231n9, 232n17, 233n19, 236n34
Levine, Gary, 197n2
Levy, Harriet, 65, 70, 79, 80, 219n30, 220n39
Levy, Meyer, 12–13
Lewis, Wyndham, 8, 9, 87, 206n28, 207n32
Lewisohn, Ludwig, 30
Linett, Maren, 5, 169
Literature and Dogma (Arnold), 27–28, 33, 34
Lombroso, Cesar, 203n9

"Making of Americans, The" (Stein): alterations to, 62; hidden Jewish traditions in, 49–55; middle-class traditions in, 55–61

Making of Americans, The (Stein): abstractions used in, 59–60, 95, 105; Anglo-Saxon type in notebooks for, 65–68; and Arnold's influence on Stein, 4; authorial type in notebooks for, 81–85; avant-garde writer as Jewish type in, 101–4; "beginning again" in, 105–13; Brother Singulars as Jewish pariahs in, 95–100, 117–22; earthy Jewish type in notebooks for, 69–74; "funny" in, 232n14; genealogy of Jewish types in notebooks for, 62–64, 85–86, 88–90, 215–16nn5–11, 216n15; "The Gradual Making of The Making of Americans," 213n31; ideal of beauty in, 87–88; identity of narrator of, 91; Jewish origins of families depicted in, 89, 221n4, 221–22n7; Jewish types at beginning of, 95–100; Jewish types in notebooks for, 62–90, 186, 215–16nn5–11, 216n15; long sentences in, 95–96; moral Calibanism of David Hersland in, 113–17; moral Caliban type in notebooks for, 79–81; Napoleon in notebooks for, 82, 186, 244n13; narrator as pariah in, 90–91, 96–98; narrator of, as Jewish type, 90–92; pronouns in, 116–19, 225–26n30; queerness in, 94–96, 98–99, 102–4, 194, 224n18, 224n20, 224n23; reticence of narrator in, 223–24n16; revisions to, 89, 221nn3–4; size of, 87; as statement on observing human nature, 91–92; Stein changes intentions for, 214n2; as Stein family memoir, 89; Stein's fatness compared to, 199n17; truth-teller Jewish type in notebooks for, 74–79; and understanding origins of modernism, 5–6

Malcolm, Janet, 3, 164, 232n16
Maquis, 165–66, 167–69, 172–80, 238–39n48, 242n65
Marrus, Michael R., 154, 170–71, 231n4, 233–34n22, 234–35n26, 235–36nn29–30, 236–37n37, 237n39, 240n57, 243–44n7
Marseilles, mass deportations from, 159–60, 176, 237nn38–39
Matisse, Henri, 68, 80, 83, 216n10, 219n32
Mayer, Oscar, 68
McBride, Henry, 132
Melancholia, 105–6, 207n35
Menorah Society, 32

Metropolitan Museum of Art, 181–82, 242–43nn1–2
Meyer, Steven, 4, 90, 112, 225n29
Middle class: association of Jews with, 45–47, 211n11; and domestic stability, 125–26; and Jewish heredity in "The Making of Americans," 57–61
Mill, John Stuart, 222n13
Miller, Matt, 197n4
Moad, Rosalind, 226n2, 227n13
Modernism: characteristics of, 6–7; and criticism of Stein, 7–9; experimentation in, 7; Jewish tradition and, 192–95; *The Making of Americans* and understanding origins of, 5–6
Moral Calibans, 70, 79–81, 113–17, 216n13, 219n30
Morel, Bénédicte Auguste, 202n3
"Mountain boys," 165–66, 167–69, 172–80, 238–39n48, 242n65
Münsterberg, Hugo, 14–15, 20

Naming: in Jewish tradition, 51; in *The Making of Americans*, 107–8; Stein on, 108
Napoleon, 82, 142, 155, 185–86, 244–45nn13–14
Nationalist Jewish lexicon, 133–42
Némirovsky, Irène, 149–50, 234n22, 239n49
New York Daily News, 181
New York Times Magazine interview, 153, 183, 186
Nordau, Max, 24, 203–4n12, 208n37
Notebooks for *The Making of Americans*: Anglo-Saxon type in, 65–68; authorial type in, 81–85; earthy Jewish type in, 69–74; genealogy of Jewish types in, 62–64, 85–86, 88–90, 215–16nn5–11, 216n15; moral Caliban type in, 79–81; Napoleon in, 186; truth-teller Jewish type in, 74–79
Nouns, renaming, 108. *See also* Pronouns

"Object as object," seeing, 67, 70, 82, 84
Odile, Saint, 178, 242n67
Olson, Liesl, 149, 237n38
"One," used by *The Making of Americans* narrator, 103–4, 112, 118–19
Ophüls, Marcel, 176–77
Oppenheimer, Adele, 201n29
Oppenheimer, Ben, 201n29
Orderliness, 174, 241n61
"Orientalizing of Europe," 154–55
Ostier, André, 246n25
OTTO lists, 190, 245n18

Pach, Walter, 71
Palestine, 133, 137–41, 229n27
Pariah(s): Arendt on Jewish, 88, 92–94, 122, 222n12; Brother Singulars as Jewish, 95–100, 117–22; "conscious," 95–100, 222n12; David Hersland as, 114–15; fraternal relationship between parvenus and, 102–3; narrator of *The Making of Americans* as "conscious," 88–89
Paris, France, 193–94
Paris, Václav, 186
Paris Peace Conference (1919), 133–34, 138, 229n28
Parvenus, 88, 92, 93–94, 102–3
Patrie, 191, 246nn23–24
Paxton, Robert O., 154, 170–71, 231n4, 233–34n22, 234–35n26, 235–36nn29–30, 236–37n37, 237n39, 240n57, 243–44n7
Peddlers / peddling, 50–51, 61, 194–95, 212n19. *See also* Jewish types
Perloff, Marjorie, 125, 126, 226n1
Pétain, Philippe, 144–47, 167, 173–75, 177, 178, 182, 186–89, 241n63, 245nn15–16
Picabia, Francis, 243n3
Picasso, Pablo, 68, 70, 78–79, 83, 109, 214n34, 222–23n14, 227n9
Pollak, Francis, 201n29, 206n26

Pondrom, Cyrena, 226n1
Pound, Ezra, 6, 7–8, 9, 125, 199n18, 243n5
Poznanski, Renée, 151, 230n1, 237n38, 240n58
Pragmatism, 48, 84, 85, 220n40
Prickett, Stephen, 22
Pronouns: and Jewish pariah types in *The Making of Americans* epilogue, 117–19; Stein's use of, 103–4, 111–12; switch to impersonal, in *The Making of Americans*, 116–17, 225–26n30
Propaganda, 163–64, 238n46
Proust, Marcel, 61, 214n33, 222n9
Purrmann, Hans, 71

Queerness: of Brother Singulars, 39–40, 57–58, 194, 210n4; of the Hersland patriarch in *The Making of Americans*, 224n18; and homosexuality's comparison to avant-garde writing in *The Making of Americans*, 104; "interesting" conflated with, 212n25; and the narrator in *The Making of Americans*, 94–96, 97–99, 102–4; in servant girl character, 224n20, 224–25n23; of Stein, 225n25. *See also* Homosexuality
Queneau, Raymond, 241n61

Racial difference, Jews and "scientific" theories of, 20–21, 23–28
Racial metaphors, in *Q.E.D.*, 43–45, 210n6
Racial separatism (Jewish), advocated by Stein, 15, 32–36, 96, 201n31
Ragussis, Michael, 202n6
Raleigh, John Henry, 30
Reality, war and sense of, 155–61
Rebellion, filial, 55–56
Refugees, 169–72, 236n35, 236–37n37, 239nn50–51
Renan, Ernest, 10, 23, 33, 201n2, 202n3
Renoir, Jean, 150
Repetition: importance of, to Stein's authorial development, 83–85; in *The Making of Americans*, 59–60, 95–96, 97, 101–3, 109–10; as metaphorically Jewish practice in Stein works, 41; relation to insistence, 210n7; in "A Sonatina Followed By Another," 129
"Report of a Visit to the Camps of Women and Children in the Cape and Orange River Colonies," 237n40
Richards, Grant, 223–24n16
Robbins, Bruce, 6
Roché, Henri-Pièrre, 71, 218–19n26
Romantic Jewish lexicon, 127–33, 227n7, 227n14
Rome, 47–48
Rosenshine, Annette, 65
Royce, Josiah, 220n37
Ruddick, Lisa, 73, 89, 210n4, 225n27
Ryan, Donna, 237n39

Santayana, George, 30, 220n37
Schmitz, Neil, 225–26n30
Schoenbach, Lisi, 197–98n4
Sedgwick, Ellery, 208n38, 228n19
Self-understanding (Socratic), 27, 49–50, 206n26
Sentences, Stein's use of long and repetitive, 95–96
Servant girl question, 100, 224n22
Servant girls, 99–104, 224–25nn20–24
Service du Travail Obligatoire (STO), 151, 236n36
Sevareid, Eric, 230n2, 239n40
Sex and Character (Weininger), 24–25, 75
Sex segregation, in synagogues, 38
Sexual dimorphism, 70–71
Shaw, George Bernard, 24
Shaw, Patrick, 233n19
Shem, 136
Sitwell, Edith, 199n18
Sivain, Maurice, 156–57
Slezkine, Yuri, 211n17, 212n23
Slote, Sam, 60, 214n33
Smedman, Lorna, 126–27

Social Darwinism, 23, 24
Socratic aphorism, 27, 49–50, 206n26
Solomons, Leon, 26, 68, 71, 207n35, 225n29
Spencer, Herbert, 10, 23, 216n11, 223n16
Spies, S. B., 160
Stein, Allan, 63, 76, 217n6
Stein, Amelia (Milly) Keyser, 12, 13, 200n24
Stein, Daniel, 12
Stein, Fred, 71, 201n29
Stein, Gertrude
—life and career: adolescent "bookish life" of, 219n27; Arnold's influence on, 2, 3–4, 21, 22, 28–32, 40–41, 194; childhood and wartime displacements of, 125–26, 156, 227n13; considerations as Jewish writer, 1, 3, 197n2, 232n16, 233n19; criticisms by modernist contemporaries, 7–9, 198n12, 198–99n14, 199nn16–18; described as "queer," 225n25; education at Harvard/Radcliffe, 14–15, 16, 20, 30–31, 45, 65, 70, 105, 201n29, 214–15n4, 220n37; education at Johns Hopkins, 20, 37, 207n35, 208n37; false reports of Hitler Nobel Peace Prize nomination by, 244n9; family and early life of, 12–14; fatness criticized, 199n17; under German Occupation, 143–44, 230nn1–2, 231n6, 235–36n33; Jewish identity of, 11–12, 31, 150–51, 218n21, 232n16, 233n19; lack of recognition for, 61, 131, 198n9; masculine identification of, 38–39, 71; nationality of, 171, 183, 190–91, 200n27; Ostier portrait of, 246n25; Picasso portrait of, 223n14; reception of, 1–2, 189–91, 198nn10–11, 245n17; as refugee, 171–72; scholarly views on, 3; scholarship on, 4; threatened with internment, 156–59, 235–36nn33–36; 2011–2012 debates over WWII politics and writings, 181–89, 192–94, 242–43nn1–5, 244n8, 246n26; WWII politics of, 144–45, 146–80, 181–89, 191–93, 230–31n3, 235n28, 242–43nn1–5, 244nn8–10, 244–45n14, 247n28; WWII publications of, 189–92, 245–46n20, 246nn23–24
—works: "As Fine as Melanctha," 69–70, 227n12; *The Autobiography of Alice B. Toklas*, 113, 146–47, 223n14, 242–43n64; "Ballade," 190; "Coal and Wood," 138, 139–41, 228n15, 229n30; "Composition as Explanation," 87; "Cultivated Motor Automatism: A Study of Character in Its Relation to Attention," 201n31; "Degeneration in American Women," 208n37; *Everybody's Autobiography*, 154, 212n21, 222n9; "Geography," 142; *The Gertrude Stein First Reader*, 190, 245–46n20; "The Gradual Making of The Making of Americans," 213n31; "Have They Attacked Mary. He Giggled," 131–32, 228n18; "Introduction to the Speeches of Maréchal Pétain," 145, 188–89; "IRELAND," 228n19; "Land of Nations," 135–36, 228n19; "Lifting Belly," 128; "Look At Us," 130–31, 228n15; "The Modern Jew," 15, 20, 32–37, 238n45; "More League," 228n19; *The Mother of Us All*, 241n62; *Mrs. Reynolds*, 144, 145, 146, 148, 178, 190, 232n15, 235–36n33, 236n35, 240n56, 240–41n60, 242n69; *Paris France*, 192, 193, 245–46n20; "Plays," 200n26; "Poetry and Grammar," 127; "Portraits and Repetition," 210n7; *Q.E.D*, 29–30, 39, 41–55, 59, 65, 210n6, 212n25; "A Radical Expert," 135, 136; "The Revery of the Zionist," 133–34, 136–37, 228nn19–20, 229n23, 229n26; "A Sonatina Followed By Another," 128–29; *Tender Buttons*, 123, 126, 226n1; *Three Lives*, 9, 69–70, 100, 126, 223n16; "The Winner Loses," 145, 147, 187, 231n9; "World Series," 133, 228n19; *Yes Is for a Very Young Man*, 145,

Stein, Gertrude—*continued*
  149, 165, 232n15, 233n21, 242nn65–66;
  "Yet Dish," 226n3. *See also* "Making
  of Americans, The" (Stein); *Making
  of Americans, The* (Stein); *Wars I Have
  Seen* (Stein)
Stein, Leo, 36–37, 65, 127, 200n24,
  206–7n31, 208n37, 209n42, 211n12,
  215n5, 225n25, 225n29, 237n40; Arnold's
  influence on, 30, 37; on Jew complex,
  14; on modern Jewish writer, 37; reads
  Nordau, 208n37; Stein's classification of,
  70, 71, 78, 79, 81, 218n26
Stein, Michael, 63, 71, 109, 132
Stein, Sally (Sarah), 63, 65, 219n32
Stein, Simon, 13, 51
"Steins Collect: Matisse, Picasso, and the
  Parisian Avant-Garde, The" exhibit,
  181–82, 242–43n1
Stendhal, Renate, 247n28
Stern, Maurice, 71
Stimpson, Catharine, 209n2
Stocking, George, 22
Suleiman, Susan, 182
Swartz, Shirley, 152
Swift, Jonathan, 206n27
Synagogues, Stein on separation of sexes
  in, 38

Taine, Hippolyte Adolphe, 10, 203n10
Tavernier, René, 230n2
This Land Is Mine, 150
Thompson, Virgil, 200–201n28
Toklas, Alice: on afterlife, 200–201n28;
  on black market, 240n56; under German Occupation, 143, 146–47, 150,
  235–36n33; in Mallorca, 227n13; and
  Napoleonic type, 244n13; as refugee,
  171–72; Stein's classification of, 65,
  76–78; Stein's concerns over health of,
  227n12; on Stein's Jewish identity, 45,
  218n21; and Stein's romantic Jewish lexicon, 127–31, 227n7, 227n14; on Stein's

sentence lengths, 96; threatened with
  internment, 156–59, 235–36nn33–36
"Tomlinson" (Kipling), 219n31
Top nature, 76
"To see things as they are," 28–29
"Tradition and the Individual Talent"
  (Eliot), 40
Trilling, Lionel, 202n7, 202–3n8
Troy, William, 213n30
Trubowitz, Lara, 5
Truth tellers, 74–79, 178–79. *See also* Jewish types
Turner, Kay, 227n7

Ulysses (Joyce), 7, 29, 60–61, 101, 104
Unlikely Collaboration: Gertrude Stein, Bernard Faÿ, and the Vichy Dilemma (Will),
  144, 183, 229n26, 231n5, 243n2

Van Dusen, Wanda, 144
Van Puymbroeck, Birgit, 192, 230–31n3
Van Vechten, Carl, 200n27
Veblen, Thorstein, 92
Vichy regime, 143–44, 147, 151–52, 181–82,
  186–89, 191, 230nn1–2, 234–35n26,
  236–37n37–39. *See also* German Occupation; *Wars I Have Seen* (Stein)
Vignale, François, 246n23
Voices poems, Jewish lexicon in, 123–27;
  nationalist Jewish lexicon, 133–42;
  romantic Jewish lexicon, 127–33, 227n7,
  227n14

Wagner-Martin, Linda, 217n19
Wald, Priscilla, 4, 107, 226n31
Walker, Jayne, 73, 217n19, 220n36
Warren, Lansing, 183, 186
Wars I Have Seen (Stein): criticisms of,
  149–50, 233n19; Dreyfus Affair as shorthand for antisemitism and imprisonment in, 161–69; Jews as symbols of
  refugeeism in, 169–72; mass displacements and concentration camps in,

155–61; organization of, 152; publication of, 190, 232n17; semantic and semitic landscapes in, 152–55, 161; Stein's daily life recorded in, 147–52; Stein's identification with *maquis* in, 172–80; Stein's Jewish identity in, 150–52, 232n16; Stein's threatened internment recounted in, 156–59, 235–36nn33–36; style of, 148–49, 152–53, 232–33nn17–18, 233n20; war as surreally "funny" situation in, 145–48, 187; as wartime documentary, 146–50, 232–33nn17–18
Watson, Dana Cairns, 150, 226n2
Weininger, Otto, 24–26, 36, 74, 75, 76, 77, 205nn20–21, 219n27
Wendell, Barrett, 31–32, 209n42
Whitehead, Jessie, 133, 229n30
Whittier-Ferguson, John, 150, 232n18
Wieviorka, Annette, 151, 234n24
Wilde, Oscar, 71, 204n12, 213n28, 238n42
Will, Barbara: *Gertrude Stein, Modernism, and the Problem of "Genius,"* 4; on "The Revery of the Zionist," 136, 229n23, 229n26; on Stein's classification of Toklas, 76; on Stein's friendship with Faÿ, 191; on Stein's Jewish identity, 232n16; on Stein's translations of Pétain, 189; and Stein's wartime politics, 144, 181, 183; *Unlikely Collaboration: Gertrude Stein, Bernard Faÿ, and the Vichy Dilemma*, 144, 183, 229n26, 231n5, 243n2; on "The Winner Loses," 231n9
Williams, Raymond, 22
Williams, William Carlos, 198n10
Wilson, Edmund, 8–9, 69, 87, 200n27
Wineapple, Brenda, 31, 73, 217n19
Wings of the Dove (James), 29–30
Wisse, Ruth, 197n2
Woolf, Virginia, 40, 169, 199n18
World War I, 132–34, 137–41, 145, 146, 187, 227n13, 228n19, 229nn28–29

Zionism, 133–34, 137–38, 244n9
Zox-Weaver, Annalisa, 186, 242n67
Zukofsky, Louis, 15, 197n2, 199n18, 244n12

AMY FEINSTEIN teaches English at a public high school in New York City. Her edition of Gertrude Stein's 1896 essay, "The Modern Jew Who Has Given Up the Faith of His Fathers Can Reasonably and Consistently Believe in Isolation," appeared with critical introduction in *PMLA*. She has published articles in *James Joyce Quarterly*, *Modern Fiction Studies*, *Shofar: An Interdisciplinary Journal of Jewish Studies*, and the edited volume *Radical Poetics and Secular Jewish Culture*.

CPSIA information can be obtained
at www.ICGtesting.com
Printed in the USA
BVHW042300240723
667704BV00002B/14